Basic Statistical Concepts

Second Edition

Albert E. Bartz

Concordia College
Moorhead, Minnesota

Macmillan Publishing Company
New York
Collier Macmillan Publisher
London

To
Sally,

who has always been
significantly different

Contents

Foreword

This edition of *Basic Statistical Concepts* is clearly written with the student in mind. This is apparent in several ways:

First, the explanatory material is *complete*. The author has done an unusually good job of developing this subject without leaving explanatory "holes." Fundamental concepts are defined carefully, and the text leads directly from one concept to the next, showing how basic statistical ideas are interrelated. Students will find, I think, that they can learn basic statistics without recourse to other sources.

Second, the text succeeds in making mathematical ideas and procedures approachable to students with a wide variety of backgrounds. Statistics is — inescapably — a branch of mathematics, and one must learn some mathematical ideas in order to use and interpret statistics properly. In this text, however, each statistical idea is introduced in a familiar context. Well-chosen examples demonstrate that fundamental statistical principles — averages, variability, correlation, and probability — are simply formal treatments of familiar, everyday concepts. Very likely, the failure of other books to make this point effectively contributes to statistics' well-known unpopularity among students. The illustrative examples included here should reassure students that computations they will perform require little more than ordinary arithmetic skills.

Third, I think this text strikes several balances in a way that is particularly appropriate for students in behavioral science and education programs. There is a nice balance between practical applications and statistical theory. Enough methods are included to equip students to understand and do research in their disciplines, but few enough methods are presented that basic ideas will not be obscured. The examples are simple enough for the beginner to follow, but not so simple as to seem unrealistic. No book can manage all of these balances optimally for all students, but this book will succeed very well for most students.

New York   Marty J. Schmidt

Preface

Revising a textbook can be a traumatic experience. An author must make whatever significant changes have been suggested by some users of the text but, at the same time, not alienate other users who are perfectly content with the first edition. A number of substantial changes, described at the end of this preface, have been made in this second edition, but the three central emphases of the first edition remain:

1. *Student-centered approach.* Deliberate attention has been paid in this text to the development of techniques that will assist the student in grasping statistical concepts. A series of **Notes** set off in shaded portions call the student's attention to helpful hints and suggestions that will aid him or her in understanding a concept, avoiding errors, and developing computational skills. This is intended to be not a gimmick, but rather a solid educational technique to supply the association and the reinforcement at precisely the right time in the learning process. Another learning aid is

the inclusion at the end of each chapter of one or more **Sample Problems,** showing collected data, decision steps, calculations, and conclusions for the various statistical techniques. These techniques – in addition to the step-by-step progression from simpler to more complex material, the attempt to combine an intuitive approach with the usual mathematical development, and the **Study Questions** and **Exercises** for each chapter – should provide the learner with ample exposure to the conceptualizations and calculations necessary for proficiency in statistical techniques.

2. *Selection and presentation of topics.* A 10-year-old girl, returning a book on penguins to the public library, remarked to the librarian, "This book told me more about penguins than I really cared to know." Many texts have included much more material than can reasonably be covered in a typical one-semester or two-quarter course in introductory statistics. The topics chosen for this text are concepts that form the foundation for measurement in education and the behavioral sciences. However, each instructor may have individual preferences, and a different order of topics may be used or some of the later topics may be omitted or abbreviated at the instructor's discretion. Most of the chapters here are organized to include an introduction to the concept with several familiar illustrations, progressing to formulas that define or demonstrate the concept, and concluding with computational formulas, worked examples, and applications and limitations of the concept.

3. *Simplified language.* The idea for this text began in 1958 with a small manual, *Elementary Statistical Methods for Educational Measurement.* It was intended as a supplement for textbooks in tests and measurements and attempted to lead the student down statistical pathways in a language and style that caused as little trauma as possible. As subsequent editions appeared, more and more material was added and an increasing number of users suggested the addition of inferential techniques employing the same simplified language. While it is one thing to discuss percentiles and an entirely different thing to describe a two-way ANOVA, I have attempted to present both kinds of material in an uncomplicated, narrative style, with a profusion of lucid examples. A considerable portion of the material may seem redundant to the mathematically sophisticated student (and to the teacher examining this copy for possible adoption!), but, in teaching the introductory statistics course for 20 years, I have found that a certain amount of redundancy is not only desirable but essential for realizing optimum gain as the student progresses through the material. There is a differ-

ence between a "watered-down" approach and one that attempts to be rigorous yet readable. I have attempted to present the traditionally difficult and more complex material in the same manner as the easier concepts.

Aside from this text's central emphases, there is one further point to be noted. This is the day of the pocket calculator, and, since many students own or at least have access to one, machine formulas are given wherever appropriate and little emphasis is given to grouped-data techniques. However, grouped-data methods are still used on occasion, so they are presented at the ends of the appropriate chapters.

A note of gratitude is due all the users of the first edition who filled out questionnaires and answered queries on suggestions for improvement. It is largely the result of their efforts that this edition includes study questions for each chapter, sections on one-tailed t tests, Tukey's procedure for multiple comparisons of means, and the two-way ANOVA, as well as a number of minor changes. I am grateful to Ann Seivert for her critical yet sensitive editing of the manuscript for both editions. I especially thank Dr. Gary Narum, of North Dakota State University, and Dr. George Seifert, of Bowling Green State University, for their many helpful suggestions. And I am grateful to my wife, Sol, for typing the manuscript and providing ideas for research applications in special education. And last of all, I want to thank the students who semester after semester have willingly and good-naturedly served as guinea pigs while numerous teaching techniques were tried. They continued to prove that a lot of learning still goes on in a formal classroom setting, both for the students and the instructor!

Moorhead, Minnesota   Albert E. Bartz

To the Student

It is a strange phenomenon, but a surprising number of college students who enthusiastically tackle such diverse college subjects as archaeology, music theory, and metaphysics are reduced to a quivering mass of collective insecurity when confronted with a required course in statistics. A "weakness" in mathematics is often given as a blanket excuse, and this would be a legitimate reaction to a course that stressed the mathematical theory underlying each concept and the derivation of all formulas for a given statistic. However, this textbook for your current statistics course assumes no mathematical training beyond your first high school algebra course. And when it is necessary to manipulate some mathematical symbols, each step is shown and carefully explained.

But there is no denying the fact that a first course in statistics can be difficult, simply because the subject matter is new to most of you. As a result, this text has been organized deliberately to facilitate the understanding of each new concept. The beginning chapters contain the simpler material, and succeeding chapters become progressively more complex. However, there is a logical progression from one chapter to the next, so even the more complex concepts will not prove too difficult if you make certain that you completely understand the material in each chapter before going on.

Teaching by example has been shown to be an effective educational tool, so plan to spend time looking over each example and coordinating it with the text narrative. The **Study Questions** will help you to focus your reading on the important concepts in each chapter. The **Sample Problems** at the end of each chapter should help tie together the concepts presented, and you should work the **Exercises** only after you understand the entire chapter.

Because the material in the earlier chapters is somewhat simpler, you may have a natural tendency to devote less time to these chapters and to neglect the **Exercises.** This can be unfortunate. Because the later chapters will require more time and effort, it is essential not to get behind in your work at any time in the course. If you keep up with the daily assignments on both the reading and the problems, you'll find that the material will be less difficult to learn and much easier to remember.

Good luck!

1 Some Thoughts on Measurement

"There are three kinds of lies: lies, damned lies, and statistics."

Disraeli

Any statistician with a normal amount of sensitivity must shudder a little whenever he sees this quotation from one of England's great prime ministers. It, of course, implies that part of a statistician's duties is to bend the data in some form or fashion to prove whatever point needs proving. Even if you were not acquainted with Disraeli's pessimistic viewpoint, you have at least heard statements such as "You can prove anything with statistics" or "Figures don't lie, but liars can figure."

It is not surprising, then, that the average person has a jaundiced view of statistics and statisticians. In Figure 1-1 we note that even Charlie Brown is not immune from the attitudes of the lay public toward statisticians.

The Need for Statistics

It is hoped that a first course in statistics will clear up some of the misconceptions about statistics mentioned in the opening paragraphs. There are

©1974 United Feature Syndicate, Inc.

Figure 1-1
Even the comics reflect the public's attitude about statistics.

three general objectives that you should hope to achieve through this introductory course. It is expected that you will (1) be able to read the professional literature in your field of study, (2) appreciate the fact that statistics is a necessary tool for research, and (3) develop an increased ability to identify situations where statistics are used in an inappropriate or misleading manner. Let us examine these three objectives in detail.

Professional Literature

As your course of study progresses, you are in the process of becoming a professional in your chosen field, and you will be expected to read the professional literature in books and journals. Since statistics are used to communicate results of surveys, experiments, and tests, you must be able to understand what an author is saying by means of graphs, averages, correlation coefficients, *t* tests, and the like. You can no longer "skip the hard places," as you might have done back in grade school, but will have to be able to read — and understand what you are reading — to be a professional. And since statistics permits the most concise and exact way of describing data, you can expect that the majority of your professional reading will use a statistical analysis of some sort.

Research Tool

Statistics is a necessary tool for all research, where *research* is broadly defined. Whether you are a classroom teacher, guidance counselor, social caseworker, physiological psychologist, or personnel manager, a rudimentary knowledge of statistics is a prerequisite for analyzing data. As education and the behavioral sciences move increasingly toward a quantitative approach, the results of research studies of all kinds become the basic diet for everyone in the field. The days of armchair speculation are numbered, and more and more hard-nosed research results will be demanded as evidence for a particular point of view.

Misleading Statistics

While we are all rather suspicious of claims using such statistics as "Three out of four doctors recommend ... " or " ... dissolves 50% more stomach acid than ... ," there are times when data manipulation is not so obvious. One candidate for ease of misinterpretation is the graphical method, and several examples are shown in Figures 1-2 and 1-3.

Figure 1-2 shows the familiar *pictogram,* where the height of the figures represents the amount of the quantity being graphed — in this case, the number of members of several church denominations in one small midwestern state. On first examination of the graph you would probably conclude that denomination A has anywhere from 6 to 10 times as many members as either B or C. The graph is misleading

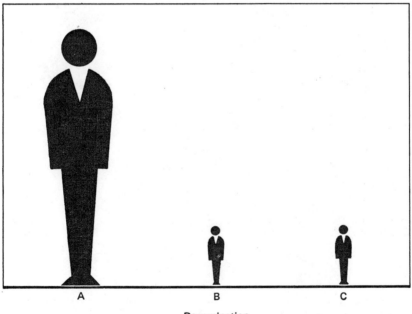

Denomination

Figure 1-2
Pictogram for church membership among three religious denominations.

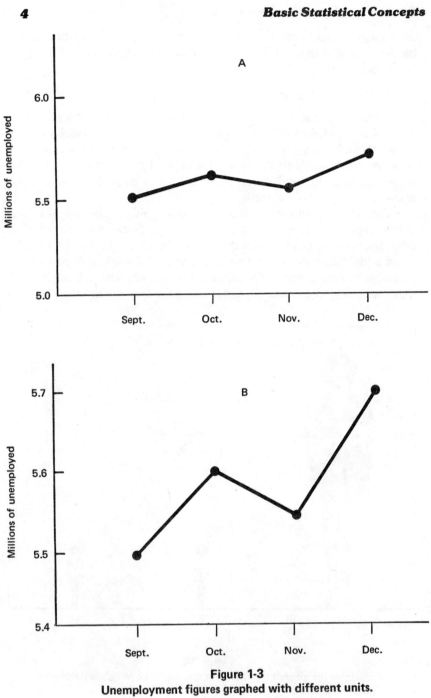

Figure 1-3
Unemployment figures graphed with different units.

because you are being influenced not by the *height* of the figures alone but by the proportionate *space* they occupy. Actually, the height of the figure representing denomination A is correct. The figure is just over 4 times taller (representing 78,426 members) than either B (18,192 members) or C (17,513 members).

Two graphs representing unemployment figures for the last 4 months of a year are shown in Figure 1-3. Both graphs are constructed from the same basic data, but they differ with respect to the units of measurement on the vertical axis. Someone who wished to demonstrate that there is no cause for alarm might represent the data by graph A. Since the units in this graph are large, an increase of 200,000 unemployed causes little change from September to December. On the other hand, someone who wished to exaggerate the increase in unemployment would demonstrate that point by means of graph B, where the smaller units magnify the change of 200,000.

The inappropriate use of graphical methods demonstrated above is only one example of how statistics can be misleading. As you develop expertise with the statistical concepts to be presented in the following chapters, you will become familiar with the appropriate applications for each statistic and will be sensitized to possible uses and abuses in the presentation of data.

The Importance of Measurement

The growth in importance of the physical sciences in the last few decades has been in part due to increased precision of measurement. The different teams of astronauts could not have explored the surface of the moon were it not for the ability of scientists to measure time, space, and matter with extreme precision. A visit to any facility for research in biology, medicine, or any other scientific discipline would show a large amount of floor and counter space devoted to precision measuring devices of one kind or another.

Although we do not claim the same degree of precision as the natural sciences, measurement is of supreme importance in education and the behavioral sciences as well. The use of statistical methods enables us to make *quantitative* statements about data that could not be formulated by any other means. The football coach who says he has a "big" team is making a less precise statement than one who states that the average weight of his defensive line is 250 pounds. To say that John is older than Joe is not as informative as saying that John is about a year older than Joe. And saying that John is 11 months and 3 days older than Joe would give us information of even greater precision. Similarly, we make quantitative statements about Pete's I.Q. test score. Judy's reading readiness score, Ted's anxiety level, and Helen's college grade-point average.

So far we have been using the term *statistics* in several different ways, and at this point it might be helpful to sort out exactly what we mean. An acquaintance of mine informs his classes that "we calculate statistics from statistics by statistics." If we stop and look at the meaning of each usage of the word, this confusing slogan will make great sense.

1. "We calculate statistics..." What he means here are the results of a computation: the graphs and percentiles and correlation co-efficients. These are the final figures that tell us what a particular batch of data means.

2. "...from statistics..." The term here refers to the data, the collection of numbers that constitute the raw material we work with. They may be test scores, reaction times, frequency of divorces, or number of juvenile delinquents, or what have you.

3. "...by statistics." The last use of the term is the process or method that we use to get our averages, percentiles, or the like. Formulas have been derived and methods have been developed so that we follow a certain procedure and perform the necessary calculations to obtain the desired result.

The emphasis in this text will be on the first and third uses of the term. As the concepts are introduced in the following chapters, we will study the *method* or *process* that is appropriate for the desired results and learn how the *end product* tells what we need to know about our data. Viewed in this way, the task of statistics *is to reduce large masses of data to some meaningful values.* Whether we are working with 20 algebra test scores, 200 freshmen entrance exam scores, or 200,000 automobile driver records, our objective is the same—to come up with some meaningful values that tell us something about our set of data.

The second use of the term, the statistics as *raw data* or *scores,* will not be discussed at any great length in the chapters to follow. Since this text is written to cover broadly the concepts applied to education and the behavioral sciences, it must be left to each individual discipline to define the kinds of data that characterize its own peculiar domain. It must be emphasized that the statistical process yielding a statistical result will never be any better than the raw material on which it is based. The computer programmer's lament, "Garbage in, garbage out," is a cliché to be remembered. An average or a correlation coefficient or any other statistic will never give respectability to a group of raw data that is essentially inaccurate.

Nevertheless, from time to time we will take a look at some *general* considerations that may tend to bias the raw data and thus influence the accuracy of the final results. We will devote several of the remaining sections in this chapter to this problem, as well as noting the limitations of each statistic in the following chapters.

The Descriptive and Inferential Approaches

The field of statistics has traditionally been divided into two broad categories—descriptive and inferential (sampling) statistics. After you have completed this first course, you will see that these two categories are not mutually exclusive and that there is a great deal of overlap in what may be labeled "descriptive" and what may be labeled "inferential." However, it is useful at this point to distinguish these two concepts.

Descriptive Statistics

We noted earlier that the task of statistics in general was to reduce large masses of data to some meaningful values. In terms of descriptive statistics this would mean that these meaningful values *describe* the results of a particular sample of behavior. We might use statistics to describe the distribution of scores on a ninth-grade algebra exam, the distribution of weights of the entire football squad at a local high school, or the incidence of Asian flu among all college students at a particular university. Your grade-point average, minimum checking account balance (sometimes a little too descriptive), and rank in high school graduating class are also descriptive statistics. The purpose of a descriptive statistic, as you can see, is to tell us something about a particular group of observations.

Inferential Statistics

In the study of inferential statistics we find our attention shifting from describing a limited group of observations to making *inferences* about the population. We will define *sample* and *population* precisely and in more detail in later chapters, but for now let us say that a sample is a smaller group of observations drawn from the larger group of observations, the population. For example, if we are conducting a poll on voting preferences, we might choose 100 voters out of a certain neighborhood. In this case the 100 voters would constitute our sample, while *all* possible voters in that neighborhood would make up the population. The task, then, of inferential statistics is to draw inferences or make predictions concerning the population on the basis of data from a smaller sample. In the case of the poll of voters, we are not particularly interested in the 100 voters but rather in making a prediction of how *all* the eligible voters in that neighborhood would vote. Similarly, if a research project is conducted by an automobile manufacturer to determine which of two designs of rear turning signals is easier to see, a sample of 500 drivers might be tested on their reaction time to the two types of lights. The engineers are not concerned only with the sample of 500 drivers but with how these results can be used to predict how *all* drivers will react.

Whether a given statistic is descriptive or inferential depends on the *purpose* for which it is intended. If a group of observations (heights, I.Q. scores, birth rates) is used merely to describe an event, the statistics calculated from these observations would be *descriptive*. If, on the other hand, a sample is selected (hence the term *sampling statistics*) with the intent of predicting what the larger population is like, the statistics would be *inferential*.

This text was designed to present both the descriptive and inferential approaches. Descriptive statistics, for example, would be found in measuring classroom performance (achievement tests), stock market trends, baseball records, and vital statistics. But as much a part of our life as these statistics are, I guess we would have to say that we are most often interested in the inferential approach.

We are rarely content as students of behavior merely to *measure* some characteristic but would rather use a single observation or a small number of observations to make statements about the world in general. We may measure Susie's I.Q., Jim's grade-point average, and Pete's sociability, and, using these as descriptors, put them to good use in advisement or counseling. But quite often we go beyond a mere description and contemplate such things as how Susie's low socio-economic level has affected her I.Q. test performance, how Jim's grade-point average is related to his father's achievement motivation, and what effect Pete's being an only child has on his introversion-extroversion score. It is the inferential approach that can help us answer questions such as these, and the majority of the chapters to follow will describe techniques designed to measure these variables.

Measurement and Scales

Ever since our early childhood years we have been bombarded by numbers. We probably began by learning to count our fingers, graduated to toes, and continued into elementary school, sharpening our skills in the marvelous numerical system. We've reached a point now where we feel relatively comfortable with numbers because we have been adding and subtracting and multiplying and dividing for years.

Occasionally the numbers that we worked with in arithmetic classes represented something concrete like ducks or money or people, but more often than not we worked with just simple rows or columns of digits. This bothered us not at all and we performed arithmetic operations on acres of numbers with the sole objective of getting the right answer.

We would now like to apply our quantitative skills to observations of behavior, but before we perform arithmetic manipulations on numbers that represent something (e.g., test scores) we have to be aware of the properties that these numbers have. We cannot blindly manipulate a set of numbers without knowing something about their properties and what the numbers represent. Somewhere back in your arithmetic training a teacher no doubt said you couldn't add apples and oranges together. This probably didn't make much of an impact on you at the time (other than the fact that you have successfully avoided adding apples and oranges), but the statement could not be more true than in the field of measurement. We must be sensitive to precisely what the numbers represent.

Measurement is formally defined as the *assignment of numbers to objects or events according to certain prescribed rules.* Once this has been done, the numbers have certain properties of which we must be fully aware as we perform the arithmetic operations. We treat these numbers differently and with varying degrees of precision, depending upon what they represent. The number *9* representing the hardness of a rock sample is different from a glove size of 9 or nine items correct on a short geography quiz.

A very convenient way of looking at the properties that a given number may have is to examine four kinds of scales that describe different levels of precision in treating numbers. These are called, in increasing order of precision, *nominal, ordinal, interval,* and *ratio* scales. Each type of scale represents a way of assigning numbers to objects or events, and the description of each type below shows the rules that were applied.

Nominal Scale

The simplest and most elementary type of measurement uses the nominal scale. Numbers are assigned for the sole purpose of differentiating one object from another. Steve has a book locker labeled 80, Joe wears basketball jersey number 22, and Dave is taking his motorbike for a trip on U.S. Highway 40. The nominal scale has only the property of differentiating one object or event from another.

In fact, it would not be necessary to use *numbers* to differentiate the categories. We could just as easily use letters of the alphabet, nouns, or proper names. When we categorize groups as male/female or freshman/sophomore/junior/senior, for example, we are categorizing according to a nominal scale.

When numbers are used in a nominal scale, we would not dream of adding them together or trying to calculate an average, because this scale does not have the necessary properties to enable us to do so. People would start avoiding you if you went around stating that the average basketball jersey number at the NCAA tournament was 37.63 or that the sum of the U.S. Interstate Highway numbers traveled on your vacation last summer was 208! In a similar vein book locker number 80 is not twice as large as book locker 40, and Joe's basketball jersey number 22 does not mean he is only half as good as his teammate wearing jersey number 44.

Such examples may seem to be belaboring the obvious, but these extreme situations are used to make you fully aware of the single property of the nominal scale—that of differentiating one object or event from another. Crude as it may be, this scale is still a form of measurement and will be useful in certain statistical techniques.

Ordinal Scale

As the term implies, measurements in an ordinal scale have the property of *order*. Not only can we differentiate one object from another as in the nominal scale, but we can specify the *direction of the difference*. We can now make statements using "more than" or "less than," since our measuring system has the property of order, and the objects or events can be placed on a continuum in terms of some measurable characteristic.

The *ranking* of objects or events would be a good example of an ordinal scale. A third-grade teacher, for example, might rank Ann, Beth, and Cindy as 1, 2, and 3, respectively, on the trait of sociability. As a result of the teacher's ranking, we know that Ann is more sociable than Beth and Beth is more sociable than Cindy. This is a definite improvement over the nominal scale, where no indication of the *direction* of the difference could be made. Under a nominal scale, all we could say is that Ann, Beth, and Cindy are different in sociability.

But note that our scale still does not permit us to say *how much* of a difference exists between two or more objects or events. Ann may be just slightly more sociable than Beth, while Cindy may be considerably less sociable than either. Yet the ranks of 1, 2, and 3 do not communicate this information. In this example, there would be hardly any difference between ranks 1 and 2, while there would be a large difference between ranks 2 and 3.

As another example, consider an art critic ranking three paintings in terms of their realism. He could conceivably give the most realistic a rank of 1, the next most realistic a rank of 2, and so on. According to the critic, the paintings may have been very reliably put into their proper order in terms of realism, but there is no way to assess the *amount* of realism or to say that one is twice as realistic as another. This is an example of an ordinal scale.

Interval Scale

The most important characteristic of an interval scale is equality of units. This means that there are equal distances between observation points on the scale. Not only can we specify the direction of the difference, as we did in the ordinal scale, but we can indicate the amount of the difference as well. A very common example of an interval scale is our familiar Fahrenheit temperature scale. There are equal intervals between the points on the scale, and the difference between 30° and 34° is the same as the difference between 72° and 76°. We can also say that an increase from 50° to 70° is twice as much as an increase from 30° to 40°. With the interval scale we can now assess the *amount* of the difference between two or more objects or events, something we could not do with the ordinal scale.

Many of the measurements that characterize education and the behavioral sciences are of the interval type. For example, most test scores (in terms of number of items correct) are treated as if they were based on interval measures.

Ratio Scale

The ratio scale has all the characteristics of the interval scale plus an *absolute zero*. With an absolute zero point we can make statements involving ratios of two observations, such as "twice as long" or "half as fast."

In the Fahrenheit temperature scale discussed above, we *cannot* say, for example, that a temperature of 80° is twice as warm as one of 40°. This is due to the fact that the Fahrenheit temperature scale has only an arbitrary zero, not an absolute zero. A ratio scale must have a meaningful absolute zero. If John Swift can jog 2 miles in 12 minutes, but it takes Joe Sludge 24 minutes, we know that John can run twice as fast. But in intelligence testing, for example, we cannot say that a person with an I.Q. of 100 is twice as intelligent as someone with an I.Q. of 50. This is because zero intelligence cannot be defined, and thus there is no absolute zero point. Most physical scales such as time, length, and weight are ratio scales, but very few behavioral measures are of this type.

Comparing the Four Scales

Table 1-1 summarizes the characteristics of the four types of scales, and, as you can see, each successive scale possesses the characteristics of the preceding scales.

It is easy to get the impression that the ideal measurement would be in a ratio scale and that measurements in the other three scales are something to be avoided if at all possible. While this may be the theoretical goal or ideal of measurement purists, we are faced with the fact that most behavioral measures miss this ideal by a significant amount, and practical considerations require our making the most of the precision that we do have. As was stated earlier, many of the measurements that we deal with in education and the behavioral sciences are treated as interval measures. However, a good part of our data is of the ordinal type, and even the nominal scale serves us very well. If a teacher ranks his students on "social participation," or a poll taker asks her respondents to indicate their preferences of political candidates' views on some national issue, or a football coach judges his backfield candidates on their proficiency, all are making use of ordinal measures. And any study involving categorization according to some attribute (men/women, freshman/senior, alcoholic/social drinker/teetotaler) would involve the nominal scale.

Table 1-1
Characteristics of Measurement Scales

Scale	Properties
Nominal	Indicates a difference
Ordinal	Indicates a difference
	Indicates the direction of the difference
	(e.g., more than or less than)
Interval	Indicates a difference
	Indicates the direction of the difference
	Indicates the amount of the difference
	(in equal intervals)
Ratio	Indicates a difference
	Indicates the direction of the difference
	Indicates the amount of the difference
	Indicates an absolute zero

As the various statistical methods are covered in the chapters to follow, you will notice very soon that a lot of information can be obtained from measurements that do not meet the theoretical ideal of a ratio scale. The important thing is that you must be aware of what sort of scale a given body of measurements represents and use the statistical procedures that are appropriate for that scale. After you have done this, the statistics that you do obtain can provide a wealth of meaning about a given set of measurements, whether they are nominal, ordinal, interval, or ratio in nature.

Some Statistical Shorthand

Statistics, like many other disciplines, has developed its own set of symbols or notation to help summarize or condense words and statements in an efficient manner. As the different statistical concepts are presented in the chapters to follow, each abbreviation or symbol will be defined and will continue to be used throughout the text. One set of symbols is so common that it might be a good idea to spend a little time at this point covering them in some detail, because they will be appearing in almost every chapter. These symbols are collectively called *summation notation,* and they are simply a way of expressing some simple mathematical operations in a very efficient way. Those of you with a mathematics background that included summation notation may skip this section.

Variables

Table 1-2 shows a group of test scores made by a number of students. The test score is the *variable* (so called because the scores *vary* from student to student) and is denoted by the letter X. Each test score in the column is one of the values of the variable X.

In order to identify *which* value of X we are considering, we give a tag or label to each value by attaching a *subscript* to X that corresponds to its position in the column (Table 1-2). X_1 is the value of the test score in the *first* row and student #1 received a score of 72, so we say that $X_1 = 72$. Similarly, X_3 is the score of student #3, so $X_3 = 83$. In order to be able to express the *general* case of any student's score, we use the subscript i. Thus X_i (read "X sub i") means *any* value of the variable, and it corresponds to a score made by *any* student who has the general number designated by i. So X_i could be the score made by the 5th student, the 23rd student, or the 99th student. If you have trouble visualizing the ith student, just picture the values of X as be-

Table 1-2
Summation Notation

Student #	X (Test Score)
1	72
2	31
3	83
4	42
5	57
6	91
7	42
8	31
.	.
.	.
i	X_i
.	.
.	.
N	X_N

Adding all values: $(X_1 + X_2 + X_3 + \ldots + X_N) = \sum\limits_{i=1}^{N} X_i$

Adding the first five values: $(X_1 + X_2 + X_3 + X_4 + X_5) = \sum\limits_{i=1}^{5} X_i$

Adding the third through the sixth: $(X_3 + X_4 + X_5 + X_6) = \sum\limits_{i=3}^{6} X_i$

longing to particular people. Then your values of X could be X_{Joe}, X_{Pete}, and so on, while X_i would be $X_{Someone}$!

The last row in a set of numbers always contains the final observation. This row is denoted as N, and the corresponding score is X_N. So the score of the Nth student in Table 1-2 is X_N. If there were a total of 50 students, N would be 50, and the score of the 50th student would be X_{50}.

Since N is always the last row containing an observation, the symbol N is also used to denote the number of observations. If there is a group of 75 scores, we say that $N = 75$, or if 29 rats are run in a maze-learning experiment, $N = 29$. It is a convenient way of expressing the *size* of the group.

The letter X is usually used to express a variable quantity (test scores, I.Q.s, heights, etc.), but theoretically we could use A, B, C, J,

K, or any uppercase letter to stand for the variable. Traditionally, the letters X, Y, and Z have been used in statistics to express a variable, with the letter X being the most common. In a later chapter we will have occasion to use both X and Y, when we need to identify two variables that are being studied simultaneously—such as height and weight or grade-point average and socioeconomic level.

Summation Notation

Many statistical techniques require the *addition* of columns or rows of numbers, so it is worthwhile to examine a shorthand way of expressing addition. This shorthand method is called *summation notation.*

The Greek letter sigma (Σ) is used to signify the addition of a group of quantities, and it means "sum of." Thus ΣX means "sum of the X values." If the X values are 5, 17, 22, and 25, $\Sigma X = 69$. It is just a shorthand way of saying, "The sum of the X values is 69."

It is often convenient to express quantities in *general,* so that the terms apply to any group of numbers. It is for this reason that it is necessary to define summation notation a little more precisely. Let us consider the case where we have a *single* column (or row) of numbers such as is shown in Table 1-2.

The symbol for adding any row or column of X values is $\sum_{i=1}^{N} X_i$.

This rather imposing little set of symbols simply says, "Add up the values of X, starting with the first and stopping with the one called N." Note that the subscript of X is i. The $i = 1$ under the sigma symbol is the *starting* point for the addition. It is, in effect, telling you to start adding with the first value of X (when $i = 1$), go on to the next, and continue adding each value to the total. The *stopping* point is the value at the top of the sigma symbol. Since N is the stopping point, you are to keep adding the column until you get to the last value, or N.

In other words, when you see $\sum_{i=1}^{N} X_i$, it is saying, "Take the value X_1, then X_2, and add the two. Then take X_3, and add it to the previous two. Then take X_4, and add it to the total, and so on, until you come to the value labeled X_N. You add X_N to the total and then you stop." You have then completed the operation that $\sum_{i=1}^{N} X_i$ calls for.

Suppose that you want the sum of the first five values. You would then want to begin with $i = 1$ as usual and end with the fifth value, so your summation sign would be $\sum\limits_{i=1}^{5} X_i$. If this were applied to Table 1-2, you would take $X_1 = 72$ and add $X_2 = 31$, $X_3 = 83$, $X_4 = 42$ and stop with $X_5 = 57$. So the value of $\sum\limits_{i=1}^{5} X_i$ would be $72 + 31 + 83 + 42 + 57$, or $\sum\limits_{i=1}^{5} X_i = 285$. In a similar fashion $\sum\limits_{i=3}^{6} X_i$ would start with $X_3 = 83$ and would sum all values through $X_6 = 91$, so $\sum\limits_{i=3}^{6} X_i = 273$.

In an introductory text such as this, most of the uses of the operation of addition will involve adding *all* the numbers in a *single* column, so there is little need to specify the starting and stopping points in a summation operation. If you are going to add *all* the numbers, the starting point will always be $i = 1$ and the stopping point will always be N. For that reason it is customary to omit the limits from the summation symbol and use only Σ, since what is to be added is understood. For example, when ΣX is called for, it simply means that you are to add all the X values. Since ΣX is easier to write and less confusing to read than $\sum\limits_{i=1}^{N} X_i$, we will use the abbreviated form throughout the text except for one occasion in Chapter 11. However, this one occasion will be very important, so it was essential to present the elements of summation at this point.

Concluding Remarks

It would be unrealistic to expect a first course in statistical methods to transform a beginner into a polished researcher or research analyst. If you find that one of your primary interests is conducting research, you will undoubtedly choose one or more additional courses in this area. Since different texts and different instructors may use other systems of notation and methods of approach in the advanced courses, it is difficult to write an introductory text that will prepare everyone equally well for future courses that they may take. The approach used by this text is to present the material in an intuitive fashion, stressing the understanding of basic concepts, so that there will be maximum transfer to the next course you take. Symbols may differ and formulas may be slightly altered, but if you understand the elementary principles presented in this text you should be able to make the transition to an advanced course with a minimum of discomfort.

Study Questions

1. How would you respond to the statement that you can prove anything with statistics?

2. Differentiate the various meanings of *statistics*.

3. What is the difference between inferential and descriptive statistics?

4. What are the characteristics of the four kinds of measurement scales?

Exercises

1. Indicate whether the types of data described below are nominal, ordinal, interval, or ratio.
   a. Elapsed time in seconds
   b. Daily temperatures in degrees Celsius
   c. Judges' rankings on the "best" Siamese at a cat show
   d. Heights on July 4 of different varieties of corn
   e. I.Q. scores of a cerebral palsy group and a normal birth group
   f. Room numbers at the Holiday Inn
   g. Test scores on an achievement test
   h. Identifications of children who have had chicken pox

2. Write the summation symbol you would use to express the following operations.
   a. For a column of test scores, (X), you want to add all the scores from the 5th one through the 21st
   b. Each student's score (X) is squared, and you would like to add all these squared scores
   c. You would like to add the first six scores in a column

3. Describe precisely what operations are indicated by the following symbols.

   a. $\displaystyle\sum_{i=3}^{8} X_i$

b. $\displaystyle\sum_{i=1}^{N} Y_i^2$

c. $\sum X$

2 Frequency Distributions and Graphical Methods

In the last chapter we noted that one of the tasks of statistics was to describe a mass of numbers in a meaningful way. The mass of numbers may represent such diverse measurements as test scores, survey results, medical records, or reaction times—but they are similar in that the final computer printouts, scoring sheets, or file folders result in a batch of numbers that defy any reasonable attempt to make sense out of them. Consider Table 2-1, which shows the results of an achievement examination in English.

Notice how difficult it is to get any meaning out of this collection of scores. With some effort we can find the highest score, 97, or the lowest score, 61. But we would be hard pressed indeed to find out where the concentrations of scores were, or how many students scored above 85, or how many people had a score of 82. In short, this collection of data gives us precious little information about the performance of the group on the English exam. So, to bring a semblance of order to a group of observations, we resort to a technique which is often used to display

Table 2-1
English Achievement Exam Scores

69	70	72	62	78
71	85	72	73	91
71	61	85	82	82
82	81	74	79	90
66	88	82	86	83
89	94	86	76	75
81	79	93	76	80
68	81	64	87	80
95	75	84	90	92
88	97	86	68	67

this kind of information in a meaningful way—the *frequency distribution*.

Frequency Distributions

Basically the frequency distribution is simply a table constructed to show *how many times* a given score or group of scores occurred. For example, we could set up a table where the highest score is at the top and the lowest at the bottom, with all possible scores in between, and indicate how often each score occurred. Such a table is called a *simple frequency distribution,* and this technique is shown for the English scores in Table 2-2.

While the simple frequency distribution may be convenient for a teacher assigning grades, the *pattern* of the distribution does not emerge as it should. It is still difficult to readily see the concentrations of scores in such a distribution.

The most common form of the frequency distribution is the *grouped frequency distribution,* which is shown for the English achievement scores in Table 2-3. Note that instead of displaying how often *each* score occurred, the scores have been grouped into intervals (thus the name *grouped* frequency distribution) and the number in the frequency column *f* tells how many scores are in the given interval. For example, in Table 2-3, eight students had scores from 90 through 99.

Unfortunately, Table 2-3 has only four intervals, resulting in a frequency distribution that does not tell us very much about the pattern of distribution of our English scores. It would be better to have a frequency distribution with more and smaller intervals. Such an example

Table 2-2
Simple Frequency Distribution of English Achievement Scores

Score	f	Score	f
97	1	78	1
96	0	77	0
95	1	76	2
94	1	75	2
93	1	74	1
92	1	73	1
91	1	72	2
90	2	71	2
89	1	70	1
88	2	69	1
87	1	68	2
86	3	67	1
85	2	66	1
84	1	65	0
83	1	64	1
82	4	63	0
81	3	62	1
80	2	61	1
79	2		

Table 2-3
A Poor Illustration of a Grouped Frequency
Distribution of English Achievement Scores

Scores	f
90–99	8
80–89	20
70–79	14
60–69	8
	$N = 50$

is shown in Table 2-4, where there are now eight intervals. Notice that this frequency distribution gives us a better idea of the spread and concentration of our scores. We can easily see the clustering of scores

Table 2-4
A Better Illustration of a Grouped Frequency Distribution of English Achievement Scores

Scores	f
95–99	2
90–94	6
85–89	8
80–84	12
75–79	7
70–74	7
65–69	5
60–64	3
	N = 50

about the center of the distribution, with fewer and fewer scores at the extreme ends of the distribution.

Defining Some Terms

Before we can get at the business of constructing frequency distributions, we must define some concepts that are essential to understanding the nature of the data to be displayed in a frequency distribution. The concepts described below will all refer to the frequency distribution of the English achievement scores of Table 2-4.

Real Limits and Apparent Limits

The top interval in Table 2-4 is 95-99, with a frequency of 2. In other words, two students scored somewhere from 95 through 99, the *apparent limits* of this interval. The next interval shows six scores from 90 through 94. However, to preserve the continuity of our measuring system for calculations to be discussed later on, we cannot leave a gap between 94 (the top score in the 90-94 interval) and 95 (the lowest score in the 95-99 interval). For this reason, it is understood that the *real limits* of any interval extend from *½ unit below the apparent lower limit to ½ unit above the apparent upper limit.* Thus the real limits of the 95-99 interval are 94.5 and 99.5, while the real limits of the 90-94 interval are 89.5 and 94.5. The real lower limit is designated L and the real upper limit is U. So for the 60-64 interval, $L = 59.5$ and $U = 64.5$. There will be more said about real limits in a later section on continuous and discrete data.

Midpoints

The exact center of any interval is called its *midpoint,* abbreviated *MP.* The *MP* of any interval is found by adding the apparent upper limit to the apparent lower limit and dividing by 2. In Table 2-4, the *MP* of the 75-79 interval is 77 (75 + 79 divided by 2), and the *MP* for the 80-84 interval is 82.

Interval Size

The *size* of the interval, denoted by the symbol *i*, is the distance between the real lower limit and the real upper limit. In other words you can determine the size of the interval simply by subtracting L from U. For example, in Table 2-4, using the 70-74 interval, you would calculate $i = U - L = 74.5 - 69.5 = 5$. Note that *i* is the same for all the intervals in Table 2-4. And, in Table 2-3, you will note that the interval size is 10 $(99.5 - 89.5 = 10)$.

Frequency

It should be obvious by now that frequency (the symbol is f) simply indicates how many scores are located in each interval. In Table 2-4, $f = 8$ for the 85-89 interval, indicating that eight students scored between 85 and 89.

Number

As was mentioned in the last chapter, in connection with summation notation, the number of scores in a distribution is denoted by the symbol N. In Table 2-4, $N = 50$. Note that N is the total of all the frequencies for the different intervals; that is, $\Sigma f = N$.

Constructing the Frequency Distribution

The first step in constructing a frequency distribution from any group of data is to locate the highest and the lowest score. For the data of Table 2-1, the two extremes are 97 and 61. This gives us $97 - 61 = 36$. Then we add 1 to the difference between the highest and lowest scores $(36 + 1 = 37)$, because simple subtraction ignores the real limits of a score. Technically, we should subtract 60.5 from 97.5 to obtain the range, 37. A convenient rule of thumb is to have from 8 to 15 intervals, depending on the size of the group. With only 50 scores 8 intervals will serve very nicely, while for a group of 200 you might get more information from your frequency distribution if you used from 12 to 15 intervals.

After you have calculated the range between the highest and lowest scores, the next step is to determine i, the size of the interval. This you do by dividing the range by the number of intervals you wish to employ. For the English scores the range of 37 divided by 8 would give 4.6 or 5, which is the interval size used in Table 2-4. *The choice of the number of intervals and the size of the interval is quite arbitrary.* Had you decided to use 10 intervals for the English scores, the interval size would be $i = 37/10 = 3.7$ or 4. However, 4 is seldom used for i, and most commonly you will see i values of 3, 5, 10, 25, 50, and other multiples of 10.

Since the choice of the number of intervals and i is arbitrary, your main concern is to have your frequency distribution display as much information as possible concerning concentrations and patterns of the scores. Obviously, the top interval should contain the highest score, and the bottom interval the lowest score. The bottom interval begins with a multiple of the interval size. The lowest score among those of Table 2-4 might be 60, 61, 62, 63, or 64, but the interval would still begin at 60.

After you have determined the size of i and the number of intervals you will use, you simply place the intervals in a column labeled "Scores" at the left side of a worksheet and then begin going through the data, placing a tally mark by the interval in which each score lies. Each entry in the frequency column is simply the addition of these tally marks for each interval. Your original worksheet for the English scores

Table 2-5
Worksheet for Frequency Distribution of
English Achievement Scores

Scores	Tally	f
95–99	I I	2
90–94	⊔⊢⊓ I	6
85–89	⊔⊢⊓ I I I	8
80–84	⊔⊢⊓ ⊔⊢⊓ I I	12
75–79	⊔⊢⊓ I I	7
70–74	⊔⊢⊓ I I	7
65–69	⊔⊢⊓	5
60–64	I I I	3
		$N = 50$

would look like Table 2-5, and the finished product would, of course, look like Table 2-4.

Continuous vs. Discrete Data

The data which constitute the raw material for studies in education and the behavioral sciences are numbers representing quantities such as reaction time, I.Q., age, test scores, and the like. It is convenient at this time to point out that some of the measurements that describe an individual's characteristics are *continuous* and some are *discrete*.

If the precision of a measurement or observation depends upon the accuracy of the measuring instrument, we say we have continuous data. For example, in measuring an individual's reaction time in pushing the brake pedal on a driving simulator in response to a red light, we may get a reaction time of 0.32 seconds. However, if we had a more accurate clock we might measure the same reaction as 0.324 seconds, or even as 0.3241 seconds. Or, in a similar vein, a person's height might be 5'10", but with a better measuring instrument we might find it to be 5'10.3" or even 5'10.317".

In any case we usually report just how accurate our measures are. If our reported reaction time is 0.32 seconds, we note that the measure is accurate to the nearest hundredth of a second. If our height is 5'10", we note that it is accurate to the nearest inch. Whenever we work with continuous data, we must be conscious of the *real limits* of the reported values, which extend from one-half unit below the reported value to one-half unit above. In the example above, any reaction time between 0.315 and 0.325 is reported as 0.32 seconds. Or any height from 5'9.5" to 5'10.5" would be reported as 5'10". If the measurement answers the question "How much?" we are talking about continuous data.

However, if data is of the *frequency* or *counting* type (and answers the question "How many?") we are speaking of *discrete* data. If there are 33 divorces for 100 marriages, or 17 auto fatalities in December, or 183 cases of Asian flu, then we have discrete data. There are no "in between" values, since you cannot have 0.35 of a divorce, or ½ a case of the flu. This does not stop the statistician from reporting fractional values, and you may have read of an average family size of 4.08 persons, or that the average worker may change jobs 3.8 times before retiring. This, of course, can be meaningful, provided you remember that the basic data consisted of discrete numbers. Later on in the text you will find that for purposes of calculation it will be necessary to assume that, for example, 3 children means between 2.5 and 3.5

children—but deep in our hearts we know that these are discrete data, and the fractions are for computational purposes only.

One very common type of measure deserves special consideration—that of test scores, especially those reported in number of items correct. If a student gets 43 items correct out of a possible 60 items, it sounds as if we are dealing with discrete data, since you cannot get 0.13 of an item correct. However, test scores in terms of items correct are considered continuous data *since the underlying variable that is being measured is assumed to be continuous*. A 60-item test may be measuring mathematics achievement, and it is assumed that the amount of achievement is continuous, with a score of 43 extending from 42.5 to 43.5. We are simply assuming that some students scoring 43 may have slightly less achievement than what is represented by the 43 but still greater than what is represented by a score of 42. Those with slightly more achievement than a score of 43, but not quite enough to obtain a score of 44, would still get a score of 43. So, when the underlying variable is assumed to be continuous, it is meaningful to consider a score of 43 extending from 42.5 to 43.5.

Graphing the Frequency Distribution

Our noble ancestor who first uttered the now-threadbare cliché about a picture being worth a thousand words was undoubtedly looking at the first graph. One can hardly read an assignment in a textbook or scan a newspaper or magazine without running into a graphical presentation of one form or another. Because graphical methods are such an important part of the statistical tools of the educator or behavioral scientist, it is essential that we spend considerable time and energy on this topic. There are many different kinds of graphs, but we will focus our attention on two main types—graphs that display the frequency distribution and graphs that represent a functional relationship between two variables.

By inspecting the frequency distribution of the English scores in Table 2-4, we can see that a few people made low scores and a few made high scores, but the majority of the scores are concentrated toward the middle of the distribution. It is difficult, however, to picture the entire distribution as a whole. For example, certain irregularities in the distribution may easily escape a casual glance. Since a pictorial representation of the data enables us to see the pattern of the distribution almost instantaneously, it is desirable to graph the frequency distribution. The most common graphical methods for the frequency distribution are the *histogram* and the *frequency polygon*.

Histogram

The histogram is similar to the old, familiar bar graph that you have seen quite frequently, and it can be interpreted in much the same way. Figure 2-1 shows a histogram based on the frequency distribution of the English scores of Table 2-4. Note that the height of each column represents the *frequency* in each interval.

When we examine the histogram of the English scores in Figure 2-1, we see that it is not symmetrical and that the shape is irregular. However, there is a tendency for many scores to fall toward the center of the distribution, with progressively fewer scores as you move in either direction from the "hump." We also see that there is a wide variation in the scores.

Certainly, if we worked at it long enough we could get the above information from the frequency distribution itself, but the graphical method gives us this information at a glance. And in a later section, when we get into the topic of the different kinds of shapes that distributions may take, it will be much easier to compare several graphs instead of frequency distributions.

The steps in the construction of a histogram are:

1. Lay out an area on a sheet of graph paper that corresponds roughly to the proportions of Figure 2-1. It is a good practice to have the

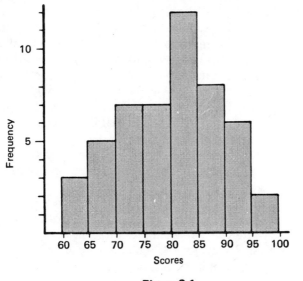

Figure 2-1
Histogram of English achievement scores.

height of the graph about three-fourths of the width. The horizontal line, called the x-axis or the abscissa, is drawn long enough to include all of the scores plus a little unused space at each end. Label this axis "Scores" and put a number of scores at appropriate intervals (60, 65, 70, etc., are logical choices here).

2. At the left end of the x-axis draw a vertical line (the ordinate, or y-axis). Divide the y-axis into units so that the largest frequency will not quite reach the top of the graph. Number these units and label this axis "Frequency."

3. Now you can complete the histogram simply by drawing lines parallel to the x-axis at the height of the frequency for each interval and connecting the lines to the x-axis by vertical lines to the *real* limits of the intervals. For example, as shown in Figure 2-1, three people scored in the 60-64 interval, so the horizontal line above this interval is drawn 3 units up from the x-axis, and vertical lines extend down to the real limits of 59.5 and 64.5.

4. Give the histogram a title, either above or below the figure. The title should be a clear statement of what the histogram represents.

Frequency Polygon

Probably most pictorial representations of the frequency distribution take the form of the *frequency polygon,* which is a line graph instead of the bar-type graph of the histogram. The frequency polygon for the distribution of English scores is shown in Figure 2-2.

Note that we get the same information from the frequency polygon as we did from the histogram, that is, the concentrations and spread of the scores. Since most graphs of the frequency distribution are frequency polygons, it might be a good idea to become thoroughly acquainted with the construction of the frequency polygon described below. Especially note that the points plotted in Figure 2-2 are directly above the *midpoint* of each interval and that the polygon drops down to the baseline (zero frequency) at both ends of the graph.

The steps in the construction of the frequency polygon are:

1. Lay out the area for the graph with the proper proportions and label the x- and y-axes just as you did for the histogram.

2. Instead of drawing a bar corresponding to the frequency for each interval as you did for the histogram, place a *dot* above the *midpoint* of each interval. For example, three persons scored in the 60-64 interval. $MP = 62$ for this interval, so you would place a dot opposite a frequency of 3 and above the score of 62. After you place the points for all intervals, simply connect the points with straight lines.

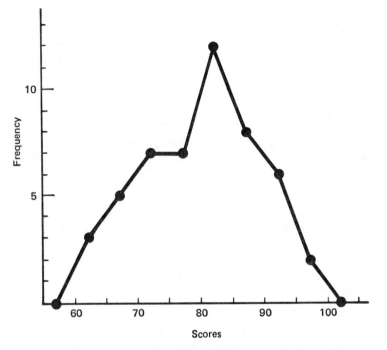

Figure 2-2
Frequency polygon of English achievement scores.

Note 2-1
Where Do the Scores Lie?

We have to remember that in gaining a bit of efficiency we have lost a little accuracy. Note that when scores are placed in a frequency distribution (and graphed as a polygon or histogram) the *identity* of an individual score is lost. In the English test data we see that five individuals scored between 65 and 69. Once the data is in the form of a frequency distribution we cannot determine the exact values of the individual scores. We only know that the five scores lie somewhere in the 65-69 interval. Several statistical techniques to be presented later on will make different assumptions regarding the precise location of the scores in an interval. But we will leave that for a later section and for now will note that the frequency polygon shown in Figure 2-2 assumes that the *average* of all the scores in any interval falls at the *midpoint* of that interval.

3. It is mathematically incorrect and artistically unsatisfying to leave the polygon suspended in mid-air, so the curve connecting the points drops down to the baseline at the extreme ends of the distribution. The curve touches the baseline at the *midpoint* of the adjacent interval, whose frequency, of course, is 0. For example, on the right side of Figure 2-2 the curve connects the point at 97 (the midpoint of the 95-99 interval) with the x-axis at 102 (the midpoint of the nonexistent 100-104 interval). The same method is used to connect the point at 62 with the x-axis at 57.

   Cautions on graphing. A certain amount of care has to be exer-

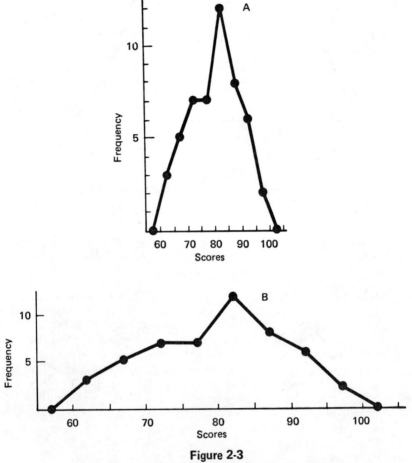

Figure 2-3
**Graphical distortion produced by improper proportion
in English achievement scores.**

cised in transforming the ordinary frequency distribution into a frequency polygon. The greatest single error committed by the novice is in using incorrect proportions in drawing the graph. In the last section we noted that the height of the graph should be about three-fourths of the width. It is essential to follow this convention, since most graphs that you will be examining in books and journal articles will have the same general proportion. It is a lot easier to analyze someone else's graph if you have been using a similar layout and format all along.

Figure 2-3 shows the English scores represented in two incorrectly drawn frequency polygons. Polygon A has the scale of the ordinate too great with respect to that of the abscissa, while polygon B is just the reverse. While these figures are obvious exaggerations, it must be noted that it does not take much deviation from the three-fourths rule of thumb to produce a distortion which interferes with interpreting the graph.

Comparing two distributions. One very common use of the frequency polygon is in presenting data from two frequency distributions with approximately equal values of N. This procedure permits a comparison of two sets of scores on the same variable, in addition to providing information on each distribution separately. Just such a comparison is shown in Figure 2-4 for coordination test scores for a group of 90 seventh-grade girls and 85 seventh-grade boys. Note the ease with which you can make direct comparisons regarding the relative abilities of the two groups and the spread and concentrations of scores.

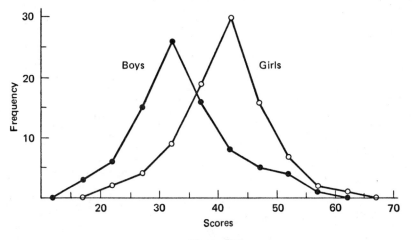

Figure 2-4
Coordination scores for seventh-grade boys and girls.

It is obvious from the graph that the ability of the girls as shown by this particular coordination test is superior to that of the boys.

Typical and Not-so-typical Frequency Distributions

The Normal Curve

You have all heard of, and undoubtedly used, the term *normal curve*. Many physiological measurements (height, weight, length of nose, number of eyelashes) and behavioral measurements (I.Q. scores, reaction time, aptitude test scores) are normally distributed in the population. By "normally distributed" we mean that the frequency polygon for the distribution of measurements closely approximates the mathematical model shown in Figure 2-5. This bell-shaped, symmetrical curve is called a *normal curve*. If this were a frequency polygon of test scores, it would show the typical concentration of scores in the middle of the distribution, with fewer and fewer scores as you approach the extremes. For example, if this curve represented the distribution of the heights of American adult males, the curve would be the highest (greatest frequency) around 5'9'' and would get progressively lower (smaller and smaller frequency) as you got out towards 6'5'' or 5'1''. And the curve would almost touch the baseline (very small frequency of occurrence) at a height of 7'1'' or 4'8''.

The frequency polygon of the English scores of Figure 2-2 bears only a slight resemblance to the normal curve. When we have only 50 scores we must expect a lack of symmetry in the distribution. If the

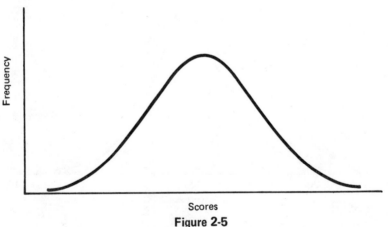

Scores
Figure 2-5
A normal curve model.

English test had been given to 500 students, we would expect that some of the irregularities would disappear, resulting in a smoother, more symmetrical curve. And if the test scores were obtained from several thousand individuals, the resulting frequency polygon would come even closer in appearance to the normal curve model of Figure 2-5.

Even though the data with which we will most often be working will never be exactly normally distributed, we will find that the normal curve model has some very useful properties in relation to our data. In fact, these properties are a foundation for a very important part of statistical techniques, and we will have occasion to devote an entire chapter to these properties later on in the text.

Skewness

There will be times when a graph of the frequency distribution will not have the typical, symmetric bell shape with the majority of scores concentrated at the center of the distribution. Instead you might find that the majority of the scores are clustered at either the high end or the low end of the distribution. This concentration of scores at one end or the other of the distribution is called *skewness*.

If the scores are concentrated at the upper end of the distribution so the tail of the curve skews to the *left*, we say that the curve is

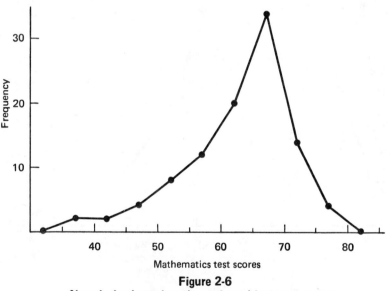

Figure 2-6
Negatively skewed mathematics achievement scores.

negatively skewed. Figure 2-6 shows the results of a national achievement exam in mathematics given to all ninth-graders in a school system enrolled in accelerated classes in mathematics. As you can see, there is a large concentration of high scores with progressively fewer low scores as you go to the left. This graph is telling us that the exam was too easy for the majority of the students, which was to be expected, since they are in accelerated classes.

If the scores are clustered at the lower end of the distribution so the tail of the curve skews to the right, we say that the curve is *positively skewed.* Positive skewness is characterized by a preponderance of low scores, such as would occur if a difficult test were administered to an average group or an ordinary test administered to a remedial group. Another set of data that is usually positively skewed is the distribution of earned incomes. Figure 2-7 shows an obviously positive skew, since the majority of incomes fall between $7,500 and $15,500, which are at the lower end of the distribution, while other incomes extend a considerable distance to the right.

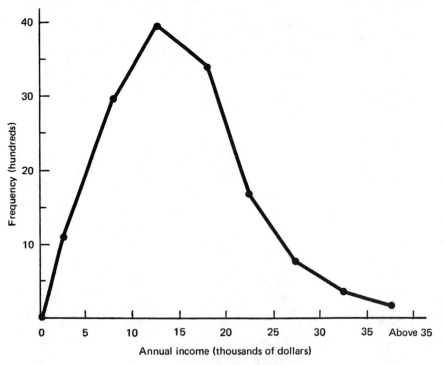

Figure 2-7
Positively skewed annual income distribution of 14,000 workers.

If we examine the frequency polygon of the English scores in Figure 2-2, we see that there is a very slight negative skewness, since there are a few more scores near the upper end of the distribution. This type of skewness is quite common in academic situations, especially in college-level classes. Since most college classes represent quite a high level of ability, there usually will be more higher scores than lower scores. To put it another way, there usually are more A and B letter grades than D and F grades.

We have been using the "eyeball" method for examining the skewness of a distribution, and this may be perfectly adequate in most situations. However, if you want a more precise, mathematically defined method for measuring the amount of skewness, see one of the books listed in the References.

Note 2-2
Remembering Which Skewness Is Which

A handy device for determining whether a curve is negatively or positively skewed is to look at the *tail* of the curve (the tail is on the opposite side from the concentration of scores). If you remember your algebra, you know the direction *left* is negative, so if the tail goes to the left, the skewness is negative. If the tail points to the right, since the direction *right* is positive, you have positive skewness. In checking this with Figures 2-6 and 2-7, note that in Figure 2-6 the tail points to the left (negative skewness) while in Figure 2-7 it points to the right (positive skewness).

Kurtosis

Another property of a frequency distribution besides the amount of symmetry (symmetry is the opposite of skewness) is its *kurtosis*. When we speak of kurtosis we are referring to the "peakedness" or "flatness" of a frequency polygon. If the curve has a very sharp peak, it indicates an extreme concentration of scores about the center, and we say that it is *leptokurtic*. If the curve is quite flat, it would tell us that while there is some degree of concentration at the center there are quite a few scores that are dispersed away from the middle of the distribution; we say the curve is *platykurtic*. The curve that represents a happy medium is a *mesokurtic* curve. The normal curve model of Figure 2-5 is mesokurtic. All three degrees of kurtosis are shown in Figure 2-8.

We ordinarily do not worry too much about the type of kurtosis in a set of data from test scores, surveys, and experiments, where we

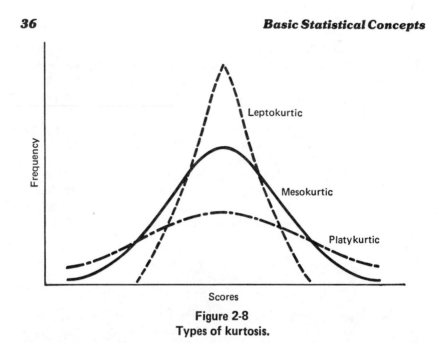

Figure 2-8
Types of kurtosis.

are interested in describing the performance of a group of individuals. However, when we consider theoretical issues in sampling procedures and statistical tests in later chapters, we will come back to the concept of kurtosis.

Note 2-3
Remembering Which Kurtosis Is Which

A colleague of mine uses some vivid imagery to illustrate the different types of kurtosis. He notes that the platykurtic curve is flat and rounded like the back of a duckbilled platypus. The other type of kurtosis reminds him of a kangaroo, since the leptokurtic curve looks as if it is "lepping" around. He claims that not a single student has forgotten the difference between platykurtic and leptokurtic curves!

J-Curves

Before leaving our discussion of the shapes of frequency distributions, we should make note of a special type of extreme skewness—the J-curve. The J-curve hypothesis of social conformity was first proposed by Floyd Allport and is related to conforming behavior among groups of people. The large majority of scores fall at the end of the scale representing socially acceptable behavior, while the small minority of scores represent a deviation from this social norm.

If we were to keep track of the amount of time that 100 drivers parked in a No Parking zone, we would find that the great majority of them would be there for just a few minutes while they ran an "emergency" errand in a nearby store. However, there would always be several that would park for a longer period of time while they ran a few errands, hoping that the local traffic patrol would not come by in their absence. And there might even be a couple of drivers who would be completely oblivious to the parking regulations and leave their cars while they went to a movie.

The J-curve for this example is shown in Figure 2-9, and you will note that the curve resembles a backward letter J. This type of curve can be found in a number of situations where a group standard can be quantified and deviations from the social norm observed. Some examples might be the speed with which drivers approach a stop sign, the time of arrival at a concert or religious service, and the number of drinks consumed during the social hour preceding a banquet.

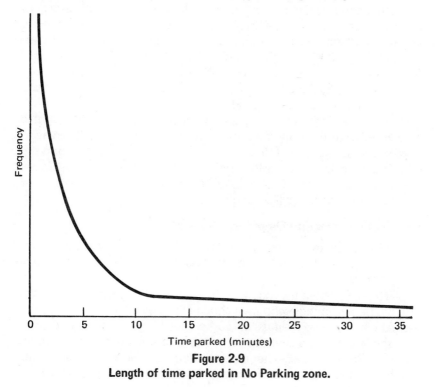

Figure 2-9
Length of time parked in No Parking zone.

Graphing the Functional Relationship

After spending considerable time and energy on frequency distributions and the graphical methods for displaying such data, we will have to shift our frame of reference slightly in order to take up the topic of graphing a *functional relationship*. We will be directing our attention not to a pictorial representation of the frequency distribution but rather to a pictorial image of the *relationship* between two variables.

In the broadest sense we might say that the objective of educators and behavioral scientists is to discover functional relationships between variables. An educator might be interested in knowing if the number of siblings (brothers and sisters) that a child has will have an effect on his social relationships in nursery school. If an investigator finds that the only child has more difficulty in getting along with others than the child with two siblings, we say that he has demonstrated a *functional relationship* between the two variables of number of siblings and amount of social adjustment.

An economist might be interested in learning what effect the amount of leisure time has on the individual's expenditures for recreational items such as snowmobiles, speedboats, camper trailers, and the like. If she finds that people working a 48-hour week spend 3% of their take-home pay on recreation while those working a 36-hour week spend 7%, we say that she has found a functional relationship between hours worked and leisure expenditures.

In still another example, an engineering psychologist might be concerned with the brightness of a car's brake lights and the reaction time of the driver in the following car. If he finds that the reaction time of 100 drivers decreases as the brightness of the brake light is increased, we would say that he has established a functional relationship between reaction time and brake light brightness.

Independent and Dependent Variables

In all of the examples above we have noted that there is a relationship between two variables — the *independent* variable and the *dependent* variable.

The independent variable is the one that is manipulated in some way by the researcher, who may choose to compare an only child with a child who has two siblings, or workers working a 48-hour work week with those working a 36-hour work week, or three different brightness levels of brake lights. The *independent variables* are, respectively, number of siblings, length of work week, and brake light brightness.

The dependent variable is dependent (hence the name) upon the value of the independent variable. It is always a measurement of some sort—in the examples above it would be the amount of social adjustment, amount of money spent on recreation, and the speed of reaction. It is sometimes called the *response variable,* since it is always the measure of some type of response. If there is a relationship between the independent and dependent variables, we note that the dependent variable changes in response to changes in the independent variable. As the researcher varies the independent variable, he notes that the dependent variable, which he is measuring, also changes.

These changes are best shown in the form of a graph such as Figure 2-10. As we mentioned earlier a researcher might be investigating how the reaction time of a driver to a brake light depends on the brightness of the brake light. Note that the dependent variable (reaction time) is plotted on the ordinate while the independent variable (brake light brightness) is plotted on the abscissa. As you can see from the graph, when a dim brake light is used as a stimulus, the response time is about 0.35 seconds. The driver's response is somewhat faster when a moderately bright brake light is used, and his response is the fastest (about 0.30 seconds) when a bright brake light is used. There is no doubt about it—the researcher has demonstrated a functional relationship between the two variables. Reaction time does in-

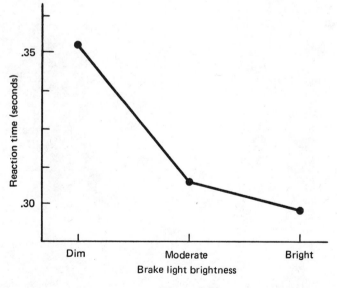

Figure 2-10
Reaction time to three brake light systems.

deed depend on the brightness of the stimulus, and the graph displays this functional relationship very efficiently.

The rules for graphing functional relationships are pretty much the same as for graphing the frequency distribution as far as proportion, labeling of axes, and so on. And, as mentioned above, the dependent variable—what the researcher is measuring—always goes on the ordinate. One important difference that should be noted is that the curve does not drop down to 0 at the baseline as was the case with the frequency polygon. If it did this in Figure 2-10, for example, it would imply that we had some measurements at other brightness levels than dim, moderate, and bright. Since reaction times were not measured at "very dim" or "very bright," we cannot extend the curve to those points.

The above discussion was not intended to be a thorough and exhaustive presentation of the topic of functional relationships. A complete treatment of functional relationships and different types of variables more properly belongs in a textbook of experimental design or advanced statistics. Our purpose for considering the topic at this point was twofold: a discussion of graphical methods would not be complete without it, and there will be several occasions in future chapters when we will want to consider ways to measure the *amount* of relationship that exists between two variables.

Sample Problem

One hundred college students enrolled in high-ability classes in freshman English were given a national English achievement examination. Their scores are listed below:

88	84	85	90	82	82	89	83	78	84
82	80	73	84	79	83	83	85	87	89
66	83	83	77	84	80	74	82	74	76
86	85	77	87	77	79	72	78	74	86
81	80	89	75	86	67	82	81	76	79
88	64	79	76	87	83	85	80	73	81
84	83	70	86	78	78	81	85	85	71
72	74	83	75	62	68	83	84	87	84
83	81	82	81	82	80	86	86	88	68
86	79	85	76	78	87	81	80	83	72

To construct a frequency distribution from this data, we first note that the highest score is 90 and the lowest is 62. With a range of $90 - 62 + 1 = 29$, we could use 11 intervals, with $i = 3$. If we wanted $i = 5$, we would only have 6 intervals, which would be too few to give a complete picture of the data.

Since the lowest score was 62, the bottom interval would be 60-62. We simply list the 11 intervals in a column and go through the table of raw data, placing a tally mark beside the interval where each score falls. The worksheet is shown at the left, and the finished product is at the right.

Scores	Tally	Scores	f
90-92	I	90-92	1
87-89	++++ ++++ I	87-89	11
84-86	++++ ++++ ++++ ++++ I	84-86	21
81-83	++++ ++++ ++++ ++++ ++++	81-83	25
78-80	++++ ++++ ++++ I	78-80	16
75-77	++++ IIII	75-77	9
72-74	++++ IIII	72-74	9
69-71	II	69-71	2
66-68	IIII	66-68	4
63-65	I	63-65	1
60-62	I	60-62	1
			$N = 100$

The frequency polygon for this data is shown in Figure 2-11. Note that for easy readability the score values chosen are in multiples of 5, even though $i = 3$ for this distribution. Also note that the points are plotted above the midpoint values for each interval.

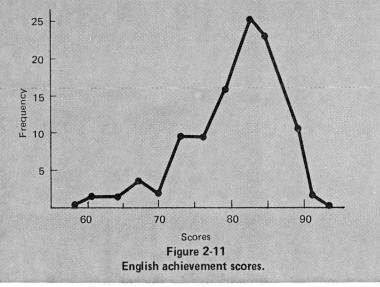

Figure 2-11
English achievement scores.

> In analyzing the frequency polygon we note that there is a rather marked degree of negative skewness; that is, the tail skews to the left. But the preponderance of high scores is to be expected, since these are test scores of a group considerably above average in ability.

Study Questions

1. What is the difference between a simple frequency distribution and a grouped frequency distribution?

2. List the steps you would use in constructing a grouped frequency distribution.

3. What is the difference between continuous and discrete data? Give an example of each.

4. Describe the construction of a histogram.

5. In what ways is a frequency polygon different from a histogram?

6. Define negative and positive skewness, and give examples of each.

7. In a graph, on what axis is the independent variable located? The dependent variable?

Exercises

1. A group of ninth-graders is given a general science exam. Construct a grouped frequency distribution from these scores.

47	49	52	40	48	47	37	47	46	45
35	32	25	35	41	40	30	26	27	42
37	36	36	32	41	42	20	31	29	28
32	37	37	42	27	21	43	22	32	20
38	39	43	38	29	34	16	44	34	33
29	44	30	31	39	32	30	33	23	34
42	24	22	33	28	35	23	31	24	22
25	26	32	27	16	22	36	17	32	34
28	31	23	15	21	17	19	37	14	39
30	27	26	25	16	18	12	13	38	33

2. A group of eighth-graders in several accelerated classes was given a mathematics proficiency examination. The scores for the 54 students are shown below. Construct a grouped frequency distribution for these data.

89	97	94	84	87	83
80	84	87	93	78	77
96	79	81	78	81	91
72	96	86	85	80	86
87	88	82	71	93	77
78	76	79	92	92	81
82	87	90	69	79	88
85	74	83	86	63	66
83	82	75	80	81	80

3. For the intervals below give the real lower and upper limits, the midpoint, and the size of the interval.

   a. 110-119
   b. 46-48
   c. 1.5-1.9
   d. 50-74
   e. 0.02-0.04
   f. 100-149
   g. 70-74
   h. 20-49
   i. 19.0-19.4
   j. 86-87

4. Indicate whether the types of data described below are likely to be discrete or continuous.

   a. Number of children of each of 1,000 married graduates of a public high school
   b. Average height of the Los Angeles Lakers
   c. Batting averages of the New York Mets
   d. Frequency of accidents at downtown intersections for each hour during the Christmas holidays
   e. Tabulation of cavities for a hundred 10-year-olds using electric toothbrushes
   f. Daily hours of sunshine during the period from September 21 to December 21

g. Incidence of auto thefts by month reported to police during the last 3 years
h. Average distance driven to work by urban commuters
i. Monthly incidence of strep throat reported to a university health center
j. Frequency of participation in extracurricular activities by college freshmen

5. Draw a histogram on a sheet of graph paper for the frequency distribution of the general science exam scores in exercise 1.

6. Using graph paper, draw a frequency polygon based on the mathematics exam scores in exercise 2.

7. Indicate the shape of the curve (normal or negatively or positively skewed) that you might find in the following data.

   a. A fifth-grade teacher inadvertently administers a test of sixth-grade spelling words
   b. Gifted students in a creative writing class are given the verbal subtest of an intelligence test
   c. A computer printout shows the current checking account balances for all checking customers of the Last National Bank
   d. Seventh-graders at a local junior high school are given a mechanical aptitude test
   e. A nationwide mathematics exam is given to 1,000 students at a college with a selective admissions policy
   f. Diagnostic reading test scores are tabulated for all fourth-graders in a school district

8. College students wearing glasses were compared with those wearing contact lenses on their reaction time in pushing a switch when a stimulus light came on. The lights were located at different positions in the visual field. One light was at center (0°), and the others were at 20°, 40°, 60°, and 80° to the left and right of the center light. Use graph paper to plot the functional relationship between reaction time (in milliseconds) and position in the visual field, and note the differences between those wearing glasses and those wearing contacts.

	(Left)				Position				(Right)
	80°	60°	40°	20°	0°	20°	40°	60°	80°
Contacts	576	570	554	545	540	544	548	560	579
Glasses	597	578	564	550	542	548	558	576	595

3 Central Tendency

Hardly a day goes by that we do not hear some reference to the concept of "average" performance. Energy-conscious drivers inform us that their cars will average 30 or 40 miles per gallon, while sports fans are forever discussing some ballplayer's batting average or earned run average or their own bowling average. And even the little girl shopping for a Mother's Day gift may explain to the salesclerk that she wants a blouse for her "average-size" mother. Figure 3-1 suggests the degree to which measures of average performance affect the lives of all of us.

The "average" used so frequently by the layperson is part of the concept of *central tendency*. As you saw in the last chapter, frequency distributions, along with the histogram and the frequency polygon, are valuable devices which enable us to extract meaning from a mass of data. However, we would like more efficient ways of expressing our results than a mere picture of the distribution as a whole. Specifically, we would like to have a statistical method that would yield a *single value* which would tell us something about the entire distribution.

©1974 United Feature Syndicate, Inc.

Figure 3-1
The concept of central tendency is even noted in the comic strips.

Such a single value is called a *measure of central tendency.* It is the single value which best describes the performance of the group as a whole. For example, the average income in a community might be $14,500, or the average weight of the defensive linemen of the Minnesota Vikings might be 248 pounds, or the average test score in an educational psychology course might be 83.2. All of these single values cited have one thing in common: they are values that best characterize the group as a whole. No person actually had a score of 83.2 on the educational psychology exam, but the average of 83.2 is the best single value that represents the performance of that group of students.

There are a number of measures of central tendency, all designed to give representative values of some distribution. In this chapter we will concentrate on three of the most commonly used: the arithmetic mean, the median, and the mode. But keep in mind as we discuss the characteristics of these measures of central tendency that our eventual aim will be to find one that best describes the performance of the group as a whole.

Mean

The *average,* referred to a bit earlier, is more correctly called the *arithmetic mean,* or often just the *mean.* I am sure you remember from an arithmetic class of many years ago that to calculate the mean you simply add up all the numbers and divide by how many numbers there are. So, if you paid 69¢, 49¢, 98¢, 59¢, and 95¢ for five items in the supermarket, the average or mean price paid per item would be $3.70 divided by 5, or 74¢.

However, statisticians tend to get a little nervous when terms are not precisely defined, so another set of observations (10 scores on an art history quiz) is shown in Table 3-1, with previously defined terms

Table 3-1
Calculation of the Mean of an Art History Quiz

X
2
7
8
6
3
6
2
3
8
5
$\Sigma X = \overline{50}$

$$\overline{X} = \frac{\Sigma X}{N} = \frac{50}{10} = 5$$

ΣX and N. As mentioned in an earlier chapter, ΣX is the symbol for the sum of the X values, and N is the number of values. In Table 3-1, the addition of the X values yields $\Sigma X = 50$, and N is, of course, 10. The formula for the mean, whose symbol is $\overline{X}$ (say "X bar"), would be:

$$\overline{X} = \frac{\Sigma X}{N} \qquad (3\text{-}1)[1]$$

which simply states that we obtain the mean by summing all the X values and dividing by N, the number of observations. So, for the data of Table 3-1, the mean would be:

$$\overline{X} = \frac{\Sigma X}{N} = \frac{50}{10} = 5$$

So what does the mean mean? What does $\overline{X} = 5$ in Table 3-1 tell us about the data? In short, we would say that the value of 5 is the best single value which describes this group of scores. Since these observations were scores on a short quiz made by 10 students, we would conclude that a score of 5 is the best single value that represents the performance of this group as a whole.

Another useful feature of the mean is that it makes it possible to compare an individual's score with the scores of the rest of the group. Did he score above the mean or below it? Is she above average or below average? How far above or below is she? We can answer these ques-

[1]Computational formulas in the text will be identified by a number that indicates the chapter number and the location of the formula in the chapter. Thus, formula 3-1 is the first formula listed in Chapter 3.

tions in terms of *deviation* or distance from the mean. In Table 3-2 are listed the same 10 scores along with the individuals that made each score. In addition to the column of scores (*X*) there is another column (*x*), which shows how far each score is from the mean. These distances are calculated by the formula

$$x = X - \overline{X}$$

which simply says that to find each individual's deviation score, *x* (read "little *x*," which is not a term of endearment but signifies a lowercase *x*), we subtract the mean from each raw score. For example, individual A's deviation score would be -3 (2 minus 5), indicating that his raw score is located 3 score units below the mean. Similarly, B's deviation score would be 2 (7 minus 5), and we know that her raw score of 7 is 2 units above the mean of 5. By raw score we mean the scores that are obtained directly from the test.

The reason for belaboring the obvious in the previous paragraph is to demonstrate that *the algebraic sum of the deviation scores is always 0.* Note that the sum of the *x* column in Table 3-2 is 0. This is the formal definition of the arithmetic mean. It is calculated in such a way that it is directly in the center of these deviations, making the algebraic sum of these deviations 0. In our usual notation $\Sigma x = 0$.

This is best shown by the illustration in Figure 3-2. Note that the mean is the fulcrum and that the entire group of observations is in balance.

We need to make one last point about the calculation of the mean.

Table 3-2
Quiz Raw Scores Expressed as Deviation Scores

Individual	X	x
A	2	-3
B	7	2
C	8	3
D	6	1
E	3	-2
F	6	1
G	2	-3
H	3	-2
I	8	3
J	5	0
	$\Sigma X = 50$	$\Sigma x = 0$

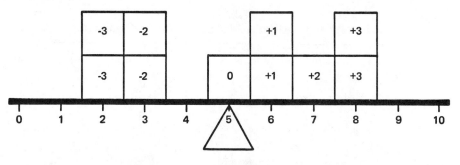

Figure 3-2
Arithmetic mean expressed as a balancing point.

In Chapter 1, if you remember, quite a case was made for the necessity of determining what level of precision we have in a group of data, that is, whether the observations are from a nominal, an ordinal, an interval, or a ratio scale. As was mentioned, we need to know this information before we can calculate any statistic based on the data. As you progress through this text, you will note that for each statistic discussed there will always be an accompanying comment on what type of data is appropriate for a given statistic. So with this in mind, we conclude that since the mean takes into account the distances between observations the measurements from which the mean is calculated must be at least of the interval type. A mean calculated from ordinal data (e.g., mean rank) may be misleading.

Median

The median is probably most familiar to you as the 50th percentile. *The median is the value that exactly separates the upper half of the distribution from the lower half.* It is obviously a measure of central tendency in that the median is the point located in such a way that 50% of the scores are lower than the median and the other 50% are greater than the median. It is important to note that while the mean was the exact center of the *deviations* or distances of the scores from the mean the median is the exact center of the scores themselves.

If the set of data contains an *odd* number of untied scores, as shown in distribution A in Table 3-3, the median is simply the central score when they are *ranked* in order of magnitude. In the example shown, *Med* = 12, since 12 is the point that exactly separates the upper and lower halves of the distribution.

Table 3-3
Calculation of the Median When There Are No Tied Scores

A (N is odd)	B (N is even)
21	13
19	12
14	9
12	4
11	3
8	1
5	
Med = 12	Med = (4 + 9)/2 = 6.5

If, as shown in distribution B, there are an *even* number of untied scores, the median is exactly halfway between the two centermost values. Since 4 and 9 are on either side of the center, the value of the median would be 6.5. In other words Med = 6.5 is the point that exactly separates the upper and lower halves of the distribution.

The calculation of the median becomes more involved when there are some tied scores, especially if they are at or near the median. It then becomes necessary to use the method of interpolation to find the exact location of the median. This method is presented later on in this chapter when *grouped-data* methods are defined.

The median is a valuable measure of central tendency for measurements that are only of the ordinal type. Since no assumptions are made concerning distances between observations, it is meaningful to talk about median ranks, for example. So the median is an appropriate measure of central tendency for data that are ordinal or above.

Mode

The French expression *à la mode* literally means in vogue or in style. And that is exactly what the mode is—*the score that is made most frequently,* or seems to be "in style." It is classed as a measure of central tendency since a glance at a graph of the frequency distribution (e.g., Figure 2-2, in the last chapter) shows the grouping about a central point, and the mode is the highest point in the hump, or the most frequent score. The mode is easily obtained by inspection, but it is the crudest measure of central tendency and is not used as often as either the mean or the median. Table 3-4 shows 14 physical fitness proficiency scores, and we note that the mode is 21, since that score appears most often. However, there are three scores of 19, so it is necessary to distinguish between the *principal mode* and the *secondary mode*. Whenever there are two peaks or concentrations in a frequency distribution, we have what is known as a *bimodal distribution*. For example, if we were to measure the heights of a random sample of high school seniors, we would very likely get a bimodal distribution—one peak corresponding to the concentration about an average for girls and another peak for boys.

The chief value of the mode lies in the fact that it is easily obtained by inspection and is useful in locating points of concentration of like scores in a distribution. The mode may be calculated from measurements that are of the nominal type or above.

Comparing the Mean, Median, and Mode

If a measure of central tendency is a single value that best represents the performance of the group as a whole, which single value should be used? If you compute the mean, median, and mode for the

Table 3-4
Determining the Mode of the Physical Fitness Scores

X	
24	
23	
22	
21	
21	Principal Mode = 21
21	
21	
20	
19	
19	Secondary Mode = 19
19	
18	
17	
16	

Note 3-1
The Effect on the Mean of Adding a Constant

If some number, such as 3 (in other words, a constant), is added to all the scores in a distribution, the mean is increased by the amount of the constant. For instance, the mean of the scores 5, 2, 9, 6, and 3 is 25/5 = 5. If the constant 3 were added to each score you now would have 8, 5, 12, 9, and 6, with a mean of 40/5 = 8. Stated symbolically, if a constant C is added to each score in a distribution with a mean $\overline{X}$, the mean of the new distribution will be $\overline{X} + C$. This fact probably does not come as a startling revelation to you, but in later chapters we will have occasion to make use of this peculiar property of the mean. For the mathematically inclined, the proof is very simple. Given the mean of a set of scores:

$$\overline{X} = \frac{\Sigma X}{N} = \frac{X_1 + X_2 + \ldots + X_N}{N}$$

a constant is added to each score:

$$\overline{X} = \frac{(X_1 + C) + (X_2 + C) + \ldots + (X_N + C)}{N}$$

Combining terms, and noting that the sum of a constant is equal to N times the constant:

$$\overline{X} = \frac{\Sigma X + \Sigma C}{N} = \frac{\Sigma X + NC}{N} = \frac{\Sigma X}{N} + \frac{NC}{N}$$

So the mean of the new distribution is

$$\overline{X} = \frac{\Sigma X}{N} + C = \overline{X} + C$$

same set of scores, you very rarely will find that all three are identical. Which one will give us the "best single value" that describes the entire distribution?

The answer to this question is by no means a simple one. First of all, we can ignore the mode since it is a rather crude measure of central tendency. This leaves the mean and median to be considered, and, as you probably have guessed, the mean is most often given as a measure of central tendency. Whenever you see the term *average* used in books, magazines, and newspapers in describing some distribution, most often the author is referring to the mean.

However, there are many instances where the median is a valuable statistic. It is not affected by extreme or atypical values as much as is the mean, so it is very useful in situations where the distribution is either positively or negatively skewed. For example, suppose we would like to calculate the average income for people living in a small mid-western town. Let us assume that in this community there is one millionaire and the rest of the residents are earning what we would judge to be ordinary incomes. This is a slight exaggeration, but it will serve to illustrate the usefulness of the median when distributions are markedly skewed. The mean, since it takes into account the exact value of each score, would be unduly influenced by the millionaire's income, and this measure of central tendency would be much too high. The median, on the other hand, is the center of the distribution and would not be affected very much by the addition of a single score at the extreme end. Clearly, the median would give the most accurate picture of the income for this situation.

The ability of the median to resist the effect of skewness is demonstrated in Table 3-5. In column B an extreme score of 100 has been added to the distribution of seven scores in column A. Note that with the addition of this extreme score, the median changes very little, from 8 to 8.5, while the mean jumps from 8.1 to 19.6.

The relationship of the mean and median in skewed distributions is demonstrated in Figures 3-3 and 3-4. The negatively skewed distribution of mathematics achievement scores discussed in the last chapter is reproduced in Figure 3-3. Note that the mode has the highest value, 67, while the mean is at 62.9, and the median is in between the two at 64.9. This illustrates a general rule: *In negative skewness, the mean is the lowest value of the three measures of central tendency.*

In Figure 3-4 the distribution of incomes of 14,000 workers discussed in the last chapter as an example of positive skewness is reproduced. Note that the mode is the lowest value, at $12,500, the median is $13,815, and the mean is the highest, at $15,200. *In positive skewness, the mean is the highest value of the three measures of central tendency.*

As you can see from the last two examples, the mean is affected greatly by the extreme or atypical scores in a skewed distribution, since it is "pulled" in the direction of the atypical values. It is for just this reason that the median is the preferred measure of central tendency when there is a marked degree of skewness in the distribution. It is much more likely to be the best single value that describes the distribution as a whole.

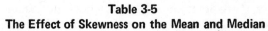

Table 3-5
The Effect of Skewness on the Mean and Median

A	B
14	100
12	14
9	12
8	9
7	8
5	7
2	5
$\Sigma X = \overline{57}$	2
	$\Sigma X = \overline{157}$
$\overline{X} = 57/7 = 8.1$	$\overline{X} = 157/8 = 19.6$
$Med = 8$	$Med = 8.5$

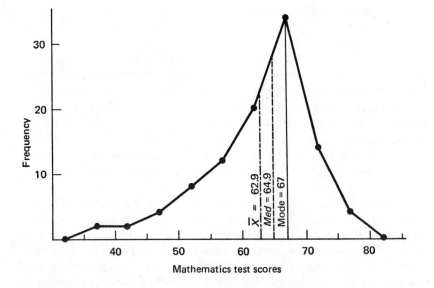

Figure 3-3
Three measures of central tendency in negative skewness.

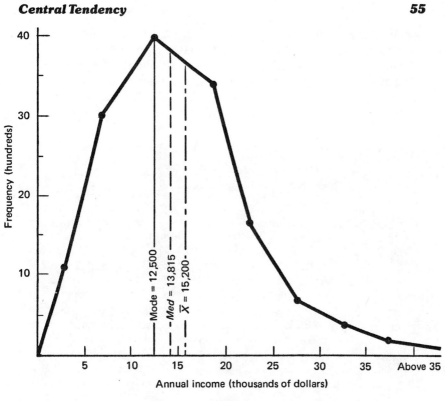

Figure 3-4
Three measures of central tendency in positive skewness.

Stability

If the median is the preferred measure of central tendency in skewed distributions, why isn't it used all the time for all distributions? The answer to this question is that the *mean* is the most *stable* of the three measures of central tendency. By stability, we mean that in *repeated sampling* the means of the samples will tend to vary the least among themselves.

A complete treatment of *sampling* and *populations* will be coming up in a later chapter, but for the time being we can illustrate this concept by an example. If we took repeated samples of some variable in the population (e.g., I.Q. scores of 100 10-year-olds, chosen at random) and calculated the three traditional measures of central tendency for various batches of samples, each containing 100 I.Q. scores, we would find that the means would be most like each other. Since we often want to estimate what the population value is from just one sample, we naturally would want to use the measure of central tendency that is the most reliable or consistent. So the mean is used most often as the measure of central tendency, since it fluctuates the least from sample to sample.

Note 3-2
Rounding Off Measures of Central Tendency

How many significant digits should you report when you calculate a measure of central tendency? The mean, since it is obtained by dividing ΣX by N, could have a whole string of digits to the right of the decimal point. For example, if $\Sigma X = 93$ and $N = 7$, you could report the mean as 13.3 or 13.29 or 13.286 or 13.2857, depending upon your enthusiasm for division. The problem is that the more digits you include, the more precision is implied – and the precision may be totally unwarranted. For that reason it is conventional to report measures of central tendency to *one more decimal place* than you have in your raw data. So for test scores that are whole numbers, such as 84, 72, and so on, your mean might be 58.6. And if your data consisted of reaction time measured in hundredths of seconds, such as 0.37, 0.29, and so on, your mean might be 0.326. The median is treated in a similar fashion.

Calculating a Mean for Several Groups

There will be occasions when you will want to calculate a mean from a number of other means. For example, if the mean reading test score for a group of fourth-graders is 31.3, and for a group of fifth-graders it is 42.7, what is the mean for the combined group of fourth- and fifth-graders? With only this information, *you cannot calculate a combined mean.* You cannot simply "average" the two means to get a combined mean for the two groups (except in the unlikely event that the values of N for the two groups are identical). In order to calculate the combined mean for a group of means, you must know the size of each sample, or N. Then the formula is:

$$\overline{X} = \frac{N_1\overline{X}_1 + N_2\overline{X}_2 + N_3\overline{X}_3 + \ldots}{N_1 + N_2 + N_3 + \ldots} \qquad (3\text{-}2)$$

where N_1 is the size of sample 1,
   $\overline{X}_1$ is the mean of sample 1,
   N_2 is the size of sample 2,
   $\overline{X}_2$ is the mean of sample 2,
and so on.

Table 3-6 shows the means for a motor coordination test for three groups of 10-, 11-, and 12-year-olds, and our objective is to find the combined mean for all 80. Note that in the calculation of the combined mean the mean of each separate group is multiplied by its own N. The sum of these products is then divided by the combined N, giving a mean of 21.1 for all three groups together. This is obviously different from what you would have obtained if you had incorrectly "averaged" the three means themselves.

Table 3-6
Calculation of a Combined Mean for Motor Coordination

10-year-olds	*11-year-olds*	*12-year-olds*
$N\ =\ 10$	$N\ =\ 30$	$N\ =\ 40$
$\overline{X}_1\ =\ 17$	$\overline{X}_2\ =\ 20$	$\overline{X}_3\ =\ 23$

$$\overline{X} = \frac{N_1\overline{X}_1 + N_2\overline{X}_2 + N_3\overline{X}_3}{N_1 + N_2 + N_3}$$

$$= \frac{10(17) + 30(20) + 40(23)}{10 + 30 + 40}$$

$$= \frac{170 + 600 + 920}{80} = \frac{1,690}{80}$$

$$\overline{X} = 21.1$$

Note 3-3
What the Combined Mean Formula Really Means

The formula for finding a mean of means is very easy to remember if you stop and note that $N\overline{X} = \Sigma X$. In other words, all that we are doing is converting the data for each group back to the original sum of the scores. After we have done this for all the groups, we add the individual sums together to get one grand sum of the scores, or a combined ΣX. This is then divided by the combined N for all groups, and the result is the ordinary mean, $\frac{\Sigma X}{N}$.

By the way, the process of multiplying each $\overline{X}$ by its own N is called *weighting* the mean by its N. This makes sense if you refer to Table 3-6 and note that there are only ten 10-year-olds, while there are forty 12-year-olds. Since there are many more 12-year-olds, their mean should have a greater *weight* in the calculation of the combined mean. Or, stated another way, the mean of 23 is weighted by an N of 40, while the mean of 17 is weighted by only 10. We will have occasion to refer to the process of weighting in later chapters.

Grouped-Data Techniques for Measures of Central Tendency

There are times when it is convenient to be able to calculate measures of central tendency for data that is in the form of a grouped frequency distribution. The computational techniques for grouped data are valuable as a shortcut method if a calculator is not available, and they may be an absolute necessity for determining measures of central tendency when you have only the grouped frequency distribution from a newspaper article or some other summary report. You will quite often encounter grouped frequency distributions in news magazines and annual reports of corporations.

The computational formulas use terms which were introduced in the discussion of grouped frequency distributions in Chapter 2, and it might be a good idea to review the meaning of such terms as *MP, L, i, f,* and *N*. The calculation of the three measures of central tendency is illustrated below.

Mean

The calculation of the mean from a grouped frequency distribution of 50 reading readiness scores is shown in Table 3-7. Note that this is an ordinary frequency distribution, with the addition of two more columns, *d* and *fd.*

To obtain the entries in the *d* column, it is necessary to choose one of the intervals as a starting point, so a *0* is placed in the *d* column opposite the interval chosen. *Any* interval can be chosen, but it is usually preferred to choose one in the center of the distribution since this results in smaller numbers for your calculations. In Table 3-7 we have picked the 70-74 interval and placed a *0* in the *d* column.

Table 3-7
Calculation of the Mean from Grouped Reading Readiness Scores

Scores	f	d	fd	
85–89	1	3	3	
80–84	3	2	6	+15
75–79	6	1	6	
70–74	15	0		
65–69	12	-1	-12	
60–64	8	-2	-16	
55–59	3	-3	- 9	-45
50–54	2	-4	- 8	
	N = 50		Σfd = -30	

$$\bar{X} = MP + i\left(\frac{\Sigma fd}{N}\right)$$

$$= 72 + 5\left(\frac{-30}{50}\right)$$

$$= 72 + (-3)$$

$$\bar{X} = 69$$

The next step is to count up by units from this 0 ($+1$, $+2$, etc.) until you reach the top of the distribution. Then count down from the 0 (-1, -2, etc.) until you reach the bottom of the distribution. These numbers simply tell us how many intervals a given interval is from the starting point.

To obtain the entries in the *fd* column, simply multiply each *f* by each *d* for every interval. Thus in Table 3-7, $1 \times 3 = 3$, $3 \times 2 = 6$, and so on. Do the same for all the intervals, remembering that some of the *fd* values will be negative since some of the *d* values are negative.

The next step is to obtain the algebraic sum of the *fd* column. Add the positive values (15) and the negative values (—45) and obtain the sum. This quantity is known as Σfd, and in Table 3-7 $\Sigma fd = -30$.

The formula for finding the mean from grouped data (as in Table 3-7) is

$$\bar{X} = MP + i\left(\frac{\Sigma fd}{N}\right) \qquad \text{(3-3)}$$

where MP is the midpoint of the interval at the starting point,
    i is the size of the interval,
    N is the number of scores,
    Σfd is the sum of the fd column.

Substituting the data from Table 3-7 into the formula, we get

$$\bar{X} = 72 + 5\left(\frac{-30}{50}\right)$$
$$\bar{X} = 72 + (-3)$$
$$\bar{X} = 69$$

The starting point for the 0 in the d column of Table 3-7 was the 70-74 interval, but any interval would have resulted in a mean of 69. As a check on the accuracy of calculations, you might choose a different interval as the starting point and see if you obtain a mean of 69. For example, if you started at the 55-59 interval, then MP would be 57, i would be 5, N would be 50, and Σfd would be 120. So no matter which interval is used for the starting point, the mean will always be the same.

It was stated in Chapter 2 that in using a grouped frequency distribution we lost a little accuracy because we did not know the identity of the individual scores. What effect does this have on the accuracy of a mean calculated from grouped data? The formula for the mean from grouped data assumes that the average of all the scores in any interval falls at the midpoint of that interval, so we expect a small, but usually not serious, discrepancy between a mean calculated from the raw data and one calculated after the data have been grouped into a frequency distribution. The mean for the raw data on which Table 3-7 was based is actually 68.94, compared with 69 using the grouped-data formula. So in this case the discrepancy is negligible.

Median

Since the median is the 50th percentile, we want to find the point in a frequency distribution that separates the top half of the scores from the bottom half.

Median for the grouped frequency distribution. Table 3-8 shows the calculation of the median, or the 50th percentile (P_{50}), for a group of 54 driver-training test scores. Note the *cum f* (cumulative frequency) column, which is simply the addition of the frequencies in each interval as you count up from the bottom. For example, there are 2 scores in the 40-44 interval and 3 scores in the 45-49 interval, so the cumulative frequency for the 45-49 interval is 5. There are 6 scores in

Table 3-8
Calculation of the Median from Grouped Driver-training Scores

Scores	f	cum f	Calculations
75–79	2	54	(A) 50% of 54 = 27
70–74	4	52	
65–69	8	48	(B) 2 + 3 + 6 + 15 = 26
60–64	14	40	
55–59	15	26	(C) $0.5N$ – cum f = 27 – 26 = 1
50–54	6	11	
45–49	3	5	(D) f_{50} = 14
40–44	2	2	
	$N = 54$		(E) L = 59.5

$$Med = L + i\left(\frac{0.5N - \text{cum } f}{f_{50}}\right)$$

$$= 59.5 + 5\left(\frac{1}{14}\right)$$

$$= 59.5 + .4$$

$$Med = 59.9$$

the 50-54 interval, so the cumulative frequency for the 50-54 interval is 11, since in *that interval and below* there are 11 scores. Technically speaking, there are 11 scores below 54.5, the exact upper limit of that interval.

The first step in the calculation of the median is to take 50% of N. In step A, $0.50 \times 54 = 27$. The next step is to count up from the bottom in the *cum f* column by adding each frequency until we get as close to 27 as we can, without exceeding 27. In step B we see that $2 + 3 + 6 + 15 = 26$. If we went up one more f value, we would go beyond 27, so we must stop here. This tells us that the median, or P_{50}, is in the *next interval* — somewhere between 59.5 and 64.5.

The next step is to subtract the frequencies that we have just totaled from the value that we actually needed. We needed 50% of N, or 27, but we could total only 26. So in step C, $27 - 26 = 1$.

Next we inspect the interval that contains the median and find out the frequency for this interval. Looking at Table 3-8 we note that there are 14 scores in the 60-64 interval. We call this value f_{50}, the frequency of the interval containing the 50th percentile. Thus, in step D, $f_{50} = 14$.

Finally, we determine the exact lower limit, L, for the interval containing the median. Since this interval is 60-64, $L = 59.5$.

The formula for the median is:

$$Med = L + i \left(\frac{0.5N - \text{cum} f}{f_{50}} \right) \qquad \textbf{(3-4)}$$

where L is the exact lower limit of class containing the median,

   i is the size of the interval,

   $0.5N$ is 50% of the size of the group,

   cum f is the number of scores below the interval containing the median,

   f_{50} is the frequency of the interval containing the median.

From the example in Table 3-8,

$$Med = 59.5 + 5 \left(\frac{27 - 26}{14} \right) = 59.5 + 5 \left(\frac{1}{14} \right)$$

$$= 59.5 + \frac{5}{14}$$

$$= 59.5 + 0.4$$

$$Med = 59.9$$

So the median, or P_{50}, is 59.9, and we say that 50% of the distribution falls below 59.9.

The preceding section on the calculation of the median will be much clearer if we look at a graphical interpretation as shown in the histogram of the driver-training scores in Figure 3-5.

Note that 50% of N, or 27, includes the four lowest intervals, with frequencies of 2, 3, 6, and 15, whose sum is 26. Since this leaves us 1 short of the required 27, we must go part of the way into the next interval to obtain the value of the median. There are 14 scores in this interval so we go 1/14 of the way into the 60-64 interval. (This leaves a single observation below the dotted line of Figure 3-5 and 13 above.)

Since this interval is 5 units wide ($i = 5$), the median is the lower limit of 59.5 + 1/14 of the interval of 5, which would be 59.5 + (1/14) (5) = 59.9. The dotted vertical line shows the location of the median, and, as you can see, this point divides the distribution into two equal halves, with 27 observations on each side and a score of 59.9 as the dividing point.

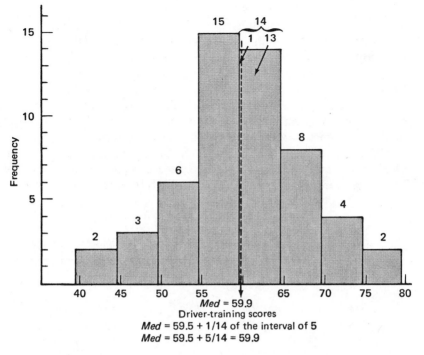

Med = 59.9
Driver-training scores
Med = 59.5 + 1/14 of the interval of 5
Med = 59.5 + 5/14 = 59.9

Figure 3-5
Histogram of driver-training scores showing calculation of the median.

An important assumption that is necessary when the median is calculated from grouped data is that in a given interval the scores are spread evenly over the interval. For example, in the 55-59 interval in Table 3-8, it is assumed that of the 15 scores in this interval, there would be three 55's, three 56's, and so on. Since the formula for the median is one that involves *linear interpolation,* this assumption is necessary. Though this condition is not always present in every interval, it appears that slight deviations from this assumption will not greatly affect the accuracy of the median calculated in this fashion.

Median for the simple frequency distribution. The same technique used for the grouped data of Table 3-8 is followed when you have ungrouped data but some of the scores are tied. A simple frequency distribution is constructed from these scores, and the formula for the median is simply a way of interpolating among the score values to determine the point that divides the distribution exactly into two equal parts. Table 3-9 shows the calculation of the median for a set of scores with several tied values.

Note that in calculating the median for ungrouped data in this way, you have a simple frequency distribution with $i = 1$. You proceed in the same fashion as you did in calculating the median for a grouped frequency distribution and find 50% of N, which would be $0.50 \times 15 = 7.5$. Counting up from the bottom in the f column, you total 7 in the *cum f* column at and below a score of 22. This tells you that the median is somewhere between 22.5 and 23.5, since a frequency of 7.5 is somewhere in that interval. To find the exact center of the distribution, then, you must go 0.5 of a score into the next interval. Since there are two scores in the 22.5-23.5 interval, you go into the

Table 3-9
Calculation of the Median with Ungrouped Data and Tied Scores

Ungrouped Scores	Scores	f	cum f
16, 23, 24,	27	1	15
26, 25, 27,	26	1	14
25, 24, 22,	25	2	13
17, 19, 23,	24	2	11
21, 21, 20	23	2	9
	22	1	7
	21	2	6
	20	1	4
	19	1	3
	18	0	2
	17	1	2
	16	1	1
	$N = 15$		

$$Med = L + i\left(\frac{0.5N - \text{cum } f}{f_{50}}\right)$$

$$= 22.5 + \frac{7.5 - 7}{2}$$

$$= 22.5 + 0.25$$

$$Med = 22.75 \text{ or } 22.8$$

interval a distance amounting to 0.5/2, which is 0.25, and this amount is added to the lower limit of the interval, 22.5, which would make 22.5 + 0.25, or 22.75. This is the point which divides the distribution exactly in half.

Mode

As we noted earlier, the mode is the score that appears most frequently in a distribution of scores. Since the actual identity of each individual score is lost when the scores are grouped in a frequency distribution, we can only make an assumption concerning the value of the mode when we use grouped data.

This value is called the *crude mode,* and it is simply the midpoint of the interval with the greatest frequency. In other words we find the interval that contains the greatest number of scores and assume that the midpoint of the interval was the score made most often. You can see why this value is called the *crude* mode. Since the mode itself is crude, the term *crude mode* is redundant—something like *dirty dirt.*

In Table 3-7, the interval containing the greatest number of scores is 70-74, so the crude mode would be 72. And, in Table 3-8, the crude mode would be the midpoint of the 55-59 interval, or 57.

Some Concluding Remarks

There should be no doubt in your mind what the purpose of a measure of central tendency is. Quite clearly, it is an attempt to find the best single value that represents the performance of the group as a whole. A measure of central tendency of 57.5 would be the best single value that describes the performance of a group of high school seniors in terms of number of items answered correctly on a college entrance exam, or a group of white rats in terms of number of seconds taken to run a maze, or a group of job applicants in terms of number of pegs correctly placed in a manual dexterity test.

The problem arises when a decision must be made concerning *which* measure of central tendency is the best one to use for a given set of data. The mean, because it is the most stable measure of central tendency, is preferred in most cases. Since, as we indicated in Chapter 1, we are often interested in making inferences concerning the population, the mean is preferred because it is the most reliable. However, as we noted in the case of skewed distributions, the mean may not be the most representative value, and for this reason the median may give a better picture of the distribution as a whole.

Sample Problem #1

Twenty students are given a short geography quiz, with the results shown below. Calculate the mean, median, and mode for this set of scores.

9	17	20	21	17
14	20	15	25	13
21	26	25	21	22
13	21	22	10	12

Mean: $$\bar{X} = \frac{\Sigma X}{N} = \frac{364}{20} = 18.2$$

Median: Since the ungrouped data above contains several tied scores it is necessary to group them into a simple frequency distribution.

X	f	cum f	X	f	cum f
26	1	20	17	2	9
25	2	19	16	0	7
24	0	17	15	1	7
23	0	17	14	1	6
22	2	17	13	2	5
21	4	15	12	1	3
20	2	11	11	0	2
19	0	9	10	1	2
18	0	9	9	1	1

$$N = 20$$

$$Med = L + 1\left(\frac{0.5N - \text{cum} f}{f_{50}}\right)$$

$$= 19.5 + \left(\frac{10 - 9}{2}\right)$$

$$Med = 20$$

Mode: The most frequent score was 21.

Sample Problem #2

In the **Sample Problem** in Chapter 2, 100 scores on a mathematics achievement test were grouped into a frequency distribution. The frequency distribution is repeated below. Calculate the mean, median, and mode for these scores and use the three values to identify the kind of skewness present.

Scores	f	d	fd		cum f
90-92	1	3	3		100
87-89	11	2	22	$\Big\}+46$	99
84-86	21	1	21		88
81-83	25 .	0			67
78-80	16	− 1	− 16		42
75-77	9	− 2	− 18		26
72-74	9	− 3	− 27		17
69-71	2	− 4	− 8	$\Big\}-102$	8
66-68	4	− 5	− 20		6
63-65	1	− 6	− 6		2
60-62	1	− 7	− 7		1
	$N = 100$		$\Sigma fd = -56$		

Mean: The d and fd columns are added to the frequency distribution, and the 81-83 interval has been arbitrarily chosen as the starting point. The products of f and d are entered in the fd column, and the algebraic sum of the fd column is found to be -56. Substituting in the formula for finding the mean from grouped data:

$$\bar{X} = MP + i \left(\frac{\Sigma fd}{N} \right)$$

$$= 82 + 3 \left(\frac{-56}{100} \right)$$

$$= 82 - 1.68$$

$$X = 80.32 \text{ or } 80.3$$

Median: Taking 50% of N gives $0.50 \times 100 = 50$. Counting up in the cum f column, we find that the median is somewhere between 80.5 and 83.5, since the 50th score lies somewhere in the next interval above 78-80, and 42 scores are at and below that interval. This gives $0.5N - \text{cum} f = 50 - 42 = 8$, and there are 25 scores in the interval containing the median, so $f_{50} = 25$. Substituting in the formula for finding the median from group data:

$$Med = L + i \left(\frac{0.5N - \text{cum} f}{f_{50}} \right)$$

$$= 80.5 + 3 \left(\frac{50 - 42}{25} \right)$$

$$= 80.5 + .96$$

$$Med = 81.46 \text{ or } 81.5$$

Mode: The crude mode would be the midpoint of the interval with the largest frequency, the 81-83 interval. Mode = 82.

Skewness: By comparing the three measures of central tendency and examining the frequency distribution, we observe a marked degree of negative skewness. The mode is 82, the median is 81.5, and the mean, which is pulled to the left by the atypical low scores, is 80.3.

Study Questions

1. What is meant by the concept of central tendency?

2. How does the mean differ from the median?

3. What does $\Sigma x = 0$ mean?

4. When might the median be preferred to the mean?

5. In calculating a mean for several groups, each individual mean is weighted. What does this mean?

6. Figure 3-5 shows how the median is interpreted in a histogram. How does this figure relate to the definition of the median?

Exercises

1. The data below are preexercise heart rates for 10 middle-aged men. Calculate the mean and demonstrate that $\Sigma x = 0$.

78	74
72	67
81	73
68	78
75	79

2. A survey of family incomes among occupational groups was conducted, and the results are shown below. What was the mean income for all groups combined?

Salesmen	Carpenters	Dentists	Clergymen
$N = 42$	$N = 15$	$N = 9$	$N = 14$
$\bar{X} = \$26,800$	$\bar{X} = \$20,480$	$\bar{X} = \$36,600$	$\bar{X} = \$18,900$

3. Ten laundromat customers are asked to rank three brands of laundry detergent (a rank of 1 indicates most preferred). Calculate
   median ranks for the three detergents to find which brand is most
   preferred.

Customer	Brand A	Brand B	Brand X
1	3	1	2
2	3	2	1
3	1	2	3
4	2	3	1
5	3	2	1
6	1	3	2
7	3	1	2
8	2	3	1
9	2	1	3
10	3	1	2

4. A depth perception test was administered to 20 college freshmen
   taking part in a driver safety experiment. The error in aligning two
   vertical rods (in millimeters) was measured, and these error scores
   are shown below. Calculate the mean, median, and mode, and
   indicate what type of skewness, if any, is present.

5	8	10	16
5	8	11	17
6	8	11	19
6	9	12	21
8	10	14	24

5. A sample of a hundred 12-year-olds was given a hand strength
   test. Use the appropriate grouped-data formulas to calculate the
   mean, median, and mode for this distribution.

Scores	f
80-84	1
75-79	2
70-74	4
65-69	9
60-64	14
55-59	22
50-54	20
45-49	18
40-44	7
35-39	3
	N = 100

6. A distribution of vocabulary test scores for 85 sixth-grade boys is given below. Calculate the mean, median, and mode for this distribution.

Scores	f
55-59	1
50-54	4
45-49	5
40-44	8
35-39	16
30-34	26
25-29	15
20-24	6
15-19	3
10-14	1
	N = 85

7. For the statistics reported below, indicate whether you would expect the distribution to be approximately normal, negatively skewed, or positively skewed.

   a. Mean is 79.3, median is 75.4, mode is 72
   b. Mean is 25.6, median is 24.9, mode is 25
   c. Mean is 128.74, median is 132.68, mode is 135
   d. Mean is 16, median is 12, mode is 9
   e. Mean is 50.3, median is 49.6, mode is 50

4 Percentiles and Norms

In the last two chapters we have been talking about scores and groups of scores, raw scores, and frequency distributions. We have taken for granted that a score describes some property of an individual — reading readiness, I.Q., clerical aptitude, or reaction time — but we have neglected to emphasize that a score has meaning only in relation to the rest of the group. The entire distribution provides a frame of reference for interpreting the individual score.

Let us say that little Johnny comes dashing home to tell his mother that he got a score of 35 on a nationwide achievement test in arithmetic. How should mother react? Obviously, she would want more information before she decides to give him some money for an ice cream sundae or take away his TV privileges for the evening. Clearly what Mom wants to know is just where her Johnny stands in relation to the rest of his class or in comparison with boys of similar age all over the nation.

It is for just this purpose that *derived scores* have been developed. A derived score is one that allows us to infer where it is located in some score distribution.

As you saw in the last paragraph a raw score does not give us this information. In the present chapter we will be concerned with several kinds of derived scores, while others will be discussed in later chapters. Just remember that the use of a derived score is an attempt to make a single score more meaningful by providing a frame of reference for purposes of comparison.

The section to follow will describe percentiles and age-grade norms as derived scores, and a section at the end of the chapter will treat the calculation and graphing of percentiles and percentile ranks from grouped data.

How Norms Are Constructed

Before a test developer promotes his new test and markets it as a nationwide standardized test, he must first construct a set of *norms* based on the population for which it is intended. He may administer the test to a representative sample of several thousand third-graders, high school sophomores, government clerical workers, or army recruits—depending on the type of test. While we cannot go into the intricacies of how these samples are chosen, let us say that the group of individuals on which the norms are based is an accurate, representative sample of the population that will eventually be taking the test. *It is the set of scores from this representative sample that constitutes the norms for a particular test.*

For example, the publisher of a well-known college ability test contacted the psychology department of a large number of colleges and universities and asked them to choose 20 freshmen and 20 sophomores at random from the student body and administer the examination. These results were forwarded to the publisher and the score distribution became the norms for this standardized test of college ability. A student taking the test in the future could now be compared with her fellow college students from all over the nation.

In another case the norms for a well-known intelligence test were constructed from the test results of 3,000 children between the ages of 6 and 12. Since it was believed that the occupational level of the fathers was a variable that affected test performance, the occupational level of the children's fathers in this group of 3,000 were checked against six occupational classifications of males in the latest U.S. Census. These groups were professionals, semiprofessionals, businessmen, farmers, skilled laborers, and slightly skilled or unskilled laborers. Since there were differing proportions of men in these groups, the percentage of children with fathers of a certain occupation in the sample had to match that of the general population. For example, if 5% of all employed males were in the professional group, then 5% of the children in the sample must have fathers in the professional group. As a result of this rather elaborate sampling procedure the I.Q. norms were expected to be accurate and representative of children from ages 6 to 12 on this standardized intelligence test.

Note 4-1
What Is Standard in a Standardized Test?

There are many misconceptions about the term *standard* in regard to a standardized test. The most common, no doubt, is that the norms accompanying a standardized test somehow form a standard or ideal against which performance is compared. It is as if the classroom teacher or a test examiner is the judge and jury for each person's test result and will determine if each examinee is performing up to par. While this may be the case when certain test results are used for guidance purposes (for example, in counseling the underachiever or the overachiever), the term *standardized* simply refers to the physical conditions under which the test is administered. In order to make certain that the examinee's performance can be accurately compared with the set of norms, it is essential that the test be administered under very precise, controlled, standard conditions. The examiner's manual is very detailed in this respect, demanding a comfortable testing room, adequate lighting, instructions that must be followed to the letter, precise, accurate timing of portions of the test that have time limits, and a host of other controlled conditions. All are factors that must be equivalent from administration to administration to ensure the accuracy of the set of norms to be used in evaluating an examinee's performance.

When norms are used to evaluate an individual score, the comparison often is made in either age or grade equivalent scores, or in percentile rank. These are described in detail in the sections to follow.

Age-Grade Norms

When a test developer uses the biographical data included on the test's answer sheet to determine the average grade in school or average chronological age for a particular distribution of test scores, the norms are called, respectively, grade norms or age norms. That is, for any given grade in school or age in years, the set of norms states the *average* raw score achieved by the sample. So, in Table 4-1, showing age-grade equivalents on a standardized arithmetic test, a raw score of 25 on the

Table 4-1
Age-Grade Equivalents on an Arithmetic Achievement Test

Raw Score	Grade	Age	Raw Score	Grade	Age
50	8.0	13-4	30	4.0	9-4
49	7.6	13-0	29	4.0	9-3
48	7.3	12-9	28	3.8	9-2
47	7.1	12-6	27	3.8	9-0
46	6.8	12-2	26	3.6	8-11
45	6.5	11-11	25	3.5	8-10
44	6.2	11-7	24	3.5	8-8
43	6.0	11-5	23	3.3	8-7
42	5.8	11-2	22	3.3	8-6
41	5.6	10-11	21	3.1	8-5
40	5.4	10-8	20	3.0	8-4
39	5.2	10-6	19	3.0	8-3
38	5.0	10-4	18	2.8	8-2
37	4.9	10-3	17	2.8	8-1
36	4.7	10-1	16	2.7	8-0
35	4.7	10-0	15	2.5	7-11
34	4.5	9-10	14	2.3	7-9
33	4.3	9-9	13	2.2	7-8
32	4.3	9-7	12	2.1	7-7
31	4.1	9-6	11	2.0	7-6

arithmetic achievement test was the average for students in the sample who were in the fifth month of the third grade or who were 8 years, 10 months of age.

When this test is used to evaluate a student's arithmetic achievement, the norms are interpreted in just this way. We enter the norms with the raw test score and determine what grade equivalent score or age equivalent score corresponds to that raw score. Again, using the example of Johnny with his score of 35, we find that his arithmetic achievement score is comparable to that of the "average" 10-year-old, or the "average" fourth-grader during the seventh month of the fourth grade. All that is left to do in order to interpret Johnny's raw score is to find out his age and grade. If he has just turned 9 years of age, or if he is just beginning the fourth grade, we would say that he is definitely above average in his grasp of arithmetic.

However, caution must be exercised in interpreting age-grade norms. It would be tempting to say that since Johnny is performing as well as the average 10-year-old, he would have the same knowledge of arithmetic fundamentals that the average 10-year-old has. This is *not* necessarily true, and this is the reason quotation marks appeared around the word *average* in the preceding paragraph. Johnny's superior score, which was equal to that of the average 10-year-old, is very likely due to his superior mastery of the material at his own level. He picks up more points at this level than would the average student who is a year older, but he would not do as well on more advanced material that is completely foreign to him. In spite of this shortcoming, age-grade norms are valuable in comparing progress of children in a classroom setting.

Percentile Norms

Probably even more familiar and more widely used are percentile norms. The test publisher administers the test to a large number of examinees to obtain norms, and an individual score is located in regard to the *percentage of the distribution falling below it.* Many tests have several sets of norms, depending on the purpose of the test. For example, a test of mechanical skills might have norms based on the performances of a group of diesel mechanics at a trade school or a group of high school senior home economics students or a class of college sophomores in a predentistry curriculum.

The percentile is a way of expressing the location of a particular raw score in a distribution. In the last chapter we found that the median is that point in a distribution below which lie 50% of the scores. In exactly the same way we could calculate points below which lie 20%, 43%, 68%, or any percentage of the scores. These points are called *percentiles* and are usually denoted by the symbol P_p, where P is a percentile and the subscript p is the percentage of the cases below that point. P_{20} (read "a percentile of 20" or the "20th percentile"), for example, is the point below which lie 20% of the scores. Similarly, P_{68} would be the point below which lie 68% of the scores. Obviously, the median would be P_{50}.

To use percentile norms all we have to do is enter the table of norms with the test score and find what percentage of the distribution (the standardization sample) falls below. Table 4-2 shows a set of norms for a particular college entrance examination developed by the American College Testing Program (ACT). A student who obtains a test score of 18 would be positioned in the distribution in such a way that 44% of the college-bound high school students have scores lower than his. Stated another way, P_{44} is a score of 18.

You will often run across the term *percentile rank* (*PR*) in a discus-

Table 4-2
ACT Percentile Ranks for College-bound High School Students

Standard Score	Percentile Rank	Standard Score	Percentile Rank
33	99.9	19	50
32	99.8	18	44
31	99.4	17	38
30	98.7	16	33
29	97	15	27
28	95	14	22
27	92	13	17
26	88	12	13
25	84	11	9
24	79	10	6
23	74	9	4
22	68	8	2
21	62	7	1
20	56		

From *Using ACT on the Campus* (Iowa City, Iowa, 1974), p. 12. Copyright 1974 by the American College Testing Program. Reprinted by permission of the publisher.

sion of percentiles. To avoid confusion, just remember that if you want to know the *score* below which a *given percentage* of the distribution falls, you are talking about a percentile. Thus, the 44th *percentile* in Table 4-2 is a score of 18. If you are interested in knowing what *percentage* falls below a *given score*, you are dealing with the score's *percentile rank*. Therefore, in Table 4-2, the percentile rank of a score of 18 is 44.

It frequently happens that the norms established for a nationwide standardized test may not be appropriate for a particular sample of examinees. For example, if a private college has rather strict admissions policies, the personnel deans may be interested in knowing how a high school student's entrance exam score compares to the scores obtained by students who were admitted to the college the year before. For this reason the school may construct its own norms, called *local norms*, based on its own student body. In this way the admissions board would know how well the individual compares with students already at the institution. Just such a set of local norms is shown in Table 4-3, for the ACT college entrance examination. Compare these local norms with the national norms of Table 4-2, to see how a selective admis-

Table 4-3
ACT Percentile Ranks for a Local Institution
(Based on a freshman class, *N* = 1,078)

Standard Score	Percentile Rank	Standard Score	Percentile Rank
31–36	99	20	36
30	98	19	29
29	97	18	23
28	94	17	17
27	90	16	12
26	86	15	7
25	79	14	5
24	72	13	4
23	64	12	2
22	55	5–11	1
21	45		

sions policy would alter the norms used to describe an individual's performance. For example, a score of 20 has a percentile rank of 56 on the national norms but a rank of only 36 on the local norms. Thus, a student with this score would find that, nationally, 56% of the distribution have scores lower than hers while, at a more selective school, only 36% are lower than hers.

Another use of percentiles is to compare an individual's own performance on two or more tests. The percentile rank is valuable here because it is impossible to compare raw scores directly. Knowing that an individual scored 27 on a reading test, 54 on an arithmetic achievement test, and 128 on a mechanical aptitude test does not help us know his relative strengths or weaknesses. However, if we know that his three scores were at the 76th, 53rd, and 83rd percentiles respectively, we know quite a bit about his performance in relation to that of the rest of the examinees.

Percentile Bands

An occasional test publisher, in a fit of honesty, recognizes that a test score is subject to error. We will spend considerable time on errors of measurement in Chapter 14, on the subject of test construction, but, for now, let us assume that a test score, like any measurement of height or volume or weight, is subject to some degree of error. Our honest test publisher admits to the possibility of error, so instead of listing a single percentile rank he identifies each raw score with a *percentile band*. This is to be interpreted according to the following definition: "Two out of three times, the individual's *true* score (i.e., with no measurement error) lies within the limits of the percentile band." Additional explanations of this concept of the probable value of a true score will be forthcoming in Chapter 14.

Table 4-4 shows the national norms for the Cooperative English Test, and, as you notice, the test scores are accompanied by a percentile band. For example, a test score of 157 has a band extending from a percentile rank of 29 to a rank of 52. This means that two out of three times the individual's *true* score would lie in such a way that from 29% to 52% of the distribution is below that point. Such a range of values may seem outrageously imprecise when we are trying to assess an individual's performance, but a percentile band is only admitting a very real fact of life—there are errors in measuring performance—and stating the norms in this manner is one way of recognizing these errors.

While percentile bands may at first be confusing to work with, it is helpful to realize that the *most likely* location of an individual's true score is near the middle of the percentile band. For example, in Table 4-4, an observed score of 158 could have a true score that falls between the percentile ranks of 36 and 59, but it is more likely to be near a percentile rank of 45 or 50 than near the extreme limits of 36 or 59.

The concept of a percentile band should remind us that we need

Table 4-4
Total Score Percentiles on the Cooperative English Test

Score	Percentile Band	Score	Percentile Band
180–182	99–100	158–159	36–59
178–179	97–99.8	156–157	29–52
176–177	95–99.4	154–155	23–44
174–175	91–99	152–153	19–36
172–173	86–97	150–151	14–29
170–171	80–95	148–149	10–23
168–169	74–91	146–147	7–19
166–167	67–86	144–145	5–14
164–165	59–80	142–143	3–10
162–163	52–74	140–141	2–7
160–161	44–67	138–139	1–5

to use caution in comparing two individuals with slightly differing scores. To say, for example, that Joe's score of 169 indicates poorer English achievement than Carol's score of 171 violates what is known about errors of measurement. We simply cannot make this fine a discrimination without additional evidence.

The theory behind the construction of percentile bands presented above has been necessarily brief; additional concepts remain to be covered in future chapters. Hopefully, everything will fall into place when the topic of test construction is covered in Chapter 14.

A Final Word about Norms

Earlier in the chapter you noted the use of sampling procedures to obtain norms against which an individual's score could be compared. While samples of a population constitute most norms (e.g., 485 ninth-grade industrial arts students or 1,730 government clerk-typists), there is an increasing use of entire test populations as normative groups. The use of computers and associated data-handling devices has made it possible to tabulate percentile ranks for an entire year's crop of test results. While much smaller samples could give almost the same degree of accuracy, it is not unusual to have the norms accompanying a test based on huge numbers of examinees. For example, the college entrance exam norms of Table 4-2 are calculated from test results of over two million examinees. This seems to be a trend among test publishers whose tests are widely used and very popular. You must admit that a "sample" of over two million is impressive indeed!

Calculating Percentiles and Percentile Ranks from Grouped Data

Before we approach the calculation of *percentiles* and *percentile ranks* from a grouped frequency distribution, it might be valuable to repeat the distinction between the two concepts. If you wish to know what score is the point below which a given percentage of the distribution falls, you are interested in a *percentile*. If you wish to know what percentage of the distribution falls below a given score, you are concerned with *percentile rank*. If you have trouble discriminating, remember:

Percentile: Given the percentage, find the score.
Percentile Rank: Given the score, find the percentage.

Hopefully, the sections to follow will clear up any confusion between the two concepts, as well as showing their method of calculation from a grouped frequency distribution. And, in keeping with our attention to the type of measurement scale with which a given statistic can be used, we note that percentiles and percentile ranks can be calculated from data ordinal or above in nature.

Calculating Percentiles

Given the percentage, find the score. Let us say that we would like to find what score separates the bottom 65% of the distribution from the top 35%. In other words we would like to find the score in the distribution that is the 65th percentile, or P_{65}. The computational steps are shown in Table 4-5 for the 50 reading readiness scores mentioned in an earlier chapter. Note that the technique for calculating percentiles is the same as for calculating the median in the last chapter—which makes sense, since the median is a percentile (P_{50}).

The first step is to calculate the percentage of N shown by the percentile. In step A, 65% of 50 is 32.5.

Table 4-5
Calculation of a Percentile from Grouped Reading Readiness Scores

Scores	f	cum f	Calculations
85–89	1	50	(A) 65% of 50 = 32.5
80–84	3	49	(B) 2 + 3 + 8 + 12 = 25
75–79	6	46	(C) $0.65N$ – cum f = 32.5 – 25 = 7.5
70–74	15	40	(D) f_{65} = 15
65–69	12	25	(E) L = 69.5
60–64	8	13	
55–59	3	5	
50–54	2	2	
	$N = 50$		

$$P_{65} = L + i\left(\frac{0.65N - \text{cum } f}{f_{65}}\right)$$

$$= 69.5 + 5\left(\frac{32.5 - 25}{15}\right)$$

$$= 69.5 + \left(\frac{37.5}{15}\right)$$

$$= 69.5 + 2.5$$

$$P_{65} = 72$$

The next step is to count up from the bottom of the f column by adding each frequency until we get as close to 32.5 as we can without exceeding it. In step B we see that $2 + 3 + 8 + 12 = 25$ in the *cum f* column. If we went up one more f value, we would go beyond 32.5, so we must stop here. This tells us that the score corresponding to P_{65} is in the *next* interval — somewhere between 69.5 and 74.5.

Next we subtract the frequencies we have totaled from the value which we actually need. Thus, in step C, $0.65N - \text{cum} f = 32.5 - 25 = 7.5$.

Next we inspect the interval that contains P_{65} and find out the frequency for this interval. In Table 4-5 there are 15 scores in the interval 70-74, so we call this value f_p, the frequency of the interval containing the given percentile. Thus in step D, $f_{65} = 15$.

Finally, we determine the exact lower limit, L, for the interval containing P_{65}. Since this interval is 70-74, obviously $L = 69.5$

We are now ready to substitute into the formula below.

$$P_p = L + i \left(\frac{pN - \text{cum} f}{f_p} \right) \qquad (4\text{-}1)$$

where L is the exact lower limit of class containing P_p,

   i is the size of the interval,

   pN is the desired percentage of the size of the group,

   cum f is the number of scores below the interval containing the percentile,

   f_p is the frequency of the interval containing P_p.

For our example in Table 4-5,

$$P_{65} = L + i \left(\frac{0.65N - \text{cum} f}{f_{65}} \right)$$

$$= 69.5 + 5 \left(\frac{32.5 - 25}{15} \right)$$

$$= 69.5 + \left(\frac{37.5}{15} \right)$$

$$= 69.5 + 2.5$$

$$P_{65} = 72$$

So, as we see from this example, $P_{65} = 72$. In other words 65% of the scores fall below a score of 72. You may calculate other percentiles by means of the above formula simply by changing step A and multiplying N by whatever percentage you wish to find.

A graphical approach to understanding the calculation of per-centiles is shown in the histogram of the reading readiness scores of Figure 4-1. The approach is identical to that of Figure 3-5, where we used a histogram to clarify the calculation of the median.

Note that 65% of N, or 32.5, includes the four lowest intervals, with frequencies of $2 + 3 + 8 + 12 = 25$. Since this leaves us 7.5 scores short of the required 32.5, we must go part way into the next interval to obtain the value of P_{65}. There are 15 scores in this interval, so we go 7.5/15 of the way into the 70-74 interval. (This leaves 7.5 scores below the dotted line of Figure 4-1 and 7.5 above.)

Since this interval is 5 units wide ($i = 5$), P_{65} is the lower limit of $69.5 + 7.5/15$ of the interval of 5, which would be $69.5 + (7.5/15)(5)$ $= 72$. The dotted vertical line shows the location of P_{65}, and, as you can see, this point divides the distribution so that 32.5 scores (65%) are below the score of 72 and 17.5 scores (35%) are above.

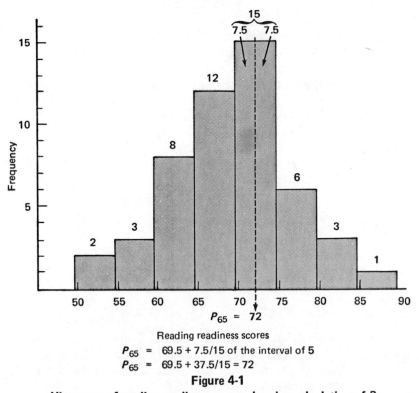

Reading readiness scores

$P_{65} = 69.5 + 7.5/15$ of the interval of 5
$P_{65} = 69.5 + 37.5/15 = 72$

Figure 4-1

Histogram of reading readiness scores showing calculation of P_{65}.

Calculating Percentile Ranks

Given the score, find the percentage. Let us say that for the frequency distribution shown above we would like to find what percentage of the distribution falls below a score of 83. In other words we would like to know the *percentile rank* of a score of 83. The computational steps shown in Table 4-6 illustrate the use of formula 4-2 for finding the *PR* of a score.

In calculating the percentile rank of a score, the first step is to subtract the exact lower limit of the interval containing the score from the score itself. In Table 4-6, the score of 83 is in the 80-84 interval, so the lower limit of this interval is 79.5. Following step A, $83 - 79.5 = 3.5$.

Next, divide the answer in step A by the width of the interval, *i*. In Table 4-6, $i = 5$, so $3.5/5 = 0.7$.

Then multiply the answer in step B by the number of cases in the interval. In Table 4-6, the frequency of the 80-84 interval is 3, so $0.7 \times 3 = 2.1$.

Now add the result obtained in step C to the number of observations below the interval containing the score. There are 46 scores in the *cum f* column below this interval, so for Table 4-6 the result would be $2.1 + 46 = 48.1$. In other words, there are 48 cases that fall below a score of 83.

Since we want to know what *percentage* falls below the score, we have to convert the result of step D to a percentage. To do this we divide by the total *N* and multiply by 100, and, in Table 4-6, this would give $(48.1/50) \times 100 = 96.2$. This means that a score of 83 is located in the distribution in such a way that 96.2% of the scores fall below that point; that is, the *PR* of a score of 83 is 96.2.

Table 4-6
Calculation of a Percentile Rank from Grouped Reading Readiness Scores

Scores	f	cum f	Calculations
85-89	1	50	(A) $X - L$: $83 - 79.5 = 3.5$
80-84	3	49	(B) Divide above by i: $3.5/5 = 0.7$
75-79	6	46	(C) Multiply above by *f* of interval:
70-74	15	40	$\quad 0.7 \times 3 = 2.1$
65-69	12	25	(D) Add above to cumulative *f* below interval:
60-64	8	13	$\quad 2.1 + 6 + 15 + 12 + 8 + 3 + 2 = 48.1$
55-59	3	5	(E) Convert above to a percentage: $(48.1/50) \times$
50-54	2	2	$\quad 100 = PR = 96.2$
	$N = 50$		Thus, a score of 83 has a percentile rank of 96.2.

Formula 4-2 summarizes these five steps:

$$PR = \frac{\left(\text{cum } f \text{ to } L + \frac{(X - L)}{i}f\right)}{N} \times 100 \qquad \textbf{(4-2)}$$

where cum f to L is the number of scores below the interval containing the score,

X is the score,

L is the lower limit of the interval containing the score,

i is the size of the interval,

f is the frequency of the interval containing the score.

Substituting from Table 4-6 would give

$$PR = \frac{\left(46 + \frac{(83 - 79.5)}{5}3\right)}{50} \times 100$$

$$= \frac{\left(46 + \frac{3.5}{5}3\right)}{50} \times 100$$

$$= \frac{(46 + 2.1)}{50} \times 100 = \frac{48.1}{50} \times 100$$

$$PR = 96.2$$

After you have become more familiar with the procedure for finding percentile ranks, you will note that it is just the reverse of the procedure for finding percentiles. To put it in a very general way, when you were calculating a percentile (the score below which a certain percentage fell) you multiplied that percentage times N to find out *how many* observations were below that point. You then proceeded to count up from the bottom in the f column until you arrived at the interval where the point was located. You then used a method of interpolation to find out exactly what *score* was located at that point in the interval.

In order to calculate a *percentile rank*, you simply reverse the above procedure. You begin by finding where in the interval your score is located and determining how many scores are below that point in the same interval. When this frequency is added to the cumulative frequency below that interval, you obviously have the number of scores *below* the score in question, and this, when converted to a percentage, gives the *percentile rank* of the score.

Graphical Methods for Percentiles and Percentile Ranks

The calculation of percentiles and percentile ranks described in the last section is a fairly straightforward procedure. However, you will be more likely to run into a *graphical* presentation of percentiles in the professional literature, especially when *two* frequency distributions are being compared. The graph is known as the *cumulative percentage curve,* or *ogive* (say "o-jive"). The ogive permits us to determine at a glance any percentile or percentile rank that we wish, and it is widely used in illustrating reports and articles on test scores, especially where two groups of subjects are being compared. The following sections describe how an ogive is constructed and how percentiles and percentile ranks can be determined quickly just by inspection.

Constructing the Ogive

The ogive is constructed directly from a grouped frequency distribution, like that of Table 4-7. Note that this frequency distribution is the same as that shown in Table 4-6, except a *cum percentage* column has been added.

Remember that the *cum f* column is simply the addition of the frequencies in each interval as you count up from the bottom. Technically speaking, the entry in the *cum f* column gives the number of

Table 4-7
Cumulative Percentage Distribution of Reading Readiness Scores

Scores	f	cum f	cum percentage
85–89	1	50	100
80–84	3	49	98
75–79	6	46	92
70–74	15	40	80
65–69	12	25	50
60–64	8	13	26
55–59	3	5	10
50–54	2	2	4
	N = 50		

scores *below the exact upper limit of the interval.* For example, the 25 in the *cum f* column opposite the 65-69 interval indicates that there are 25 scores below a score of 69.5. Similarly, there are 46 scores below a score of 79.5. This is an important point: the accuracy of your graph depends on this fact.

The *cum percentage* column contains the same information as the *cum f* column, except that the entries have been converted to percentages. Instead of saying that 13 scores are below 64.5, we can say that 26% of the group are below 64.5. To obtain the entries in the *cum percentage* column, you divide each entry in the *cum f* column by the total number of scores, N, and multiply by 100. So, for the entry opposite the 80-84 interval, you would calculate $(49/50) \times 100 = 98\%$. You know that 98% of the scores fall below 84.5.

After the cumulative percentage distribution has been prepared as shown in Table 4-7, the steps in the construction of the ogive are as follows:

1. Lay out the area on a sheet of graph paper with the usual proportions and label the x- and y-axes as shown in Figure 4-2.
2. Place a dot above the *exact upper limit* opposite the cumulative percentage on the y-axis for all the intervals. For example, in Figure 4-2 there is a point above 64.5 and opposite a percentage value of 26.
3. Include a point at the exact lower limit of the bottom interval opposite a percentage value of 0. In Figure 4-2 the curve drops to 0 at a score of 49.5.
4. Connect the dots by straight lines.

Reading Percentiles and Percentile Ranks from the Ogive

Once you have drawn the ogive (or you see the finished product in a book or professional journal), it is a simple matter to determine percentiles or percentile ranks directly from the graph.

If you want to find a particular *percentile,* you simply draw a horizontal line from the cumulative percentage scale on the y-axis until it intersects the curve. At the point of intersection you drop a vertical line perpendicular to the x-axis and read the score where the perpendicular line touches the x-axis. For example, in Figure 4-2 a percentile of 65, P_{65}, is found by the above method to be a score of 72.

The reverse procedure is used to determine the *percentile rank* of a particular score. You draw a vertical line from the score until it intersects

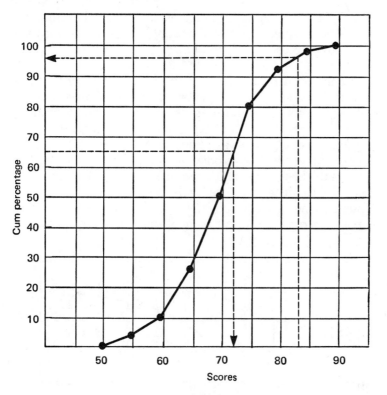

Figure 4-2
Ogive of the reading readiness scores.

the curve, and a horizontal line from that point of intersection over to the cumulative percentage scale. That point is the percentile rank of the score. For example, in Figure 4-2 the percentile rank of a score of 83 is 96.

Any percentile or percentile rank can be found in the manner described above. The accuracy of this procedure depends on how precisely the graph is drawn, but usually the results will compare favorably with the computational procedures described earlier in the chapter. Compare the results obtained from the ogive of Figure 4-2 with the computed values given in Tables 4-5 and 4-6.

Comparing Ogives for Two Different Distributions

A very useful technique which is often employed with the ogive is a comparison of two frequency distributions. In Figure 2-4 there was a comparison of the frequency polygons of coordination test scores for a group of seventh-grade boys and girls. The distributions have been converted to ogives and are shown in Figure 4-3.

It is obvious from Figure 4-3 that the coordination test performance of seventh-grade girls was superior to that of their male counterparts. But by using the techniques described above in reading percentiles and percentile ranks directly, we can gain a great deal of specific information as well and we can do such things as:

Comparing medians. A horizontal line from the 50th percentage value intersects the boys' curve at a score of 33 and the girls' curve at a score of about 41.2. The "average" girl's performance is a good 8 points higher than the "average" boy's.

Comparing scores. If the test manual states that anyone with a

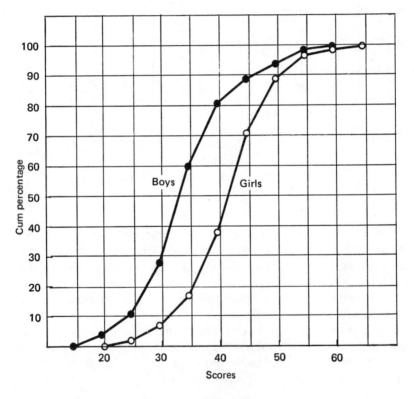

Figure 4-3
Ogives for coordination scores for seventh-grade boys and girls.

score of 27 or below should be given remedial exercises, how do boys and girls compare? A vertical line from the score of 27 intersects the girls' curve at about 4% and the boys' at about 20%. In other words only 4% of the girls but 20% of the boys would score below 27, or in the "remedial" range.

Comparing percentiles. Just as when comparing medians, you might decide to compare other percentiles. For example, what score has to be made to place a boy or girl in the top 25% of his or her group? The value that you want is, of course, the 75th percentile, P_{75}, and a horizontal line from the 75th percentage value intersects the boys' curve at a score of 38 and the girls' curve at a score of about 45.5. Comparatively speaking, the examinee would need a coordination score of at least 46 to be in the top 25% of the girls' group but only 38 to be in the top 25% of the boys'.

Deciles, Quartiles, and Other Iles

It will come as no great surprise to you to find that percentiles are based on a system of 100 units and that theoretically a percentile can take any value between 0 and 100. You should note that while the distribution is usually broken into pieces of 100 there are other systems of dividing a distribution as well. You could conceivably divide the distribution into equal halves, quarters, tenths, or whatever fraction suited your purpose. There are certain divisions which are more common than others, and these are:

Quartiles. The distribution is divided into four equal parts, with 25% of the distribution in each part, so obviously Q_1 is the same as P_{25}, Q_2 equals P_{50}, or the median, and Q_3 equals P_{75}.

Deciles. The distribution is divided into 10 equal parts, with 10% of the distribution in each part, and D_1 equals P_{10}, D_5 equals P_{50}, and so on.

There are other divisions besides the above, but they are not commonly used. Regardless of the type of division used, it must be remembered that P_{72}, or Q_3, or D_7 are *points* in the distribution, not intervals. You may score *at* the 72nd percentile, or *at* the 3rd quartile, or *at* the 7th decile, but not *in* the 3rd quartile or *in* the 7th decile. The reason for the confusion is that we tend to think of quartiles as quarters and deciles as tenths, and obviously you can score *in* the upper quarter or *in* the bottom tenth of a distribution. But, again, percentiles, quartiles, deciles, and other "iles" are *points,* and you score either at a given point (exactly Q_3, for example) or in between two points (between D_7 and D_8, for example).

Sample Problem

The frequency distribution below shows the scores made by 60 students on a social studies test. Calculate P_{35} and the percentile rank of a score of 56. Draw an ogive and use it to check the accuracy of the calculated values. Also use it to determine the value of the median.

Scores	f	cum f	cum percentage
69-71	2	60	100
66-68	6	58	97
63-65	9	52	87
60-62	12	43	72
57-59	16	31	52
54-56	8	15	25
51-53	6	7	12
48-50	1	1	2
$N = 60$			

Following the steps in Table 4-5, 35% of 60 equals 21. Counting up from the bottom, we find that the 21st score is in the 57-59 interval, whose lower limit, L, is 56.5. We needed 21 but could only count up to 15 without going into the interval containing P_{35}, so $0.35N - \text{cum} f = 21 - 15 = 6$. Since there are 16 scores in the 57-59 interval, $f_{35} = 16$. Substituting into the formula:

$$P_{35} = L + i \left(\frac{0.35N - \text{cum} f}{f_{35}} \right)$$

$$= 56.5 + 3 \left(\frac{21 - 15}{16} \right)$$

$$= 56.5 + 1.1$$

$$P_{35} = 57.6$$

We conclude that a score of 57.6 is the point that exactly separates the bottom 35% from the top 65% of the distribution.

To find the percentile rank of a score of 56, we follow the approach of Table 4-6 and formula 4-2. Subtracting the lower limit of the interval containing the score from 56 would give $56 - 53.5 = 2.5$. Dividing this result by the width of the interval yields $2.5/3 = 0.83$, and multiplying by the frequency in the interval containing the score gives $0.83 \times 8 = 6.64$. This result is added to the number of cases below the interval containing the score, so $6.64 + 7 = 13.64$. And, finally, we want to convert these 13.64 cases to a percentage, so we divide by the total N and multiply by 100: $(13.64/60) \times 100 = 23\%$.

So the percentile rank of a score of 56 is 23, meaning that 23% of the distribution scored below 56.

$$PR = \frac{\left(\text{cum}f \text{ to } L + \frac{(X - L)}{i}\, f\right)}{N} \times 100 = \frac{\left(7 + \frac{(56 - 53.5)}{3}\, 8\right)}{60} \times 100$$

$$PR = \frac{(7 + 6.64)}{60} \times 100 = \frac{13.64}{60} \times 100 = 23$$

Plotting the ogive results in the graph shown in Figure 4-4. Using the ogive to find P_{35}, we see that the vertical line across from the 35th percentage value touches the x-axis at a score of about 57.6. The percentile rank of a score of 56 is approximately 23, since the horizontal line from the curve above a score of 56 touches the y-axis at that percentage value. Both the percentile and percentile rank compare favorably with the calculated values. Finally, the median, or P_{50}, for this distribution is approximately 59.3.

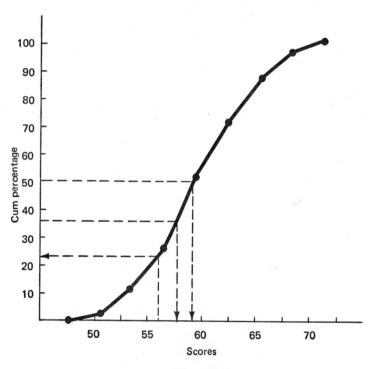

Figure 4-4
Ogive of social studies test scores.

Study Questions

1. How are age-grade norms used?

2. A student whose age is 7 years and 11 months scores 27 on the Arithmetic Achievement Test. Use the norms of Table 4-1 to determine her age-grade placement. Why would it be incorrect to say that her performance is comparable to that of the average 9-year-old?

3. What is the difference between a percentile and a percentile rank?

4. What is a percentile band?

5. What is the ogive or cumulative percentage curve?

6. Why are the points on an ogive plotted at the exact upper limit of each interval?

7. Why is it incorrect to say that someone scored "in the 3rd quartile"?

Exercises

1. The distribution below shows vocabulary test scores for 90 girls and 85 boys in fifth-grade classes in a local elementary school.

Scores	Girls f	Boys f
60-64	1	0
55-59	2	1
50-54	7	4
45-49	16	5
40-44	30	8
35-39	19	16
30-34	9	26
25-29	4	15
20-24	2	6
15-19	0	3
10-14	0	1
	$N = 90$	85

a. Calculate percentile ranks for *both* girls' and boys' scores of 26 and 51.

b. Calculate the values of P_{20} and P_{62} for *both* boys and girls.

c. Use a sheet of graph paper to draw two ogives on the *same* graph (similar to Figure 4-3) for the vocabulary test scores of girls and boys. Determine the percentile ranks and percentiles by inspection. How do they compare with the values you calculated?

5 Variability

If one thing is obvious from a casual observation of human behavior, it must be the notion of variability. Some people are short, some are tall, others are in between. One 5-year-old might be forward, aggressive, and noisy, while her playmate is withdrawn, passive, and quiet. A teacher giving a test may find that a few of his sixth-graders get top scores, a few get very low scores, and most scores cluster in the center of the group. You notice that your car averages 21 miles per gallon, but you know that on a long trip you can squeeze 26 out of it while in downtown traffic the mileage drops to a mere 13.

And not only is there variation among different people and among different things, but the same person or thing may vary from time to time in certain characteristics. While Tom Watson and Lee Trevino are capable of shooting a subpar 66, both can also score a disastrous 77 in a PGA golf tournament. Similarly, a B student will get A's on occasion and also a few C's.

We said earlier that the task of statistics was to

reduce large masses of data to some meaningful values. In Chapter 3 you saw how a measure of central tendency yielded the best *single* value that described the performance of the group as a whole. It was a value that best represented the entire group of observations. But as you noted in the first couple of paragraphs of this chapter, there is more to describing a group of observations than noting the *average* performance, since a measure of central tendency tells you nothing concerning the variation about the average. In preparing frequency distributions and calculating measures of central tendency in earlier chapters you noted that some observations fell below the mean while some were above the mean. This fluctuation of scores about a measure of central tendency is called variability.

In short, to describe a set of observations accurately we need to know not only the central tendency but also the variability of the observations. For example, let us suppose that we have two seventh-grade math teachers, Ms. Jones and Ms. Smith, who give an identical national achievement test in mathematics to their two classes. They happen to meet in the hall one day after the tests are scored, and Ms. Jones states that her class averaged 72. Ms. Smith stops short and remarks that it certainly is a coincidence because her class average was also a 72.

A naive observer would tend to say that the abilities of the two classes must be quite similar since they were equal on the achievement test. But note that nothing has been said about the variability of the two groups. It is possible that Ms. Jones has an ordinary class with several very bright students, a few slow ones, and the rest run-of-the-mill, average seventh-graders. Ms. Smith, on the other hand, could have a peculiar class that has only "average" students if the bright students have been assigned to an accelerated ability group and the slow students have a special remedial class of their own.

The frequency polygons shown in Figure 5-1 illustrate this somewhat contrived, but not uncommon, example. The scores of Ms. Jones' students are spread out over a wide range (approximately 42 to 97), since her group contains a few excellent students and several poor students. The scores from Ms. Smith's class, on the other hand, show much less dispersion (scores from 51 to 85), which is what you would expect when those students likely to make the high scores and the low scores are in special classes somewhere else in the building. In Figure 5-1 the greater variability of Ms. Jones' class is obvious, and there is no doubt that despite the fact that the two classes have equal means, the scores of Ms. Jones' students are different from those of Ms. Smith's.

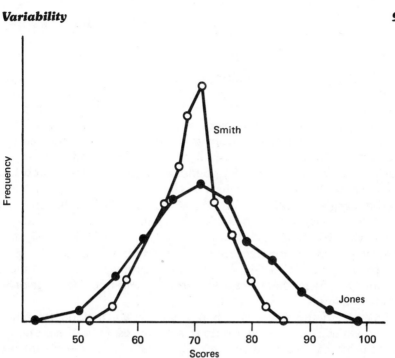

Figure 5-1
Frequency polygons for two distributions of
arithmetic achievement scores.

Clearly, a measure of central tendency is not enough to describe a distribution accurately. Some stories concerning statisticians have arisen from just this last point, and you may have heard such things as "A statistician drowned in a river whose average depth was 4 feet" or "A statistician is one who with his feet in the oven and his head in the refrigerator is, on the average, quite comfortable."

Since a measure of central tendency does not give information about the variability of a group of observations, it is necessary to have some way to measure precisely the amount of variability (scatter, dispersion, spread, variation) that is present in a distribution of scores. We would like to have a convenient and concise measure that tells us instantly something about how much the scores are spread out. The frequency polygons in Figure 5-1 tell us this, of course, but a single measure would be much more efficient. This measure would do for the characteristic of variability what the mean or median did for central tendency. Let us examine several ways of measuring variability.

Range

One of the simplest and most straightforward measures of variability is the *range*. This statistic can be calculated for measurements that are on an interval scale or above. The range is simply the difference between the *highest* and the *lowest* scores in a distribution plus 1. For example, if a distribution of weights of 100 college men showed the heaviest at 225 pounds and the lightest at 132 pounds, the range would be $225 - 132 + 1 = 94$ pounds. (Remember that we add 1 to the difference between the highest and lowest scores, since technically we should subtract $225.5 - 131.5 = 94$.) Or, in the example described previously in Figure 5-1, Ms. Jones' class had a range of $97 - 42 + 1 = 56$, while Ms. Smith's class was $85 - 51 + 1 = 35$. Obviously, this single value tells us something about the scattering or spread of scores, and the range of 56 for Ms. Jones' class indicates considerably more variability in the mathematics achievement scores than the range of 35 for Ms. Smith's.

Although the range is a handy preliminary method for determining variability, it has two serious weaknesses. First of all, one extreme value can greatly alter the range. Again looking at Figure 5-1, note that the lowest score in Ms. Jones' class is a 42. If the student making that score had been sick that day the next lowest score might have been a 50. In this case the range would be $97 - 50 + 1 = 48$, which is considerably less than the original range of 56—and all because of a flu bug.

The second, and most serious, drawback is that since the range is based on only two measures, the highest and the lowest, it tells us nothing about the *pattern* of the distribution. A good illustration of this drawback is shown in Table 5-1.

Both group A and group B have identical means, 32.5, and identical ranges, 16, but a glance at the *pattern* of the distributions shows how dissimilar they are. The scores of group A range from 25 to 40, with most of the other values clustered tightly around the mean of 32.5. Group B's scores also range from 25 to 40, but note that most of the scores are grouped at the extreme ends of the distribution. In this case the range is misleading as a measure of variability, since it says that groups A and B have equal variability while it is obvious that there are rather severe differences between the two.

It is this last point which is important for our attempt to measure variability in an accurate way. We need a method that depends on *all* the measures in a distribution, not just the two extremes. If we define variability as the fluctuation of the scores about some central point, we

Table 5-1
Two Distributions with Equal Ranges but Dissimilar
Patterns of Dispersion

Group A		Group B	
40		40	
33		39	
33	$\bar{X} = \dfrac{325}{10} = 32.5$	39	$\bar{X} = \dfrac{325}{10} = 32.5$
33		38	
33		38	
32	Range $= 40 - 25 + 1 = 16$	27	Range $= 40 - 25 + 1 = 16$
32		27	
32		26	
32		26	
25		25	
$\Sigma X = 325$		$\Sigma X = 325$	

need a method that will tell us *how much* these scores are fluctuating about that point, or how far they are from the mean. In Table 5-1 the majority of the scores of group A do not deviate very far from the mean, while those of group B are scattered quite a distance from the mean. Clearly, we need a method that will be sensitive to how far each individual observation deviates from the mean, so let us take a look at one method that might be of help in measuring the amount of deviation.

Average Deviation

You will recall from Chapter 3 that the mean was defined as the center of the deviations, and to prove it we subtracted the mean from each score. For example, if a distribution consisted of five measures, 14, 12, 9, 17, and 8, the mean would be $60/5 = 12$. Subtracting the mean from each score $(X - \bar{X} = x)$ we would get x values of 2, 0, -3, 5, and -4.

It should be obvious that if we want a measure of variability that takes into account how far each score deviates from the mean, the deviation score (x) would give us this information. If the values of x are relatively small it would indicate that there is not much variability and that the scores are near the mean, while if the values of x are large the scores must be scattered farther from the mean.

To construct a measure of variability it would be necessary only to add the x values to get an overall picture of how much variation there was. However, we noted in Chapter 3 that the sum of the deviations about the mean, Σx, is always 0. We can easily overcome this problem by ignoring the sign of the deviation score (in other words, using the *absolute* value) and then dividing this sum by N to get the average deviation. The formula for the average deviation is

$$AD = \frac{\Sigma|x|}{N} \qquad\qquad (5\text{-}1)$$

where $\Sigma|x|$ is the sum of the absolute values of the deviations from the mean,

N is the number of observations.

For the group of five scores listed earlier:

X	x	|x|
14	2	2
12	0	0
9	−3	3
17	5	5
8	−4	4
$\Sigma X = 60$	$\Sigma x = 0$	$\Sigma|x| = 14$

$$\overline{X} = \frac{\Sigma X}{N} = \frac{60}{5} = 12$$

$$AD = \frac{\Sigma|x|}{N} = \frac{14}{5} = 2.8$$

From an intuitive point of view the average deviation makes good sense. The value of 2.8 in the example above would tell us that on the average each observation deviates 2.8 units from the mean. So the average deviation is a sensible, easily understood, accurate measure of variability.

Unfortunately, it is hardly ever used. One thing that you will become aware of should you go on to more advanced courses in statistics is that all of the statistical techniques are linked together by certain theoretical foundations—and that the average deviation simply doesn't fit into this framework. So it is doubtful that you will ever see any reference to the average deviation again. The only reason that it was brought up at this point was to emphasize the use of the deviations from the mean (x) as a way of indicating the amount of variability. These deviations will be an important part of the measure of variability to be discussed in the next section.

Standard Deviation

The most widely used measure of variability is the *standard deviation*. This statistic makes use of the deviation of each score from the mean, but the calculation, instead of taking the absolute value of each deviation, squares each deviation to obtain values that are all positive in sign. You will remember from elementary algebra that when two numbers of the same sign are multiplied together the product is always positive. So when we square each of the deviations, we get positive numbers whether our original deviations were positive or negative. We add these squared deviations to obtain Σx^2 (read "sum of the squared deviations" or "sum of the little x squares"), divide the sum by N to obtain a sort of average, and then take the square root of that result in order to get back to our original units of measurement. The standard deviation may be calculated from any set of measurements that are at least of interval nature.[1]

To summarize the steps just described we can state the formula for the standard deviation as

$$S = \sqrt{\frac{\Sigma x^2}{N}} \qquad\qquad (5\text{-}2)$$

where S is the standard deviation,

Σx^2 is the sum of all the squared deviations from the mean,

N is the number of observations.

This formula for the standard deviation is called the *deviation formula* because it is calculated from the deviations themselves. In the next section formulas will be used that simplify the calculation of S by eliminating the time-consuming step of subtracting the mean from each score. But before we get ahead of ourselves let us use the deviation formula to calculate S for the set of data shown in Table 5-2. Substituting into formula (5-2) we obtain:

$$S = \sqrt{\frac{\Sigma x^2}{N}} = \sqrt{\frac{30}{8}}$$

$$S = \sqrt{3.75}$$

$$S = 1.94$$

And our standard deviation for the data of Table 5-2 is $S = 1.94$.

---

[1]The meaning of the standard deviation will become clearer when it is interpreted in terms of normal curve later in this chapter. It is simply the distance on the x-axis between the mean and the steepest part of the normal curve, (e.g., between $\bar{X}$ and -1 or $\bar{X}$ and $+1$ in Figure 5-2).

Table 5-2
Calculation of the Standard Deviation (Deviation Method)

X	x	x^2	
6	1	1	$\bar{X} = \dfrac{\Sigma X}{N} = \dfrac{40}{8} = 5$
8	3	9	
2	-3	9	
4	-1	1	$S = \sqrt{\dfrac{\Sigma x^2}{N}} = \sqrt{\dfrac{30}{8}}$
4	-1	1	
3	-2	4	
7	2	4	$S = \sqrt{3.75}$
6	1	1	$S = 1.94$
$\Sigma X = 40$	0	$\Sigma x^2 = 30$	

The example shown in Table 5-2 uses the deviation formula to obtain S. While this method was used here to show you how S is based on squared deviations from the mean, it is not often used in practice because its calculations are time-consuming and laborious. It is necessary to subtract the mean from each score, square these deviations, average them by dividing by N, and extract the square root. However, some of the concepts involved in this method, especially the sum of squares (Σx^2), will be useful to us in a later chapter. And, as was mentioned earlier, the deviation method illustrates the concept of variability very well in that each score is treated as a deviation from the mean.

Calculating the Standard Deviation (Raw Score Methods)

The method described above for calculating S employed the deviation of each score from the mean, but it was mentioned that there was a more efficient method. It doesn't take much thought to realize that the calculation in Table 5-2 would have been much more time-consuming and prone to error if ΣX had been 41 instead of 40. Then the mean would have been $41/8 = 5.125$. Consider for a moment subtracting 5.125 from each score and then squaring the deviation. Instead of pondering this plodding, time-consuming process, let us consider two alternate formulas for the standard deviation. One requires the mean of the distribution, and the other requires only ΣX and ΣX^2, which makes it especially suited for pocket calculators. Both formulas are demonstrated below for the distribution of scores in Table 5-3.

Table 5-3
Calculating ΣX and ΣX^2 for Raw Score Formulas

X	X^2
10	100
10	100
12	144
15	225
12	144
11	121
14	196
13	169
13	169
13	169
$\Sigma X = 123$	$\Sigma X^2 = 1{,}537$

$$\bar{X} = \frac{\Sigma X}{N} = \frac{123}{10} = 12.3$$

Standard Deviation — Mean Formula

The formula for calculating the standard deviation using the mean is

$$S = \sqrt{\frac{\Sigma X^2}{N} - \bar{X}^2} \qquad (5\text{-}3)$$

where S is the standard deviation,
ΣX^2 is the sum of the squared scores,
$\bar{X}$ is the mean of the distribution,
N is the number of observations.

As you can see in Table 5-3, the scores are placed in the X column, each score is squared and the square entered in the X^2 column, and the two columns are summed to obtain ΣX and ΣX^2. The mean of X is also calculated. The appropriate values from Table 5-3 are substituted into the formula

$$S = \sqrt{\frac{\Sigma X^2}{N} - \bar{X}^2} = \sqrt{\frac{1{,}537}{10} - (12.3)^2}$$

$$= \sqrt{153.7 - 151.29} = \sqrt{2.41}$$

$$S = 1.55$$

This formula is algebraically equivalent to the deviation formula (formula 5-2) and is much easier to compute because you are working with the original raw scores instead of the deviations. Notice in the above formula the ΣX^2 refers to the sum of the squares of the *raw* scores, whereas in the deviation method you added the squared *deviations*, Σx^2.

Standard Deviation – Machine Formula

Since most of you own or have access to a pocket calculator, there is an alternative to formula 5-3 that might be more convenient since it does not require the separate calculation of the mean. The *machine formula* (the term dates back to the days when desk calculators were large and cumbersome and were called machines) for *S* is

$$S = \frac{1}{N}\sqrt{N\Sigma X^2 - (\Sigma X)^2} \qquad (5\text{-}4)$$

where ΣX^2 is the sum of the squared scores,
$(\Sigma X)^2$ is the square of the sum of the scores,
N is the number of observations.

Note the difference between ΣX^2 and $(\Sigma X)^2$. The symbol ΣX^2 indicates that you are to square each individual score and then sum these squared scores. The term $(\Sigma X)^2$ indicates that you are to add all the scores first and then square that sum. To clarify these terms, let us calculate *S* for the data of Table 5-3 using the machine formula.

$$S = \frac{1}{N}\sqrt{N\Sigma X^2 - (\Sigma X)^2} = \frac{1}{10}\sqrt{10(1{,}537) - (123)^2}$$

$$= \frac{1}{10}\sqrt{15{,}370 - 15{,}129} = \frac{1}{10}\sqrt{241} = \frac{15.52}{10}$$

$$S = 1.55$$

And your result, $S = 1.55$, is the same as obtained with formula 5-3. Since pocket calculators are readily available, we will use this machine formula throughout the rest of this text.

Note 5-1
Calculating the Standard Deviation with a Pocket Calculator

If your pocket calculator has memory and square root functions, the machine formula for the standard deviation is especially easy to calculate. After you have calculated ΣX in the usual way, the quantity ΣX^2 can be obtained by squaring each number and entering the square in your M+ storage. For example, in Table 5-3 you would multiply the first score, 10, by itself to obtain 100 and enter this in the memory by pushing the M+ key. The second score, also 10, would be squared and entered into M+ and so on until you reached the last score, 13, and entered its square, 169, into M+. You would then recall memory to obtain $\Sigma X^2 = 1,537$.

You now can perform the operation called for in the machine formula, $S = \frac{1}{N}\sqrt{N\Sigma X^2 - (\Sigma X)^2}$. You would first obtain $N\Sigma X^2$ by multiplying $10 \times 1,537$ and storing the 15,370 in M+. Next you would calculate $(\Sigma X)^2$ by multiplying $123 \times 123 = 15,129$ and subtract this from the memory by pushing the M− key. The next step would be to recall the result, 241, from the memory and press the square root key to obtain 15.52. The last step, dividing by N, 10, would yield 1.552, the standard deviation for the data of Table 5-3.

Now that we have spent the time and effort on the calculation of S, what does it do? What does it tell us about a distribution of scores? Obviously, it tells us in a relative fashion *how much* the scores in a distribution deviate from the mean. If S is small, there is little variability and the majority of the observations are tightly clustered about the mean. If S is large, the scores are more widely scattered above and below the mean. One of the primary uses of S is to compare two or more distributions with respect to their variability. Let us repeat Table 5-1, where we noted that groups A and B had equal ranges but the scores were distributed differently in the two distributions. The results are shown in Table 5-4.

There can be no doubt that S is sensitive to the pattern of scores in a distribution. The scores of group A are tightly clustered about the mean and S is 3.38. Compare this with 6.34 for group B, where the scores are more widely dispersed from the mean. We have accomplished what we said we would do, that is, develop a measure of variability that reflects the distance each score deviates from the mean. S is just this measure. The importance of S cannot be overemphasized,

Table 5-4
Comparing the Standard Deviations of Two Different Distributions

Group A		Group B	
X	X^2	X	X^2
40	1,600	40	1,600
33	1,089	39	1,521
33	1,089	39	1,521
33	1,089	38	1,444
33	1,089	38	1,444
32	1,024	27	729
32	1,024	27	729
32	1,024	26	676
32	1,024	26	676
25	625	25	625
$\Sigma X = 325$	$\Sigma X^2 = 10,677$	$\Sigma X = 325$	$\Sigma X^2 = 10,965$

$$\bar{X} = \frac{\Sigma X}{N} = \frac{325}{10} = 32.5$$

$$\bar{X} = \frac{\Sigma X}{N} = \frac{325}{10} = 32.5$$

$$S = \frac{1}{N}\sqrt{N\Sigma X^2 - (\Sigma X)^2}$$

$$S = \frac{1}{N}\sqrt{N\Sigma X^2 - (\Sigma X)^2}$$

$$= \frac{1}{10}\sqrt{10(10,677) - (325)^2}$$

$$= \frac{1}{10}\sqrt{10(10,965) - (325)^2}$$

$$= \frac{1}{10}\sqrt{1,145}$$

$$= \frac{1}{10}\sqrt{4,025}$$

$$= \frac{33.84}{10}$$

$$= \frac{63.44}{10}$$

$$S = 3.38$$

$$S = 6.34$$

and, if there are some concepts that are still not clear, it would be a good idea to review the preceding sections before going on to the next topic.

Variance

Before leaving the section on measures of variability, we should take a quick look at a measure of variability that will be of considerable

> ### Note 5-2
> ### Rounding Off the Standard Deviation
>
> It was noted in Chapter 3 that the mean is conventionally rounded off to one more decimal place than you have in your set of raw data. It is conventional in calculating the standard deviation to round off the result to *two* more decimal places than the raw data contain. So for whole numbers, such as the test scores of Table 5-4, the mean is 32.5 while the standard deviation is reported as 3.38. And, if you had a set of reaction time scores measured in hundredths of seconds, your mean might be 0.326 with a standard deviation of 0.0942.

importance in later chapters. This measure is called the *variance,* and it is simply the square of the standard deviation. In Table 5-2, you will note that the deviation formula[2] for the standard deviation is

$$S = \sqrt{\frac{\Sigma x^2}{N}}$$

and so the formula for the variance is simply

$$S^2 = \frac{\Sigma x^2}{N}$$

For the data of Table 5-2, S is 1.94, and the variance, S^2, is 3.75.

We will have occasion to discuss the concept of variance in several future chapters, but, for the time being, consider variance (S^2) as just another method for describing the amount of variation in a set of scores. For example, in Table 5-4, S^2 for group A is $(3.38)^2 = 11.45$, while for group B it is $(6.34)^2 = 40.25$. Obviously, there is greater variability in the scores of group B than in those of group A.

The Standard Deviation and the Normal Curve

It was noted earlier that frequency distributions of much of the data in education and the behavioral sciences approximate the normal curve. The normal curve will be discussed in excruciating detail in the next chapter, but at this point it will be helpful to see the relationship of S and the normal curve. If we assume that a body of data is approximately normally distributed, we can gain still more information from S

[2]In Chapter 7 we will point out the important difference between dividing Σx^2 by N or by $N - 1$ to obtain the variance.

about the variability in the distribution. Consider Figure 5-2, where a normal curve is shown with S units on the baseline.

In the normal curve of Figure 5-2, the mean is erected from the baseline, and this vertical line divides the distribution into two equal parts. In other words 50% of the scores lie below the mean (to the left) and 50% above the mean (to the right). Vertical lines are also erected from the baseline corresponding to the different S units, so that the area under the curve (number of scores, for example) between 1 S unit below the mean and 1 S unit above the mean is approximately 68% of the total area. (In other words, if 1,000 scores were normally distributed, approximately 680 would be between -1 and $+1 S$. Similarly, approximately 95% of the distribution lies between -2 and $+2 S$ units from the mean, and about 99% of the distribution lies between -3 and $+3 S$ units from the mean. These statements are represented graphically in Figure 5-3.

Let us apply this approach to an actual set of data such as that shown in Figure 5-4. The scores in the frequency polygon were the results of a cultural affairs test administered to a large number of high school seniors. The mean was 72 with an S of 8. With what we know about the normal curve, we can make statements to the effect that 68% of the students scored between $\overline{X} \pm 1\ S$, or 72 ± 8, or between 64 and 80. In the next chapter we will spend considerable time on the normal curve; it was introduced at this point to show where S fits in when variability is being studied in a distribution that approximates the normal curve.

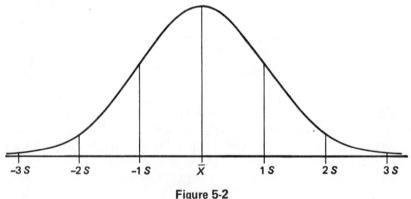

Figure 5-2
Normal curve with mean and S units.

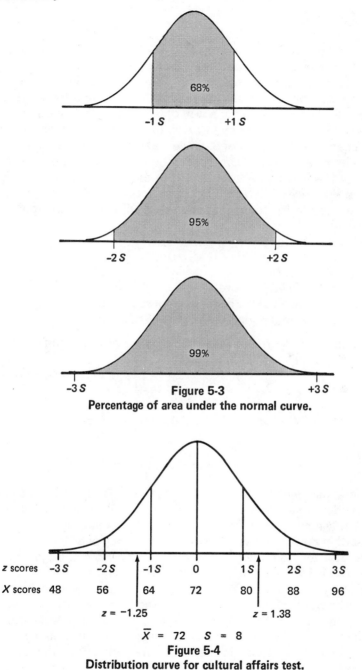

Figure 5-3
Percentage of area under the normal curve.

$\overline{X}$ = 72   S = 8
Figure 5-4
Distribution curve for cultural affairs test.

z Scores

It is a little awkward in discussing a score or observation to have to say that it was "2 standard deviations above the mean" or "1.5 standard deviations below the mean." To make it a little easier to pin-point the location of a score in any distribution, the z score was developed. The z score is simply a way of telling how far a score is from the mean *in standard deviation units.* In Figure 5-4 the distribution had a mean of 72 and an S of 8. Since a z score tells how far the score is from the mean in S units, a score of 80 in Figure 5-4 is a z score of $+1$, since it is 1 S unit above the mean. Similarly, a score of 56 is a z score of -2 since it is 2 S units below the mean.

The formula for converting any score (X) into its corresponding z score is

$$z = \frac{X - \overline{X}}{S}$$
(5-5)

where z is the z score,
  X is the observed score,
  $\overline{X}$ is the mean of the distribution of scores.
  S is the standard deviation of the distribution.

Again, from Figure 5-4, what would be the z score for an observed score of 83? Using the above formula:

$$z = \frac{X - \overline{X}}{S} = \frac{83 - 72}{8} = \frac{11}{8} = 1.38$$

In Figure 5-4 what would be the z score for an observed score of 62?

$$z = \frac{X - \overline{X}}{S} = \frac{62 - 72}{8} = \frac{-10}{8} = -1.25$$

Note that when a z score is positive it is located *above* the mean, and when negative it is *below* the mean. Observe the location of these last two z scores in Figure 5-4. If you have difficulty understanding just what a z score is, remember that it is a way of telling how much a score deviates from the mean in S units. The score of 62 just calculated above is 1.25 standard deviations below the mean.

The most compelling reason for using a z score is to make comparisons between different distributions. Knowing that John got a score of 78 on a mathematics achievement test, 115 on a natural science aptitude test, and 57 on an English usage exam tells us nothing about his performance in relation to the rest of the group. But if the distributions on the three tests in this test battery were similar (e.g., approxi-

---

Note 5-3
Finding the Observed Score When z Is Given

There will be times when you will have to calculate the observed score when the z score is known. For those of you not particularly proficient in algebra, the z score formula can be reworked so that you solve for X. By appropriate manipulation the equation $z = \dfrac{X - \overline{X}}{S}$ yields $X = z(S) + \overline{X}$. For example, from Figure 5-4, what score corresponds to a z score of -1.75? Solving for X you get

$$X = z(S) + \overline{X} = -1.75(8) + 72 = -14 + 72 = 58$$

Thus, 58 is the score which corresponds to a z of -1.75.

---

mately normal, such as you would expect on a nationally administered test), you can make direct comparisons by using the z score approach. For example, Table 5-5 shows the means and standard deviations for the three tests just mentioned.

In comparing z scores for the three tests you would first calculate the z scores for the three as follows:

Mathematics: $\quad z = \dfrac{X - \overline{X}}{S} = \dfrac{78 - 75}{6} = \dfrac{3}{6} = 0.5$

Natural Science: $\quad z = \dfrac{115 - 103}{14} = \dfrac{12}{14} = 0.86$

English: $\quad z = \dfrac{57 - 52}{4} = \dfrac{5}{4} = 1.25$

So we find that John, in terms of the rest of the group, did best on the English test and poorest (though still above average) on the mathematics exam.

Table 5-5
Means, Standard Deviations, and John's Scores (X) on Three Tests

Mathematics	Natural Science	English
$\overline{X} = 75$	$\overline{X} = 103$	$\overline{X} = 52$
$S = 6$	$S = 14$	$S = 4$
$X = 78$	$X = 115$	$X = 57$

Because a z score can be interpreted in relation to the rest of the distribution without knowledge of the observed scores themselves, z scores will be used frequently throughout the rest of this text. Their relation to the normal curve, which you were introduced to in Figure 5-4, will be explained further in the next chapter.

Other Standard Scores

The z score above is a *derived* score, since it is derived from the original score units. (Remember that the percentile ranks discussed in the last chapter were also derived scores.) It is also referred to as a *standard score*, since it is based on standard deviation units. However, there are several minor disadvantages in the use of the z score. There are negative values for any scores below the mean, the mean of the z score distribution is 0, and the z scores are decimal fractions—all of which results in a certain amount of computational complexity.

A number of other standard score systems have been devised which do not have these disadvantages. These are listed (along with the familiar z scores for comparison) in Table 5-6.

The standard scores of Table 5-6 are only a small sample of possible standard score systems in current use. However, they are all related to the z score, since they still tell us the basic fact—how far any score deviates from the mean in standard deviation units.

The z score formula is used to determine how many S units a given score in one of the distributions above deviates from the mean. Where in the CEEB distribution, for example, does a score of 437 lie?

$$z = \frac{X - \overline{X}}{S} = \frac{437 - 500}{100} = \frac{-63}{100} = -0.63$$

Table 5-6
Typical Standard Score Systems

z scores:	$\overline{X} = 0$	$S = 1$
T scores:	$\overline{X} = 50$	$S = 10$
General Aptitude Test Battery (GATB):	$\overline{X} = 100$	$S = 20$
College Entrance Exam Board (CEEB):	$\overline{X} = 500$	$S = 100$

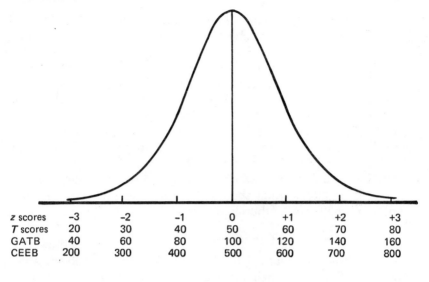

z scores	-3	-2	-1	0	+1	+2	+3
T scores	20	30	40	50	60	70	80
GATB	40	60	80	100	120	140	160
CEEB	200	300	400	500	600	700	800

Figure 5-5
The normal curve and standard scores.

Thus a CEEB score of 437 lies 0.63 of a standard deviation below the mean of 500. Similarly, a *T* score of 62 yields a *z* of 1.2, which indicates it is 1.2 *S* units above the mean. Figure 5-5 shows the relationship of various derived scores to the normal curve.

Standard Deviation: Miscellaneous Topics

Negative Numbers under the Radical Sign

In computing *S* using the raw score formulas, you may get a negative number under the radical sign after you have subtracted $\bar{X}^2$ from $\Sigma X^2/N$ in the formula using the mean, or $(\Sigma X)^2$ from $N\Sigma X^2$ in the machine formula. If this should happen, *you have made a mistake*. You must recheck your work, perhaps the addition of the X^2 column, to find the error. Whether you are using the mean formula or the machine formula, a negative number under the radical sign indicates an error in your calculations.

A Rough Check for Accuracy

In Figures 5-3 and 5-4 you noted that the $\bar{X} \pm 3$ *S* units just about covered the entire range of scores under the normal curve, since 99%

of the total area lies between -3 and $+3$ S units. We can make use of this fact to exercise a rough check on the accuracy of our calculations of S for a group of scores. For an approximately normal distribution, S should be about one-sixth of the range, when N *is quite large.*

But, when you are working with only 50 or 100 scores, you will find that S is about one-fourth or one-fifth of the range. So, when you calculate S for a distribution containing 72 scores where the lowest score is 25 and the highest is 88, you would know that S should be about 13 to 16 for the range of 64. If your S turned out to be 2.53 or 27.69, you would probably want to recheck your work for possible errors. This will not work every time because some distributions will have peculiar, non-normal shapes, but for most situations the one-fourth-to-one-fifth rule of thumb will be helpful.

Effect of Adding a Constant to Each Score

It can be shown that when a constant is added to each score in a distribution S remains unchanged. The addition of a constant to each score does not change each score's relative position with respect to the new mean, and, since S is based on deviations from the mean, the deviations themselves would remain unchanged. Table 5-7 shows distribution A with its mean and S and distribution B, where the constant 3 has been added to each score of distribution A. The deviation

Table 5-7
Adding a Constant Does Not Affect the Standard Deviation

Distribution A			Distribution B (A + 3)		
X	x	x^2	X	x	x^2
9	3	9	12	3	9
7	1	1	10	1	1
6	0	0	9	0	0
5	-1	1	8	-1	1
3	-3	9	6	-3	9
$\Sigma X = 30$	0	$\Sigma x^2 = 20$	$\Sigma X = 45$	0	$\Sigma x^2 = 20$

$$\bar{X} = 6 \qquad\qquad\qquad\qquad \bar{X} = 9$$

$$\varepsilon = \sqrt{\frac{\Sigma x^2}{N}} = \sqrt{\frac{20}{5}} = \sqrt{4} = 2 \qquad S = \sqrt{\frac{20}{5}} = \sqrt{4} = 2$$

method for calculating S is used so you can see that the deviations remain unchanged.

As you remember from Chapter 3, the addition of a constant to every score *did* alter the mean in that the mean increased by an amount equal to the constant. However, this addition of a constant, as shown in Table 5-7, does not change the standard deviation.

Note 5-4
Using the Table of Squares and Square Roots

If you do not have access to a calculator, you may wish to use Table A in Appendix 2, which contains squares and square roots of numbers from 1 to 1,000. If you want to find the square or square root of a number, you obviously look up the number in the N^2 or $\sqrt{N}$ column.

There are some slight complications in obtaining the square root if the number is not listed in the N column. What, for example, is the square root of 3.75, or of 3,270, or of 40.5, or of 876,525?

1. For finding the square root of numbers such as 3.75, where there is a single digit followed by a decimal point and one or two digits (e.g., 6.9 would be 6.90), it is only necessary to look up the entire number without the decimal point in the N column and read from the $\sqrt{N}$ column. For example, the square root of 375 is 19.36. To find the square root of 3.75, just move the decimal point to the left *one* place, to get 1.936.

2. To find the square root of four-digit numbers ending in 0, such as 3,270, look up the number in the N column for the first *three* digits, and find the square root in the $\sqrt{10N}$ column. For example, you would find 327 in the N column, and the square root of 3,270 in the $\sqrt{10N}$ column would be 57.18.

3. When the number contains two digits, a decimal point, and one final digit, as does 40.5, look up the entire number without the decimal point (405) in the N column and read from the $\sqrt{10N}$ column, to get 63.64. Then to find the square root of 40.5 simply move the decimal point to the left *one* place to get 6.364.

4. To find the *approximate* square root of any whole number up to 1,000,000 use the table in the reverse order—that is, look up the number in the N^2 column and read the square root in the N column. For example, to find the square root of 876,525 you would find approximately that number in the N^2 column opposite the N of 936.

It is a good idea to make a quick check of your calculations anytime that you are working with square roots. Simply multiply your square root by itself to see if the product equals the number of which you wished to extract the square root.

Semi-interquartile Range

There are times when it is convenient to be able to examine the variability of a group of observations about the *median* rather than the mean. Such a measure of variability is the *semi-interquartile range* (sometimes called the quartile deviation, or *Q*), which can be used with any data that is appropriate for the median, that is, with data that is of an ordinal nature or above.

The semi-interquartile range is one-half the distance between Q_3 and Q_1 (or P_{75} and P_{25}). The formula for Q is

$$Q = \frac{P_{75} - P_{25}}{2} \tag{5-6}$$

In a normal distribution we would expect that about 50% of the observations would be covered in the range $Med \pm Q$. For example, in **Sample Problem #2** at the end of this chapter, the median is 32.5. If P_{75} were 35.7 and P_{25} were 29.3, Q would be calculated as

$$Q = \frac{P_{75} - P_{25}}{2} = \frac{35.7 - 29.3}{2} = \frac{6.4}{2} = 3.2$$

We would then assume that approximately 50% of the distribution would be between 32.5 ± 3.2, or between 29.3 and 35.7.

The semi-interquartile range has not been a popular statistic in recent years, but you still may run across it in older books and journal articles. Because of its limited use, we will not have any more to do with it.

Standard Deviation from Grouped Data

As we noted in Chapter 3, there are times when we might want to calculate statistics directly from a frequency distribution. The calculation of *S* from a frequency distribution involves only one step beyond those required for calculating the mean. It might be a good idea to review the technique for calculating the mean from grouped data presented in Chapter 3. Table 5-8 shows the same data that was used to illustrate the calculation of the mean in Table 3-7, but a new column, fd^2, has been added.

After you have completed the steps described earlier in the calculation of the mean, it is only necessary to compute the entries in the fd^2 column. To obtain each fd^2 entry, multiply each fd by the corresponding d value. In Table 5-8, $3 \times 3 = 9$, $2 \times 6 = 12$, and so on for the

Table 5-8
Calculation of the Standard Deviation for Grouped Reading Readiness Scores

Scores	f	d	fd		fd²
85–89	1	3	3		9
80–84	3	2	6	+15	12
75–79	6	1	6		6
70–74	15	0			
65–69	12	-1	-12		12
60–64	8	-2	-16	-45	32
55–59	3	-3	- 9		27
50–54	2	-4	- 8		32
	$N = 50$		$\Sigma fd = -30$		$\Sigma fd^2 = 130$

rest of the distribution. Remember, fd^2 means fd times d, not fd times fd. For example, the entry in the 80-84 interval is $2 \times 6 = 12$, not $6 \times 6 = 36$. Also note that all the entries in the fd^2 column are positive. There are no negative numbers, because multiplying a negative d by a negative fd results in a positive answer. For example, in the 55-59 interval, $-3 \times -9 = 27$. The next step is to add the fd^2 column to obtain $\Sigma fd^2 = 130$.

The formula for the standard deviation from grouped data is

$$S = i\sqrt{\frac{N\Sigma fd^2 - (\Sigma fd)^2}{N^2}} \tag{5-7}$$

where S is the standard deviation,
  i is the size of the interval,
  N is the number of scores,
  Σfd^2 is the sum of the fd^2 column,
  Σfd is the sum of the fd column.

For the frequency distribution of Table 5-8,

$$S = i\sqrt{\frac{N\Sigma fd^2 - (\Sigma fd)^2}{N^2}}$$

$$= 5\sqrt{\frac{50(130) - (-30)^2}{(50)^2}}$$

$$= 5\sqrt{\frac{6{,}500 - 900}{2{,}500}}$$

$$= 5\sqrt{\frac{5{,}600}{2{,}500}}$$

$$= 5\sqrt{2.24}$$

$$= 5(1.5)$$

$$S = 7.50$$

Sample Problem #1

Fifty high school students are chosen at random from the junior class at a local high school and are given an examination on their knowledge of current events. Their scores are listed below. Calculate the mean, range, and S for this distribution.

X	X^2	X	X^2	X	X^2
9	81	12	144	18	324
11	121	12	144	31	961
11	121	25	625	22	484
22	484	14	196	30	900
6	36	22	484	23	529
29	841	26	676	15	225
21	441	33	1,089	20	400
8	64	4	16	20	400
35	1,225	24	576	32	1,024
28	784	26	676	9	81
10	100	2	4	27	729
25	625	13	169	30	900
1	1	22	484	10	100
21	441	19	361	21	441
28	784	26	676	15	225
34	1,156	16	256	37	1,369
19	361	16	256		

Summary: $\Sigma X = 990$ $\Sigma X^2 = 23{,}590$ $N = 50$

Mean: $\overline{X} = \dfrac{\Sigma X}{N} = \dfrac{990}{50} = 19.8$

Range: Range $= 37 - 1 + 1 = 37$

Standard Deviation:

$$S = \frac{1}{N} \sqrt{N\Sigma X^2 - (\Sigma X)^2} = \frac{1}{50} \sqrt{50(23,590) - (990)^2}$$

$$= \frac{1}{50} \sqrt{1,179,500 - 980,100} = \frac{1}{50} \sqrt{199,400}$$

$$S = \frac{446.54}{50} = 8.93$$

As a rough check on the accuracy of our calculation of S, let us ask if our value is about one-fourth to one-fifth of the range. One-fourth of the range of 37 would be 9.25 while one-fifth would be 7.4, so our value of 8.93 appears reasonable.

If John Jones scored 14 on this test, what would be his z score? And if Mary Smith was told that her z score was 1.37, what was her score on the test?

John Jones: $X = 14, z = ?$

$$z = \frac{X - \overline{X}}{S} = \frac{14 - 19.8}{8.93} = \frac{-5.8}{8.93} = -0.65$$

Mary Smith: $z = 1.37, X = ?$

$$X = z(S) + \overline{X} = 1.37(8.93) + 19.8 = 12.23 + 19.8$$

$$X = 32.03, \text{ or } 32$$

Sample Problem #2

A group of 90 seniors takes a college entrance examination and the data is compiled in the grouped frequency distribution shown. Calculate the mean and standard deviation, using the appropriate grouped-data formulas.

Scores	f	d	fd	fd^2
42-44	2	4	8	32
39-41	3	3	9	27
36-38	12	2	24	48
33-35	20	1	20	20
30-32	24	0		
27-29	16	-1	-16	16

24-26	9	-2	-18	36
21-23	4	-3	-12	36
	$N = 90$		$\Sigma fd = 15$	$\Sigma fd^2 = 215$

Mean: $$\bar{X} = MP + i\left(\frac{\Sigma fd}{N}\right) = 31 + 3\left(\frac{15}{90}\right)$$
$$= 31 + 0.5 = 31.5$$

Standard Deviation: $$S = i \sqrt{\frac{N\Sigma fd^2 - (\Sigma fd)^2}{N^2}} = 3\sqrt{\frac{90(215) - (15)^2}{(90)^2}}$$

$$= 3\sqrt{\frac{19,350 - 225}{8,100}} = 3\sqrt{\frac{19,125}{8,100}}$$

$$= 3\sqrt{2.36} = 3(1.54)$$

$$S = 4.62$$

Study Questions

1. Why can't a measure of central tendency adequately describe a distribution of scores?

2. Why is the range a rather crude measure of variability?

3. Define what is indicated by Σx^2.

4. What is the difference between ΣX^2 and $(\Sigma X)^2$? Demonstrate the difference in these two operations by choosing five numbers and calculating both values for each.

5. Suppose you have a test that has been administered to thousands of students. The mean score is 50 and the standard deviation is 10. Redraw Figure 5-4 using these new test data.

6. What does $z = 1.54$ indicate? What about $z = -2.73$?

7 One hundred physical education students are measured for hand grip strength, with the weakest at 81 pounds and the strongest at 190 pounds. What should be the approximate value of the standard deviation for this distribution?

Exercises

1. Calculate the standard deviation for the 10 quiz scores shown below, using the three different formulas described in this chapter.

9	3
11	7
16	8
8	6
2	1

2. Fifteen subjects in a problem-solving experiment are measured on how long it takes to form a word from a scrambled set of letters. Calculate the mean and standard deviation (machine formula) for these scores.

15	13
12	11
11	10
11	14
14	13
11	11
12	13
13	

3. A geology lab quiz is given to 17 students. Calculate the mean and standard deviation (by the machine formula) for this distribution.

19	15
15	16
16	13
17	14
14	10
9	16
16	12
18	12
17	

4. The mean of a popular mental ability test is 100 with a standard deviation of 16. Sketch the normal curve, and mark off standard deviation units as in Figure 5-4. The following exercises are based on this distribution.

   a. Joan's score is 120. Calculate her z score, and locate it on your sketch.

   b. What z score corresponds to a mental ability score of 88? Locate it.

   c. Bill's z score is 1.75. Calculate his mental ability score and locate it.

   d. What mental ability score corresponds to a z score of -1.50? Locate it.

   e. If the distribution of mental ability scores is normal, the *middle* 68% of the scores should lie between what two scores?

   f. The middle 95% of the mental ability scores should be between what two values?

5. Susan scores 115 on the GATB, 627 on the CEEB, and 61 on a test using the T scale. On which scale did she perform the best? (Refer back to Table 5-6.)

6. A mechanical aptitude test was given to 80 junior high school students enrolled in an industrial arts curriculum. Use appropriate grouped-data formulas to calculate the mean and standard deviation for this distribution.

Scores	f
50-54	1
45-49	2
40-44	4
35-39	7
30-34	13
25-29	23
20-24	9
15-19	9
10-14	8
5-9	3
0-4	1
	$N = 80$

6 The Normal Curve

We have had several occasions in previous chapters to refer to the normal curve in a cursory fashion, but it is necessary at this point to devote an entire chapter to this much maligned and misunderstood statistical concept. Technically, this chapter is not consistent with the rest of the text as far as presenting techniques for either describing a set of data or making inferences about the nature of the population. Rather, it is a necessary interruption in order to introduce a mathematical concept that is a foundation for many statistical concepts, and it is essential to insert the material at this point. This chapter is somewhat similar to the interruption of an auto mechanic's on-the-job training with a study unit on the theory of automotive electronics. Comparatively speaking, we will temporarily put aside our statistical wrenches and screwdrivers for a short dissertation on the properties of the normal curve.

In previous chapters we noted that many physiological and psychological measurements were "normally" distributed; that is, a graph of the mea-

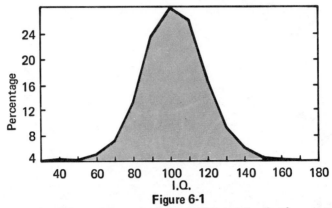

Figure 6-1

Stanford-Binet I.Q. scores of 1937 standardization group. From L. M. Terman and N. Merrill, *Stanford-Binet Intelligence Scale* (Boston, 1960), p. 18. Copyright 1960 by Houghton Mifflin Co. Used by permission of the publisher.

surements took on the familiar symmetrical, bell-shaped form. The graph of I.Q. test scores shown in Figure 6-1 is but one of the countless examples of such a distribution.

The Normal Curve as a Model

One of the reasons for the tremendous progress of the sciences over the last few decades has been their utilization of *mathematical models*. Without getting bogged down in technical jargon, we can say that scientists are overjoyed when the data of whatever they happen to be observing "fit" a particular mathematical model that they have chosen. Astronomers noted very early that the orbital path of planets seemed to be elliptical in form (an oval is one type of an ellipse), and by using this model they were able to predict such things as eclipses and the existence of, at that time, still undiscovered planets. In a similar way, physicists and other scientists have used such mathematical models as exponential or logarithmic functions, wave motion, and ballistic mechanics to study the behavior of electrons, light, body motion, and other natural phenomena. And — here is the point of the whole discussion — mathematical models were used to help scientists *picture* or *visualize* the nature of the data and to enable them to *predict* the outcome of data to be gathered in the future.

Applications of the normal curve were developed in much the same way. Borrowing from the work of several earlier mathematicians (see **Note 6-1**), Adolphe Quetelet (1796-1874), a Belgian mathematician and astronomer, was the first to note that the distribution of certain body measurements appeared to approximate the normal curve. He found that the heights of French soldiers and chest circumferences of Scottish soldiers yielded frequency distributions that fit the characteristic bell-shaped curve. Sir Francis Galton (1822-1911) continued with Quetelet's approach and studied the distributions of a wide variety of physical and mental characteristics. Quetelet, Galton, and countless researchers in innumerable investigations since those early days have made good use of the normal curve model to describe a set of data and to predict the results of future investigations.

So, why are we so excited (or, at least, mildly enthusiastic) over the possibility of using the normal curve as a model for data in education and the behavioral sciences? Simply because, if we can assume that the *population* of measurements from which we draw our sample is normally distributed, we can make use of the known properties of the normal curve both to visualize our data and to make predictions based on our sample. And since prediction is such an important part of statistics, we shall examine in detail the properties of this mathematical concept, the normal curve, in the remainder of this chapter.

Note 6-1
Origin of the Normal Curve

The noble art of mathematics was very early applied to problems in probability posed by gamblers. One very knotty problem concerned such questions as "What is the probability that in 10 flips of a coin heads will result 6 times?" or "What is the probability that in 20 throws of a die a '2' will show 7 times?" While solutions to these simple problems occurred quite early, it remained for a general application to cover the impossible calculations involved in answering a question such as "What is the probability that in 12,000 tosses of a coin heads will occur 1,876 times?" In 1733 Abraham de Moivre (1667-1754) developed a mathematical curve which would predict the probabilities of events associated with such things as flipping coins and rolling dice. The curve that de Moivre developed was, of course, what we now call the normal curve.

You may also have seen this curve referred to as the "Gaussian curve," after C. F. Gauss (1777-1855), who developed the normal curve independently of de Moivre in 1809. His interest was primarily in errors of measurement or observation in astronomy, and he noted that the curve described a distribution of errors. But, as was mentioned earlier, it was probably Quetelet who first applied the curve to a variety of physical data.

Some Characteristics of the Normal Curve

Since the normal curve is a mathematical function, it has a formula, which is

$$y = \frac{1}{\sigma \sqrt{2\pi}} e^{-\frac{(X - \mu^2)}{2\sigma^2}}$$

where y = height of the curve,

σ = standard deviation of the population,

π = pi, or 3.14,

e = natural logarithm, approximately 2.718,

X = any score value,

μ = the population mean.

Admittedly, the formula is an imposing one, and fortunately we will have very little to do with it as such. It is mentioned here so that we are aware of the fact that the normal curve is indeed a mathematical function, and because we must call attention to some of the terms in the formula.

There is a whole family of normal curves, depending on the values for the population mean (μ) and the population standard deviation (σ). That is, we can change the position of the curve on a scale of measurement by altering the mean, or we can change the spread of the curve by altering the standard deviation. We could have a normal curve by substituting into the formula a mean of 10, 50, or 100 and a standard deviation of 2, 17, or 29, or any value that suited our fancy.

In Figure 6-2 a normal curve with a mean of 0 and a standard deviation of 1 is shown. This is called the *unit normal curve*, and it is the

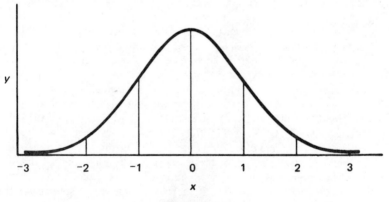

Figure 6-2
The unit normal curve.

one we will be working with throughout this chapter. It is called the unit curve because the *area* under the curve is exactly equal to 1 square unit. As we shall see later, using this area of exactly 1 will simplify our computations greatly.

Note that the units on the abscissa of Figure 6-2 are the familiar *z* scores that we dealt with in the last chapter. As you discovered then, a *z* score is a way of specifying a location on the scale that holds for whatever mean or standard deviation you have. The *z* score simply tells where a particular value lies in terms of standard deviation units from the mean. For example, in Figure 6-2, a *z* of 2.5 is obviously 2.5 standard deviations to the right of a mean of 0. (If having a mean of 0 bothers you, consider the mean as a point that is 0 standard deviations from the mean!)

Area under the Curve

The last characteristic of the normal curve that we will be concerned with is an important one indeed—that of determining the amount of *area* under the curve. We will find ourselves using this technique throughout the remaining chapters in the text, and it might be an understatement to say that any student of statistics *must* show at least a minimum level of competency in working with normal curve areas.

Some of the areas under the curve are obvious, and a quick glance at Figure 6-2 should reveal that, if the total area under the curve is 1.00, then 0.50 must be the area to the left of the mean and 0.50 the area to the right of the mean. Also, as you may remember from the last chapter, we found that about 68% of the total area (0.68 in decimal terms) is under the curve between a *z* of −1 and a *z* of +1, 95% between *z* scores of −2 and +2, and about 99% between *z* scores of −3 and +3.

However, we are usually interested in the "in between" values, and we must resort either to some high-level mathematics or a table of normal curve areas to determine the answers to such questions as "How much of the area under the curve lies between the mean and a *z* of 1.53?" or "How much of the area under the curve lies between a *z* of −2.38 and a *z* of 1.92?" Fortunately, we have Table B in Appendix 2, which makes it very simple to answer a variety of questions relating to normal curve areas. Note that the left side of the pairs of columns in Table B lists the *z* score, and the entry opposite gives the area under the normal curve *between that z score and the mean.* So to answer the question "How much of the area lies between the mean and a *z* of 1.53?" you simply look up the *z* value of 1.53 in Table B and note that

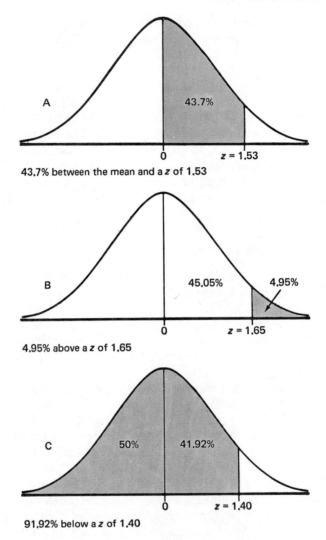

43.7% between the mean and a z of 1.53

4.95% above a z of 1.65

91.92% below a z of 1.40

Figure 6-3
Determining areas under the normal curve.

0.4370 or 43.7% of the total area is included under the curve between those points. The shaded area in Figure 6-3A illustrates this graphically.

The z scores of Table B are all positive, but since the curve is perfectly symmetrical we use the same tabled values for negative z scores. For example, if we wanted to know the area under the curve between the mean and a z of −1.53, we would get the same answer as above—43.7%. The only thing that would be different would be the location of the shaded area in Figure 6-3A, and we would see that the area under consideration would be to the *left* of the mean, between −1.53 and the mean.

Two techniques will be demonstrated in the following sections, with variations of each illustrated in Figures 6-3 through 6-5. Basically, we have two approaches: we either know the z score and use Table B to find an area, *or* we know the area and use Table B to determine the appropriate z score.

Given a z Score, Find the Area

In the preceding section Table B was described as giving a direct answer to finding the area under the curve between a z score and the mean, and the answer was illustrated in Figure 6-3A. The following examples show how to determine the area *above* or below a z score or *between* z scores.

Figure 6-3B—How do you find the area under the curve above a positive z value (or below a negative z)? You cannot read the value directly from Table B, since the areas in Table B are *between z and the mean*. In this case you must *subtract* the tabled value from 0.5000. For example, if you want to find what percentage of the area under the curve lies above a z of 1.65, the tabled value from Table B is 0.4505. But this value is the area between z and the mean, so you must subtract 0.4505 from 0.5000 to obtain 4.95%, which is the area above a z of 1.65. Figure 6-3B demonstrates this graphically. A similar approach would be used to find the area below a negative z value.

Figure 6-3C—How do you find the area below a positive z score? In this case it is necessary to add the tabled value to 0.5000 since the value in Table B gives only the area from the z value down to the mean. Figure 6-3C shows how this is done to answer a question such as "What percentage of the area under the curve lies below a z of 1.40?" Table B shows the area from a z of 1.40 down to the mean to be 0.4192, which, when added to 0.5000, would give 91.92% of the area below a z of 1.40.

To determine the percentage of the area *between* two z scores it is necessary to use one of two techniques, depending on whether the z scores are on the same side of the mean or on opposite sides.

Figure 6-4A—How do you determine the area under the curve between two z scores on different sides of the mean? Figure 6-4A shows how you would find the area between a negative z and a positive z, for example, −1.20 and 1.96. Since Table B gives the area from the z

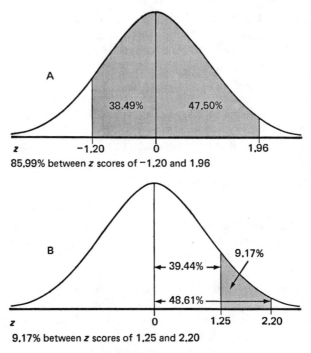

A

38.49%   47.50%

z   −1.20   0   1.96

85.99% between z scores of −1.20 and 1.96

B   9.17%

◄— 39.44% —►

◄— 48.61% —►

z   0   1.25   2.20

9.17% between z scores of 1.25 and 2.20

Figure 6-4
More areas under the normal curve.

score to the mean, it is only necessary to add the two areas to arrive at the answer. As you can see, the area between the mean and a z of −1.20 is 0.3849, and the area between the mean and a z of 1.96 is 0.4750, for a total area between the two of 0.8599 or 85.99%.

   Figure 6-4B—How do you determine the area under the curve between two z scores on the same side of the mean? You simply subtract the smaller area from the larger area. For example, if we wish to determine the area between a z score of 1.25 and 2.20, we look up the tabled value for 2.20 and find that 0.4861 of the total area lies between the mean and a z of 2.20. We then look in Table B for the area between the mean and a z of 1.25 and find the value to be 0.3944. We then subtract 0.3944 from 0.4861 to show that 0.0917 or 9.17% of the area lies between a z of 1.25 and 2.20. This is illustrated graphically in Figure 6-4B.

Given an Area, Find the z Score

   The preceding section just about exhausts all the possible ways in which Table B can be used when the z score is known and we wish to

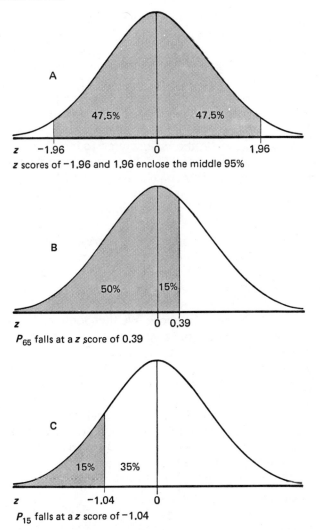

z scores of −1.96 and 1.96 enclose the middle 95%

P_{65} falls at a z score of 0.39

P_{15} falls at a z score of −1.04

Figure 6-5
Still more areas under the normal curve.

find the area. However, there are many occasions when we will have a known percentage of area under the curve and will use Table B to find the appropriate z score. Such occasions are obviously the reverse of the problems described in the preceding section, but the same general logic is used. Only the procedure is changed, in that you go to Table B with a percentage of area and look for a z. Figure 6-5 shows several examples of how Table B can be used in this way.

Figure 6-5A—How do you find what z scores form the boundaries of a centrally located area? All you have to do is divide the area by 2 (since Table B gives values only for one-half of the curve) and look up the z score that corresponds to that value. For example, the middle 95% of the area is between what two z scores? Figure 6-5A shows that one-half of the area, or 47.5%, would be on either side of the mean. We then go to Table B and look in the *area* column to locate 0.4750 and find that the z score that marks off 47.5% of the area from the mean is 1.96. And since the curve is symmetrical we know that a z score of −1.96 would mark off 47.5% of the area below the mean. So we conclude that z scores of −1.96 and 1.96 are the boundaries enclosing the middle 95% of the distribution.

Figure 6-5B—How do you find the z score corresponding to a given percentile? In an earlier chapter we noted that a percentile is a point below which lies a given percentage of the distribution. So to answer the question "What is the z score that corresponds to the 65th percentile, or P_{65}?" we note that in Figure 6-5B, since 50% of the distribution is below the mean, 15% would be above. We then look up 15% in the *area* column of Table B, because the areas shown in Table B are between the mean and the z value. We find that the exact value of 0.1500 is not listed in Table B, so we take the value *closest* to 0.1500, which is 0.1517, and see that the corresponding z score is 0.39. So the z score at P_{65} is 0.39.

Figure 6-5C—What if the percentile is below the mean? As you can see, the situation is a little different if the percentile falls below the mean, at P_{15}, for instance. Since the areas of Table B are between the mean and the z score, it is necessary to subtract 0.1500 from 0.5000 to get 0.3500 with which to enter Table B. The nearest value in Table B is 0.3508 and the corresponding z score is 1.04. Since the percentile in question is below the mean, the z value for P_{15} is −1.04.

It should be evident by now that in any problems involving normal curve areas it is a good idea to draw a rough sketch of the curve, both so you can follow the procedure (i.e., use Table B correctly) and so you get a pictorial representation that helps you visualize the reasoning behind the procedure. In some of the practical applications to follow, we will find such a pictorial approach very helpful in visualizing variables that otherwise would be difficult to understand.

Some Practical Applications

The preceding section was basically a set of instructions on the use of a normal curve table, at best a mechanical and mathematical procedure. We have already seen that the scientist is looking for mathematical models for understanding and predicting, so we now turn to a very important activity of behavioral scientists—applying the normal curve to actual data.

If we can assume that our set of scores is a random sample from a population that we believe is normally distributed, we can use the known characteristics of the normal curve to predict all sorts of things about the variables we are measuring. And, as we noted in Chapter 2, much of the data of a psychological and physiological nature is normally distributed in the population. But in the remaining sections of this chapter we must keep in mind the distinction between the mathematical model and the distribution of observed data. The mathematical characteristics of the normal curve printed in Table B (z scores and corresponding areas under the curve) apply to the model only, and the accuracy of our predictions regarding the real world depends on how close the population "fits" the normal curve model.

With these reservations in mind, let us use the normal curve model in a practical setting. If you will refer to Figure 6-1 you will remember that we used this sample of tested I.Q. scores to demonstrate that many test score distributions seem to fit the normal curve fairly well. The mean of this distribution of I.Q. scores is approximately 100, with a standard deviation of 16. With only this information (and the assumption of a normal distribution) we can make a number of predictions based on the normal curve model.

Figure 6-6A—If an individual with a tested I.Q. of 70 or below is considered mentally retarded, what percentage of the population would be classified as mentally retarded? The first step in answering this question is to convert the score of 70 to a z score. The formula given in Chapter 5 for a z score was $z = (X - \overline{X})/S$. So a score of 70 in the distribution of I.Q. scores would have a z of:

$$z = \frac{X - \overline{X}}{S} = \frac{70 - 100}{16} = \frac{-30}{16} = -1.88$$

Referring to Figure 6-6A and Table B you can see that a z of -1.88 is below the mean and the area between z and the mean is 0.4699. But the question asked concerned the population *below* 70, so we must subtract 0.4699 from 0.5000 to get 0.0301. Thus, we would conclude that 3.01% of the population has a tested I.Q. of 70 or below.

Figure 6-6B—If an I.Q. of 140 or above is necessary for a person to be considered mentally gifted, what percentage of the population is mentally gifted? Since we need a z score to enter Table B we find that the z score corresponding to an I.Q. of 140 is

$$z = \frac{X - \bar{X}}{S} = \frac{140 - 100}{16} = \frac{40}{16} = 2.50$$

Using Table B and Figure 6-6B, you note that 0.4938 of the area is between the mean and the z of 2.50, leaving 0.0062 or 0.62% of the

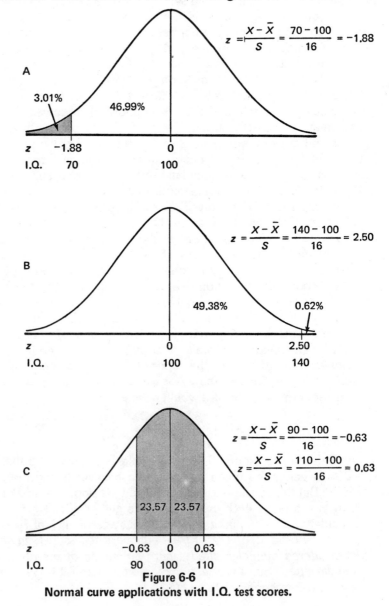

Figure 6-6
Normal curve applications with I.Q. test scores.

area above the z score. So we conclude that 0.62% of the population would have tested I.Q. scores above 140.

Figure 6-6C—If the range of "average" I.Q. scores is 90 to 110, what percentage of the population is considered average in intelligence? Converting I.Q. scores to z scores we get

$$z = \frac{X - \overline{X}}{S} = \frac{90 - 100}{16} = \frac{-10}{16} = -0.63$$

$$z = \frac{X - \overline{X}}{S} = \frac{110 - 100}{16} = \frac{10}{16} = 0.63$$

We see that the area of the curve in question is that between z scores of -0.63 and 0.63. Referring to Table B we find that 0.2357 of the area lies between the mean and a z of 0.63. Since the curve is symmetrical we know that the same area lies between the mean and a z of -0.63, for a total area of $0.2357 + 0.2357$, or 0.4714. So we conclude that 47.14% of the population would have I.Q. scores between 90 and 110.

The examples above are just three of many possible ways in which z scores can be calculated from actual score distributions to tell us something about the variable in the population. Quite often an additional step is taken when there are predictions to be made on a given sample. If, for example, the I.Q. score data of Figure 6-1 is based on a random sample of 1,500 school children, we could convert the percentages obtained in the above examples to actual numbers to find *how many* in the sample should score above or below or between certain z values. In the example illustrated in Figure 6-6A we found that 3.01% of the population should have I.Q. scores below 70. *If we can assume that our sample approximates the normal curve* (and the shape of Figure 6-1 shows that this is not a bad assumption), we need only multiply the sample size of 1,500 by 3.01% to find that we would expect approximately 45 children to have I.Q. scores of 70 or below. Similarly, in Figure 6-6B, there should be approximately 9 with scores of 140 or above $(1,500 \times 0.0062)$ and, in Figure 6-6C, approximately 707 with I.Q. scores between 90 and 110 $(1,500 \times 0.4714)$. So you can see that the normal curve can be used to make predictions about what will occur in a large, approximately normally distributed sample, as well as what can be theoretically expected in the population.

The careful reader will note that the three examples above were similar in that a decision had to be made about the location of a score in the distribution, the score was converted to a z score, and Table B was used to find the percentage of area above, below, or between the

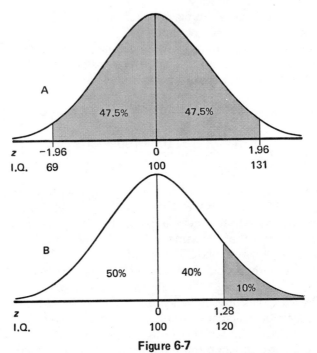

Figure 6-7
More normal curve applications with I.Q. test scores.

z scores. In terms of the earlier section on the use of Table B, we are again saying, "Given a z, find the percentage." The reverse procedure—"Given a percentage, find the z"—can also be used in practical applications, and Figure 6-7 illustrates this fact.

Figure 6-7A—The middle 95% of the population have I.Q. scores between what two values? Dividing the distribution into two equal parts on each side of the mean gives 47.5% on each side. Table B shows us that the z scores corresponding to these areas are −1.96 and 1.96, so we know that the middle 95% have I.Q. scores between z values of −1.96 and 1.96. However, the question is stated in terms of I.Q. scores, not z scores, so we must convert our z values to I.Q. scores, and we find:

$$X = zS + \overline{X} = -1.96\,(16) + 100 = -31.36 + 100 = 68.64$$

$$X = zS + \overline{X} = 1.96\,(16) + 100 = 31.36 + 100 = 131.36$$

So, as Figure 6-7A indicates, the middle 95% of the population have I.Q. scores between 69 and 131.

Figure 6-7B—How high does an individual's I.Q. have to be to place among the top 10% of I.Q. scores? By drawing a quick sketch you can see at a glance that we want the score that corresponds to the 90th percentile, since that would divide the bottom 90% from the top 10%. As Figure 6-7B shows, we use Table B to find the z score that marks off 40% of the area, and we note that the closest value to 40% is 0.3997 and its corresponding z score is 1.28. Converting the z score to an I.Q. score we find:

$$X = zS + \overline{X} = 1.28(16) + 100 = 20.48 + 100 = 120.48$$

And we conclude that an individual must have an I.Q. score of at least 120 to be considered in the top 10% of the population.

Probability and the Normal Curve

As we noted earlier in the chapter, especially in **Note 6-1,** the development of the normal curve was directly linked to some practical applications involving probability—mostly questions that gamblers might ask on the probability of the flip of a coin or the roll of a die. While a complete treatise on probability is beyond the intended scope of this text, it will be helpful to become acquainted with some of the terms used in probability, since we must be aware of just how the normal curve can assist us in making probability statements.

Coins, Cards, Dice, and People

A formal discussion of probability would make the subject seem unfamiliar to most of you, but, whether you are aware of it or not, we are constantly surrounded by probability statements. In a single evening the news, weather, and sports on television might all contribute statements directly related to probability. The news reporter might comment on the increase in car insurance rates, the weatherman will report a 30% chance of rain for the next 24 hours, and the sports commentator will note that the boxer being interviewed is a 5-to-1 favorite for tomorrow's middleweight match. And if, during a TV commercial, the reigning Dairy Princess spins a wheel to determine the lucky winner of a prize Holstein cow, we will have seen demonstrated all the different types of probability in a single evening! With these examples in mind, let us sort out two different types of probability.

Theoretical. This type of probability is undoubtedly the most familiar to us, since we all have flipped coins, rolled dice, drawn a playing card from a deck, and maybe even, like the Dairy Princess above, had a chance to spin a roulette wheel. We define probability, p, in this case by the following formula:

$$p = \frac{\text{number of ways the event in question can occur}}{\text{number of events possible}}$$

So the probability of getting heads in the flip of a coin is $1/2$, since the 1 event is getting heads on a normal coin, and the total number of events possible (represented by the 2) is a head and a tail. Similarly, the probability of rolling a "4" on one toss of a die is $1/6$, since only one side of a die has four spots while there is a total of six possible sides on the die. The probability of drawing an ace of spades from a well-shuffled deck would, of course, be $1/52$, while the probability of drawing any ace from the deck would be $4/52$. The typical roulette wheel has 38 numbered spaces and 1 blank space, so the probability that your number will come up on a fair spin of the wheel is $1/39$.

While we have been using *fractions* to illustrate the above probability situations, it is conventional to state probabilities in terms of *proportions*. So, instead of $p = 1/2$, $p = 1/6$, or $p = 1/52$, it is more common to see $p = .50$, $p = .17$, or $p = .02$. A quick glance at the general probability formula above should demonstrate that the probability of a "certainty" or "sure thing" is 1.0. Thus, the probability of flipping *either* a head *or* tail is $2/2$ or 1.0.

One lucky by-product of stating probabilities in terms of proportions is that they are so easily converted to percentages when we talk about frequency of occurrence in the "long run." For example, if the probability of rolling a "4" in one throw of a die is $p = .17$, we can expect a "4" to appear approximately 17% of the time. Or, in the long run, we could expect to pull an ace of spades from a well-shuffled deck approximately 2% of the time. There are advantages to thinking of probabilities in terms of percentages, as we shall see when we apply probabilities to areas under the normal curve.

Empirical. The characteristic which differentiates empirical probability from theoretical is that empirical probabilities can be calculated only from previous observations. How would one calculate the probability that the next baby born at a given hospital will be a boy? If records for the past five years show 7,223 babies born at this hospital, 3,720 of them boys, our empirical probability that the next birth will be a boy would be $p = 3,720/7,223 = .515$. Or, again using the "long run" concept, we would say that 51.5% of the births would be boys.

In a similar fashion, the weatherman's prediction of a 30% chance of rain is based on a number of past situations when meteorological conditions were identical to present conditions. Some precipitation occurred in the surrounding area on 30% of the occasions when these conditions were present, so he is predicting that $p = .30$ for some rain during the next 24 hours. (Not everyone comprehends this system, as illustrated by Figure 6-8.) The same interpretation can be applied to the car insurance rates and the betting results for the boxer. Past results (amount of insurance claims or amount bet on the boxer to win vs. amount bet on him to lose) in each case determine the probability associated with each event.

Reprinted by permission of Jefferson Communications, Inc., Reston, Virginia.

Figure 6-8
Probability statements in weather forecasts are not universally understood.

It should be clear by now that the way to compute an empirical probability is simply to calculate the percentage of times that the event in which you are interested has occurred in past situations and convert that percentage to a proportion. So, if you find that there are 800 freshmen, 680 sophomores, 578 juniors, and 492 seniors at a college with a total enrollment of 2,550, you would simply convert these to percentages to find that there are 31% freshmen, 27% sophomores, 23% juniors, and 19% seniors. Thus, the probability that a name drawn at random from the student directory will be that of a senior would be $p = .19$, since 19% of the student body are seniors.

Reading Probabilities from the Normal Curve Table

We can go directly from the normal curve areas of Table B to statements of probability. For example, what is the probability of a z score being greater than 1.0? Since 0.1587 of the area of the normal curve lies above a z of 1.0 (0.5000 − 0.3413), the probability of a z score being in this region is simply $p = .1587$ or .16. Stated another way, 16% of the z scores are above 1.0, so the probability of any one z score being above 1.0 is .16.

What is the probability of a z score being between −1.96 and 1.96? Since 95% of the area under the curve is between these two values, $p = .95$ that any z score would be between those values.

It should be obvious by now that in any of the previous examples where we calculated a percentage of the area under the curve we could easily make a probability statement. In Figure 6-6A, for example, we found that 3.01% of the population would have an I.Q. score of less than 70. Thus the probability that a person selected at random would have an I.Q. score below 70 is $p = .03$. Similarly, in Figures 6-6B and 6-6C, $p = .006$ that a person would have an I.Q. score above 140, and $p = .47$ that an individual would have a score between 90 and 110.

Odds and Ends

Any observer of the American sporting scene is aware of a unique way of stating the probability of success in a sporting event—in terms of the "odds for" or "odds against" a particular outcome. A football power might be a 2-to-1 favorite, a horse might be a 40-to-1 long shot, or the chances of filling out a spade flush in your friendly poker game might be 1 in 25. Of course, such statements are not limited to sporting events or games of chance but are often made about political elections, weather forecasts, and any other event where the outcome is something less than a certainty.

Undoubtedly, most of these statements are rather subjective, as shown by Figure 6-9, and are based upon hunches, past experiences, and the like. For example, in horse racing, the "morning line" of a newspaper contains the day's picks by one or more sportswriters, and statements like "Whirligig is a 100-to-1 long shot" simply imply that this creature may not even make it from the stable area to the starting gate. However, in some cases, actual data may be involved; thus the fact that a sample of voters has given two-thirds of their votes to one candidate may lead to a statement that "Senator Blank is a 2-to-1 favorite."

©1974 United Feature Syndicate.

Figure 6-9
An example of a subjective odds statement.

It would be interesting to continue discussing horseflesh and gambling, but we will have to confine our treatment of the topic to theoretical probability and areas under the normal curve. We will then be able to use "odds for" or "odds against" as just another way of stating probability. A homely way of stating the *odds for* an event to occur would be

Frequency of occurrence to Frequency of nonoccurrence

Thus, the *odds for* obtaining a "3" in the roll of a die would be 1 to 5, since out of six possible ways the die can land 1 is the frequency of the specified event and 5 is the frequency of the remaining events. In a similar fashion, the *odds for* drawing an ace of spades from a deck of cards would be 1 to 51, and the *odds for* drawing any ace would be 4 to 48. And you might note that the *odds for* flipping a head, with an unbiased coin, would be 1 to 1; that is, the odds are even. In all cases note that the total frequency in the odds statement adds up to the total number of ways *any* event can occur. That is, 1 to 5 = 6 sides, 1 to 51 = 52 cards, etc.

The *odds against* an event occurring are given simply by reversing the *odds for* statement. The *odds against* rolling the "3" are 5 to 1, and the *odds against* drawing the ace of spades are 51 to 1.

When odds statements are made concerning areas under the normal curve, we are able to go directly from probability to odds by using 100 as the base figure. For example, we noted that about 68% of the area under the curve lies between z's of -1.0 and 1.0. We then stated that the probability of a z score chosen at random being between -1.0 and 1.0 was $p = .68$. Thus the *odds for* a z score being between -1.0 and 1.0 are 68 to 32. Similarly, in Figure 6-6, the *odds for* an individual having an I.Q. of less than 70 would be 3 to 97, the *odds for* an individual having an I.Q. greater than 140 would be less than 1 to 99 (actually 6 to 994), and the *odds for* an individual having an I.Q. between 90 and 110 would be 47 to 53.

Some Concluding Remarks

As was mentioned earlier, the discussion of probability in this chapter is a very superficial treatment of the topic. We did, however, spend quite a bit of time with the normal curve, both examining its mathematical properties and applying these characteristics to some practical situations. But you still must be aware of the fact that we have just barely scratched the surface as far as the normal curve goes. By using this normal curve model, mathematical statisticians have been able to solve a number of theoretical issues that would otherwise be extremely tedious, if not impossible. Many of the techniques to be discussed in later chapters are based on such a theoretical foundation. If this topic has whetted your appetite for a mathematical approach to statistics, by all means pursue the matter with your favorite mathematics department.

Sample Problem

A manufacturer of hockey equipment is designing a new set of protective gear for college hockey players, and the design engineers have collected physical measurement data on 1,800 college players. The mean chest circumference for this group is 39 inches, with a standard deviation of 2.5 inches. Assume that this group is a random sample of all players and that the distribution is normal.

What percentage of the population has a chest measurement of over 44 inches?

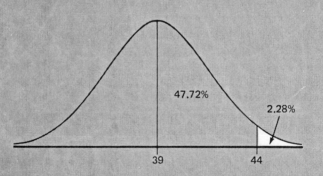

After drawing the curve, we calculate the z score for 44, which is $z = (44 - 39)/2.5 = 2.0$. In Table B we note that 47.72% of the area is between a z of 2.0 and the mean, leaving a total of 2.28% with a chest measurement of more than 44 inches.

If an engineer wants his design to fit the middle 99% of all players, what range of chest measurements will be covered?

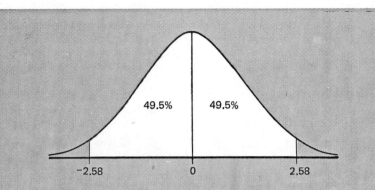

The middle 99% would be divided so that 49.5% of the distribution is on either side of the mean. In Table B we see that z scores of −2.58 and 2.58 are the boundaries for this 99%. Converting the z scores to chest measurements, we have

$$X = zS + \overline{X} = -2.58(2.5) + 39 = 32.6$$
$$X = 2.58(2.5) + 39 = 45.5$$

So we conclude that the design would have to be adjustable from 32.6 inches to 45.5 inches in order to fit the middle 99% of the players.

A husky lad claims that he is in the top 1% in chest expansion. What would his measurement have to be in order for him to make this claim?

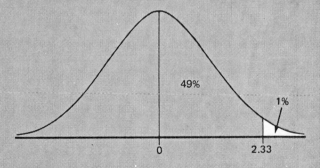

From the drawing and Table B we note that 49% of the area would be between the mean and the point needed, which would give a z score of 2.33. Converting the z score to inches, we would have

$$X = zS + \overline{X} = 2.33(2.5) + 39 = 44.8$$

His chest measurement would have to be 44.8 inches.

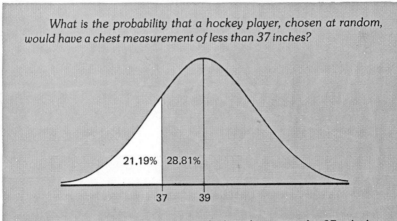

What is the probability that a hockey player, chosen at random, would have a chest measurement of less than 37 inches?

21.19%   28.81%

37   39

After drawing the curve, we calculate the z score for 37, which is $z = (37 - 39)/2.5 = -0.8$. In Table B we note that 28.81% of the area is between the mean and a z of -0.8. This would leave 21.19% below this point, so the probability that anyone chosen at random would have a chest measurement of less than 37 inches would be $p = .21$.

Study Questions

1. What are the reasons for using mathematical models in science?

2. What do we mean when we say there is a family of normal curves?

3. What is the unit normal curve?

4. Describe the process of finding the area under the normal curve between two positive z scores.

5. Differentiate theoretical from empirical probability.

6. How are odds statements used in theoretical probability? In empirical probability?

Exercises

1. What percentage of the area under the normal curve lies within the boundaries given:

    a. Between the mean and a z of 1.00

    b. Between the mean and a z of −1.96

    c. Between z scores of −1.28 and 2.06

    d. Between z scores of 1.42 and 2.25

    e. Above a z of 2.58

    f. Below a z of 1.63

    g. Above a z of −1.15

2. A college entrance examination is given to thousands of high school seniors. The mean of the scores is 50 with a standard deviation of 10. Assume that this distribution is normal.

    a. What percentage of the group scored below 35?

    b. A small college with questionable admissions policies announces that they will accept anyone who scores above 30 on this exam. What percentage of the group is eligible for admission to this college?

    c. Jane Doe announces that her test score is in the top 10% of the distribution. How high does her score have to be for her to make this statement?

    d. A vocational counselor suggests that no one scoring in the bottom 30% consider going to college. This group would have scores below what value?

    e. The middle 95% of the group has exam scores between what two values?

    f. What exam score would be at the 85th percentile?

    g. A name is pulled at random from the thousands who took the exam. What is the probability that this person scored 67 or above?

    h. What are the *odds for* someone scoring 67 or above?

3. What is the probability of someone drawing either an ace or a king from a deck of playing cards?

4. There are 50 cars in a parking lot — 11 Chevrolets, 9 Fords, 5 Plymouths, 4 Buicks, 3 Pontiacs, and 18 foreign cars. A woman crosses the street and enters the lot to retrieve her car.

    a. What is the probability that she is the owner of a Chevrolet?

    b. What is the probability that she owns a foreign car?

    c. What are the odds for her owning a foreign car? Odds against?

5. In a normal curve what is the probability of obtaining any of the
   following at random?
   a. A z of 1.0 or greater
   b. z values between −1.96 and 1.96
   c. A z value of 2.58 or greater
   d. z values between −2.58 and 2.58
   e. A z value of −1.96 or less

7 Sampling Theory

As the guard changes at Buckingham Palace, so must we change emphasis in our treatment of statistical topics. Earlier we noted the distinction between descriptive statistics and inferential statistics, and it is with this chapter that we begin to be concerned about making *inferences* about the *population* instead of being content merely to describe a particular distribution of data. To be sure, descriptive statistics are useful—even indispensable—for a teacher measuring the performance of a class of algebra students or a college administration calculating grade-point averages, but, as Chapter 1 pointed out, educators and behavioral scientists often gather evidence from samples for the express purpose of generalizing their results to the population.

Descriptions vs. Inferences

If a social psychologist wants to know the relationship between TV violence and aggression in children, or if a guidance counselor wants to know if participation in extracurricular activities is an indicator of a healthy self-image, or if a personnel manager wants to see if performance on a manual dexterity test will predict job success on the assembly line, all three will undoubtedly select a group of individuals, gather data, and generalize the results from the small sample to a much larger population.

Note that the difference between descriptive statistics and inferential statistics is not in the *kind* of statistical measures employed but in the *purpose* for doing the measuring. If your intent is merely to describe a distribution of data, you will construct a frequency distribution and frequency polygon in order to picture the distribution and you will calculate a mean, median, or mode to discover its central tendency and a standard deviation to find its variability. All of these procedures, of course, *describe* the distribution.

Now, if your purpose is to make *inferences* about a population, you will still calculate means and standard deviations, but your interest will focus on how well these statistics estimate a *population* mean and standard deviation. The rest of this chapter will be devoted to procedures for taking samples and for estimating the population values by using the sample statistics.

The terms *sample* and *population* have been used rather informally in the preceding discussion, and you have probably assumed by now that a population consists of *all* the members of a group while a sample is a somewhat smaller group, selected from that population. While this distinction is essentially correct, it is not complete, and more precise definitions are needed.

A *population* is a group of elements that are alike in one or more characteristics as defined by the researcher. A population could be all the college students in the U.S., or all the voters in a state, or all the seventh-graders in a school system, or all the dairy cattle in a county. Or, in terms of the social psychologist, the guidance counselor, and the personnel manager mentioned earlier, the populations could be all the preschool children in the Midwest, all the junior high school students in a metropolitan school district, or all the welding machine operators in automotive assembly plants owned by General Motors. The important thing to remember is that the population is defined by a researcher *for a particular purpose* and *all* the elements satisfying the criteria are members of that population. Size alone does not determine whether or not a group of elements is a population, although in practice most populations turn out to be rather large.

A *sample*, on the other hand, is a group of elements that is selected from the population and is *smaller* in number than the size of the population. A sample may be chosen in a number of ways, and you can have random samples, stratified samples, or cluster samples. Each type involves a different procedure for determining how the data are to be gathered, and the following section describes the different sampling procedures.

Types of Samples

Random Samples

The random sample is chosen in such a way that *each element in the population has an equal chance of being in the sample.* This is an important definition and one that must be strictly followed before the procedures outlined in this chapter can be applied. But how does one draw a random sample in practice?

As an example, let us say that we would like to interview a random sample of college students on a given college campus about their attitudes toward the college administration. While it would be simple to stand in the entrance to the student union and pick the first 50 students that come by, the result would *not* be a random sample. The fact that many polls are conducted in just this fashion does not make it right, and we must look for a more statistically defensible procedure. There are two generally acceptable ways of obtaining a random sample—a table of random numbers and a "counting-off" technique. The random number method is preferred, although the counting method will usually approximate a random sample.

Table of random numbers. Table L in Appendix 2 is a collection of random numbers, random in that any digit or any grouping of four digits bears no relationship to any other digit or grouping of digits in the table. In other words, in terms of our definition of a random sample, in any position in the table, each digit from 0 to 9 has an equal chance of appearing.

To obtain a random sample from a college population of 5,000 students we would first obtain a listing of all students and assign each one a number from 1 to 5,000. We would then enter Table L at a point determined by chance (a colleague of mine closes his eyes and stabs at the page with his fingertip or a pencil). From this starting point, we would take as many numbers from the columns as we needed for our sample. If we ran across a duplicate number, we would ignore it and go on to the next one. If we wanted one-, two-, or three-digit numbers, we would use the same procedure but would take only the first one, two, or three digits of the four-digit numbers. The students with the numbers corresponding to the ones we selected would constitute our sample.

Counting-off procedure. The technique described above can be quite time-consuming when the populaton is large; assigning a number to all the names in a metropolitan telephone directory, for instance, would require great dedication. In such a case it may be more convenient to use a counting-off procedure and take every hundredth or every thousandth name in the list. For example, if we wanted a random sample of 200 from a population of 60,000, we would take every 300th name. A counting-off procedure is used frequently in consumer surveys, where a questionnaire may be inserted in every 30th box of the manufacturer's product or mailed along with a monthly billing to every 10th credit card customer.

Sometimes referred to as "systematic sampling," this procedure involves entering a directory or list of names by making the first draw a random one. For example, if we wanted a sample of 50 from a list of 500 names, we would need every 10th name on the list. The starting place for counting would be determined by a table of random numbers, so we would choose a number from 1 to 10 at random. If the number 6 came up, we would begin our drawing at the 6th name on the list and take every 10th name after that.

Stratified Random Sampling

When the results of the poll or experiment are likely to be affected by certain characteristics of the population, a stratified random sample is often used. For example, if a campus survey is conducted and the attitudes being evaluated would depend on sex, year in school, size of high school graduating class, and family income, it would be essential to have the sample contain the proportions that exist in the campus population. A number of subgroups would be set up (e.g., freshman women from a high school graduating class of 300 to 399 whose annual family income is between $20,000 and $30,000), and *random* samples would be drawn from each of the subgroups in such a way that the size of each subgroup in the sample was proportional to the size of the same subgroup in the total campus population. This, of course, would result in a sample that is a miniature population, with all relevant characteristics represented.

While stratified sampling may require a colossal amount of work, it is essential in many instances where a *representative* sample is required. In Chapter 4 we noted that the sample of children used in constructing norms for an I.Q. test was *stratified* according to the father's occupation, since it was known that I.Q. depends upon socioeconomic status. Similarly, in voter polls prior to an election, stratified samples need to have proportionate representation of Democrats and Republicans, of men and women, and of relevant variables such as education, income, ethnic group, and the like.

Cluster Sampling

In practice it may be very difficult to stratify a population on a nationwide basis, so cluster sampling is often used. Whereas the members of a given stratum or subgroup of the stratified sample are alike (all men, or all Democrats, etc.), a cluster is itself composed of the different variables. An example might help clarify this distinction.

Let us say that we would like to construct a set of national norms for a test that we have developed and would like fourth-graders from all over the nation to be represented in the sample. Clusters could be any intact unit such as states, counties, or legislative districts, but we would probably choose to use school districts as our "population" of clusters. As you can see, each school district would have fourth-graders enrolled in one or more elementary schools, and all the variables affecting the test scores (e.g., socioeconomic level, sex, age) would be represented in the cluster.

After the clusters had been defined, a random sample of clusters would be chosen in the first stage of sampling, and additional random sampling would be used to select particular schools, classrooms, or even individuals within a class that would make up our final sample. Again, as with stratified sampling, our objective is to achieve a sample that is *representative* of the population.

One popular national polling service uses more than 300 voting precincts for its samples. These would be considered clusters, since they contain a certain proportion of each sex, political preference, ethnic group, socioeconomic level, and so on. Within these clusters random samples can be taken; for example, every fourth dwelling on the block might be polled.

Some Concluding Remarks on Samples

Before progressing to the mathematics of sampling theory, you should be aware of some terms and concepts that you may encounter in reference to sampling.

Size of Sample

All other things being equal, a sample is more likely to be accurate (i.e., to faithfully describe the population characteristics) as it increases in size. Size alone does not insure an accurate sample (as we will note below when we take up the topic of *biased* samples), but it is safe to say that if we follow the rules in obtaining whatever type of sample we are working with, a larger sample will more accurately reflect the characteristics of the population. You will have to accept this statement on faith for stratified and cluster samples, but later in the chapter we will have occasion to demonstrate mathematically the effect of size of a random sample on accuracy of results.

Biased Samples

Any time that our samples contain a systematic error, they are said to be *biased*. A very common example of bias in sampling is the case in which copies of a questionnaire are mailed out to a number of people and only a fraction of the total are sent back. It is entirely possible that those returning the questionnaire, thereby volunteering to have their data examined, are different in some respect from those who do not return them. The classical study on sexual behavior in men by Kinsey was criticized by some on just this point; the critics felt that those men willing to divulge such information in explicit detail were somehow different from the ordinary male in the population.

Perhaps the most famous example of biased sampling occurred in a voting preference poll sponsored by the *Literary Digest* in 1936. On the basis of a huge sample of voters gleaned from automobile registration records and telephone directories, the magazine predicted that Alf Landon would easily defeat Franklin D. Roosevelt in the 1936 presidential election. The systematic error in this poll was that voters who did not own automobiles or have telephones—the people who were most likely to vote for FDR and his social reform policies—were not represented in the sample. They did vote, however, and Roosevelt was elected by an overwhelming majority.

Incidental Sampling

Much of the data constituting the foundation for theories in education and the behavioral sciences is from studies using college students. It seems that introductory psychology courses are a very handy source of subjects for an infinite variety of experiments, and it is the rule rather than the exception to have each student participate in one or more experiments as a course requirement. Critics of this technique are quick to point out that college sophomores in the introductory psychology course may not be representative of even college students in general, to say nothing of the population at large. Whenever such *incidental sampling* is employed (grade school classes, a college faculty, county welfare recipients, etc.), it is difficult, to say the least, to generalize to a population of all grade schools, college faculties, or welfare recipients. The particular sample at hand may be unique, so that the results of a study simply cannot be generalized to a larger population without serious error. Thus, if incidental sampling must be used because of cost considerations, great pains must be taken to examine the sample for any possible biases. Otherwise, it could be the *Literary Digest* poll all over again!

Sampling with Replacement

When random samples are drawn from a comparatively small population, it is usually necessary to replace the observation before taking the next one. If your population consists of a deck of cards, a bag of colored marbles, numbers in a hat, or the like, you should return the card or whatever to the group before making another draw. For example, let us say a bag contains 15 yellow, 3 blue, and 2 red marbles. The probability of drawing a blue marble would be 3/20 or $p = .15$. However, if you didn't get a blue on your first draw, the probability of getting a blue on the second draw depends on whether or not you return the first marble to the bag. If you don't, the probability is now 3/19 or $p = .16$. Similarly, the probability of pulling an ace from a well-shuffled deck is 4/52 or $p = .077$. If you don't get an ace on the first draw and do not replace the card, the probability on the second draw is now 4/51 or $p = .078$. The differences due to nonreplacement in the above examples are small, but nonreplacement could affect your calculations in a complex probability problem.

Parameters vs. Statistics

In the sections to come we will have occasion to talk about means, medians, standard deviations, and other characteristics of samples, as well as means and standard deviations of a population. We will attempt to avoid confusion by referring to these measures of central tendency and variability as *statistics* when they describe a *sample* and as *parameters* when they describe a *population*. In other words the mean and standard deviation of a sample are *statistics*, and their namesakes in the population are *parameters*. To aid us in identifying which are which, we use the lowercase Greek letter μ (mu) for the population mean and the lowercase Greek letter σ (sigma) for the population standard deviation. As before, $\overline{X}$ and S are the sample mean and standard deviation, respectively.

Estimating the Population Mean

Much of the energy expended in inferential statistics goes toward the *estimation* of population parameters. This estimation process is necessary because in most cases it is virtually impossible to measure an entire population due to its size and ever-changing nature. If one wants to know the average I.Q. of high school seniors, manual dexterity of aerospace electronics technicians, reading readiness scores of 6-year-olds, or what have you, the respective populations are so large and inaccessible that the only reasonable procedure is to take a random sample and estimate the population values from this sample alone.

While this procedure may seem questionable to you, it is the only practical approach to the problem. Statisticians have worked out the necessary formulas, tested mathematical models, and developed techniques to enable us to take a sample, calculate its mean, and estimate with a given degree of certainty how well this sample $\overline{X}$ estimates the "true" mean or population mean, μ. The following sections will describe the theory behind the techniques and the methods to be followed in estimating population parameters.

The Sampling Distribution

Let us suppose that we would like to know the average height of all adult males in a large midwestern university. We follow the rules listed earlier for obtaining a random sample and, using a sample size of 100, we come up with a mean of 69.2 inches and a standard deviation of 2 inches. The sample $\overline{X}$ of 69.2 is called *an unbiased estimate of the population mean, μ.* By *unbiased*, we mean that if we continued to take samples like the one we just did the *mean of all these sample means* would approach the value of the population mean.

After we have gathered our data and calculated the sample mean, we ask, "How good an estimate of the population mean is our sample mean of 69.2 inches?" "Is it too high?" "Too low?" "Just about right?" Since we rarely know the true mean (population mean) we can never answer these questions exactly, but we can make a *probability statement* about its most likely value.

In order to do this we must first indulge in a bit of fancy. Let us perform a hypothetical exercise in which we continue to take samples of size 100 and calculate the mean of each sample. Keeping track of these means, we might get

$$\overline{X}_1 = 69.2$$
$$\overline{X}_2 = 68.7$$
$$\overline{X}_3 = 69.6$$
$$\overline{X}_4 = 68.5$$

and so on.

If we continued to do this for an *infinite* number of samples (you see why it is a *hypothetical* exercise), the following would occur:

1. A batch of means, called a *sampling distribution of means*, would result.
2. The mean of this sampling distribution, $\bar{X}_{\bar{X}}$ (say "mean of means"), would be the same as the population mean, μ.
3. The batch of sample means would be normally distributed around the mean of the distribution, $\bar{X}_{\bar{X}}$, with a standard deviation of $\sigma/\sqrt{N}$.

This last point summarizes the *central limit theorem*, and it is an important foundation for much of our work in statistical inference. Stated more precisely, the central limit theorem in this instance says that *if a population has a mean μ and a standard deviation σ, then the distribution of sample means drawn from this population approaches a normal distribution as N increases, with a mean $\bar{X}_{\bar{X}}$ and a standard deviation $\sigma/\sqrt{N}$.* Regardless of the shape of the population from which we draw our samples, the sampling distribution of means will be normal, *if the sample size is sufficiently large.* What is a "sufficiently large" sample? There is no easy answer, because the required sample size depends on the shape of the population distribution. You will find some statistics texts specifying an *N* of 30, and others an *N* of 50; certainly an *N* of 100 would remove all doubt about the resultant shape of the sampling distribution. In any event, the central limit theorem enables us to solve sampling problems without worrying whether or not the population from which we are sampling is normal.

The three characteristics of a sampling distribution noted above are of primary importance, so let us look at each in greater detail.

Sampling distribution of means. We would note as we calculated mean after mean that most of them tended to cluster about some central point, just as our frequency distributions tended to do back in Chapter 2. We should not be surprised that all the samples do not have the same mean; we expect that because of *chance* fluctuations the means will tend to vary slightly. Just as we would not expect to get 5 heads and 5 tails every time we flipped a coin 10 times, we also do not expect that all sample means would be the same.

Note 7-1
Chance, "Dumb Luck," and Sampling Error

There will be a number of occasions in the remaining chapters when we will be talking about *chance* or *sampling error*. Decisions must be made to determine whether some result is due to chance (i.e., sampling error), or whether the result represents a real departure from purely chance fluctuations. If you regularly take a coffee break with a friend and flip a coin to see who pays, you expect in the long run to win about half the time. In other words, who winds up paying on a given day is strictly due to "chance." But, as you well know, there might be times when one of you will win, three, or even four days in a row. Such fluctuations can still be chance effects and would be called, simply, "sampling error."

On the other hand, if your friend seems to win the toss 90% of the time, you would probably demand to examine her coin, since such a departure from what you expect to happen "just by chance" leads you to suspect something other than an unbiased coin toss. But where do you draw the line? How much of a deviation from a 50-50 split do you endure before you can say that there is something uncanny about your friend's coin-tossing ability? 60-40? 70-30? 80-20? At what point do you say that the deviation is no longer sampling error but is a *real* nonchance happening? Decisions such as these are typical of inferential statistics, and we will be spending considerable time on just how such decisions are made.

Let us assume that the mean of means, $\overline{X}_{\overline{X}}$, in our hypothetical exercise on the height of adult males in a midwestern university turned out to be 69 inches. We would notice that many of the sample means would be quite close to $\overline{X}_{\overline{X}}$, say 68.7, 69.2, or 68.6. However, we would also notice that a few of the sample means would be scattered a little farther away from $\overline{X}_{\overline{X}}$, such as 66.2 or 70.1. And an occasional sample mean would be as far away as 65.1 or 72.3. We expect the sample means to be distributed in this fashion, *and this scattering of $\overline{X}$'s about $\overline{X}_{\overline{X}}$ is due to sampling error.*

The mean of means. The mean of the sampling distribution of means, $\overline{X}_{\overline{X}}$, is the same as the population mean, μ. What we are saying is that if we take all possible samples of a given size from a population and calculate the mean of each sample the mean of all these sample means is equal to the population mean. The mathematical proof for the relationship between $\overline{X}_{\overline{X}}$ and μ is beyond the scope of this text, but this is a handy relationship, as we shall soon see.

Normal sampling distribution. Since the sampling distribution of means is normal, we can use the characteristics of the normal curve that we noted back in the last chapter. For example, we could say:

1. 68.26% of all the sample means would fall between -1 and 1 standard deviation from the mean, $\overline{X}_{\overline{X}}$.
2. 95% of all the sample means would fall between -1.96 and 1.96 standard deviations from the mean, $\overline{X}_{\overline{X}}$.

3. 5% of all the sample means would fall outside the same interval, -1.96 and 1.96 standard deviations from the mean, $\bar{X}_{\bar{X}}$.

And, similarly, the probability statements we made concerning the normal curve would apply to this sampling distribution as well.

1. The probability that a sample mean falls between $\bar{X}_{\bar{X}} \pm 1$ standard deviation would be .68.
2. The probability that a sample mean falls between $\bar{X}_{\bar{X}} \pm 1.96$ standard deviations would be .95.
3. The probability that a sample mean falls *outside* the same interval, $\bar{X}_{\bar{X}} \pm 1.96$ standard deviations, would be .05.

With these probability statements in mind, let us get back to our original question, "How well does our sample mean of 69.2 inches estimate the true mean?" In Figure 7-1, the hypothetical sampling distribution of means is shown with its mean, $\bar{X}_{\bar{X}}$, of 69. Basically, we are asking, "Where in this distribution of sample means does our mean of 69.2 fall?"

Standard Error of the Mean

As you can see from Figure 7-1, we could locate our sample mean of 69.2 and make probability statements about where it falls, *if we knew the standard deviation of this distribution*. If the standard deviation were 1 inch, 69.2 inches would be very close to $\bar{X}_{\bar{X}}$, but, if the standard deviation were 0.1 inch, the sample mean of 69.2 inches would be 2 standard deviations above $\bar{X}_{\bar{X}}$.

The standard deviation of this sampling distribution of means is called the *standard error of the mean*[1] and, as we noted earlier, is given by

$$\sigma_{\bar{X}} = \frac{\sigma}{\sqrt{N}} \qquad (7\text{-}1)$$

where $\sigma_{\bar{X}}$ is the standard error of the mean,

σ is the standard deviation of the population from which the samples were drawn,

N is the size of the *sample*.

However, this formula is not usually used, because we generally do not know the value of the population standard deviation, σ. As a result, we resort to an alternate formula which permits us to use our *sample* standard deviation, S, and we can then estimate the standard

---

[1] The term *standard error of the mean* may sound awkward, but it is to be interpreted as any other standard deviation. We could just as well say "standard deviation of the mean," but convention is convention, and we will have to learn to live with the standard *error* of the mean. The important thing is that *standard error of the mean* means the standard deviation of the sampling distribution of means.

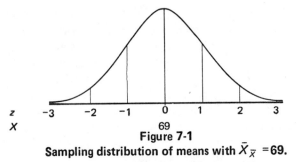

Figure 7-1
Sampling distribution of means with $\bar{X}_{\bar{x}} = 69$.

deviation of the sampling distribution of means. The formula for this estimate is

$$s_{\bar{X}} = \frac{S}{\sqrt{N-1}}$$ (7-2)

where $s_{\bar{X}}$ is the standard error of the mean,[2]
    S is the standard deviation of our *sample*,
    N is the size of the *sample*.

Note that the above formula calls for $N - 1$ instead of N in the denominator. Later on in the chapter we will look at the reason for using $N - 1$ in more detail, but for now we will simply say that it "corrects" for the fact that the sample standard deviation, S, tends to be smaller than the population standard deviation, σ.

Once we have calculated the standard error of the mean, $s_{\bar{X}}$, we can make probability statements about where our sample mean falls in the sampling distribution and, by inference, just how good an estimate of the population mean our sample mean is. As an example let us assume that our sample of 100 college men ($N = 100$) showed $\bar{X} = 69.2$ and $S = 3$.

To calculate the standard error of the mean we substitute into the formula:

$$s_{\bar{X}} = \frac{S}{\sqrt{N-1}} = \frac{3}{\sqrt{100-1}}$$

$$= \frac{3}{\sqrt{99}} = \frac{3}{9.95}$$

$$s_{\bar{X}} = 0.3$$

Some Trial Estimates of μ

Now, with our sample mean, $\bar{X}$, of 69.2 and our standard error,

$s_{\overline{X}}$, of 0.3, is it possible for the population mean, μ, to be 69? Figure 7-2A shows the sampling distribution with $\overline{X}_{\overline{X}}$ of 69 and its standard deviation ($s_{\overline{X}}$) of 0.3. If the true mean (remember that $\overline{X}_{\overline{X}} = \mu$) is actually 69, where does our sample mean of 69.2 lie?

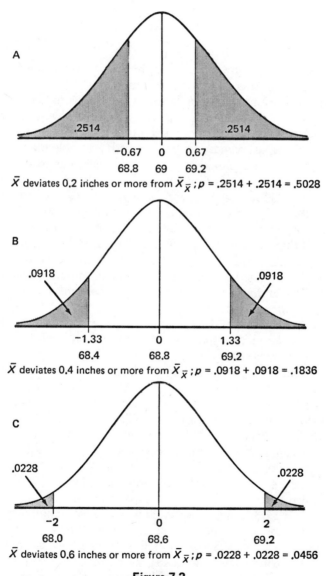

A

.2514   .2514

| −0.67 | 0 | 0.67 |
| 68.8 | 69 | 69.2 |

$\overline{X}$ deviates 0.2 inches or more from $\overline{X}_{\overline{x}}$; p = .2514 + .2514 = .5028

B

.0918   .0918

| −1.33 | 0 | 1.33 |
| 68.4 | 68.8 | 69.2 |

$\overline{X}$ deviates 0.4 inches or more from $\overline{X}_{\overline{x}}$; p = .0918 + .0918 = .1836

C

.0228   .0228

| −2 | 0 | 2 |
| 68.0 | 68.6 | 69.2 |

$\overline{X}$ deviates 0.6 inches or more from $\overline{X}_{\overline{x}}$; p = .0228 + .0228 = .0456

Figure 7-2
Sample mean with different hypothesized true means.

The *z* score is used to determine where in the distribution our mean of 69.2 is located. However, the usual *z* score formula, $z = (X - \bar{X})/S$, must be modified slightly in order for us to use it in a sampling distribution. Since the mean is $\bar{X}_{\bar{X}}$, the standard deviation is the standard error of the mean, $s_{\bar{X}}$, and the "score" is our sample mean, $\bar{X}$, the *z* formula would now read

$$z = \frac{\bar{X} - \bar{X}_{\bar{X}}}{s_{\bar{X}}}$$

(7-3)

It is still the same old *z* score, but the terms in the formula are changed to apply to a sampling distribution.

The *z* score for our sample mean of 69.2 would be $z = (69.2 - 69)/0.3 = 0.67$. In other words, it is approximately two-thirds of a standard deviation from the hypothesized true mean of 69. Since by sampling error it is just as easy to wind up with a sample mean 0.2 inches *below* $\bar{X}_{\bar{X}}$, we can rephrase our original question as follows: "What is the probability that any sample mean would deviate from the population mean by 0.2 inches or more?" Using Figure 7-2A and Table B we see that the sample means in the sampling distribution that deviate 0.2 inches or more are shown *below* a *z* score of -0.67 and above a *z* of 0.67, and that 50.28% of the normal curve area lies outside these two points. In other words, 50.28% of all sample means would fall outside these two *z* values, so *the probability that a sample mean, picked at random, would deviate 0.2 inches or more from this hypothesized true mean of 69 inches is .5028.*

From these results does it seem likely that the true mean is actually 69 inches? Remember that we do not know the exact value of the true mean but are simply hypothesizing a value and, on the basis of our sample, trying to make a decision about the most likely value of the true mean.

Suppose that we had hypothesized that the true mean was 68.8 inches. We then would have the situation shown in Figure 7-2B. With our sample mean again of 69.2, our question would now be "What is the probability that any sample mean would deviate from this hypothesized population mean by 0.4 inches or more?" If the true mean were in fact 68.8, the sampling distribution would look like Figure 7-2B, and we could calculate a *z* score for our sample mean of 69.2 as $z = (69.2 - 68.8)/0.3 = 1.33$. Since the deviation could be either plus or minus (again, remember that from a sampling point of view we are just as likely to get a sample mean that is 0.4 inches *below* the mean as one that is 0.4 inches above the mean), we can see from Figure 7-2B that this area is represented under the curve below a *z* of -1.33 and above a z of 1.33. We then conclude that if the true mean were 68.8, 18.36% of all the means in this sampling distribution would fall outside the two z scores of −1.33 and 1.33, or outside 68.4 and 69.2, so $p = .1836$ that any sample mean would fall outside these values.

With these results is it possible that the true mean could actually be 68.8? Is it possible with a sample mean of 69.2 to have a population mean that is only 68.8? Let us postpone an answer to these questions until we look at one more example.

Suppose that we had hypothesized that the population mean was 68.6 inches with the hypothetical frequency distribution shown in Figure 7-2C. With our sample mean again of 69.2, what is the probability that a sample mean, drawn at random, would deviate 0.6 inches or more from the true mean? The z score for our sample mean of 69.2 would now be $z = (69.2 - 68.6)/0.3 = 2.0$. Again, since this much of a deviation from the mean could be below the mean, we see in Figure 7-2C that this area is represented under the curve below a z of −2.0 and above a z of 2.0. We then conclude that if the true mean were actually 68.6, only 4.56% of all sample means in this sampling distribution would fall outside the two z scores of −2.0 and 2.0, or outside 68.0 and 69.2. The probability, then, of any sample mean chosen at random being outside these two values is $p = .0456$.

Sampling Error vs. a Real Difference

At last we have come to the point where we can make a decision about how good our sample mean is as an estimate of the population mean. (Again, keep in mind that we do not know the actual value of the population mean.) In Table 7-1 are the results of our three hypothetical estimates of the population mean, along with the probability of a sample mean deviating by as much as or more than our sample mean of 69.2 does. Examine this table carefully and, at the same time, inspect the three sampling distributions of Figure 7-2.

Note in Table 7-1 and Figure 7-2 that the farther away the hypothesized population mean is from our sample mean, *the smaller the probability that a given sample mean, drawn at random, would deviate by that amount or more*. On the basis of these three examples we note that:

1. When we hypothesized a population mean of 69 inches, we saw that more than 50% of all sample means would miss μ by as much as (or more than) our mean of 69.2 did. Since the probability of any sample mean, chosen at random (as ours was), deviating by as much as or more than that was .5028, we would conclude that it is entirely possible that the population

Table 7-1

Hypothesized Population Means and Associated Probabilities
of a Greater Deviation Than Our Sample Mean of 69.2 Inches

Hypothesized Population Mean	Amount of Deviation from μ	Probability of Deviation
69 inches	0.2 inches or more	p = .5028
68.8 inches	0.4 inches or more	p = .1836
68.6 inches	0.6 inches or more	p = .0456

mean is in fact 69, and our sample mean of 69.2 represents *sampling error* due to chance effects present in any sampling situation.

2. When we hypothesized that μ = 68.8 inches, we saw that about 18% of all sample means would miss μ by as much as or more than 0.4 inches. The probability, then, of any sample mean deviating by that much or more than that was p = .1836, and we would probably conclude that it would be entirely possible for μ to be 68.8 and that our sample mean of 69.2 is due to sampling error. But, noting that fewer sample means (18% vs. 50%) deviate by this larger amount, we begin to feel a little uneasy about one of two possibilities. Either we doubt our hypothesis about the value of μ, or we wonder about the accuracy of our sample mean.

3. When we hypothesized that μ = 68.6 inches, we noted that less than 5% of all the sample means would miss μ by as much as 0.6 inches or more. The probability of any sample mean, chosen at random, deviating by this much or more is p = .0456, and now we really begin to feel uneasy. Our sample mean deviates by so much that less than 5% of the sample means deviate by this much or more by *sampling error*. There are two possibilities, as indicated in statement 2.

   a. The population mean could really be 68.6 and our sample mean of 69.2 is a rare occurrence, one of the few that we expect would deviate this much by sampling error.

   b. Our hypothesis is dead wrong. We have made a big mistake in hypothesizing the value of the population mean.

It turns out that we have the utmost faith in our sample mean, so, if the discrepancy between our sample mean and some hypothesized population mean is too large, *we must reject the hypothesized population mean as being untenable.* When there is a conflict between the value of the sample mean and the hypothesized population mean, we will go along with the sample mean.

Note 7-2
How Large a Difference Is Still Due to Chance?

An example may be helpful in illustrating the dilemma posed in statements 3a and 3b on p. 162, where we were faced with the problem of determining if the discrepancy between our sample mean of 69.2 and a hypothesized population mean of 68.6 was due to sampling error.

Let us imagine that you have a friend who claims to have extrasensory perception (ESP). To test this ability you take two slips of paper and write an A on one and a B on the second. You hand him the two slips of paper, *face down*, and ask him to put them in the proper order (i.e., A first, then B) without looking at the writing. Let us say that he performs this task successfully. Does this demonstrate ESP ability?

Before you decide, let us take a careful look at his task. We know that there are only two possible ways that he can respond—he can put them down on the table as A, then B, or he can lay them down as B, then A. Whether he has ESP or not, only one of the two orders is correct, and we say that he would be right 50% of the time *just by chance*. The probability that he would be correct just by chance would, of course, be $p = .50$. If he were correct on this simple task, we would be unimpressed, since anyone, ESP or no, would be right 50% of the time.

But let us make the task a little more difficult. Suppose we had decided to use three slips of paper, lettered A, B, and C, and required him to put them in order in the same manner. There are now six possible ways in which he could place them on the table—ABC, ACB, BAC, BCA, CAB, and CBA. Since only one of these orders is correct, we know that the probability of his being correct, *just by chance*, is 1/6, or $p = .17$. If he were correct, we would probably still be unimpressed, since anyone would be right 17% of the time just by chance.

We could make the task still more difficult by requiring him to order correctly four, five, six, or more slips of paper. The probabilities are given below.

Number of Slips	Possible Orders	Probability of Correct Order
2 AB	2	$p = 1/2 = .50$
3 ABC	6	$p = 1/6 = .17$
4 ABCD	24	$p = 1/24 = .042$
5 ABCDE	120	$p = 1/120 = .008$
6 ABCDEF	720	$p = 1/720 = .001$

The point of this whole discussion is this: there is *no time* that you can say that your friend's performance is not due to chance and is definitely due to ESP. If he picks up four slips of paper and places them in the correct order, we begin to suspect him of possessing some kind of strange power, but we definitely cannot say that it is not chance, since it is still possible (4 chances out of 100) that the result is simply due to chance. If the test is set up with five slips, the probability due to chance of his ordering them correctly is pretty slim (8 chances out of 1,000), but it is still possibly a chance effect. The same reasoning applies to the test with six slips, but note that the correct order would happen just by chance only 1 time out of 1,000 ($p = .001$).

So, you ask, when is the result definitely, positively, irrevocably due to ESP (or whatever is responsible for your friend's strange ability) and *not* due to chance? You *never* know for certain; you just have varying degrees of certainty that the result could have happened by chance alone. If the probability of a result happening by chance is .042, we are more certain that this result could have happened by chance than a result whose probability due to chance was .008. Clearly, what we need are some guidelines to help us make our decision as to whether chance is responsible for our results.

Significance Levels

It should be obvious by now that the crux of the whole problem is where to draw the line. At what point do you say that your result is such a rare occurrence that it is highly unlikely to be sampling error? When do you start rejecting the notion that the discrepancy is due to sampling error? Fortunately, statisticians have rallied to our cause and have proposed the concept of *significance levels*. Simply stated, a significance level is the probability that a result is due to sampling error, *and, if this probability is small enough, we reject the notion that sampling error is the cause.* We then conclude that there is a real difference between our result and what would logically be expected by chance. Traditionally, these significance levels have been set at .05 and .01.

.05 significance level. If the probability that our result happened by chance is .05 or less, we say that our results are significant at the .05 level. If the discrepancy between our result and what would be expected by chance alone would happen 5% of the time or less, we reject the notion that it is sampling error.

.01 significance level. If the probability that our result happened by chance is .01 or less, we say that our results are significant at the .01 level. If the discrepancy between our result and what would be expected

by chance alone would happen 1% of the time or less, we reject the notion that it is sampling error.

Statisticians will be the first to admit that these levels are set in an arbitrary manner, but at least they represent some guidelines to use in making a decision. Let us apply these guidelines to our earlier problem—that of determining how good our sample mean is as an estimate of the population mean, μ.

The Confidence Interval Approach to Estimating μ

In an earlier example we tested various hypothesized values of the population mean and observed the hypothetical sampling distributions for possible population means of 69, 68.8, and 68.6 inches. We noted that as the hypothesized values deviated more and more from our sample mean of 69.2, the probability that we would obtain a sample mean that deviated by as much as or more than ours grew smaller and smaller.

So why not hypothesize a population mean that is the *same* value as our sample mean? With our sample mean of 69.2 and a population mean of 69.2, we would not have to worry at all about sampling error. Whenever we wished to estimate μ from a sample $\overline{X}$, all we would have to do is say that the most likely value of the population mean is the value of our sample mean.

However practical this approach may sound, there is an error in this type of reasoning. The population mean is a *fixed* value, *and it is the sample means that deviate about this fixed value.* As you saw in Figure 7-2, for any given value of μ, the sample means were normally distributed about this point. So instead of talking about possible values that μ may take, given our sample $\overline{X}$, we are better off in setting up a *confidence interval* in which the true mean probably lies.

As an example let us use the information presented in Figure 7-2C, where we hypothesized a population mean of 68.6 and noted that 95.44% of all sample means fell between this mean $\pm 2s_{\overline{X}}$, or between 68.0 and 69.2. You will remember from the last chapter that in a normal curve the interval $\overline{X} \pm 1.96S$ contained 95% of the cases and $\overline{X} \pm 2.58S$ contained 99% of the cases. So, in a similar manner, we could calculate the interval about the hypothetical sampling distribution with its mean of 68.6. This interval would be $\overline{X}_{\overline{X}} \pm 1.96s_{\overline{X}}$, or $68.6 \pm 1.96(0.3) = 68.6 \pm .59$, or 68.01 to 69.19. So we would say that 95% of the sample means would fall between 68.01 and 69.19 if the population mean were 68.6. Similarly, with the interval of $\overline{X}_{\overline{X}} \pm 2.58s_{\overline{X}}$, we would have $68.6 \pm 2.58(0.3)$, or 67.83 to 69.37. In this case we can say that 99% of the sample means would fall between 67.83 and 69.37.

However, when we use the confidence interval approach, we set up an interval with the *sample mean as the center*. The proof for this bit of algebraic maneuvering is shown in **Note 7-3** for the benefit of the curious. Whether you understand the proof or not, we now have a technique which allows us to feel reasonably certain that the population mean is included in an interval, without having to start out by hypothesizing a specific value for μ.

95% confidence interval. To determine the 95% confidence interval, we simply calculate the interval

$$\bar{X} \pm 1.96s_{\bar{X}} \tag{7-4}$$

where $\bar{X}$ is the *sample mean* and $s_{\bar{X}}$ is the standard error of the mean. So, for our sample mean of 69.2 and standard error of 0.3, we would have

$$\begin{aligned}
\bar{X} \pm 1.96s_{\bar{X}} &= 69.2 \pm 1.96\,(0.3)\\
&= 69.2 \pm .59\\
&= 68.61 \text{ to } 69.79
\end{aligned}$$

Since the probability is .95 that the population mean is included in all intervals similarly constructed from all possible sample means, we are reasonably certain that the population mean is between 68.61 and 69.79.[3]

99% confidence interval. To determine the 99% confidence interval, we calculate the interval given by

$$\bar{X} \pm 2.58s_{\bar{X}} \tag{7-5}$$

which gives

$$\begin{aligned}
\bar{X} \pm 2.58s_{\bar{X}} &= 69.2 \pm 2.58\,(0.3)\\
&= 69.2 \pm .77\\
&= 68.43 \text{ to } 69.97
\end{aligned}$$

Since the probability is .99 that the population mean is included in all intervals similarly constructed from all possible sample means, we are even more certain (than with the 95% interval) that the population mean is between 68.43 and 69.97. Or, stated in still another way, if we continued to take more and more samples of the same size, we would find that 99 out of 100 times the population mean would be included in the interval.

[3] We might be tempted to say that the probability is .95 that μ is between 68.61 and 69.79. However, mathematicians remind us that meaningful probability statements are made only about variables (such as $\bar{X}$) and not fixed values (such as μ).

Comparing the two confidence intervals. In practice, which of the two intervals do you use? Note that the 99% confidence interval is *wider* (68.43 to 69.97) than the 95% confidence interval (68.61 to 69.79). This is to be expected, since in order to be more certain you must have a slightly wider interval. We have sacrificed some precision in order to be more certain, so, as a colleague of mine has stated, "You are more and more certain of less and less."

Note 7-3
Proving That the Confidence Interval
Is around the Sample Mean, $\bar{X}$

Remembering that in a sampling distribution 95% of the sample means (in terms of z scores) fall inside the interval,

$$-1.96 \leq z \leq 1.96$$

But $z = \dfrac{\bar{X} - \bar{X}_{\bar{X}}}{s_{\bar{X}}}$, so we can write

$$-1.96 \leq \frac{\bar{X} - \bar{X}_{\bar{X}}}{s_{\bar{X}}} \leq 1.96$$

Considering first the left side of the inequality, and multiplying by $s_{\bar{X}}$:

$$-1.96 s_{\bar{X}} \leq \bar{X} - \bar{X}_{\bar{X}}$$

We add $\bar{X}_{\bar{X}}$ to both sides of the inequality to obtain

$$\bar{X}_{\bar{X}} - 1.96 s_{\bar{X}} \leq \bar{X}$$

and add $1.96 s_{\bar{X}}$ to both sides to get

$$\bar{X}_{\bar{X}} \leq \bar{X} + 1.96 s_{\bar{X}}$$

We now go through the same procedure with the right side of the original inequality, multiplying first by $s_{\bar{X}}$ and then by adding $\bar{X}_{\bar{X}}$ to both sides to obtain

$$\bar{X} \leq 1.96 s_{\bar{X}} + \bar{X}_{\bar{X}}$$

And subtracting $1.96 s_{\bar{X}}$ from both sides we get

$$\bar{X} - 1.96 s_{\bar{X}} \leq \bar{X}_{\bar{X}}$$

We now put together both sides to obtain

$$\bar{X} - 1.96 s_{\bar{X}} \leq \bar{X}_{\bar{X}} \leq \bar{X} + 1.96 s_{\bar{X}}$$

Thus, we can see that the interval $\bar{X} \pm 1.96 s_{\bar{X}}$ will contain (in the long run) $\bar{X}_{\bar{X}}$ or μ (remember that $\bar{X}_{\bar{X}} = \mu$) 95% of the time.

Let us use the confidence interval approach in several examples and see how it helps us in estimating the population mean, μ. Suppose that we administer a college entrance exam to a random sample of 200 high school seniors ($N = 200$), with the following results: $\bar{X} = 102, S = 12$.

The 95% confidence interval, $\bar{X} \pm 1.96s_{\bar{X}}$, requires us to calculate first the standard error of the mean, $s_{\bar{X}}$, as follows:

$$s_{\bar{X}} = \frac{S}{\sqrt{N-1}} = \frac{12}{\sqrt{200-1}} = \frac{12}{\sqrt{199}} = \frac{12}{14.11} = 0.85$$

Substituting into the interval formula yields

$$\bar{X} \pm 1.96s_{\bar{X}} = 102 \pm 1.96(0.85)$$
$$= 102 \pm 1.67$$
$$= 100.33 \text{ to } 103.67$$

and we can be reasonably certain that the population mean is in that interval.

To calculate the 99% confidence interval, we substitute to obtain

$$\bar{X} \pm 2.58(0.85) = 102 \pm 2.19$$
$$= 99.81 \text{ to } 104.19$$

and we are even more certain that this interval contains the population mean.

As a second example, let us say that a friend of yours feels that college women are much taller today than 10 years ago and claims that the average coed's height is 5′6″. To check out the claim you take a random sample of 50 college women ($N = 50$), with the results $\bar{X} = 65$ inches, $S = 2.5$ inches. Is your friend's claim correct? With what degree of confidence?

Calculating the standard error of the mean and both the 95% and 99% confidence intervals would give

$$s_{\bar{X}} = \frac{S}{\sqrt{N-1}} = \frac{2.5}{\sqrt{49}} = \frac{2.5}{7} = 0.36$$

95% Confidence Interval: $\bar{X} \pm 1.96s_{\bar{X}} = 65 \pm 1.96(0.36)$
$$= 64.29 \text{ to } 65.71$$

99% Confidence Interval: $\bar{X} \pm 2.58s_{\bar{X}} = 65 \pm 2.58(0.36)$
$$= 64.07 \text{ to } 65.93$$

In this example we can be very confident that μ is included in the interval 64.07 to 65.93. We would have to deny our friend's claim that the average coed is 66 inches tall, since we are reasonably certain that the population mean is in the 64.07 to 65.93 range and 66 is outside that interval.

Confidence Intervals and Significance Levels

A few paragraphs ago we had occasion to consider the concept of levels of significance, and we noted that this concept referred to the probability of a result being caused by sampling error. Let us consider this last example of women's heights to show how confidence intervals, significance levels, and sampling error are related.

We note that your friend's claim that the average coed's height is 66 inches is really a hypothesized value for the mean of the population of college women. However, our random sample of 50 women yields a mean of 65. Our question is "If the population mean is in fact 66, could we through sampling error come up with a sample mean of 65?" Using the 99% confidence interval we found that we are reasonably certain that the population mean is included in the 64.07 to 65.93 interval, *which does not include 66.*

So we are again faced with the dilemma of determining whether the discrepancy between the hypothesized population mean of 66 and our sample mean of 65 is one of sampling error or whether the hypothesized population mean is incorrect. If we use the 95% confidence interval, the probability that all possible intervals include the population mean is .95. But this also means that the probability is .05 that they do *not* include the population mean. Similarly, with the 99% confidence interval, the probability is .01 that these intervals do not include the population mean.

Since the discrepancy between a possible $\mu = 66$ and our sample $\overline{X} = 65$ is such a rare occurrence (happening less than 1% of the time just by sampling error), we conclude that the discrepancy is *not* sampling error but that the hypothesized μ is incorrect. But there is a slight chance (probability less than .01) that we are wrong and that the discrepancy *is* due to sampling error.

We can summarize by making two general statements. With the 95% confidence interval, in the long run we stand to be in error 5% of the time; that is, 5% of the time our intervals will *not* contain the population mean. If we use the 99% confidence interval, we could be wrong 1% of the time; that is, 1% of the time our intervals would *not* contain the population mean.

These points can best be illustrated in the graph shown in Figure 7-3, where a number of random samples have been taken from a population and a confidence interval has been constructed about the mean

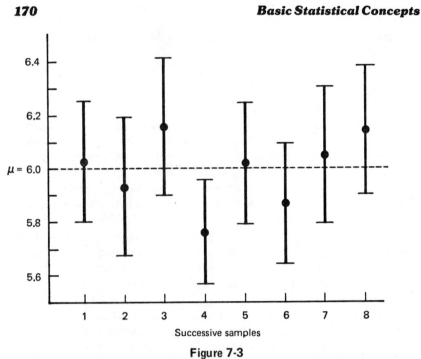

Figure 7-3
Interval estimates of a population mean of 6.0 from successive samples.

of each sample. The dot in the center of each interval represents the mean, and the bars are the lower and upper limits of the interval. Notice that most of the intervals include the population mean of 6.0. However, sample 4 has a confidence interval that does *not* include a μ of 6.0. If we use the 95% confidence interval, we expect that 5% of the samples will *not* include μ and, like sample 4, will miss μ on either the high end or low end. If we use the 99% confidence interval, we expect that 1% of the samples will not include μ.

Standard Error and Size of Sample

In previous sections we have looked at how we go about the business of estimating an unknown population mean on the basis of the data from a single sample. You have seen that we do not attempt to specify a *single* value for μ but rather an *interval* in which μ is most likely included. It should be obvious that we would like to have the confidence interval as *narrow* as possible, since we then have a better idea of what the population mean "really" is. Knowing that the I.Q. of the average college sophomore is between 110 and 130 is not very helpful; an interval of 118 to 123 would give us a much clearer picture of what is going on.

What factors are responsible for reducing the width of the interval (without causing a less stringent probability level, such as .90 or .80) so we can more accurately pinpoint the population mean? In examining the formula for the standard error of the mean:

$$s_{\bar{x}} = \frac{S}{\sqrt{N-1}}$$

you note that S and N are the two variables affecting $s_{\bar{x}}$ and consequently the confidence interval itself. We could reduce the size of $s_{\bar{x}}$ either by *decreasing* the standard deviation of the sample or by *increasing* the size of the sample. Since we usually do not have any control over the amount of variability in a given sample, we must concentrate our efforts on increasing the sample N. Table 7-2 shows how the confidence interval is reduced as you go from a sample size of 10 to 20 to 50. It follows that we would like to have our sample size as large as possible.

Table 7-2
Decreasing the 95% Confidence Interval by Increasing Sample Size

Sample

$\bar{X} = 60$ $S = 5$

If $N = 10$: $s_{\bar{x}} = \dfrac{S}{\sqrt{N-1}} = \dfrac{5}{\sqrt{9}} = \dfrac{5}{3} = 1.67$

$\bar{X} \pm 1.96s_{\bar{x}} = 60 \pm 3.27 = 56.73$ to 63.27

If $N = 20$: $s_{\bar{x}} = \dfrac{S}{\sqrt{N-1}} = \dfrac{5}{\sqrt{19}} = \dfrac{5}{4.36} = 1.15$

$\bar{X} \pm 1.96s_{\bar{x}} = 60 \pm 2.25 = 57.75$ to 62.25

If $N = 50$: $s_{\bar{x}} = \dfrac{S}{\sqrt{N-1}} = \dfrac{5}{\sqrt{49}} = \dfrac{5}{7} = 0.71$

$\bar{X} \pm 1.96s_{\bar{x}} = 60 \pm 1.39 = 58.61$ to 61.39

Other Sampling Distributions

The bulk of this chapter has been spent on the sampling distribution of means, the standard error of the mean, and estimated confidence intervals for the population mean. We could go into depth for other statistics, such as the median, standard deviation, and proportion. However, in an introductory text it is just not possible to cover all these topics, and you are referred to any advanced statistics text for a treatment of these sampling distributions. But the method of approach is similar for each statistic. Each has its own sampling distribution with its standard deviation being, for example, the standard error of the median or standard error of the proportion.

In light of an earlier discussion we might briefly examine the formula for the standard error of the median, which is

$$s_{Med} = \frac{1.253S}{\sqrt{N-1}}$$

Note that the standard error of the median is approximately 1.25 times as large as the standard error of the mean. You will recall that in an earlier discussion we noted that the mean was a more *stable* measure of central tendency than was the median. This should now be obvious, since the confidence interval using the standard error of the mean about the population *mean* is narrower than the confidence interval using the larger standard error of the median about the population *median*. This is just another way of saying that *means* of repeated samples will vary less than will the *medians* of repeated samples.

Estimating the Population Variance

Back in Chapter 5 the concept of *variance* was introduced, and we saw that the variance of a distribution was simply the square of the standard deviation. In other words, variance is another method of showing the variability of a set of scores around the mean of the distribution.

However, it is much more than just another method of measuring variability, and we will have occasion to use this important concept in a number of applications in the remaining chapters of this text. For this reason let us carefully consider the development of the concept in the following sections, first demonstrating a *biased* estimate of the population variance for the data of Table 7-3 and then an *unbiased* estimate.

Biased Estimate of Population Variance

In examining the scores of Table 7-3 we note that the procedure for calculating the variance, S^2, is identical to the technique we used in computing the standard deviation using the deviation formula in Chapter 5 except that we do not take the square root of $\Sigma x^2/N$. To calculate the variance you subtract the mean from each score, square each deviation, add the squared deviations to obtain Σx^2, and finally divide by N. In other words, the variance is simply the average of the squared deviations from the mean. In Table 7-3, the value $S^2 = 12.8$ represents how much, on the average, each score deviated from the mean in squared units. As it stands, the S^2 in Table 7-3 is a *descriptive statistic*, describing the variability of that distribution of scores.

Let us suppose, however, that the 10 scores are a random sample from some population and we are interested in estimating the population variance from this sample. If we do this, we must note that the variance, S^2, is a *biased* estimate of the population variance, σ^2. We noted

Table 7-3
Biased and Unbiased Estimates of the Population Variance

X	x	x^2
14	5	25
13	4	16
11	2	4
11	2	4
10	1	1
9	0	—
8	-1	1
7	-2	4
6	-3	9
1	-8	64
$\Sigma X = 90$	0	$\Sigma x^2 = 128$
$\bar{X} = 9$		

Biased Estimate:

$$S^2 = \frac{\Sigma x^2}{N} = \frac{128}{10} = 12.8$$

Unbiased Estimate:

$$s^2 = \frac{\Sigma x^2}{N-1} = \frac{128}{10-1} = 14.22$$

in an earlier section that the sample mean, $\overline{X}$, is an *unbiased* estimate of the population mean, μ, because as more and more samples are drawn from the population the mean of the sample means tends to approach the value of the population mean. Such is not the case with the biased variance estimate, S^2, since this variance (shown in Table 7-3) *tends to underestimate the population variance. S^2 is, on the average, too small* and obviously would give a misleading picture of the population distribution. (Note also that the *standard deviation* of a sample, S, is also a biased estimate of the population *standard deviation, σ*.)

But why are S and S^2 of a sample consistently smaller than their population counterparts, σ and σ^2? The answer lies in the probability of obtaining extreme cases in a small sample. Let us use a rather homely example to illustrate how this might happen. If you took a small random sample of the heights of males on a college campus, you would not be likely to find the 7'2" basketball star or the 4'6" midget wrestler in your sample. But it is precisely these extreme observations that contribute a large squared deviation to the variance of the population. And since these rare cases are not likely to show up in a small sample, the amount of variability in the sample is going to be less than the variability in the population.

Unbiased Estimate of Population Variance

The calculation of an *unbiased* estimate of the population variance involves only a minor change in the formula. For the unbiased estimate, Σx^2 is divided by $N - 1$ instead of by N. The term $N - 1$ is called the *degrees of freedom*, a rather strange term that we will define later, in Chapter 10. For now, however, we say that an unbiased estimate of the population variance can be made from the sample through division of Σx^2 by its degrees of freedom. Note that the symbol s^2 (lowercase s) is used instead of S^2 as the symbol indicating an *unbiased* estimate.

Again, if the 10 scores in Table 7-3 are a random sample from some population, the *unbiased* estimate of the population variance is calculated as $s^2 = 14.22$. Note that the effect of dividing Σx^2 by $N - 1$ is to increase the size of the variance and to bring it in line with the actual population variance, σ^2. However, if we take the square root of s^2, we get $s = \sqrt{\Sigma x^2/(N - 1)}$, which is *still* a biased estimate of the population standard deviation, σ. We might note that $s = \sqrt{\Sigma x^2/(N - 1)}$ is slightly *less biased* than $S = \sqrt{\Sigma x^2/N}$, but it is still a biased estimate.

In summary, then, we would say that

$$S = \sqrt{\frac{\Sigma x^2}{N}}$$ (5-2)

is a biased estimate of the population standard deviation, σ,

$$S^2 = \frac{\Sigma x^2}{N}$$ (7-6)

is a biased estimate of the population variance, σ^2,

$$s^2 = \frac{\Sigma x^2}{N-1}$$ (7-7)

is an unbiased estimate of the population variance, σ^2.

Random vs. Representative Samples

Let us close out this chapter by recalling an earlier discussion of the topic of a representative sample. We noted that a representative sample was a "miniature" population that contained all the relevant characteristics of the population. Now that we have covered a number of topics on random sampling, we should remember that a random sample may or may not be a representative one; that is, a random sample may not necessarily be an accurate representation of the population. Using again the example of a "population" of colored marbles, let us say that a bag contained 50 blue, 30 red, and 20 yellow marbles. A sample of 10 that contained 5 blue, 3 red, and 2 yellow would certainly be a representative sample. On the other hand, it would be entirely possible for a *random* sample to contain 10 blue marbles (remember sampling error?) and obviously not be representative of the population at all.

So why don't we *always* use stratified or cluster sampling, where we are likely to obtain representative samples, and dispense with random sampling altogether? The reason is that we know the shape of the sampling distribution for random samples and can estimate its standard deviation in order to set up confidence intervals, but we do not always know the nature of the distribution for other kinds of samples. As a result we may freely use representative samples for opinion polls, consumer surveys, and the like, but when we need to set up confidence intervals for estimating population means, we resort to the old reliable random sample.

Sample Problem #1

A random sample of 145 freshmen at State University, taken by the University Bookstore, showed that the average amount paid for textbooks during a certain semester was $72.74, with a standard deviation of $12.60. Calculate the 95% confidence interval for the true mean.

The first step is to calculate the standard error of the mean, $s_{\bar{X}}$:

$$s_{\bar{X}} = \frac{S}{\sqrt{N-1}} = \frac{12.60}{\sqrt{145-1}} = \frac{12.60}{\sqrt{144}} = \frac{12.60}{12}$$

$$s_{\bar{X}} = 1.05$$

The 95% confidence interval, $\bar{X} \pm 1.96 s_{\bar{X}}$, would give

$$72.74 \pm 1.96(1.05)$$
$$72.74 \pm 2.06$$
$$\$70.68 \text{ to } \$74.80$$

So we would be reasonably certain that the average amount paid by a freshman at State University for textbooks during this semester was between $70.68 and $74.80.

Sample Problem #2

A school psychologist takes a random sample of 50 sixth-graders from all the elementary schools in a school system. He administers a standardized intelligence test with the results shown below. Given the sample, is it possible that the true mean I.Q. of the population is actually 100? (Use the 99% confidence interval.)

$$N = 50$$
$$\bar{X} = 107$$
$$S = 14$$

The standard error of the mean, $s_{\bar{X}}$, would be calculated as

$$s_{\bar{X}} = \frac{S}{\sqrt{N-1}} = \frac{14}{\sqrt{50-1}} = \frac{14}{\sqrt{49}} = \frac{14}{7}$$

$$s_{\bar{X}} = 2$$

The 99% confidence interval is given by $\bar{X} \pm 2.58 s_{\bar{X}}$, or

$$107 \pm 2.58(2)$$
$$107 \pm 5.16$$
$$101.84 \text{ to } 112.16$$

We would be reasonably certain that the true mean I.Q. is between 101.84 and 112.16. Since the hypothesized mean of 100 is not
in this interval, we would have to reject the notion that the true value
is 100. But considering the meaning of significance levels there is a
slight chance that the true mean is *not* in the 101.84 to 112.16
interval.

Study Questions

1. What is the difference between a *sample* and a *population*?

2. Nine hundred freshmen are enrolled at a small private college.
   Describe the procedure you would use in obtaining a random
   sample of 50 using Table L in Appendix 2.

3. What is the difference between stratified random sampling and
   cluster sampling?

4. Differentiate among the terms *sample*, *sampling distribution*, and
   population.

5. State the central limit theorem as it applies to a sampling distribution of means.

6. What is meant by *sampling error* or *chance*?

7. Why is formula 7-2 preferred to formula 7-1 for calculating the
   standard error of the mean?

8. Why is it necessary to set arbitrary significance levels (e.g., .05 or
   .01) to resolve the sampling error-real difference dilemma?

9. What happened to the size of the confidence interval in Table 7-2
   as you increased the sample size from 10 to 50? Why do we want
   this interval as narrow as possible?

10. S^2 is a *biased* estimate of the population variance. What does this
    mean? How would you calculate an *unbiased* estimate?

Exercises

1. What is the probability that a sample mean will deviate by $\pm 1.96 s_{\bar{X}}$ or more from the population mean?

2. In a sampling distribution of means, $\bar{X}_{\bar{X}} = 80$ and $s_{\bar{X}} = 2.5$. What percentage of the sample means will deviate from $\bar{X}_{\bar{X}}$ by 5 or more?

3. A random sample of 145 grade-point averages is taken from second-semester freshmen at a large university. The sample mean is 2.92 with a standard deviation of 0.60. Calculate the 95% confidence interval for the true mean.

4. The personnel manager of a large bank administers a clerical aptitude test to 50 job applicants, with a mean of 71 and a standard deviation of 14. A friend who helped develop the test tells the personnel manager that the population mean would be 75. In light of these results, could the population mean be 75? (Use the 95% confidence interval.)

5. A national survey of 10,000 college freshman males showed a mean height of 70 inches with a standard deviation of 2.1 inches. Establish the 95% confidence interval for the true mean.

6. Calculate an *unbiased* estimate of the population variance using the scores from Table 5-3. How does this value compare with the biased estimate?

8 Correlation

If we looked back over the contents of several earlier chapters we would recall that all discussions to date have concerned a *single* distribution. Frequency distributions, measures of central tendency, measures of variability—all have given us information about a single distribution of scores. At this point it is necessary to shift our emphasis to cases involving *two* distributions, and in this chapter and the next we will be concerned with measuring the amount of *relationship* between *two* distributions of scores.

While the phrase "relationship between two distributions" may sound unfamiliar to you, the concept of relationships between variables is an integral part of our everyday language. We commonly hear relational statements such as "He'll make a good salesman because of his gift of gab," or "She will be an excellent pianist; look at her slender, delicate fingers," or even "Of course he's got a temper — all redheads are that way." In these statements, relationships are implied between sales ability and verbal skills, manual dexterity and hand shape, and temper and hair color.

The above examples probably belong more properly in the category of folklore than statistics, but let us consider some other common examples of relationships between variables. Haven't we all, at some time or another, heard questions such as "What is the relationship between high school grades and college success?" or "What is the relationship between your I.Q. and your ability to remember?" or "What is the relationship between college entrance exam scores and college performance?"

Questions such as these about relationships can be answered by a statistical technique called *correlation*. If there is a relationship between two variables, such as high school grades and college success, we say that they are *correlated*. The statistical techniques to be developed in Chapters 8 and 9 will demonstrate two major functions of correlation. First, we would like to develop techniques that indicate the *strength* or *amount* of the relationship, so that a single value will tell us at a glance how two variables are related. Second, we would like to be able to *predict* scores on one variable from knowledge of another variable. For example, if there is a relationship between high school grades and college success, we would like to be able to actually predict an individual's college grades on the basis of his high school grades.

Before beginning such an ambitious undertaking, let us first consider the meaning of correlation by looking at two approaches to this new concept. The first is an intuitive approach, and the second is a graphical method, called a *scattergram*.

An Intuitive Approach

Let us use a rather homely example of correlation and assume that we would like to see if there is a relationship between athletic ability and scholastic ability. Are good athletes also good students? Or are the best athletes poor students, while the poorer athletes are good students? To test our hypotheses we choose five college football players and have the coaches rank them on their football ability. (Obviously, we would want more than five subjects in an actual experiment, but such a small number will make our illustration easier.) After the coaches have ranked the five on football ability, we consult the Registrar's Office and obtain the players' grade-point averages (GPA's), which are a measure of their academic success. We then rank the five on their scholastic ability and get the results shown in Table 8-1.

Note that Al was the best football player and also the best student

Table 8-1
Ranks on Football Ability and GPA: Positive Correlation

Player	Football Ability	GPA
Al	1	1
Bob	2	2
Carl	3	3
Don	4	4
Ed	5	5

of this small sample. Bob was second best at both, and so on down to poor Ed, who brings up the rear as the poorest football player and the poorest student. This is an illustration of *perfect positive correlation.* It is *perfect* because there are no reversals or changes from the 1-1, 2-2, 3-3, 4-4, 5-5 pairs of ranks, and it is *positive* because both variables *increase together.* If you are high on one variable, you are high on the other, and, if you are low on one, you are low on the other. *Perfect positive correlation is denoted by a coefficient of +1.00.* (We will come back to the meaning of a coefficient later, but for now regard it as a descriptive number.)

But let us suppose that our little experiment had turned out just the opposite way and the rankings on football ability and GPA resulted in the data shown in Table 8-2.

As you can see, there is a definite relationship here, but in just the opposite direction. Al, who is the *best* in football, has the *worst* GPA, the second *best* football player has the second *worst* GPA, and so on down to Ed, who is the worst football player but has the highest GPA. This is an illustration of *perfect negative correlation.* It is *perfect* because

Table 8-2
Ranks on Football Ability and GPA: Negative Correlation

Player	Football Ability	GPA
Al	1	5
Bob	2	4
Carl	3	3
Don	4	2
Ed	5	1

there are no changes or reversals from the best-worst, second best-second worst, third best-third worst, etc., pairs of ranks, and it is *negative* because as one variable *increases* the other *decreases*. The better one is at football, the poorer he is at getting grades. *Perfect negative correlation is denoted by a coefficient of* -1.00.

And, of course, there is the possibility that we would find no relationship at all between football ability and GPA. Al might be the best at football and the third best student, while Carl might be the third best at football and the second best student. In other words, there might be no pattern of relationship shown in the data. Thus there would be no correlation, and the coefficient would be simply 0, indicating no relationship.

The first two examples illustrate the extreme cases, where the correlation was either perfect positive or perfect negative, that is, 1.00 or -1.00. In practice we find that correlation coefficients may take any value between -1.00 and 1.00, such as $-.80$, .43, or .70. These three hypothetical examples are shown on a continuum in Figure 8-1 and might illustrate the correlation between juvenile delinquency and socioeconomic level $(-.80)$, manual dexterity and assembly line production (.43), and height and weight (.70).

Let us ponder further the correlation between height and weight. What does a correlation coefficient of .70 tell us about the data? Any coefficient less than perfect means that there have been some reversals or changes in the relative ranking. In Table 8-1, for example, suppose that Carl had a GPA ranking of 4 while Don's GPA ranking was 3. This reversal would result in a coefficient that was less than 1.00, but it would still be quite high and would still be positive, maybe around .90. We would still say that the relationship between football ability and GPA was "high" and "positive." We would say that the better

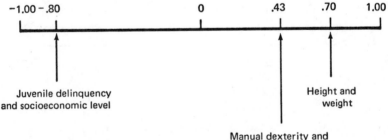

Figure 8-1
Some possible correlation coefficients on a continuum from -1.00 to 1.00.

players "tended to be" the better students while the poorer players "in general" were poorer students.

As there get to be more and more reversals in the relative ranks, we find that the correlation gets lower and lower. In our height-weight example with a coefficient of .70, we would note that, in general, taller people are heavier and shorter people are lighter—but there are an ample number of reversals, with some tall, skinny, light people and some short, stocky, heavy people.

There are two important characteristics of a correlation coefficient to keep in mind when evaluating a relationship—first its *sign* and then its *size*. If the sign is positive, we know that as one variable increases so does the other. So, if the relationship between height and weight or between manual dexterity and assembly line performance is positive, we know that tall people tend to be heavier than short people, or that factory workers with high dexterity scores will produce more units than their lower-scoring fellow workers. If, on the other hand, the sign is negative, we know that as one variable increases, the other decreases. Thus, if the correlation between coordination and age is negative for people over age 40, we know that as age increases, coordination decreases. And, in the example shown in Figure 8-1, the negative relationship between juvenile delinquency and socioeconomic level indicates that as socioeconomic level increases, the incidence of juvenile delinquency decreases.

The *size* of the coefficient, as we noted earlier, indicates the *amount* of relationship. In Tables 8-1 and 8-2, there were no reversals in relative ranking, and the resultant coefficients were a perfect 1.00. As there get to be more and more changes in the relative rankings, the coefficient becomes lower and lower until it finally reaches 0, indicating no relationship between the variables. The correlation of .70 between height and weight, as we saw earlier, indicated that "in general" tall people tended to be heavier and short people lighter, but there would be a number of exceptions. The correlation of .43 between manual dexterity and assembly line performance shows a considerably poorer relationship than that between height and weight. We would still say that there is a tendency for good manual dexterity to be matched with good assembly line production, but there are a lot of exceptions.

The Graphical Approach

There is always something appealing about an intuitive approach to an unfamiliar topic, but, unfortunately, we cannot stop with the preceding section but must push on to a graphical and a mathematical interpretation of correlation. The intuitive approach was presented to provide a frame of reference for discussing correlation in general terms, and many of the concepts to be discussed in future sections will be a little more familiar because of that earlier treatment.

The graphical approach to correlation uses a *scattergram*. A scattergram is simply a graph showing the plotted pairs of values of the two variables being measured. In keeping with mathematical convention, we designate the vertical axis (the ordinate) as Y and the horizontal axis (the abscissa) as X, and plot each X,Y pair for all the pairs in our data. As an illustration let us say we would like to see if there is a relationship between height and weight among college males. We select a random sample of 20 college men, measure their height and weight, and enter the paired scores (X = height, Y = weight) on a data sheet, as in Table 8-3.

These X,Y pairs are plotted in the method described in Chapter 2 for graphing a functional relationship. The resulting *scattergram* is shown in Figure 8-2. Examining this scattergram you would expect the correlation to be positive (since those with greater heights tend to weigh more) and quite high. However, the correlation certainly isn't perfect, since you can find a number of reversals. Student P, for example, is 3 inches taller than student I but weighs 6 pounds less. If you will find those two points on the scattergram (Student I is at [66,159] and Student P is at [69,153]), you will see that they contribute

Table 8-3
Heights and Weights of 20 College Men

Student	X Height (inches)	Y Weight (pounds)	Student	X Height (inches)	Y Weight (pounds)
A	70	177	K	64	147
B	69	174	L	70	162
C	72	190	M	70	177
D	70	174	N	65	147
E	72	177	O	72	180
F	67	162	P	69	153
G	71	186	Q	68	168
H	67	165	R	68	150
I	66	159	S	71	168
J	70	171	T	69	159

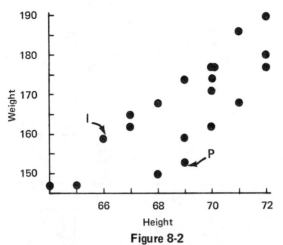

Figure 8-2
Scattergram of heights and weights.

to the "scattering" of the points away from a straight line. Anyway, there are not too many of these reversals in the height-weight data, and the actual correlation coefficient is .81, which is quite high.

Scattergrams and Size of Correlation

The height-weight data of Figure 8-2, with its correlation co-efficient of .81, illustrated a certain degree of "scattering" of the plotted points. Let us now take a look at a number of scattergrams with different patterns of plotted points and see how they are related to the size of the correlation coefficient. Four sets of data and their associated scatter-grams are shown in Figure 8-3.

Figure 8-3A. Note that with perfect positive correlation the plotted points lie on a *straight line* going from the lower left-hand corner to the upper right-hand corner. There are no reversals in X and Y; each increase in X is accompanied by a corresponding increase in Y.

Figure 8-3B. As the correlation coefficient decreases to .83, note that there is a scattering away from the straight line of graph A. The pattern of points is elliptical, but its major axis is still from lower left to upper right, indicating positive correlation. In general, low scores in X are paired with low scores in Y, and high values of X are paired with high values of Y. You can see that exceptions to this general statement contribute to the scattering away from the major axis of the ellipse.

Figure 8-3C. By the time the coefficient drops to near 0 (.09 in this example), the pattern of points is almost circular and it is difficult to tell whether the relationship is positive or negative. Note that some

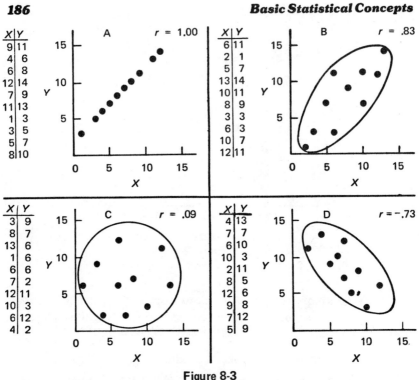

Figure 8-3
Scattergrams and size of correlation coefficients.

high values of X are accompanied by *high* values of Y while other high values of X are paired with *low* values of Y. The same can be said of lower values of X. There apparently is little or no relationship between X and Y, and this is reflected in the coefficient of nearly 0.

Figure 8-3D. When the relationship between X and Y is *negative,* you can see that the points lie in an ellipse whose major axis goes from the upper left-hand corner to the lower right-hand corner. This is, of course, due to the fact that *low* values of X are paired with *high* values of Y and *high* values of X with *low* values of Y. And since a correlation of −.73 is quite high, we do not expect much scattering away from a straight diagonal line but a rather tight ellipse, as shown.

Calculating the Pearson r (z Score Method)

We have finally reached the point where we are ready to actually calculate a correlation coefficient. There are a number of techniques used to calculate a measure of correlation, but one stands alone as far as popularity and universality go. This coefficient is called the Pearson r (after Karl Pearson [1857-1936], an English statistician), and it is derived from the z scores of the two distributions to be correlated. The Pearson r may be computed for interval or ratio data.

As an example, let us say that we would like to see if there is any relationship between proficiency in algebra and proficiency in geometry. An algebra and a geometry test are given to 10 high school sophomores, with the result shown in Table 8-4.

In Table 8-4 are 10 pairs of scores, each individual having a score on X (the algebra test) and a score on Y (the geometry test). In addition to these raw scores, a z score has been calculated for both X and Y for each individual, by the simple division of each score's deviation from its mean by the standard deviation for that distribution. For example, individual A has an X score of 14, which is 1 unit above the mean of 13. That x is then divided by the standard deviation of the X distribution, 2.5, for a resultant z score of 0.4. Similarly, A's z score on Y would be $z = (Y - \overline{Y})/S_Y = (24 - 21)/3 = 1.00$.

The next step in calculating the Pearson r is to obtain the *products*

Table 8-4
z Score Method for Calculating the Pearson r

Individual	Algebra			Geometry			
	X	x	z_X	Y	y	z_Y	$z_X z_Y$
A	14	1	0.4	24	3	1.00	0.400
B	16	3	1.2	23	2	0.67	0.804
C	17	4	1.6	25	4	1.33	2.128
D	13	—	—	21	—	—	—
E	13	—	—	20	-1	-0.33	—
F	14	1	0.4	23	2	0.67	0.268
G	14	1	0.4	23	2	0.67	0.268
H	10	-3	-1.2	18	-3	-1.00	1.200
I	9	-4	-1.6	17	-4	-1.33	2.128
J	10	-3	-1.2	16	-5	-1.67	2.004

$$\overline{X} = 13 \qquad \overline{Y} = 21 \qquad \Sigma z_X z_Y = 9.2$$

$$S_X = 2.5 \qquad S_Y = 3.0$$

$$r = \frac{\Sigma z_X z_Y}{N} = \frac{9.2}{10} = .92$$

of the pairs of z scores for each individual. Each individual's z score on X is multiplied by his or her z score on Y. For individual A, $z_X = 0.4$ and $z_Y = 1.00$, so A's $z_X z_Y$ product would be 0.4×1.00, or 0.400. Similarly, individual B would have a $z_X z_Y = 1.2 \times 0.67 = 0.804$. After $z_X z_Y$ products are obtained for all individuals, the $z_X z_Y$ column is summed and $\Sigma z_X z_Y$ is obtained.

The final step in the calculation of the Pearson r is simply to find the *mean* of these summed products of z_X and z_Y by dividing by N, the number of pairs.

$$r = \frac{\Sigma z_X z_Y}{N} \tag{8-1}$$

For the data of Table 8-4,

$$r = \frac{9.2}{10} = .92$$

With $r = .92$ we would conclude that there is a high positive correlation between X and Y in the data of Table 8-4. If a person has a high level of ability in algebra, he or she also excels at geometry.

Let us stop a moment and consider just what these $z_X z_Y$ products are telling us about the data and how they indicate the amount of relationship between two distributions. Consider three examples—high positive, low positive, and high negative correlations.

High positive values of r. If the correlation between two variables is high positive, we expect high scores in one variable to be matched with high scores in the other variable. In terms of z scores, if a person's z_X is high his or her z_Y should also be high. For example, in Table 8-4, individual C has a z_X of 1.6 and a z_Y of 1.33. This, of course, indicates that C is well above the mean in both the X and Y distributions. We also expect in a situation where r is high and positive that an individual who is low in X will also score low in Y. This point is illustrated in Table 8-4 by individual J, who had a z_X of -1.2 and a z_Y of -1.67, well below the mean in both distributions.

Note that in either example the $z_X z_Y$ products are both large and *positive*. If both of a pair of z scores are positive, the resultant $z_X z_Y$ product is, of course, positive. And, if both of a pair of z scores are negative, the resultant $z_X z_Y$ product is *still positive*. Thus, the sum of the products, $\Sigma z_X z_Y$, will be large and positive, yielding a high value of r.

Low positive values of r. In light of the preceding discussion, can you see what factors are responsible for decreasing the value of r? Just what happens as the scores become more and more scattered, as shown earlier, in Figure 8-3? Instead of a cozy arrangement of each positive z_X paired with a positive z_Y or a negative z_X paired with a negative z_Y, we now begin to see instances where some individuals scoring high on X score lower on Y. This means that some large positive z scores on X are paired with small positive z scores on Y, which, of course, eventually means a smaller $\Sigma z_X z_Y$ and a smaller r. And, as the strength of the relationship decreases still further, some individuals with a positive z_X may score *below* the mean on Y, which results in a negative z_Y. The resultant $z_X z_Y$ product for such individuals would be negative, and this would reduce the size of $\Sigma z_X z_Y$, and of r.

In the case where r is near 0, we would note that there would be about as many positive $z_X z_Y$ products as there were negative $z_X z_Y$ products, making $\Sigma z_X z_Y$ and r about 0.

High negative values of r. We noted in the introductory material to the topic of correlation that if there were a high negative correlation between two variables, high scores on X would be paired with low values on Y, and low values on X would be matched with high values on Y. In terms of z scores, note that this means that a large *positive* z score on X is paired with a large *negative* z score on Y, and a large *negative* z_X is paired with a large *positive* z_Y. As a result the $z_X z_Y$ product for most individuals will be negative. This, of course, means that the sum of the cross products, $\Sigma z_X z_Y$, will also be negative and will yield a negative r.

Calculating the Pearson r (Raw Score Methods)

The z score method, just described, for calculating r is extremely tedious and time-consuming, since computing a $z_X z_Y$ for each individual involves a number of different steps. Much more convenient techniques make use of *raw score methods*, where we deal with pairs of raw scores instead of the derived z scores. We have two formulas using raw scores — one which requires the means and standard deviations of the two distributions and one which requires only the sums of the various columns on a correlation worksheet.

Pearson r — Mean and S Formula

The formula for the Pearson r using the means and standard deviations of X and Y is

$$r = \frac{\dfrac{\Sigma XY}{N} - \overline{X}\,\overline{Y}}{S_X S_Y} \tag{8-2}$$

where N is the number of *pairs* of scores,
ΣXY is the sum of the products of each *pair* of scores,
$\overline{X}$ is the mean of the X distribution,

$\overline{Y}$ is the mean of the Y distribution,

S_X is the standard deviation of the X distribution,

S_Y is the standard deviation of the Y distribution.

All of the terms in the above formula are familiar except ΣXY, which is the sum of the products of each person's pair of scores. For example, in Table 8-5, the XY product for individual A is $14 \times 24 =$

Table 8-5
Calculating the Pearson r Using Means and Standard Deviations

Indi-vidual	Algebra X	Geometry Y	X^2	Y^2	XY
A	14	24	196	576	336
B	16	23	256	529	368
C	17	25	289	625	425
D	13	21	169	441	273
E	13	20	169	400	260
F	14	23	196	529	322
G	14	23	196	529	322
H	10	18	100	324	180
I	9	17	81	289	153
J	10	16	100	256	160

$\Sigma X = 130$ $\Sigma Y = 210$ $\Sigma X^2 = 1{,}752$ $\Sigma Y^2 = 4{,}498$ $\Sigma XY = 2{,}799$

Means:

$$\overline{X} = \frac{\Sigma X}{N} = \frac{130}{10} = 13 \qquad \overline{Y} = \frac{\Sigma Y}{N} = \frac{210}{10} = 21$$

Standard Deviations:

$$S_X = \sqrt{\frac{\Sigma X^2}{N} - \overline{X}^2} = \sqrt{\frac{1{,}752}{10} - 169} \qquad S_Y = \sqrt{\frac{\Sigma Y^2}{N} - \overline{Y}^2} = \sqrt{\frac{4{,}498}{10} - 441}$$

$$S_X = \sqrt{6.2} = 2.49 \qquad\qquad S_Y = \sqrt{8.8} = 2.97$$

Pearson r:

$$r = \frac{\frac{\Sigma XY}{N} - \overline{X}\overline{Y}}{S_X S_Y} = \frac{\frac{2{,}799}{10} - (13)(21)}{(2.49)(2.97)} = \frac{279.9 - 273}{7.40}$$

$$r = \frac{6.9}{7.40} = .93$$

336, for B it is $16 \times 23 = 368$, and so on. The sum of this column is $\Sigma XY = 2,799$. Let us repeat the data from Table 8-4 for the algebra and geometry scores and use formula 8-2 to calculate r.

Table 8-5 shows the calculated r to be .93, almost the same as the r calculated by the z score method shown in Table 8-4. The z score formula and formula 8-2 are algebraically identical, and the difference between .93 and .92 is due simply to rounding error.

Pearson r—Machine Formula

If the means and standard deviations of X and Y are not immediately available, the calculation of the Pearson r is simplified greatly with a pocket calculator and the following machine formula.

$$r = \frac{N\Sigma XY - \Sigma X \Sigma Y}{\sqrt{N\Sigma X^2 - (\Sigma X)^2} \quad \sqrt{N\Sigma Y^2 - (\Sigma Y)^2}} \tag{8-3}$$

where N is again the number of pairs and the rest of the terms are simply the sums of the X, X^2, Y, Y^2, and XY columns. Table 8-6 shows the calculation of the Pearson r for the algebra-geometry data using this machine formula. We again calculate $r = .93$, since the machine formula is algebraically equivalent to formula 8-2.

Table 8-6
Calculating the Pearson r Using the Machine Formula

Algebra	Geometry
$\Sigma X = 130$	$\Sigma Y = 210$
$\Sigma X^2 = 1,752$	$\Sigma Y^2 = 4,498$

$$\Sigma XY = 2,799$$

$$r = \frac{N\Sigma XY - \Sigma X \Sigma Y}{\sqrt{N\Sigma X^2 - (\Sigma X)^2} \quad \sqrt{N\Sigma Y^2 - (\Sigma Y)^2}}$$

$$= \frac{10(2,799) - (130)(210)}{\sqrt{10(1,752) - (130)^2} \quad \sqrt{10(4,498) - (210)^2}}$$

$$= \frac{27,990 - 27,300}{\sqrt{17,520 - 16,900} \quad \sqrt{44,980 - 44,100}}$$

$$= \frac{690}{\sqrt{620} \quad \sqrt{880}} = \frac{690}{(24.90)(29.66)}$$

$$r = \frac{690}{738.53} = .93$$

The raw score formulas are obviously preferred, since the z score method, as was mentioned earlier, requires a number of tedious steps with each score value. However, the z score formula was included to show just what the Pearson r is measuring, since with the raw score methods it is not possible to see what the individual pairs of scores are doing.

Testing r for Significance

Up to this point we have been treating r simply as a descriptive statistic, meaning that it describes the mathematical relationship between pairs of scores. This is useful, to be sure, and there are many times when we may wish to know the amount of relationship in a set of data without needing to make inferences concerning a population. However, if we wish to use correlational techniques to *predict* one variable from another, or to make inferences regarding the amount of relationship between two variables in the *population,* we find that correlation is indeed a very powerful tool in statistical analysis.

In order to be able to use correlation in this way, we must observe some rules of sampling, just as we did for the mean in the last chapter. These rules, or assumptions, are stated explicitly in Chapter 9, but for now we are concerned primarily with just one—that of a random sample from the population.

If we wanted to know, for example, the relationship between intelligence and school marks for children in the sixth grade, we would want to conduct our study with a *random* sample from a population of sixth-graders. We would then be able to generalize the results from our sample of 100 or 500 or 1,000 to the population of sixth-graders everywhere.

But we face a problem similar to that mentioned in the last chapter: does our calculated correlation coefficient represent the actual situation out there in the real world, *or is it due to sampling error?* Is it possible that in the population from which we drew our sample the true r is 0 and the r calculated from our sample is due simply to sampling error? We can answer this question, at least on a probability basis, by taking the next step in a correlational analysis—testing our obtained r for significance. Stated more formally, after we have calculated the r for our sample, we must determine if our r could have arisen by chance alone from a sampling distribution of r's whose mean is 0.

Chance correlation. The last statement above might be confusing at first, so let us use an example to help clarify some of the important concepts implicit in that statement. Imagine yourself in a room with 39 other people, taking part in a little demonstration. Forty slips of paper are numbered from 1 to 40, dropped in a hat, and mixed thoroughly. The hat is then passed around, and each of you draws a number without looking into the hat. After this is done, another 40 slips of paper, numbered from 1 to 40, are placed in the hat, and the procedure is repeated. Each of you now has two slips of paper, and we ask, "What is the relationship between the first number you drew and the second number?" Since both were random draws, you would undoubtedly say that there is no relationship at all. However, if we calculated r for the 40 pairs of numbers we would very likely not get an r that is exactly 0. It would probably be very close to 0, such as .07 or $-.02$, but it certainly does not surprise us that we do not calculate an r that is exactly equal to 0. This discrepancy, similar to that noted between a sample mean ($\overline{X}$) and the population mean (μ) in the last chapter, is due to sampling error.

Correlating numbers on slips of paper is, at best, a theoretical exercise, and we do not get very emotional about getting an r that is .07 or $-.02$ or .11 instead of exactly 0. What *does* concern us is the reverse situation, where we run a study, compute an r, and then wonder whether the "true" r in the population is really 0 and our r is due to sampling error.

Fortunately, we can use the confidence interval approach that was introduced in the last chapter to help us out of our dilemma. But, instead of taking an infinite number of sample *means* from some population and constructing a hypothetical sampling distribution of sample means, let us construct a sampling distribution of sample r's.

Sampling distribution of r. We first assume that the true r in the population from which we draw our samples is 0. If we then draw an infinite number of random samples from this population and calculate an r between the two variables we are interested in, we will have a *sampling distribution of* r. This sampling distribution of r's would be normal (if the size of each of our samples was greater than 30), its mean would be 0, and its standard deviation would be called the standard error of r, s_r.

As with the sampling distribution of means, we could then make such statements as:

1. 95% of all sample r's would fall between $0 \pm 1.96s_r$
2. 99% of all sample r's would fall between $0 \pm 2.58s_r$

The formula for the standard error of r, which is an estimate of the standard deviation of this sampling distribution of r's, is

$$s_r = \frac{1}{\sqrt{N-1}} \tag{8-4}$$

where N is the size of the sample.

For an example, let us say that we have tested a random sample of 50 high school juniors to find the correlation between their college entrance exam scores and their scores on a current events test and found $r = .45$. Calculating s_r, we find

$$s_r = \frac{1}{\sqrt{N-1}} = \frac{1}{\sqrt{50-1}} = \frac{1}{\sqrt{49}} = \frac{1}{7} = 0.143$$

We can now set up a confidence interval and say that if the population r is 0 we would expect 95% of the sample r's to fall between $0 \pm 1.96s_r$. The equation would be as follows:

$$0 \pm 1.96(0.143) = 0 \pm .28 = -.28 \text{ to } .28$$

Similarly, 99% of the sample r's would fall between $0 \pm 2.58s_r$:

$$0 \pm 2.58(0.143) = 0 \pm .37 = -.37 \text{ to } .37$$

Figure 8-4 shows this hypothetical sampling distribution with the 99% confidence interval about the hypothesized mean of 0.

But where does our sample $r = .45$ enter the picture? Note from Figure 8-4 that our $r = .45$ is *outside* this interval and, given the above assumptions, would be branded as a very rare occurrence. Specifically, if the true r in the population were indeed 0, we would obtain an r as large as or larger than .45 due to sampling error less than 1% of the time. Again, following the logic of the last chapter, we must now make a decision. Is the true r really 0 and our sample r one of those rare occurrences caused by sampling error? Or is it not sampling error at all, and is the true r some other value than 0? Since by sampling error alone, r's as large as or larger than .37 happen less than 1% of the time, we conclude that our r of .45 is not sampling error and that the true r is something larger than 0. In terms of our example, the correlation between college entrance exam scores and knowledge of current events *in the population* is not 0. In effect, we have shown that a relationship does exist on the basis of our sample.

Using Table C to test r *for significance.* The confidence interval approach outlined above is not only rather time-consuming but should be avoided if the size of your sample is less than 30. The shape of the sampling distribution of r when N is less than 30 is *non-normal,* and the normal curve values of 1.96 and 2.58 for the 95% and 99% confidence intervals would be in error. For this reason a table of r's necessary for

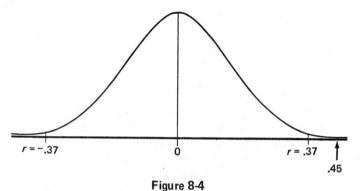

Figure 8-4
Sampling distribution of *r* when hypothesized population *r* is 0.

r to be significant at the .05 and .01 levels is printed in Table C in Appendix 2. The tabled values are to be interpreted in the same manner as in the confidence interval approach.

Before using Table C in an example, you must note that the left-hand column contains the term *degrees of freedom* (df). We had occasion to call attention to this term in Chapter 7, where we noted that the degrees of freedom was used in calculating an unbiased estimate of the population variance and was equal to $N - 1$, where N was the size of the sample. For purposes of using Table C we must remember that the degrees of freedom in calculating *r* is equal to $N - 2$, where N is the number of pairs of scores. We will have more to say later about the degrees of freedom concept, but for now just remember when you use Table C that the degrees of freedom is equal to $N - 2$.

As an example of the use of Table C, let us say that we found $r = .42$ for 25 students given a manual dexterity test (X) and a hand steadiness test (Y). Is this *r* significantly different from 0? We turn to Table C and note that for 23 degrees of freedom $(df = 25 - 2 = 23)$, *r* at the .05 level is .396 and at the .01 level is .505. These values are to be interpreted in the same way as when we constructed a confidence interval; that is, 95% of the sample *r*'s would fall between $-.396$ and .396 if the true population *r* were 0. Similarly, 99% of the sample *r*'s would fall between $-.505$ and .505 if the true *r* in the population were 0.

With our sample value of $r = .42$, we note that this is a rather rare occurrence (since *r*'s outside the $-.396$ to .396 interval occur less than 5% of the time by random sampling from a distribution whose mean *r* is 0), so we conclude that the true *r* is not 0. We can say tnat the obtained *r* of .42 is *significantly different from 0 at the .05 level.*

Note that with this size sample you would have to obtain an r of at least .505 to be able to say it was significantly different from 0 *at the .01 level*. We would conclude that the probability that our r of .42 arose through sampling error is between .01 and .05.

Establishing Confidence Intervals for the True r

After one has concluded that the obtained r is significantly different from 0, the logical next step would be to set up a confidence interval for the true r, in much the same way that we set up confidence intervals for the true mean in the last chapter. It would then be possible to make a statement that, for example, $p = .95$ that the population r is included in the interval .47 to .61. However, determining confidence intervals for the true r is a rather complicated affair, and you are referred to any advanced statistics text for this involved operation. The reason that it is not a simple, straightforward technique is that the sampling distribution is non-normal for population r's that are not 0. The sampling distribution of r becomes more and more skewed as the population r gets larger. An excellent treatment of establishing confidence intervals for the true r can be found in Guilford and Fruchter (1978).

Restrictions on Using the Pearson r

There are two restrictions on the Pearson r (other than the fact that it requires interval or ratio data) that must be kept in mind. First, the relationship between X and Y must be linear. Second, the technique requires pairs of values; that is, for every observation, you must have a value for X and a value for Y. This second restriction is self-explanatory, since you need X,Y pairs to plot a scattergram, but the linearity restriction deserves further clarification.

A linear relationship between X and Y means that the plotted points in a scattergram ascend (or descend, if r is negative) in a regular fashion such as shown in the scattergrams of Figure 8-3 (A, B, and D).

A nonlinear relationship between X and Y is shown in Figure 8-5, which plots coordination scores as a function of age. There is no doubt that there is a high degree of relationship between age and coordination. As you can see in Figure 8-5, coordination scores increase as the child gets older, up to about age 15. From 15 years of age until about 40, coordination scores stay the same, and they decline after age 40. The scattergram indicates a high degree of relationship since the points are tightly clustered, but $r = 0$ for this data, since the relationship of X and Y is curvilinear (the points are clustered about a curved line). Mathematically speaking, the Pearson r measures the amount of

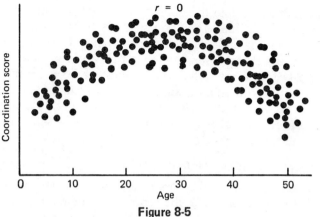

Figure 8-5
A curvilinear relationship: coordination as a function of age.

linear relationship present in two distributions, and the interpretation of *r* will be in error if the relationship between *X* and *Y* is nonlinear. It is a good practice to plot a scattergram to check for nonlinearity when using the correlational method.

The Spearman Rank-Difference Method

There is a convenient shortcut for calculating the correlation between two variables if *N* is relatively small, that is, less than 30 or so. The procedure is called the Spearman rank-difference method, and it uses the ranks of the scores instead of the scores themselves. The formula for the Spearman coefficient, r_s, is

$$r_s = 1 - \frac{6\Sigma D^2}{N(N^2 - 1)} \qquad (8\text{-}5)$$

where r_s is the coefficient (some older texts use the Greek symbol ρ),
ΣD^2 is the sum of the squared differences between ranks,
N is the number of pairs of ranks.

Calculating the Spearman r_s

The Spearman r_s can be calculated for data that are already in the form of ranks or that can be converted to ranks. Let us first consider the example of Table 8-7, where a teacher has ranked 10 children on "social responsiveness" and "conversational skills." Is there any relationship between these two variables?

Note that you obtain the quantity ΣD^2 by first listing the pairs of ranks for each individual. Then you subtract the rank on one variable from the rank on the other variable to obtain the difference (D) for each pair. You square these differences to get D^2 and sum the D^2 column to obtain ΣD^2. Note that after you substitute $\Sigma D^2 = 18$ and $N = 10$ into the formula, you subtract the resulting fraction, 0.11, from 1 to obtain $r_s = .89$. And a coefficient of .89 would indicate a strong relationship between social responsiveness and conversational skills as judged by this teacher.

Converting Existing Data to Ranks

When one or both of the variables to be correlated are measurements of one sort or another, the scores must be ranked; the highest score receives a rank of 1, the next highest a rank of 2, and so on. As an illustration of this method, let us consider the results of an interna-

Table 8-7
**The Relationship between Teacher Rankings on
Social Responsiveness and Conversational Skills**

Child	Social Rank	Skills Rank	D	D²
A	2	1	1	1
B	4	3	1	1
C	1	2	1	1
D	8	8	0	—
E	3	6	3	9
F	6	4	2	4
G	9	10	1	1
H	5	5	0	—
I	10	9	1	1
J	7	7	0	—
				$\Sigma D^2 = 18$

$$r_s = 1 - \frac{6\Sigma D^2}{N(N^2 - 1)} = 1 - \frac{6(18)}{10(100 - 1)}$$

$$= 1 - \frac{108}{990} = 1 - 0.11$$

$$r_s = .89$$

Table 8-8
Correlation between Speed Limits and Highway Fatalities
for 15 Countries

Country	Speed Limit (miles per hour)	Fatalities per 100 million miles	R_1	R_2	D	D^2
Belgium	56	10.5	7.5	6	1.5	2.25
Britain	60	4.0	5	14	9	81
Denmark	50	4.8	12	11	1	1
France	56	8.0	7.5	7	.5	.25
Greece	37	12.9	14	4	10	100
Hungary	62	14.5	3	3	–	–
Italy	68	6.4	1	9	8	64
Japan	31	4.7	15	12	3	9
Netherlands	50	6.0	12	10	2	4
Norway	50	4.2	12	13	1	1
Portugal	56	22.5	7.5	2	5.5	30.25
Spain	62	12.4	3	5	2	4
Turkey	56	32.2	7.5	1	6.5	42.25
United States	55	3.3	10	15	5	25
West Germany	62	7.9	3	8	5	25

$$\Sigma D^2 = 389.00$$

$$r_s = 1 - \frac{6\Sigma D^2}{N(N^2 - 1)} = 1 - \frac{6(389)}{15(225 - 1)}$$

$$= 1 - \frac{2,334}{3,360} = 1 - .69$$

$$r_s = .31$$

tional study on highway safety. Fifteen nations participated in the survey, and the speed limits for highways other than superhighways (converted to miles per hour) and fatalities per 100 million miles driven are listed in Table 8-8. Let us use the Spearman rank-difference method to determine the correlation between speed limits and fatality rates.

Note that, when there are tied values, *each observation is assigned* the average rank for the tied positions. For example, Hungary, Spain, and West Germany have the same speed limit, 62. Since these values occupy the rank positions of 2, 3, and 4, all three are assigned a rank of 3 in the first rank (R_1) column. Similarly, Belgium, France, Portugal, and Turkey all have a limit of 56, and these values are in rank positions of 6, 7, 8, and 9, so each is assigned the average rank of 7.5.

Is r_s Significantly Different from 0?

We have already seen that it is possible to obtain a correlation coefficient that is due to chance or sampling error, so we must test our obtained r_s to see if it is significantly different from 0. Table D in Appendix 2 lists the values of r_s that are necessary for r_s to be significantly different from 0 at the .05 and .01 levels of significance. For example, with an N of 20, the tabled value of r_s at the .05 level is .450. As before, this means that an obtained r_s of .450 or greater would happen by sampling error alone less than 5% of the time.

In our example in Table 8-8, we found $r_s = .31$. Is this significantly different from 0? Entering Table D with an N of 15, we find the tabled values of r_s at the .05 and .01 levels to be .525 and .689, respectively. Since our r_s of .31 is *less than* .525, we must conclude that a correlation coefficient of this size could have happened just through sampling error, and we would state that it is not significantly different from 0. In terms of the study, we would conclude that no relationship has been demonstrated between speed limits and fatality rate, at least for this small sample of countries.

The Meaning of r_s

The rationale for interpreting the rank-difference method is a simple one. Note that when there is perfect positive correlation between two variables the pairs of ranks for each individual would be identical. This means that all the differences (D) would be 0, the differences squared would all be 0, and the fraction $6(\Sigma D^2)/N(N^2 - 1)$ would be 0, leaving $r_s = 1 - 0 = 1$.

As the relationship drops, the differences and ΣD^2 increase and r_s, of course, gets smaller. And when there is a negative correlation the differences and ΣD^2 are very large indeed, so that the fraction to be subtracted from 1 is greater than 1, resulting in a negative r_s.

The Spearman r_s can be computed on pairs of measurements where one or both of the variables are expressed in an ordinal scale. The Spearman coefficient is nothing more than the Pearson r applied to *untied* ranks, and it would be interpreted in the same manner as the Pearson *r*. However, when some of the ranks are *tied,* the formula for r_s does not yield the same result as the formula for *r* and is only an approximation of *r*. The difference is negligible if there are not too many tied ranks. Also, since r_s is computed on ordinal data (remember that ranking yields an ordinal scale), it cannot take the place of the Pearson *r* in the regression equation or the standard error of estimate—two concepts to be discussed in the next chapter. Given these shortcomings of r_s, we are still likely to see the Spearman method used occasionally because of its computational simplicity.

Some Concluding Remarks on Correlation

Cause and Effect

If it should turn out that your calculated *r* indicates that two variables are correlated, this does not necessarily indicate a *cause-and-effect* relationship. After all, the Pearson *r* merely tells the strength of a *mathematical* relationship between *X* and *Y*: it is left to the researcher to determine the reason for the correlation. One may find that there is a correlation between socioeconomic level and school performance, or between a father's salary and his child's I.Q., but we cannot say that one causes the other unless we have additional information about the variables involved. The calculation of *r* is only the first step in a correlational study, and it indicates the *degree* to which two variables are related. The *why* of the relationship is a nonmathematical matter left up to the ingenuity of the researcher.

A very common result noted in correlational studies is that the relationship between two variables is caused by a third variable. For example, a study of the mental ages of elementary school pupils and their height in inches would indicate a substantial correlation. Such a spurious correlation, obviously, does not mean that there is any meaningful relationship between mental age and height, because the relationship is due to a third variable—the chronological age of the children. Both mental age and height increase with chronological age, and thus the relationship between mental age and height is a statistical artifact. When you read the results of correlational studies, it is a good idea to consider the possibility of other variables contributing to an obtained correlation. There are statistical techniques designed to handle this problem, and you are referred to one of the advanced texts listed in the References for information on these techniques. (See also Table 8-9.)

Restriction of Range

The correlation coefficient is highly sensitive to the range of scores on which it is calculated. As the range becomes more and more restricted, the size of the coefficient decreases. For example, a college entrance exam, given to incoming freshmen during the first week on campus, might correlate .70 with college GPA at the end of the freshman year. However, if we continue to calculate the correlation coefficient at the end of the sophomore, junior, and senior years, we would find a marked reduction in the size of r. One of the reasons for a declining r is that many of those with lower entrance exam scores would drop out of school after an unsuccessful freshman year, a few more after the sophomore year, and so on, and the range of the scores would decrease as these lower scores drop out of the picture.

Similarly, the Graduate Record Exam (GRE), used for screening applicants for admission to graduate school, correlates quite highly with success in postgraduate study. However, if we select a given graduate program (e.g., a psychology department at a large university) and attempt to correlate GRE with course grades, we would be lucky indeed to find an r as large as .30 or .35! These low coefficients are due to the fact that the range of GRE scores has been severely restricted, since only those with very high GRE scores were initially admitted to this graduate program. There are several techniques for dealing with the problem of a restricted range, but they are beyond the scope of this text, and you are referred to one of the advanced texts listed in the References.

How High Is High?

It is a very common practice to describe the strength of a correlation by such descriptive adjectives as high, low, moderate, strong, weak, and the like. And some texts encourage this practice by stating that correlation coefficients can be described according to the following scheme:

> Very high r = .80 or above
> Strong r = .60 to .80
> Moderate r = .40 to .60
> Low r = .20 to .40
> Very low r = .20 or less

While such descriptors may be convenient for summarizing a series of research studies ("The correlation between cigarette consumption and heart disease is very high"), it makes much more sense to use the actual value of the correlation coefficient itself. When asked how tall a friend of yours is, you don't answer "very tall" if you know he is exactly 6'4". You simply say that he is 6'4" tall. So, in the interest of precision, you are encouraged to use the exact value of *r* (or range of values, if more than one study is being cited) rather than the vague and somewhat ambiguous descriptors above.

Aside from scientific precision, there is another reason for avoiding descriptive terms for the strength of a correlation. Whether a correlation coefficient is high, moderate, or low depends, to a certain extent, on what variables are being correlated. For example, the correlation between two forms of an intelligence test would be considered low if *r* = .80, while the correlation between college entrance exam scores and college success would be exceedingly high with the same value of *r*. Again, the scientist can avoid confusion by stating the exact value of *r* and letting the readers make their own value judgment.

Other Correlational Techniques

In our introduction to the concept of correlation, we have just barely scratched the surface of correlational topics, and the inclusion

Table 8-9
Some Other Correlational Methods

Point-biserial r:	One dichotomous variable (yes/no; male/female) and one interval or ratio variable
Biserial r:	One variable forced into a dichotomy (grade distribution dichotomized to "pass" and "fail") and one interval or ratio variable
Phi coefficient:	Both variables are dichotomous on a nominal scale (male/female vs. high school graduate/dropout)
Tetrachoric r:	Both variables are dichotomous with underlying normal distributions (pass/fail on a test vs. tall/short in height)
Correlation ratio:	There is a curvilinear rather than linear relationship between the variables (also called the eta coefficient)
Partial correlation:	The relationship between two variables is caused by a third variable (e.g., a correlation between mental age and height, which is caused by chronological age)
Multiple R:	The maximum correlation between a dependent variable and a combination of independent variables (a college freshman's GPA as predicted by her high school grades in English, biology, government, and algebra)

of the Pearson r and Spearman r_s in this chapter was dictated mainly by the popularity of these methods. There are a wide variety of other techniques, however, developed for rather specific applications. Some are modifications of the Pearson r, while others are based on probability functions. Some of the more popular techniques and possible applications are shown in Table 8-9.

    Table 8-9 is not intended to be an exhaustive list of possible correlational methods but a sampling of the possible ways in which correlational research can be used. The serious student is referred to one of the advanced texts listed in the References, especially the text by Glass and Stanley (1970).

Sample Problem #1

A psychologist is evaluating two different tests that attempt to measure "creativity." He administers the two tests to a sample of 15 third-grade students and tabulates the number of errors made. Was there a relationship between the error scores on the two tests? (Both raw score formulas are shown.)

Student	Test X	Test Y	X^2	Y^2	XY
A	7	6	49	36	42
B	14	10	196	100	140
C	8	6	64	36	48
D	6	5	36	25	30
E	10	9	100	81	90
F	1	3	1	9	3
G	7	9	49	81	63
H	12	9	144	81	108
I	1	4	1	16	4
J	13	11	169	121	143
K	4	8	16	64	32
L	9	7	81	49	63
M	3	7	9	49	21
N	9	10	81	100	90
O	12	8	144	64	96
	116	112	1,140	912	973

Means:

$$\bar{X} = \frac{\Sigma X}{N} = \frac{116}{15} = 7.73 = 7.7 \qquad \bar{Y} = \frac{\Sigma Y}{N} = \frac{112}{15} = 7.47 = 7.5$$

Standard Deviations:

$$S_X = \sqrt{\frac{\Sigma X^2}{N} - \overline{X}^2} = \sqrt{\frac{1,140}{15} - (7.73)^2}$$
$$= \sqrt{76.0 - 59.75} = \sqrt{16.25}$$

$$S_X = 4.03$$

$$S_Y = \sqrt{\frac{\Sigma Y^2}{N} - \overline{Y}^2} = \sqrt{\frac{912}{15} - (7.47)^2}$$
$$= \sqrt{60.8 - 55.8} = \sqrt{5}$$

$$S_Y = 2.24$$

Pearson r (Formula 8-2):

$$r = \frac{\dfrac{\Sigma XY}{N} - \overline{X}\,\overline{Y}}{S_X S_Y} = \frac{\dfrac{973}{15} - (7.73)(7.47)}{(4.03)(2.24)}$$

$$= \frac{64.87 - 57.74}{9.03} = \frac{7.13}{9.03} = .79$$

Pearson r (Formula 8-3):

$$r = \frac{N\Sigma XY - \Sigma X \Sigma Y}{\sqrt{N\Sigma X^2 - (\Sigma X)^2}\,\sqrt{N\Sigma Y^2 - (\Sigma Y)^2}}$$

$$= \frac{15(973) - (116)(112)}{\sqrt{15(1,140) - (116)^2}\,\sqrt{15(912) - (112)^2}}$$

$$= \frac{14,595 - 12,992}{\sqrt{17,100 - 13,456}\,\sqrt{13,680 - 12,544}}$$

$$= \frac{1,603}{\sqrt{3,644}\,\sqrt{1,136}} = \frac{1,603}{(60.37)(33.70)}$$

$$r = \frac{1,603}{2,034.47} = .79$$

Is r Significantly Different from 0?

From Table C, we note that with 13 degrees of freedom ($N - 2 = 13$), r at the .01 level is .641. Since our value of .79 exceeds this tabled value, we conclude that $r = .79$ is significantly different from 0 at the .01 level.

Sample Problem #2

An English teacher was interested in the topic of creativity and wanted to know if there was any relationship between creativity and a person's vocabulary. She tabulated the vocabulary scores for 12 sophomores from a recent nationwide test and then ranked the 12 students for creativity on the basis of their English compositions and themes. The vocabulary scores and the creativity rankings are shown below. Was there a relationship between vocabulary and creativity?

Student	Vocabulary Score	Vocabulary Rank	Creativity Rank	D	D²
A	59	6	4	2	4
B	65	3.5	2	1.5	2.25
C	72	1	6	5	25
D	55	7	5	2	4
E	49	10	8	2	4
F	50	9	3	6	36
G	70	2	9	7	49
H	65	3.5	7	3.5	12.25
I	40	11	11	0	—
J	52	8	1	7	49
K	64	5	12	7	49
L	32	12	10	2	4

$$\Sigma D^2 = \overline{238.5}$$

$$r_s = 1 - \frac{6 \Sigma D^2}{N(N^2 - 1)} = 1 - \frac{6(238.5)}{12(144 - 1)}$$

$$= 1 - \frac{1{,}431}{1{,}716} = 1 - .83$$

$$r_s = .17$$

Is r_s Significantly Different from 0?

From Table D, we see that with an N of 12, r_s at the .05 level is .591. Since our value of .17 is less than this tabled value, we conclude that our r_s is not significantly different from 0, and there appears to be no relationship between vocabulary and creativity.

Study Questions

1. A correlation of .60 indicates a lesser relationship between two variables than one of .80. Use the intuitive approach to explain the difference in the strength of the relationship between .80 and .60.

2. How would you use the graphical approach to explain the difference of question 1?

3. The relationship between two variables is indicated by the *size* and the *sign* of the coefficient. What does this mean?

4. Describe the scattergram you would expect from the following correlation coefficients.
   a. .77
   b. −.85
   c. −1.00
   d. .02

5. A friend is using the *z* score method for calculating a Pearson *r*. You happen to glance at his data and notice that the $z_x z_y$ values for three observations are −3.071, −2.095, and −3.064. On the basis of your "random glance," what kind of relationship should his correlation coefficient demonstrate? Why?

6. In testing *r* for significance, what do you assume as the mean of the sampling distribution of *r*?

7. Under what condition would the Pearson method and the Spearman method yield identical results?

Exercises

1. Indicate whether you would expect a positive, negative, or zero correlation between the pairs of variables described below.
   a. Blood pressure reading and incidence of stroke
   b. Miles per gallon and weight of automobile
   c. College GPA and age
   d. Occupational noise level and degree of hearing loss
   e. Educational level and unemployment rate
   f. I.Q. and size of head
   g. Thickness of wall insulation and intensity of sound conducted

2. To see if there is any relationship between reading ability and manual dexterity, 15 eighth-graders are given a reading comprehension test (*X*) and a tweezer dexterity test (*Y*). The data are summarized below. Calculate the Pearson *r*, using formula 8-2.

$$X \qquad\qquad\qquad Y$$
$$\bar{X} = 10 \qquad\qquad\qquad \bar{Y} = 6$$
$$S_X = 2.6 \qquad\qquad\qquad S_Y = 1.6$$
$$\Sigma XY = 905$$

3. An industrial psychologist wants to find the correlation between a manual dexterity test (X) and assembly line performance (Y). She administers the test and assesses performance for a sample of 15 workers. Use the machine formula to calculate the Pearson r for the results summarized below.

$$X \qquad\qquad\qquad\qquad Y$$
$$\Sigma X = 90 \qquad\qquad\qquad\qquad \Sigma Y = 150$$
$$\Sigma X^2 = 578 \qquad\qquad\qquad\qquad \Sigma Y^2 = 1{,}604$$
$$\Sigma XY = 920$$

4. A sample of 15 students is measured on grip strength (X) and simple reaction time to a buzzer (Y). Calculate the Pearson r for this data first by formula 8-2 and then by the machine formula.

X	Y	X	Y
12	15	9	12
15	16	8	13
13	16	4	10
11	14	7	6
11	13	10	11
9	10	4	14
8	10	6	9
8	11		

5. A researcher found a Pearson r of .50 between reading comprehension scores and spelling test scores for 15 seventh-graders. Was this correlation significantly different from zero? (Use Table C in Appendix 2.)

6. A medical research associate is conducting a correlational study of two variables which she believes will yield a Pearson r of about .20. What is the minimum number of subjects she could use in her study so she could say her correlation is significantly different from zero at the .05 level?

7. A personnel dean at a small college believes that there is a relationship between academic performance and class attendance. He

chooses a sample of 15 students on academic probation and has each student's instructors tabulate the number of times each one misses classes during a 10-week period. Calculate the Spearman coefficient for these data and see if it is significantly different from zero.

GPA	Absences	GPA	Absences
1.80	8	1.52	10
1.90	6	1.25	15
1.80	7	1.35	14
1.65	9	1.40	12
1.87	6	.97	15
1.40	10	1.14	17
1.50	9	1.30	13
1.17	14		

9 Prediction and Regression

Prediction is a fascinating topic, as evidenced by the rapt attention we give to astrologers, medical doctors, and Super Bowl oddsmakers. And few of us can resist a quick peek at the 10-item "Are You a Good Mate?" or "Are You a Dangerous Driver?" tests in the Sunday supplement. From childhood to old age, we listen to predictions of our school success, athletic prowess, job satisfaction, and life expectancy from teachers, parents, coaches, and physicians. Some of these predictions, fortunately, do not come true.

Most of the above examples are predictions based on a multitude of factors; for example, your doctor's diagnosis may be based on 10 or 20 physiological indicators. For the purposes of our discussion in this chapter, however, we will restrict our topic to predictions made from a single variable. In the last chapter we noted that the two purposes of correlation were (1) to indicate the amount of relationship between two variables and (2) to enable us to predict one variable from the knowledge of another variable.

It is this kind of prediction that we will be concerned with here—the prediction of an individual's score on one variable on the basis of that person's score on another variable.

The Use of r in Prediction

After a significant correlation has been obtained between two variables, *X* and *Y*, we would like to be able to take a score on *X* and *predict* the associated score on *Y*. For example, if a correlation has been established between high school grade-point average (GPA) and college GPA, we would like to develop a method that would allow us to select a high school senior, calculate his GPA, and actually predict what his college GPA will be (within limits) after his freshman year. This procedure, which at first glance may appear to border on the occult, is really rather simple if one progresses step by step to the different concepts involved. Let us begin with some very basic algebra.

Equation for a Straight Line

Somewhere back in ninth-grade algebra you probably learned that the equation of a straight line was of the general form $Y = mX + b$, and you plotted various values of *X* and *Y* to get a graph similar to that of Figure 9-1. The equation of the line in Figure 9-1 is $Y = 2X + 3$, and five pairs of *X,Y* values are plotted. In the general equation $Y = mX + b$, the quantity *b* is called the *Y intercept* and *m* is the *slope* of the line. For $Y = 2X + 3$, in Figure 9-1, the *Y* intercept is 3, since the line will cross the *Y* axis at $Y = 3$. The slope of the line is 2, indicating that for an increase of one unit in X, there is an increase of two units in *Y*.[1]

This graph of $Y = 2X + 3$ shows a *functional relationship* between *X* and *Y*, with *X* as the independent variable and *Y* as the dependent variable. (It might be helpful to review the topic on functional relationships in Chapter 2.) That is, we can insert any value of *X* and *predict* the value of *Y* which is paired with that value of *X*. For example, in Figure 9-1, we can specify an *X* of 5 and "predict" that a *Y* of 13 will satisfy the equation and fall on the same straight line. Note that a similar straight line has occurred in Figure 8-3A, where *perfect correlation* is shown between *X* and *Y*. When the correlation between *X* and *Y* is *perfect* (either positive or negative) we are able to predict *Y* from *X* without error. Or in terms of the example of several paragraphs ago, if $r = 1.00$ between high school GPA and college GPA,

---

[1]There is an easy way to remember these two concepts. Go one unit to the right of your line and the *slope* is the distance you need to go up (or down) to get back on the line. The *Y intercept* is the value of *Y* when *X* is 0.

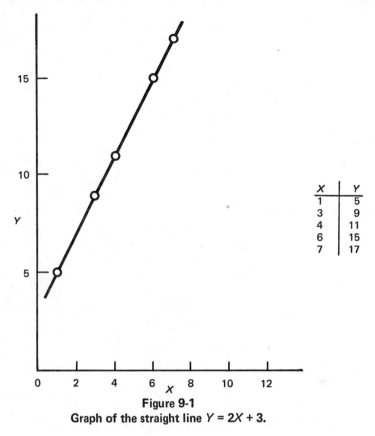

Figure 9-1
Graph of the straight line $Y = 2X + 3$.

we would be able to predict accurately your college GPA from your high school record alone!

The Prediction Equation

But back to the world of reality. How can you predict Y from X when r is not 1.00 and the points do not all fall on the straight line? The answer is simple: we calculate a straight line that "best fits" the points and from X predict the most likely value of Y. In other words, we can take a group of paired scores, regardless of the value of r (as long as it is significantly different from 0), calculate the best-fitting straight line, and for any given value of X predict the most likely value of Y.

Three sets of data are shown in the scattergrams of Figure 9-2, with the best-fitting straight lines for each set. Note that when r is high (.83) most of the points are fairly close to the line and when r is low (.09) the points are scattered well away from this line. This means that

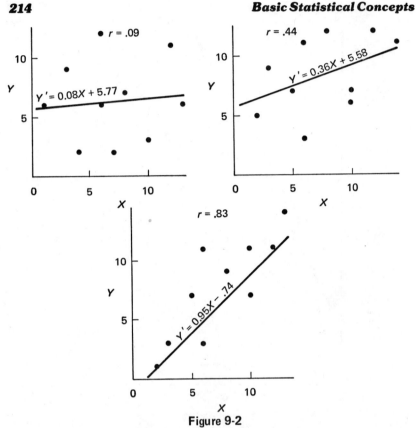

Figure 9-2
Scattergrams and best-fitting straight lines.

the higher *r* is, the *more accurate* our predictions of *Y* from a given *X* will be. We will have more to say about this accuracy later on.

The equation that will result in the best-fitting straight line for a set of paired scores is:

$$Y' = \left(\frac{rS_Y}{S_X}\right)X - \left(\frac{rS_Y}{S_X}\right)\overline{X} + \overline{Y} \qquad (9\text{-}1)$$

where *Y'* is the predicted[2] value of *Y*,
  r is the correlation between *X* and *Y*,
  S_Y is the standard deviation of the *Y* distribution,
  S_X is the standard deviation of the *X* distribution,
  X is the variable in the formula *Y = mX + b*,
  $\overline{X}$ is the mean of the *X* distribution,
  $\overline{Y}$ is the mean of the *Y* distribution.

[2]We will use *Y'* to denote any value that falls on the regression line and satisfies the equation, while *Y* will refer to any of the *observed* values of that variable in the distribution.

This formula is admittedly an imposing one, but after all the calculations have been performed, it reduces to the familiar form of $Y = mX + b$. Let us use the data of the algebra and geometry scores from Table 8-5 and calculate the best-fitting straight line that would predict an individual's geometry score (Y) from his algebra score (X). Summarizing the statistics from Table 8-5:

$$\bar{X} = 13 \qquad\qquad \bar{Y} = 21$$
$$S_X = 2.49 \qquad\qquad S_Y = 2.97$$
$$r = .93$$

Substituting into the formula we get

$$Y' = \left(\frac{rS_Y}{S_X}\right)X - \left(\frac{rS_Y}{S_X}\right)\bar{X} + \bar{Y}$$

$$= \frac{.93(2.97)}{2.49}X - \frac{.93(2.97)}{2.49}(13) + 21$$

$$= \frac{2.76}{2.49}X - \frac{2.76}{2.49}(13) + 21$$

$$= 1.11X - 1.11(13) + 21$$

$$= 1.11X - 14.43 + 21$$

$$Y' = 1.11X + 6.57$$

This equation, sometimes called a *regression equation,* yields the best-fitting straight line for the algebra-geometry data, and we can now plot this line on the scattergram for the data of Table 8-5, as shown in Figure 9-3.

To draw this best-fitting straight line, also called the *regression line,* on a scattergram, choose a *low* value of X and a *high* value of X and calculate their corresponding Y' by using the regression equation above. Looking at the scattergram of Figure 9-3, we see that X values of 10 and 16 would do nicely, so calculating Y' by substituting for X in the regression equation would give

$$Y' = 1.11X + 6.57 = 1.11(10) + 6.57 = 11.1 + 6.57 = 17.67$$
$$Y' = 1.11X + 6.57 = 1.11(16) + 6.57 = 17.76 + 6.57 = 24.33$$

These two values of Y' are located on the scattergram above X values of 10 and 16 respectively, and a straight line connects these two points. This regression line is the best-fitting straight line for this set of data, and the equation for this line is $Y' = 1.11X + 6.57$.

The regression equation can now be used to predict the most

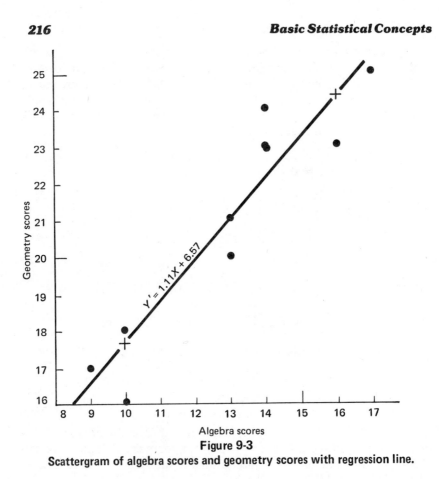

Figure 9-3
Scattergram of algebra scores and geometry scores with regression line.

likely value of Y for any given value of X. For the algebra-geometry data, we can predict the most likely geometry score (Y) from an individual's algebra score alone. For example, let us suppose that another individual takes the algebra test and scores 15. What would be her predicted geometry score (Y')? Substituting for X in the prediction equation, we would get

$$Y' = 1.11X + 6.57$$
$$= 1.11(15) + 6.57$$
$$= 16.65 + 6.57$$
$$Y' = 23.2$$

and we conclude that for the individual scoring 15 on the algebra test our best prediction of her geometry score would be 23.2. This score, of course, falls on the regression line of Figure 9-3.

> ### Note 9-1
> ### Origin of the Regression Concept
>
> Sir Francis Galton (1822-1911) undertook a series of studies of inheritance which tested some of the hypotheses of his cousin, Charles Darwin. In studying the relation between the heights of parents and the heights of their offspring, Galton noted that the heights of offspring tended to *regress* toward the mean of the general population. In general, tall parents had children who were above average in height but who were not as tall as the parents. And short parents had children who were below average in height but who generally were taller than their parents. This "dropping back" toward the general mean was often referred to as the *law of filial regression.* The term *regression* came to be used whenever the relationship between two variables was studied.

Accuracy in Predicting Y from X

In the previous sections we have been discussing the prediction of the "most likely value of Y" without ever really defining what is meant by "most likely." You have probably gathered by now that the accuracy of a predicted value of Y is somehow related to the scattering of the points about the regression line. In Figure 9-3, for example, most of the points lie *near,* but not *on,* the regression line. And if you will look back at Figure 9-2, you will note that, as r gets larger, the points are closer to the regression line.

Errors of Estimate

In fact, we can define the *error of estimate, e,* as the distance between the predicted value of Y and the observed score of Y at a given value of X. Stated algebraically, we would have

$$e = Y - Y'$$

where e is the error of estimate,

Y is the observed value for a given value of X,

Y' is the predicted value of Y for that value of X.

Let us repeat the scattergram of the algebra-geometry data in Figure 9-4 and demonstrate this error of estimate for two students, A and J. As you can see, student A has an algebra score (X) of 14 and a geometry score (Y) of 24. However, the predicted score Y' for an X of 14 is calculated as follows:

$$Y' = 1.11X + 6.57 = 1.11(14) + 6.57 = 22.11$$

so the error of estimate for student A would be

$$e_A = Y - Y' = 24 - 22.11 = 1.89$$

which indicates that the actual score of 24 is 1.89 score units *above* the predicted Y' of 22.11 on the regression line. For student J, who has an algebra score of 10 and a geometry score of 16, the predicted value of Y is 17.67, which yields an error of estimate of

$$e_J = Y - Y' = 16 - 17.67 = -1.67$$

which indicates that the actual score of 16 is 1.67 units *below* the predicted Y' of 17.67 on the regression line. These values, 1.89 and −1.67, clearly indicate the amount of error in predicting Y from X in terms of deviations from the regression line.

It would be possible to find the error of estimate for every individual and develop a statistic which would summarize the accuracy of

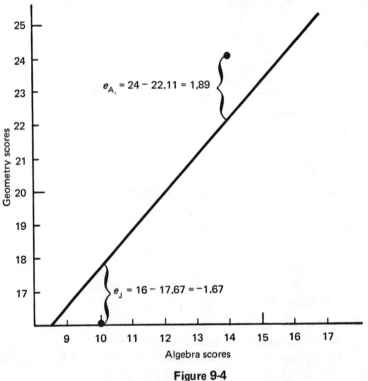

Figure 9-4
Errors of estimate for students A and J.

our predictions of Y, but such a procedure would be very inefficient and time-consuming, especially if N is quite large. It turns out that the best way to proceed is to develop a *confidence interval* approach and make a probability statement concerning the value of an individual's predicted score.

Standard Error of Estimate, s_E

Let us assume that both X and Y are normally distributed in the population. In our preceding example this would mean that ability in algebra and proficiency in geometry are normally distributed in the population, which is a rather reasonable assumption. If this is true, it can be shown that for a given value of X the actual Y values are normally distributed about a mean which lies on the regression line. In other words a predicted value of Y' is the mean of all these actual Y values, and the standard deviation of this distribution of actual Y values is called the *standard error of estimate, s_E*.

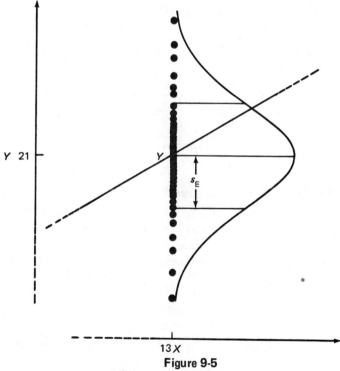

Y 21

$13\,X$

Figure 9-5
Y', s_E, and the regression line.

In an attempt to clarify this last statement let us refer to Figure 9-5, which shows a portion of the regression line for a *large* number of algebra-geometry scores. Note that for an algebra score (X) of 13 the actual geometry scores (Y) of this large sample are clustered about the mean, Y', of 21; they are normally distributed, and the standard deviation of this distribution is shown as s_E, the *standard error of estimate*.

With our expertise with the normal curve, we can make statements that for a given value of X:

1. Approximately 68% of the actual Y scores will fall between $Y' \pm 1s_E$.
2. 95% of the actual Y scores will fall between $Y' \pm 1.96s_E$.
3. 99% of the actual Y scores will fall between $Y' \pm 2.58s_E$.

The formula for the calculation of the standard error of estimate is

$$s_E = S_Y\sqrt{1 - r^2} \tag{9-2}$$

where s_E is the standard error of estimate in predicting Y from X,

S_Y is the standard deviation of the Y distribution,

r is the Pearson correlation coefficient between X and Y.

Let us use this formula for s_E to calculate the standard error of estimate for the algebra-geometry data. Substituting in the formula for S_Y and r, we have

$$
\begin{aligned}
s_E &= S_Y\sqrt{1 - r^2} \\
&= 2.97\sqrt{1 - (.93)^2} \\
&= 2.97\sqrt{1 - .86} \\
&= 2.97\sqrt{0.14} \\
&= 2.97(0.37) \\
s_E &= 1.10
\end{aligned}
$$

The Confidence Interval about Y'

Now that we have calculated s_E, we can set up a confidence interval about a predicted score, Y', in the following way. Let us go back to an earlier example, where an individual scored 15 on the algebra test and by using the regression equation we predicted her geometry score would be $Y' = 23.2$. Knowing that in a large sample of people taking the algebra test there would be 68% having Y values within the 68% confidence interval for Y,

$$Y' \pm 1s_E \tag{9-3}$$

we would calculate the 68% confidence interval for Y for an X of 15 to be

$$
\begin{aligned}
Y' \pm 1s_E &= 23.2 \pm 1.10 \\
&= 22.1 \text{ to } 24.3
\end{aligned}
$$

In other words, we are 68% certain ($p = .68$) that an individual who scores 15 on X will have a Y score between 22.1 and 24.3. We have accomplished what we set out to do: we can now make a probability statement about the interval in which a given Y score is likely to fall.[3]

Accuracy of Prediction and Size of r

For accuracy in predicting, we would like to have the confidence interval about Y' as small as possible, which means we want s_E as small as possible. A glance at the formula for s_E shows that this is a function of the size of r. When $r = 1.00$, the quantity $S_Y \sqrt{1 - r^2}$ reduces to 0, and s_E is 0. In other words, if r is 1.00, there is no error in predicting Y from X. And this is obvious, because all the points on a scattergram would fall on the regression line. As r gets smaller, the quantity $S_Y \sqrt{1 - r^2}$ gets larger, of course, and when there is no correlation ($r = 0$), s_E is the same size as S_Y, the standard deviation of the Y distribution. So we would have to conclude that the larger the value of r, the more accurate will be our predictions.

An Example of Correlational Research

The preceding sections have covered a number of topics, and it may be helpful at this point to examine an actual research study to see how the various concepts fit together. A midwestern college administered a nationally standardized entrance examination to a sample of 484 freshmen during their first week on campus. At the end of the freshman year the grade-point average (GPA) for these students was calculated. Since the administration was interested in eventually predicting college GPA from the exam scores taken the first week, the GPA was the dependent variable (Y) and the entrance exam was the independent variable (X). The means, standard deviations, and ΣXY for the 484 pairs of scores are given below. The scattergram for the data is plotted in Figure 9-6.

Exam Scores (X)	*GPA (Y)*
$\overline{X} = 22.21$	$\overline{Y} = 2.53$
$S_X = 4.00$	$S_Y = 0.67$

[3]It has been pointed out by Bobko, Sapinkoff, and Anderson (1978) that the interval $Y' \pm S_E$ is too small and implies greater accuracy than is actually the case. However, formula 9-3 is one that is generally accepted in education and the behavioral sciences, and your author has chosen not to deviate from the accepted pattern. Your instructor may choose to use the interval stated by Bobko, Sapinkoff, and Anderson, which is

$$Y' \pm S_E \sqrt{1 + \frac{1}{N} + \frac{(X - \overline{X})^2}{\Sigma x^2}}$$

where X is the individual's score on X, and the rest of the terms are as defined earlier.

$$N = 484$$
$$\Sigma XY = 27{,}884.06$$

The main interest, of course, is in the possible relationship be-tween the exam scores and the GPA's, so the very first step is the calcu-lation of r.

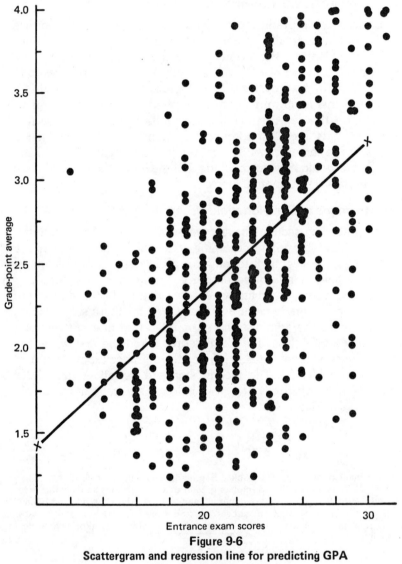

Figure 9-6
Scattergram and regression line for predicting GPA
from entrance exam scores.

$$r = \frac{\frac{\Sigma XY}{N} - \overline{X}\overline{Y}}{S_X S_Y} = \frac{\frac{27{,}884.06}{484} - (22.21)(2.53)}{(4.00)(0.67)}$$

$$= \frac{57.6117 - 56.1913}{2.68} = \frac{1.42}{2.68} = .53$$

After r has been calculated, the next step is to see if it is significantly different from 0. From Table C in Appendix 2 we note that for 400 degrees of freedom (we actually have $484 - 2 = 482$ degrees of freedom, but since Table C does not list that value, we take the next *lowest* value listed) an r must be at least .128 to be significantly different from 0 at the .01 level. Since an r of .53 is outside the $-.128$ to .128 interval, we reject the notion that the true r is 0. There is definitely a relationship between entrance exam scores and college GPA.

The next step is the calculation of the regression line. This is calculated to be

$$Y' = \left(\frac{rS_Y}{S_X}\right)X - \left(\frac{rS_Y}{S_X}\right)\overline{X} + \overline{Y}$$

$$= \frac{.53(0.67)}{4}X - \frac{.53(0.67)}{4}(22.21) + 2.53$$

$$= 0.089X - .089(22.21) + 2.53$$

$$= 0.089X - 1.98 + 2.53$$

$$Y' = 0.089X + 0.55$$

We now position the regression line on the scattergram of Figure 9-6 by substituting any two values of X and solving the equation for Y'. Let us use X values of 10 and 30 and solve for the corresponding Y' values. This would give

$$Y' = 0.089X + 0.55 = 0.089(10) + 0.55 = 0.89 + 0.55 = 1.44$$
$$Y' = 0.089X + 0.55 = 0.089(30) + 0.55 = 2.67 + 0.55 = 3.22$$

These Y' values are plotted above their respective X values on the scattergram, a straight line is drawn between the two points, and this regression line, $Y' = 0.089X + 0.55$, is the best-fitting straight line for this data.

The last step before we can make predictions about an individual's GPA is to calculate the standard error of estimate, s_E. This is calculated by

$$s_E = S_Y\sqrt{1 - r^2} = 0.67\sqrt{1 - (.53)^2}$$
$$= 0.67\sqrt{1 - .28} = 0.67\sqrt{.72}$$
$$= 0.67(0.85) = 0.57$$

On the basis of the above research, the college administration is now ready to use the entrance examination for predicting college GPA for *future* students. If John Jones enrolls as a freshman the following year and scores 24 on the entrance examination, what would be the best prediction for his college GPA at the end of his freshman year? Using the regression equation we find

$$Y' = 0.089X + 0.55 = 0.089(24) + 0.55 = 2.14 + 0.55 = 2.69$$

and setting up the 68% confidence interval about Y':

$$Y' \pm 1s_E = 2.69 \pm 0.57$$
$$= 2.12 \text{ to } 3.26$$

We would conclude that $p = .68$ that John Jones' actual GPA at the end of his freshman year would be between 2.12 and 3.26.

Assumptions for the Pearson r in Prediction

We noted in the last chapter that we had to make two assumptions before we could meaningfully apply the Pearson method — linearity of X and Y and paired X,Y data. In a similar way, assumptions must be made before the Pearson r can be used for purposes of prediction. They are:

1. The regression of Y on X is linear (linearity).
2. X and Y are normally distributed in the population (normality).
3. The standard deviation of the Y values about Y' for a given value of X is about the same for all values of Y' (homoscedasticity).

Linearity

We emphasized the importance of linearity in the last chapter, since r measures the degree of *linear* relationship between X and Y. Figure 9-7 shows the scattergram of the coordination scores as a function of age that we examined in the last chapter. But note that the "best-fitting" straight line is a horizontal line at the mean of the Y scores.[4] It is obvious that there is a high correlation between coordination scores and age, but the Pearson r is 0, because of the lack of linearity in the data. And with a regression line that is horizontal at the

---

[4]You can demonstrate this for yourself very easily by substituting $r = 0$ in the regression equation and obtaining $Y' = \bar{Y}$.

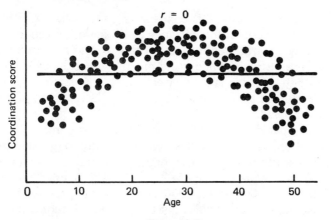

Figure 9-7
A curvilinear relationship: coordination as a function of age.

mean of the Y scores, our prediction of Y' for any value of X would be the same, $Y' = \bar{Y}$! As we noted in the last chapter, we certainly would want to draw a scattergram, in order to examine the data for possible nonlinearity.

Normality

In order to use the standard error of estimate to establish the accuracy of a predicted Y', it is necessary that X and Y be normally distributed in the population. Since the confidence interval about a predicted Y' uses the traditional normal curve values of $\pm 1.96s_E$ and $\pm 2.58s_E$, the assumption of a normal population distribution of X and Y is a logical one.

Homoscedasticity

In order for us to use s_E for any predicted Y' on the regression line, it is necessary that there be homoscedasticity in the values of Y about Y'. Homoscedasticity (this tongue-twisting term can be roughly translated as "equal spread") means that the variance of the Y values around their mean of Y' for a given value of X should be about the same for all distributions of Y values about their respective Y' values. In other words, if we were to calculate the variance (or standard deviation) of all of the Y values for a given value of X, we would expect this variance to be approximately equal to the variance of another group of Y values for some other value of X.

To better understand this concept, let us refer back to Figure 9-6, where the scattergram of the entrance exam scores and college GPA is plotted. Let us arbitrarily choose an X value of 20. The Y values for this value of X are distributed about the mean, $Y' = 2.34$, which is on the regression line. If there is homoscedasticity, the variance of this distribution should be about the same as the variance of any of the other columns of Y values.

Strictly speaking, homoscedasticity is a property possessed by samples that are very large, but we can get a very rough idea from the shape of the scattergram. The scattergram of Figure 9-6 is roughly elliptical, but the scattergram of Figure 9-8 is not. This figure shows the relationship between I.Q. and the scores on a creativity test. Note that the creativity scores (Y) are tightly clustered about the regression line for the lower I.Q. scores (X), while the creativity scores are more dispersed for the higher I.Q. scores. This would tell us that those with low I.Q.

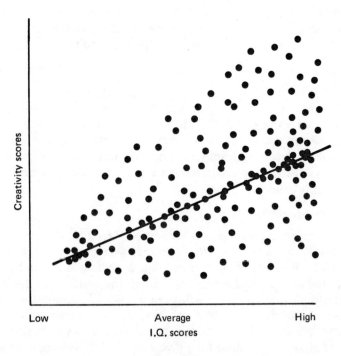

Figure 9-8
Scattergram not meeting the homoscedasticity assumption.

scores tend to score lower in creativity, while those with the higher I.Q. scores may be low, average, or high in creativity. In other words, if you have a lower I.Q., you probably are not a very creative person, but if you have a high I.Q., you may or may not be very creative. This peculiar state of affairs results in an unequal spread of Y values about the regression line, and this data would not meet the assumption of homoscedasticity.

Sample Problem

A personnel director at a large factory would like to be able to predict the performance of work inspectors on an assembly line. He develops a visual search test which requires the examinee to identify target letters in a mass of letters and numbers on 9" × 12" cards. The score is the number of errors made on 20 cards. The assembly line performance requires the inspector to reject an assembly if it has a broken connection. An error is counted if the assembly gets by the inspector before he can see the faulty part and push a reject switch. Each inspector's score is the number of errors made in a 2-hour work period.

The search test (X) is given to 15 inspectors; later, their assembly line errors (Y) are noted during a 2-hour work period. How well does the search test predict assembly line performance?

Worker	Search Test (X)	Assembly Errors (Y)	X^2	Y^2	XY
A	16	9	256	81	144
B	17	12	289	144	204
C	17	10	289	100	170
D	15	8	225	64	120
E	14	8	196	64	112
F	11	6	121	36	66
G	11	5	121	25	55
H	12	5	144	25	60
I	13	6	169	36	78
J	14	5	196	25	70
K	4	1	16	1	4
L	7	4	49	16	28
M	12	7	144	49	84
N	7	1	49	1	7
O	10	3	100	9	30
	$\Sigma X = 180$	$\Sigma Y = 90$	$\Sigma X^2 = 2,364$	$\Sigma Y^2 = 676$	$\Sigma XY = 1,232$

Means:

$$\bar{X} = \frac{\Sigma X}{N} = \frac{180}{15} = 12 \qquad \bar{Y} = \frac{\Sigma Y}{N} = \frac{90}{15} = 6$$

Standard Deviations:

$$S_X = \frac{1}{N}\sqrt{N\Sigma X^2 - (\Sigma X)^2} = \frac{1}{15}\sqrt{15(2,364) - (180)^2}$$

$$= \frac{1}{15}\sqrt{35,460 - 32,400} = \frac{\sqrt{3,060}}{15}$$

$$S_X = \frac{55.32}{15} = 3.69$$

$$S_Y = \frac{1}{N}\sqrt{N\Sigma Y^2 - (\Sigma Y)^2} = \frac{1}{15}\sqrt{15(676) - (90)^2}$$

$$= \frac{1}{15}\sqrt{10,140 - 8,100} = \frac{\sqrt{2,040}}{15}$$

$$S_Y = \frac{45.17}{15} = 3.01$$

Pearson r:

$$r = \frac{\dfrac{\Sigma XY}{N} - \bar{X}\bar{Y}}{S_X S_Y} = \frac{\dfrac{1,232}{15} - (12)(6)}{(3.69)(3.01)} = \frac{82.13 - 72}{11.11}$$

$$r = \frac{10.13}{11.11} = .91$$

Is r *Significantly Different from 0?*

From Table C, we note that with 13 degrees of freedom ($N - 2 = 13$), r at the .01 level is .641. Since our value of .91 exceeds this tabled value, we conclude that $r = .91$ is significantly different from 0 at the .01 level.

Scattergram and Regression Equation:

Figure 9-9 shows the scattergram for the data. Calculating our regression equation, we get

$$Y' = \left(\frac{rS_Y}{S_X}\right)X - \left(\frac{rS_Y}{S_X}\right)\bar{X} + \bar{Y}$$

$$= \frac{.91(3.01)}{3.69}X - \frac{.91(3.01)}{3.69}(12) + 6$$

$$= 0.74X - 0.74(12) + 6$$

$$= 0.74X - 8.88 + 6$$

$$Y' = 0.74X - 2.88$$

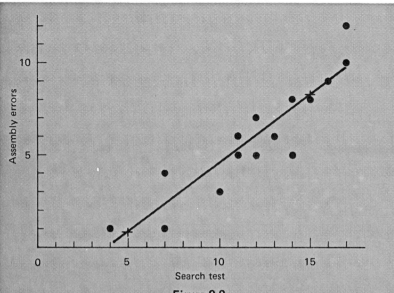

Figure 9-9
Scattergram and regression line for assembly line performance.

To plot the regression equation on the scattergram of Figure 9-9 we need to choose a small and a large value of X and solve for Y'. Using X values of 5 and 15, we get

$$Y' = 0.74(5) - 2.88 = 3.70 - 2.88 = 0.82$$
$$Y' = 0.74(15) - 2.88 = 11.10 - 2.88 = 8.22$$

We then locate the points (5,0.82) and (15,8.22) on the graph and draw a straight line between them to obtain the regression line.

John Jones applies for a job as inspector and makes 9 errors on the search test. What would be our prediction of his performance on the assembly line?

$$Y' = 0.74(9) - 2.88 = 6.66 - 2.88 = 3.78$$

How accurate is our predicted score? To set up a confidence interval around a predicted Y' score of 3.78, we calculate the standard error of estimate:

$$s_E = S_Y\sqrt{1 - r^2} = 3.01\sqrt{1 - (.91)^2}$$
$$= 3.01\sqrt{1 - .83} = 3.01\sqrt{.17}$$
$$= 3.01(0.41) = 1.23$$

The confidence interval would be calculated as follows:

$$Y' \pm 1s_E = 3.78 \pm 1.23$$
$$= 2.55 \text{ to } 5.01$$

and we would conclude that $p = .68$ that his actual error performance would be between 2.55 and 5.01.

Study Questions

1. How do you predict Y from X when all the points on the scatter-gram are not on a straight line?
2. What is meant by a *predicted value* of Y?
3. What quantities are needed to predict Y from a given value of X?
4. What is a regression equation?
5. What is the relationship between the size of the correlation and prediction accuracy?
6. What is the standard error of estimate?
7. A study showed a relationship between clerical aptitude (X) and typing speed (Y). The 68% confidence interval of Y' for an aptitude score of 27 was 57.2 to 69.3. What does this mean?
8. What are the assumptions for the Pearson r?

Exercises

1. A correlational study resulted in the following data. Calculate the regression equation.

X	Y
$\bar{X} = 71.5$	$\bar{Y} = 12.2$
$S_X = 8.4$	$S_Y = 2.4$

$$r = .70$$

2. Use the regression equation calculated in exercise 1 to predict the Y score of a person who has an X score of 68.
3. Calculate the standard error of estimate for the data in exercise 1. Use your standard error to calculate the 68% confidence interval for the predicted Y you calculated in exercise 2.
4. In **Sample Problem #1** in Chapter 8, data were shown representing pairs of scores on two different creativity tests. Calculations yielded the following:

Test X	Test Y
$\bar{X} = 7.73$	$\bar{Y} = 7.47$

$$S_X = 4.03 \qquad\qquad S_Y = 2.24$$

$$r = .79$$

a. Plot a scattergram for the pairs of scores on graph paper.
b. Calculate the regression equation and plot it on the scattergram.
c. Julie Johnson scores 4 on Text X. Use the regression equation to predict her score on Test Y.
d. Calculate the 68% confidence interval for her predicted score.

5. An investigator wants to know if there is any relationship between manual dexterity (as shown by a pursuit rotor) and a steadiness test. Performance on the pursuit rotor is given by time on target in seconds (X) during a 20-second trial. Performance on the steadiness test is the length of time in seconds that the subject can hold a stylus in an aperture before touching the side of the box (Y). Twenty volunteers give the following results:

X	Y	X	Y
12	9	2	4
11	8	8	10
17	11	13	10
11	9	2	5
12	12	14	12
8	7	5	9
15	11	10	8
9	7	4	8
7	6	10	11
11	10	13	9

a. Calculate the Pearson r for these data (use machine formulas for S_X, S_Y, and r).
b. Plot a scattergram of the data on a sheet of graph paper.
c. Test the calculated r for significance.
d. Calculate the regression equation and plot the line on the scattergram.
e. Frank is tested on the pursuit rotor and scores 14. What is our best prediction for his performance on the steadiness test?
f. Calculate the 68% confidence interval for Frank's predicted score.

10 The Significance of the Difference between Means

Much of the activity of the researcher in education and the behavioral sciences is directed at comparing the performance of two groups. A sampling of recent research studies might show investigations of differences between men and women on verbal ability, differences between only children and children from large families on introversion, and differences between college GPA's of marijuana users and those of marijuana non-users. Whenever such differences are established, that is, verified by a number of independent investigators, they become part of our body of scientific knowledge and finally find their place in books on individual differences, child psychology, or drug abuse.

Sampling Error or Real Difference?

Verification by the independent work of other researchers is an important part of the scientific method, but how does a single investigator determine whether or not he has found a real difference in the performance of two groups? For example, suppose that our researcher is trying to see if there is a difference in word comprehension between fifth-grade boys and girls. Using random samples and an appropriate comprehension test, he comes up with the following mean scores (number of words correctly identified):

Boys   Girls

$\overline{X} = 49.21$ $\overline{X} = 49.23$

We certainly would agree that there appears to be no difference between boys and girls on word comprehension. The slight difference we do observe (obviously 49.21 and 49.23 *are* different) is attributed to "chance" or "sampling error."

But what if he had obtained the following?

Boys   Girls

$\overline{X} = 49.21$ $\overline{X} = 49.27$

We would probably still conclude that the .06 difference between the two means was due to sampling error and there basically was no difference between boys and girls on word comprehension.

But just how far apart must the two means be before we can say that there is a *real* difference between the two groups? 49.21 and 49.50? 49.21 and 52.00? 49.21 and 55.00? We are faced with the same dilemma that we noted in the ESP example of **Note 7-2**. At what point do we draw the line between a sampling error and a real difference?

To help us answer this question we will have to resort to the sampling distribution, a concept first introduced in Chapter 7. Our ultimate goal is to derive a technique that will enable us to make a probability statement regarding sampling error, just as we did in Chapter 7.

The Sampling Distribution of Differences between Pairs of Means

As an example, let us say that we are interested in seeing if there is any difference between the mathematical ability of college chemistry majors and that of college biology majors. Using appropriate sampling techniques, we select a sample of 100 chemistry majors and 100 biology majors, administer a standardized mathematical aptitude test, and obtain the following results:

Chemistry   Biology

$\overline{X}_1 = 72.9$ $\overline{X}_2 = 68.4$

The obtained difference in the means of the two groups is 72.9 − 68.4 = 4.5, and we would like to know if this indicates a real superiority in mathematical ability on the part of chemistry majors, or if it is simply the result of sampling error.

At this point we do a rather strange thing. We begin by assuming that there is *no difference* in the means of the populations from which our two samples were drawn. In other words, we assume that the mean mathematical ability of the population of chemistry majors is the same as the mean mathematical ability of the population of biology majors. If μ_1 is the mean ability of the population of chemistry majors and μ_2 is the mean ability of the population of biology majors, we are assuming that $\mu_1 = \mu_2$, or $\mu_1 - \mu_2 = 0$. *This statement is called a null hypothesis,* and it simply states that there is no difference between the means of the two populations from which we drew our two samples.

If this null hypothesis is true and $\mu_1 - \mu_2 = 0$, then our obtained difference of 4.5 is just sampling error. But to see if our assumption that $\mu_1 - \mu_2 = 0$ is true, let us indulge in another bit of fancy, just as we did in Chapter 7. We will conduct a hypothetical exercise by continuing to take pairs of samples and finding the differences (D) in their means. Keeping track of these pairs, we might get the results shown below (note that we always subtract the biology mean from the chemistry mean to obtain D):

	Chemistry	Biology	D
Sample 1	73.5	73.9	−0.4
Sample 2	74.6	72.1	2.5
Sample 3	72.8	71.3	1.5
Sample 4	73.4	74.6	−1.2
Sample 5	72.9	72.9	0

and so on.

As we ran this hypothetical exercise (all the while assuming a null hypothesis, $\mu_1 - \mu_2 = 0$), we would note that some of the differences were negative, some were positive, and most would be fairly close to 0.

If we continued to do this for an *infinite* number of pairs of samples, the following would occur:

1. A batch of differences, called a *sampling distribution of differences between means*, would result.
2. The mean of this sampling distribution $\bar{D}_{\bar{x}}$ (say "mean of the differences"), would be 0.
3. The batch of differences would be normally distributed around the mean of the distribution, $\bar{D}_{\bar{x}}$, with a standard deviation of $\sqrt{\sigma_{\bar{x}_1}^2 + \sigma_{\bar{x}_2}^2}$.

Let us take a closer look at these three results.

Sampling distribution of differences between means. Even though we are assuming that the two populations have equal means, we do not expect that the sample drawn from one population will have a mean exactly identical to the mean of the sample drawn from the second population. We have grown accustomed to sampling error as a fact of life, and we would take for granted that in pairs of means, $\overline{X}_1$ will sometimes be greater than $\overline{X}_2$, and $\overline{X}_2$ will sometimes be greater than $\overline{X}_1$. This, of course, results in a distribution of differences, of which some will be negative and some positive.

The mean of the differences. The mean of this distribution of differences, $\overline{D}_{\overline{X}}$, will be 0 under our assumption that $\mu_1 - \mu_2 = 0$. As indicated in the last paragraph, we expect that some differences will be negative and others positive, with the net effect being a mean that is exactly 0.

Normal sampling distribution. Since the distribution of differences is normal, we can use the characteristics of the normal curve to show, for example, that

1. 68.26% of all the differences would fall between -1 and 1 standard deviation from the mean, $\overline{D}_{\overline{X}}$.
2. 95% of all the differences would fall between -1.96 and 1.96 standard deviations from the mean, $\overline{D}_{\overline{X}}$.
3. 99% of all the differences would fall between -2.58 and 2.58 standard deviations from the mean, $\overline{D}_{\overline{X}}$.

And, similarly, the probability statements we made concerning the normal curve would apply to this sampling distribution as well; for example:

1. $p = .68$ that any difference would fall between $\overline{D}_{\overline{X}} \pm 1$ standard deviation.
2. $p = .95$ that any difference would fall between $\overline{D}_{\overline{X}} \pm 1.96$ standard deviations.
3. $p = .05$ that any difference would fall *outside* the same interval, $\overline{D}_{\overline{X}} \pm 1.96$ standard deviations.

With these probability statements in mind, let us get back to our original problem—that of deciding whether our obtained difference of 4.5 between the mean mathematical ability of chemistry and biology majors is simply due to sampling error. The first step in determining if it *is* in fact due to sampling error is to establish *where* in the sampling distribution of differences our obtained difference is located. Figure 10-1 shows this hypothetical sampling distribution, which, under the null hypothesis of $\mu_1 - \mu_2 = 0$, has a mean, $\overline{D}_{\overline{X}}$, of 0.

Using the same logic that was introduced in Chapter 7, we need only find *where* in the sampling distribution of differences our

obtained difference falls. If it is located toward the center of the distribution (i.e., between -1.96 and 1.96 standard deviations from the
mean), we say that our obtained difference was caused by sampling
error. On the other hand, if our difference is so large that it falls way
out in either tail of the distribution (labeled "Reject" in Figure 10-1), we
know that it would be an extremely rare occurrence, and we would
wonder whether our difference is really due to sampling error after
all.

The procedure is simple indeed. We need only calculate the z
score for our difference and find its location in the sampling distribution
of differences, as in Figure 10-1. Under the null hypothesis that $\mu_1 -
\mu_2 = 0$, this sampling distribution of differences has $\bar{D}_{\bar{x}} = 0$. Now if the
z score of our difference were, for example, 1.23 or -0.67, we would
say that our difference of 4.5 points between the mean mathematical
ability of chemistry and biology majors could possibly be due to
sampling error. However, if the z score of our difference were, for
example, 1.98 or -2.37, we would say that it is a rare occurrence in a
distribution that has $\bar{D}_{\bar{x}} = 0$ and would conclude that μ_1 is not equal
to μ_2 (or $\mu_1 - \mu_2 \neq 0$), $\bar{D}_{\bar{x}}$ is not 0, and our obtained difference is a
real difference and not sampling error.

Since that last sentence above is crucial to understanding this
chapter, let us briefly examine the concepts involved by referring to
Figure 10-1.

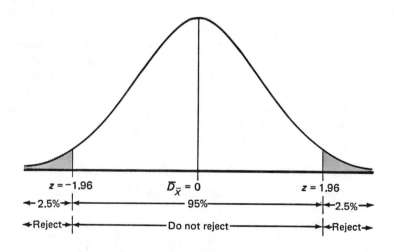

Figure 10-1
Sampling distribution of differences between means
assuming the null hypothesis ($\mu_1 - \mu_2 = 0$).

1. If there is no difference in the populations from which the samples came, the probability that any obtained difference would deviate by ±1.96 standard deviations or more is .05. (Remember that only 5% of the differences are in the two tails of the distribution beyond ±1.96 standard deviations.) These differences are in the shaded portions of Figure 10-1.

2. If, in fact, our obtained difference falls in the *unshaded* portion of the distribution, that is, between −1.96 and 1.96 in Figure 10-1, we say that our difference could be due to sampling error. Since differences with z scores between −1.96 and 1.96 standard deviations happen 95% of the time just by sampling error, we have no reason to believe that our difference is anything but sampling error. We say that the difference is not significant.

3. However, if our obtained difference falls in the region of ±1.96 standard deviations or more (the shaded portions of Figure 10-1 labeled "Reject"), we are faced with two possibilities.

   a. $\bar{D}_{\bar{x}}$ really is 0, and our difference is one of those rare occurrences that happen 5% of the time or less due to sampling error.

   b. $\bar{D}_{\bar{x}}$ is *not* 0, but some other value, and our difference tells us that there is a real difference between the two populations from which we drew our samples. In this example, we would say that the chemistry majors are higher in mathematical ability than biology majors.

4. In light of the statistical conventions mentioned in Chapter 7, we will conclude that any difference that happens 5% of the time or less by sampling error, that is, $p \leq .05$ (read "probability is equal to or less than .05"), is not due to chance at all but represents a real difference. We say that the difference is significant at the .05 level, and we reject the null hypothesis ($\mu_1 - \mu_2 = 0$) in favor of $\mu_1 - \mu_2 \neq 0$.

Standard Error of the Difference between Means

In order to know where our obtained difference is located in the hypothetical sampling distribution of differences, we need to know the standard deviation of this distribution. We can then convert our difference to a z score and locate it precisely in the sampling distribution.

The standard deviation of this sampling distribution is called *the standard error of the difference between means,* and it is denoted by the symbol $\sigma_{D_{\bar{x}}}$. This statistic is to be interpreted as our ordinary, garden variety standard deviation. For example, we know that 95% of the differences fall between -1.96 and 1.96 standard errors of the difference, or between $\bar{D}_{\bar{X}} \pm 1.96\sigma_{D_{\bar{X}}}$.

When we calculate a z score for the sampling distribution of differences, we must modify the usual z score formula, $z = (X - \bar{X})/S$. The "score" of X is now the difference, or $\bar{X}_1 - \bar{X}_2$. The mean of the sampling distribution is now $\bar{D}_{\bar{X}}$, but, as you have seen, $\bar{D}_{\bar{X}} = 0$ under our assumption of the null hypothesis. And the standard deviation of the sampling distribution is now the standard error of the difference, $\sigma_{D_{\bar{X}}}$. So our new formula for calculating a z score in a sampling distribution of differences is

$$z = \frac{(\bar{X}_1 - \bar{X}_2) - 0}{\sigma_{D_{\bar{X}}}} \tag{10-1}$$

Let us leave the computation of $\sigma_{D_{\bar{X}}}$ for a later section and examine now the use of $\sigma_{D_{\bar{X}}}$ in determining the significance of an obtained difference in the following hypothetical example. Suppose that in our study of the mathematical ability of chemistry and biology majors, we had obtained the following results.

Chemistry   *Biology*

$\bar{X}_1 = 72.6$ $\bar{X}_2 = 67.6$

$\sigma_{D_{\bar{X}}} = 5.0$

Is this difference between the means due to sampling error, or is it such a rare occurrence that we would suspect a real difference in the mathematical ability of the two groups? Our first step is to calculate a z score for the difference, which would be

$$z = \frac{(\bar{X}_1 - \bar{X}_2) - 0}{\sigma_{D_{\bar{X}}}} = \frac{72.6 - 67.6}{5} = \frac{5}{5} = 1.0$$

Since by sampling error it is just as easy to get $\bar{X}_2$ greater than $\bar{X}_1$, we will consider both tails of the curve and ask the question "What is the probability of obtaining a difference of 5 points just by sampling error from a sampling distribution whose mean is 0?" As we just noted, a difference of 5 points results in a z score of 1 (or -1 if $\bar{X}_2$ is greater than $\bar{X}_1$), and we can locate a difference of 5 points in the sampling distribution of differences as shown in Figure 10-2A. By using Table B we would see that 68.26% of the differences would fall between $-1z$ and $1z$, and 31.74% of the differences would result in z scores larger than 1, if the null hypothesis is true ($\mu_1 - \mu_2 = 0$, or $\bar{D}_{\bar{X}} = 0$). Converting the percentages to probabilities, we see that $p = .3174$ that *any* obtained difference would deviate by 5 points or more just by

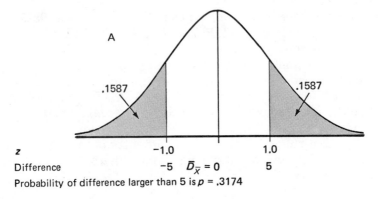

A

.1587   .1587

z   −1.0   1.0
Difference   −5 $\bar{D}_{\bar{X}} = 0$ 5
Probability of difference larger than 5 is $p = .3174$

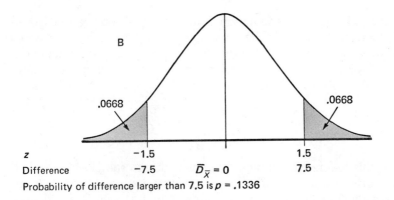

B

.0668   .0668

z   −1.5   1.5
Difference   −7.5 $\bar{D}_{\bar{X}} = 0$ 7.5
Probability of difference larger than 7.5 is $p = .1336$

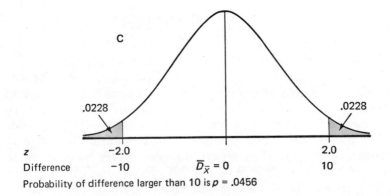

C

.0228   .0228

z   −2.0   2.0
Difference   −10 $\bar{D}_{\bar{X}} = 0$ 10
Probability of difference larger than 10 is $p = .0456$

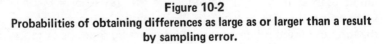

Figure 10-2
**Probabilities of obtaining differences as large as or larger than a result
by sampling error.**

sampling error. Since anything that happens 32% of the time is hardly a "rare occurrence," we conclude that the difference of 5 points in mathematical ability between chemistry and biology majors is possibly just due to sampling error.

But suppose, instead, that we had obtained the following results, shown graphically in Figure 10-2B.

$$\text{Chemistry} \qquad \text{Biology}$$
$$\bar{X}_1 = 72.6 \qquad \bar{X}_2 = 65.1$$
$$\sigma_{D\bar{X}} = 5.0$$
$$z = \frac{(\bar{X}_1 - \bar{X}_2) - 0}{\sigma_{D\bar{X}}} = \frac{72.6 - 65.1}{5} = \frac{7.5}{5} = 1.5$$

Our calculations show that our obtained difference of 7.5 between the two means results in a z score of 1.5. And what is the probability of obtaining a difference this large or larger just by sampling error from a sampling distribution whose mean is 0? By referring to Figure 10-2B and using Table B, we see that differences as large as 7.5 and larger will happen only 13.36% of the time just by sampling error, or $p = .1336$ that *any* obtained difference will be that large or larger. Since something that happens 13% of the time just by chance is not really a "rare occurrence," we would state that a difference of 7.5 points between the means of the two groups may simply be due to sampling error. But note that if the null hypothesis is *really* true ($\mu_1 - \mu_2 = 0$, or $\bar{D}_X = 0$) a difference as large as 7.5 is less likely to occur just by chance than is a difference of 5.0 (13% vs. 32%).

As a final example, let us suppose that we had obtained the following results on the mathematical ability of chemistry and biology majors.

$$\text{Chemistry} \qquad \text{Biology}$$
$$\bar{X}_1 = 72.6 \qquad \bar{X}_2 = 62.6$$
$$\sigma_{D\bar{X}} = 5.0$$
$$z = \frac{(\bar{X}_1 - \bar{X}_2) - 0}{\sigma_{D\bar{X}}} = \frac{72.6 - 62.6}{5} = \frac{10}{5} = 2$$

What is the probability of obtaining a difference of 10 points or more just by sampling error? Figure 10-2C and Table B in Appendix 2 show that we expect only 4.56% of the differences to be 10 points or more, if the null hypothesis that $\mu_1 - \mu_2 = 0$ is true. In other words, less than 5% of the differences would be this large or larger, so $p < .05$ that *any* obtained difference would be this large or larger. Since this is a relatively rare occurrence, we reject the null hypothesis that $\bar{D}_{\bar{x}}$ is really 0 and state that there is a significant difference between the average mathematical ability of the population of chemistry majors and that of the population of biology majors.

In summary, the steps involved in determining the significance of a difference are:

1. Assume the null hypothesis—that the means of the two populations from which the samples are drawn are equal ($\mu_1 = \mu_2$, or $\mu_1 - \mu_2 = 0$).
2. Calculate the z score for your obtained difference between the means of the two samples and locate it in the sampling distribution of differences whose mean, $\bar{D}_{\bar{x}}$, is 0.
3. If the resulting z score falls between $\bar{D}_{\bar{x}} \pm 1.96\sigma_{D_{\bar{x}}}$, assume that the difference in sample means is due to sampling error.
4. If the resulting z score falls *outside* the interval $\bar{D}_{\bar{x}} \pm 1.96\sigma_{D_{\bar{x}}}$, reject the null hypothesis, assume that $\mu_1 - \mu_2$ is *not* 0, and state that your obtained difference is significant at the .05 level.

Calculating the Standard Error of the Difference between Means

The standard error of the difference between means, as we noted earlier, is the standard deviation of the hypothetical sampling distribution of differences, and it is given by the following formula:

$$\sigma_{D\bar{X}} = \sqrt{\ \sigma_{\bar{X}_1}{}^2 + \sigma_{\bar{X}_2}{}^2} \tag{10-2}$$

where $\sigma_{D\bar{X}}$ is the standard error of the difference between means,
$\sigma_{\bar{X}_1}$ is the standard error of the mean of one distribution,
$\sigma_{\bar{X}_2}$ is the standard error of the mean of the other distribution.

However, we noted in Chapter 7 that the standard error of the mean, $\sigma_{\bar{X}}$, is calculated from the *population* standard deviation, so formula 10-2 is of little value to us since we rarely know the value of σ. As a result, we must have a formula for the standard error of the difference that permits us to use the standard deviations of our samples.[1] The formula which we shall use extensively is:

$$s_{D\bar{X}} = \sqrt{\frac{N_1 S_1{}^2 + N_2 S_2{}^2}{N_1 + N_2 - 2} \left(\frac{1}{N_1} + \frac{1}{N_2}\right)} \tag{10-3}$$

---

[1]Note that the symbol for the standard error of the difference is $\sigma_{D\bar{X}}$ when the standard error of the mean, $\sigma_{\bar{X}}$, is calculated from the population σ. When it is calculated from the sample standard deviation, S, we will use the symbol, $s_{D\bar{X}}$.

where S_1 is the standard deviation of the first sample,
$\quad\quad S_2$ is the standard deviation of the second sample,
$\quad\quad N_1$ and N_2 are the sizes of the respective samples.

Testing for Significance with the t Test

We must note that $s_{D_{\bar{X}}}$ is an *estimate* of $\sigma_{D_{\bar{X}}}$, and because $s_{D_{\bar{X}}}$ is based on the standard deviations of the samples, it is subject to sampling error. When the standard deviations of the populations are not known (so $\sigma_{D_{\bar{X}}}$ cannot be calculated), the normal distribution can no longer be used, which, of course, means that the z score values of 1.96 and 2.58 cannot automatically be used to describe the region of rejection in the tails of the distribution.

So, instead of the normal distribution with the usual z values, we use what is called the t distribution, and the statistical procedure is known as the t test. We calculate a t value and locate its position in the t distribution, just as we did earlier for the z score. The procedure is the same as before, but we no longer use 1.96 and 2.58 as dividing lines for acceptance or rejection of the null hypothesis. The t statistic, in fact, has the same formula as the z score used earlier, except the denominator is now $s_{D_{\bar{X}}}$.

$$t = \frac{(\bar{X}_1 - \bar{X}_2) - 0}{s_{D_{\bar{X}}}} \quad\quad\quad \textbf{(10-4)}$$

The t Distribution

The t distribution (sometimes called "Student's t," after W. S. Gossett, who published under the pseudonym "Student") looks very much like the normal curve, except that the tails for the t distribution are higher and we must go farther out to find the t values that mark off the 5% and 1% regions in the distribution. This is illustrated graphically in Figure 10-3.

Note that the normal curve has 95% of its area between the usual z scores of -1.96 and 1.96 while the t distribution shown in Figure 10-3 for a combined sample size of 6 has 95% of its area between -2.78 and 2.78. As the sample size gets larger, the t distribution looks more and more like the normal curve, and, when the N of the combined samples is about 30, the curves are approximately identical. What this means, of course, is that, as the size of your samples gets smaller, you need a larger t value to reject the null hypothesis.

Since the normal curve and the t distribution are *exactly* identical only with an *infinitely large* sample size, it has become conventional

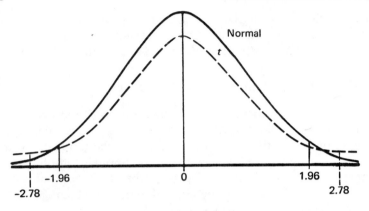

Figure 10-3
Comparison of a normal distribution and a *t* distribution (*N* = 6)
showing the 95% limits for each distribution.

always to use the *t* distribution, *regardless of sample size*. This means that we can ignore the *z* values of 1.96 and 2.58 in favor of a specific *t* value which is determined by the size of our samples or, more properly, the *degrees of freedom* in our samples.

The Degrees of Freedom (df) Concept

Before we can look at the different *t* distributions, we must become acquainted, at least superficially, with a concept known as *degrees of freedom*. Although a knowledge of advanced statistical theory is necessary to completely understand this concept, we can say that the degrees of freedom in a sample is *the number of observations that are free to vary.*

For example, if we put a restriction on a set of five numbers, such that $\Sigma X = 12$, we may pick any *four* numbers we like, but the *fifth* one is not free to vary, since it, added to the others, must meet the requirement of $\Sigma X = 12$. If we choose 3, 2, 4, and 7, we *must* use -4 as the fifth number in order to meet this requirement, since $3 + 2 + 4 + 7 = 16$ and only a -4 would yield $\Sigma X = 12$. In this case we have $N - 1$ degrees of freedom, since only one observation is restricted in meeting the requirement. Stated more formally, $df = N - 1$.

In the calculation of a *t* test, each of the two samples has $N - 1$ degrees of freedom. This means that the total *df* for *both* samples would be $(N_1 - 1) + (N_2 - 1)$, which would sum to $N_1 + N_2 - 2$. Thus, the total *df* for our samples is 2 less than the combined sample size. For example, if we had 20 students in one group and 10 students in the second group, our total *df* would be $(20 - 1) + (10 - 1) = 19 + 9 = 28$.

Using the t Table

As we noticed earlier, there is a different *t* distribution for every sample size. This would mean that we could have a table of *t* values similar to a normal curve table, for every sample size from 2 to infinity! In the interest of brevity, we do not usually consider all areas of the curve, but only those points that indicate the usual significance levels, such as .05, .01, and .001. Table E in Appendix 2 lists the *t* values which must be equaled or exceeded for these usual significance levels for various sample sizes (in terms of degrees of freedom). Note that the table gives both one-tailed and two-tailed values. Let us consider for now only the two-tailed values. We will interpret the one-tailed values later on in the chapter.

For the example above, with 28 degrees of freedom, how large must our *t* value be in order to be significant at the .05 level? From Table E, we see that for a *df* of 28, the tabled value of *t* is 2.048. We know that our calculated *t* must be at least 2.048 before we can reject the null hypothesis at the .05 level.

As another example, suppose that you had 7 students in one group and 12 in a second group. How large would your *t* value have to be in order for it to be significant at the .01 level? Again, from Table E we see that for 17 degrees of freedom ($df = 6 + 11$), we would need a *t* of at least 2.898 in order to reject the null hypothesis at the .01 level.

Calculating the t Test

While the formula for $s_{D\bar{X}}$ looks somewhat complicated, it is relatively easy to use in practice since it requires only the standard deviations of the samples and the N of each sample. Table 10-1 shows the calculation of $s_{D\bar{X}}$ and its use in determining the significance of a difference between the tested I.Q.'s of seventh-grade girls and boys.

Following the four steps listed earlier, we note in the example of Table 10-1 that a null hypothesis would state that the mean I.Q. for a population of seventh-grade boys is the same as the population mean for seventh-grade girls, or $\mu_1 - \mu_2 = 0$. A sample of 50 boys and 40 girls from these two populations shows a mean difference of $108.6 - 110.2 = -1.6$.

After calculating *t* to be -0.52, we consult Table E for 88 degrees of freedom. There are no values listed between $df = 80$ and $df = 90$, so we choose the value for 80 – the more conservative value – and note that a *t* value of ± 1.990 marks off the 5% region of rejection.

Table 10-1
Testing for Significant Differences in Mean I.Q. for Boys and Girls

Boys	Girls
$\bar{X}_1$ = 108.6	$\bar{X}_2$ = 110.2
S_1 = 14.8	S_2 = 13.9
N = 50	N = 40

$$s_{D_{\bar{X}}} = \sqrt{\frac{N_1 S_1{}^2 + N_2 S_2{}^2}{N_1 + N_2 - 2}\left(\frac{1}{N_1} + \frac{1}{N_2}\right)}$$

$$= \sqrt{\frac{50\,(14.8)^2 + 40(13.9)^2}{50 + 40 - 2}\left(\frac{1}{50} + \frac{1}{40}\right)}$$

$$= \sqrt{\frac{10{,}952 + 7{,}728.4}{88}\,(0.02 + 0.025)}$$

$$= \sqrt{212.28(0.045)}$$

$$= \sqrt{9.5526}$$

$$s_{D_{\bar{X}}} = 3.09$$

$$t = \frac{(\bar{X}_1 - \bar{X}_2) - 0}{s_{D_{\bar{X}}}} = \frac{108.6 - 110.2}{3.09} = \frac{-1.6}{3.09} = -0.52$$

t_{05}, df = 80, is 1.990

Not significant, $p > .05$

Since our calculated value of -0.52 is well within the central region (as shown in Figure 10-4), it is hardly a "rare occurrence" and we have no reason to believe that the null hypothesis should be rejected. We pronounce the obtained difference not significant, since the probability is greater than .05 ($p > .05$) that this could happen by sampling error alone.

Table 10-1 illustrated a typical research study, with the statistical logic behind the decision to conclude that an observed difference was not significant. Let us consider a recent study that led the investigators to conclude that the differences were significant. The mean GPA was calculated for a sample of 30 marijuana users and 30 non-users on a college campus. The calculations are shown in Table 10-2.

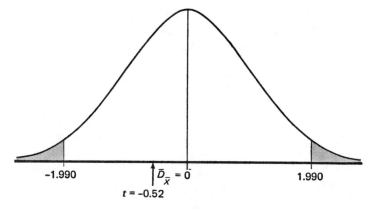

Figure 10-4
Nonsignificant difference in I.Q. scores of seventh-grade boys and
girls, with a *t* of –0.52.

In analyzing the data of Table 10-2, we would first state a null hypothesis, that the mean college GPA for the population of marijuana users would be the same as the population mean for non-users, $\mu_1 - \mu_2 = 0$. A sample of 30 marijuana users and 30 non-users from these two populations shows a mean difference in college GPA of $3.05 - 2.75 = 0.30$.

After calculating a *t* of 2.31, we note from Table E that ±2.009 marks off the 5% region of rejection (we are again conservative and use the tabled value for *df* = 50, since the value for *df* = 58 is not listed). Note that our calculated *t* of 2.31 is outside the interval, as shown in Figure 10-5. Since this is a rare occurrence, happening less than 5% of the time by sampling error (*p* < .05), we conclude that it is not likely that $\mu_1 - \mu_2 = 0$. We reject this null hypothesis in favor of $\mu_1 - \mu_2 \neq 0$ and say that there is a significant difference in the grade-point averages of marijuana users and non-users.

Significance Levels

In the preceding discussion and in the examples of Tables 10-1 and 10-2, we have seen that any difference occurring 5% of the time or less through sampling error is labeled a "significant" difference. Our concluding statement is that the difference is "significant at the .05 level," or "the null hypothesis is rejected at the .05 level." As you saw in Chapter 7, there is nothing magic about the 5% point: it is simply an arbitrary designation that has become a convention or rule of thumb. Presumably, the 6% or 4% levels could be similarly justified.

Table 10-2
Testing for Significant Differences in College GPA
among Marijuana Users and Non-Users

Non-users	*Users*
$\bar{X}_1$ = 3.05	$\bar{X}_2$ = 2.75
S_1 = 0.60	S_2 = 0.40
N_1 = 30	N_2 = 30

$$s_{D\bar{X}} = \sqrt{\frac{N_1S_1^2 + N_2S_2^2}{N_1 + N_2 - 2}\left(\frac{1}{N_1} + \frac{1}{N_2}\right)}$$

$$= \sqrt{\frac{30(0.60)^2 + 30(0.40)^2}{30 + 30 - 2}\left(\frac{1}{30} + \frac{1}{30}\right)}$$

$$= \sqrt{\frac{10.8 + 4.8}{58}(0.067)}$$

$$= \sqrt{0.2690 \; (0.067)}$$

$$= \sqrt{0.018}$$

$$s_{D\bar{X}} = 0.13$$

$$t = \frac{(\bar{X}_1 - \bar{X}_2) - 0}{s_{D\bar{X}}} = \frac{3.05 - 2.75}{0.13} = \frac{0.30}{0.13} = 2.31$$

t_{05}, df = 50, is 2.009

Significant, $p < .05$

However, many statisticians feel that there should be some way to indicate just how rare a rare occurrence is under the null hypothesis, so the .01 level and .001 level have been added to the familiar .05 level. If a difference is significant at the .01 level, we are saying that the obtained difference would happen by sampling error 1% of the time or less. Similarly, if a difference is stated as significant at the .001 level, the obtained difference would happen by sampling error 0.1% of the time or less. To summarize:

   1. If a difference would happen 5% of the time or less by sampling error but is not large enough so that it reaches the 1% level, we

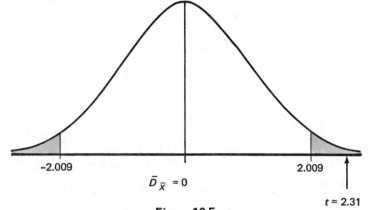

-2.009

$\bar{D}_{\bar{X}} = 0$

2.009

$t = 2.31$

Figure 10-5
Significant difference in college GPA of marijuana users and
non-users with a *t* of 2.31.

state that the difference is significant at the .05 level, or $p \leqslant$ .05 that the obtained difference would happen by sampling error, or $.05 > p > .01$ (probability of the obtained difference happening by sampling error is between .05 and .01).

2. If a difference would happen 1% of the time or less by sampling error but is not large enough so that it reaches the 0.1% level, we state that the difference is significant at the .01 level, or $p \leqslant .01$ that the difference would happen by sampling error, or $.01 > p > .001$.

3. If a difference would happen 0.1% of the time or less by sampling error, we state that the difference is significant at the .001 level, or $p \leqslant .001$.

We will have occasion in a later section to examine these various significance levels in greater detail and to show how they are involved in making decisions regarding sampling error.

Note 10-1
Statistical Significance vs. Practical Significance

When we use the term *significant difference*, our definition of *significant* is just as we have explored in the last few pages – it is simply a statement of an arbitrarily chosen probability level.

However, a statistically significant difference may have no social or practical significance whatsoever. As an example, a colleague of mine studying peripheral vision noted that some of his subjects had faster reaction times to stimuli on the left side of their visual field on Mondays and Tuesdays, while other subjects had faster reactions in their right visual field during the latter part of the week. The difference was on the order of 1 millisecond (0.001 seconds) and was significant at the .05 level! While such individual differences may be of academic interest, the practical importance of a daily variation of 1 millisecond applied to everyday situations seems somewhat trivial. We must distinguish, then, between a trival difference and one that has practical significance.

The Null Hypothesis and Other Hypotheses

We have pursued the simplest approach in testing the null hypothesis: we eventually conclude that either $\mu_1 - \mu_2 = 0$ or that $\mu_1 - \mu_2 \neq 0$. These statements are sometimes designated as H_0 for the null hypothesis and H_A for the alternate hypothesis. In other words, we assume H_0, $\mu_1 - \mu_2 = 0$, but, if the observed difference between the sample means is large enough to be significant, we reject H_0 in favor of H_A.

It is a common error to confuse the alternate hypothesis ($\mu_1 - \mu_2 \neq 0$) with a researcher's *experimental* hypothesis. An important maxim in statistical decision making is that *the rejection of the null hypothesis does not necessarily make an experimental hypothesis true*. For example, a researcher might hypothesize that elementary school pupils who had attended nursery school would get better grades than those who had not attended nursery school, due to the socializing influence of the nursery school setting.

The researcher first assumes the null hypothesis that there is no difference between the academic performance of both groups and then gathers data and runs a *t* test. If there is a significant difference between the two groups, the researcher can conclude only that $\mu_1 - \mu_2 \neq 0$. He cannot say, for example, that the children with a nursery school background get better grades because they are more conforming, or more classroom oriented, or more socially adjusted, or whatever, on the basis of the statistical test alone. The statistical procedure allows him only to reject the null hypothesis, since such a decision is based on the probability of a difference occurring by sampling error. The researcher cannot go any farther than that. He cannot use his approach to prove why a difference exists.

Assumptions Underlying the t Test

We noted in Chapter 9 that there were certain restrictions or assumptions about the data that were necessary before a Pearson r could be interpreted meaningfully. In a similar fashion, the t test has four restrictions that must be met before the t can be interpreted in the manner described in the preceding sections. These are:

1. The scores must be interval or ratio in nature.
2. The scores must be measures on random samples from the respective populations.
3. The populations from which the samples were drawn must be normally distributed.
4. The populations from which the samples were drawn must have approximately the same variability (homogeneity of variance).

Since these assumptions will be popping up in a number of other contexts, let us look at each one in some detail.

Interval or ratio data. Since means and standard deviations are calculated in the t test, the data must be at least interval in nature.

Random samples. The statistical theory underlying the t test rests heavily on an assumption of random sampling, and this assumption must be met.

Normally distributed populations. In most cases, this is a reasonable assumption, since we are fairly certain that the majority of psychological and physiological characteristics are normally distributed. Note that this is *not* the same as saying that the *samples* are normally distributed.

Homogeneity of variance. There are statistical techniques available to test the samples for homogeneity of variance, but these techniques are beyond the scope of this text. In a very rough way, we can "eyeball" the standard deviations, and, if one is more than twice as large as the other, we should question whether the homogeneity of variance assumption has been met.

In summarizing the four assumptions, we are happy to note that the t test will give fairly accurate results, even if these assumptions have been violated to a certain degree. The t test is extremely resistant to departures from normality and, to a lesser degree, departures from homogeneity of variance. If you are in doubt about whether you can run a t test on some data because these assumptions may not have been met, it may be possible to do so simply by requiring a more stringent significance level (.01 instead of .05, for example).

Note 10-2
The Origin of "Student's t Distribution"

In the early 1900's an Englishman by the name of W. S. Gossett was using sampling techniques to ensure quality control at a brewery. The typical sampling procedure involved using a normal curve distribution to set up a confidence interval for estimating the population mean, μ. This procedure required that the researcher take large samples in order to have a sample variance that was a reliable estimate of the population variance, σ^2. Presumably, Gossett tired of the tedious effort involved in taking large samples and developed the t distribution, which enabled the researcher to estimate μ with much smaller samples. He published his theory in 1908 under the pseudonym "Student," and the distribution he developed is still occasionally called "Student's t distribution."

Errors in Making Decisions: The Type I and Type II Errors

On several occasions, both in this chapter and in Chapter 7, we have examined in detail the problem of deciding whether a particular experimental result was due to sampling error or whether the observed difference between the sample means represented a *real* difference in the variables under study. We have noted that if a result could occur *by chance* 50% of the time, or 13%, or 6%, we will still attribute the results to sampling error. And, as was pointed out earlier, statisticians have conventionally used the 5% level as the cutting point; that is, if a certain result happens 5% of the time or less by chance, we will say that it is *not* sampling error but the result is a real one.

These statements should be very familiar to you by now, but let us look closely at the problems that arise when the researcher is confronted with decisions between sampling error and real results. Suppose that our researcher runs a study to see if there is any difference in reading proficiency between left-handers and right-handers. As usual, he assumes the null hypothesis ($\mu_1 - \mu_2 = 0$), gathers a sample of left- and right-handed school children, administers a reading proficiency test, and performs the necessary calculations. He now has to decide whether his findings are "significant."

Let us pause a moment to consider the choices confronting our researcher. As usual, he is faced with the two familiar possibilities: (1) there is no difference between left- and right-handers ($H_0: \mu_1 - \mu_2 = 0$ is true), and the obtained difference is one of those rare occurrences when a difference that large is due to sampling error, or (2) there is indeed a difference between left- and right-handers ($H_0: \mu_1 - \mu_2 = 0$ is *not* true).

If our researcher finds that his *t* value will occur 5% of the time or less just by sampling error, he will very likely choose (2) above and decide that there is a real difference between left- and right-handers, rejecting the null hypothesis. *But he could be wrong!* He just might have been unlucky enough to get one of those rare occurrences which happen 5% of the time or less even when the null hypothesis is true. If there is no difference between the means of the populations from which the samples were drawn, then $\mu_1 - \mu_2 = 0$ and he has made a mistake by calling his difference a significant one instead of sampling error. This mistake is called a *Type I error*. Formally defined, a Type I error is committed *if the null hypothesis is rejected when it actually is true.*

So, what is our researcher to do in order to avoid making a Type I error? In an earlier section, we noted that there are different significance levels, and a cautious, conservative researcher might very well demand that his *t* value be significant at the .01 level, or even the .001 level, in order to be more certain that he doesn't label as significant a difference that really is only sampling error.

But look what happens when he does this. Suppose he chooses (1) above and decides that his finding is due to sampling error—it may represent a *real* difference! That is to say, there may be a difference

Table 10-3
Decision Matrix for Rejecting or Not Rejecting H_0

	Decision on the Basis of Sampling	
	Reject H_0	Accept H_0
H_0 is TRUE in population	Type I error $p = \alpha$	correct
H_0 is FALSE in population	correct	Type II error $p = \beta$

between the means of the two populations which he has decided to attribute to sampling error. This error is called a *Type II error.* A Type II error is committed *if the null hypothesis is accepted when actually it is false.*

We obviously have a real dilemma here, because the more we try to avoid making a Type I error by demanding greater significance, the greater are the chances of our making a Type II error. And, if we scrupulously avoid the taint of a Type II error by not being quite so strict, the possibility of our making a Type I error is back again. Before looking at ways in which this problem is handled, let us review this complex decision process in the form of a *decision matrix* (shown in Table 10-3) and consider each of the four decision possibilities.

H_0 *is rejected when it is, in fact, true.* The upper left square of the matrix illustrates the Type I error, where the researcher decides that his *t* value is significant and rejects the null hypothesis when it really is true. The probability of making a Type I error is the same as the value of the significance level that the researcher chooses. (The Greek letter alpha, α, is used to indicate significance levels, so α can be .05, .01, .001, etc.) Thus, if $\alpha = .05$, for example, we say that the probability of a Type I error occurring is .05. A moment's reflection should show why this is true. Since 5% of the sampling distribution (with $\overline{D}_{\overline{x}} = 0$) is in the region of rejection when the researcher chooses $\alpha = .05$, if he were to label all differences as significant, he would be wrong 5% of the time (i.e., whenever the difference fell in this region). One thing must be noted: the probability of a Type I error is under the direct control of the researcher, since he is responsible for setting the significance level.

H_0 *is accepted when it is true.* The upper right square indicates a decision to accept H_0, which was a correct decision since H_0 is, in fact, true. We must be careful to note that a finding of nonsignificance does not *prove* that the null hypothesis is true. It is evidence, but it is not conclusive proof.

H_0 *is accepted when it is false.* The lower right square of the decision matrix illustrates the Type II error, where the researcher decides to accept the null hypothesis, when, in fact, the null hypothesis is false. The probability of making a Type II error is noted by the Greek letter beta, β. In an introductory text it is just not possible to go into the characteristics of β, but we should note that the relationship between α and β is not a simple one. However, it is true that as we decrease the probability of a Type I error we increase the probability of a Type II error.

H_0 *is rejected when it is false.* The lower left square indicates the correct decision to reject the null hypothesis when it is false. We gave only a passing comment to the other correct decision (accepting H_0 when it was true), but we need to devote more time to the correct rejection of the null hypothesis. The typical researcher is very much concerned with correct rejection of the null hypothesis, since she basically is seeking to establish significant relationships. In other words, if there is a difference between two variables out in the population, she wants to find it. Therefore, she wants to use a statistical test that is sensitive to these differences. *The ability of a test to reject the null hypothesis when it is false is called the "power" of a test.* Power (sometimes defined as $1 - \beta$) is a characteristic of any statistical test; the more power a statistical test has, the more likely it is to detect significant differences if they exist. So, all things being equal, a researcher will choose a statistical test that has the greatest amount of power. We will have occasion to examine other tests besides the *t* test in later chapters, and we will note the power of these tests.

Resolving the Sampling Error-Real Difference Dilemma

You have probably gathered by now that there is no easy way of determining whether an observed difference is sampling error or a real difference. But we can ask ourselves if we prefer a Type I error or a Type II error! Our choice of which error to risk is determined by the nature of the subject matter being studied.

On important theoretical issues, such as demonstrating the existence of ESP, we might wish to set our significance levels very low (α = .01 or .001). We do not want to risk our laboratory or scientific career by stating that we found some weird or bizarre result to be significant when it was really due to sampling error. In this instance we definitely prefer to avoid a Type I error (by reducing our α to .01 or .001) and to risk a Type II error.

If, on the other hand, a researcher is examining two poultry disinfectants for germ-killing ability and chicken farmers everywhere are in dire need of some kind of disinfectant, we do not really care very much if we pronounce brand A better than brand B. If we say that one is better than the other, when actually there is no difference, we are making a Type I error, but since some kind of disinfectant is sorely needed, no great problem arises from our error. Either brand A or brand B will do the job.

One very practical approach to the problem involves setting up a middle ground or buffer zone between sampling error and real differences. Guilford and Fruchter (1978) suggest that any difference that will occur by chance 1% of the time or less ($p \leq .01$) be called "significant" and any difference that happens by chance more than 10% of the time ($p > .10$) be labeled "not significant." Any result that is in between the .01 level and the .10 level should lead to a state of "suspended judgment," which demands repetition of the experiment and verification by other researchers. While such an approach has not been universally accepted, it has a lot to recommend it, and it may eventually become one of our statistical conventions.

One-tailed vs. Two-tailed Tests

The significance tests that we have discussed so far have all been *two-tailed* tests. This means that the investigator proposes a null hypothesis that $\mu_1 = \mu_2$, so, if he decides to reject the hypothesis, it may be that either $\mu_1 > \mu_2$ or $\mu_2 > \mu_1$. In other words, the null hypothesis will be rejected if the *t* value (or *z*, or other statistics to be discussed in future chapters) is either to the extreme left of the sampling distribution or to the extreme right. In Figure 10-1 you saw that the region of rejection at the .05 level was to the left of a *z* of -1.96 or to the right of a *z* of 1.96. Since both of the "tails" of the sampling distribution are involved in this decision, such an approach is called a *two-tailed* test. The null hypothesis states that $\mu_1 = \mu_2$, and the rejection of it leads us to accept the alternate hypothesis that $\mu_1 \neq \mu_2$. We are *not* stating the *direction* of the difference when we say that $\mu_1 \neq \mu_2$, only that there is a difference. If we are using the .05 level of significance, our *t* value is significant in a two-tailed test if it falls in either the top 2.5% or the bottom 2.5% of the sampling distribution of differences.

The One-tailed t Test

If an investigator predicts before collecting her data that μ_1 is greater than μ_2, the alternate hypothesis is not $\mu_1 \neq \mu_2$ but $\mu_1 > \mu_2$. Note that this not only states that there will be a difference but predicts the direction of the difference as well. Hence, it is sometimes called a *directional* hypothesis. Since our interest is in only those $\bar{X}_1 - \bar{X}_2$ differences that are positive, the region of rejection is now confined to the right end of the sampling distribution. This region of rejection is at one end of the sampling distribution only, and we have what is called a *one-tailed test* (as shown in Figure 10-6).

And when is an investigator able to predict that the difference, if it exists, will be only in one direction? The answer is not always that obvious, but in some cases a difference in the opposite direction would be virtually impossible because of prior information regarding physiology, developmental stages, maturation, or whatever. For example, if we were investigating the effect of vitamin C on the inci-

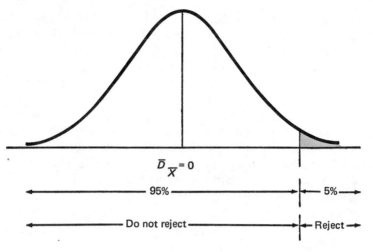

$$\bar{D}_{\bar{X}} = 0$$

95% ← → 5% →

← Do not reject → ← Reject →

Figure 10-6
Region of rejection for a one-tailed test.

dence of common colds, we would certainly have a directional hypothesis and would specify a one-tailed test. The alternate hypothesis would be $\mu_{\text{NoC}} > \mu_{\text{C}}$, that is, that those not taking vitamin C would have more colds than those taking the vitamin. It would seem unreasonable to hypothesize that $\mu_{\text{C}} > \mu_{\text{NoC}}$, that those taking the vitamin would have more colds! As a result, we are more efficient by specifying $\mu_1 > \mu_2$ as an alternate hypothesis instead of $\mu_1 \neq \mu_2$, since this approach places the region of rejection all in one tail of the sampling distribution of differences.

If a one-tailed approach is used, the *t* test is computed by *always subtracting the sample mean that was predicted to be the smaller from the sample mean that was predicted to be the larger*. In other words, the one-tailed test makes use of positive $\bar{X}_1 - \bar{X}_2$ differences only. In the two-tailed test it was immaterial whether we subtracted $\bar{X}_1$ from $\bar{X}_2$ or $\bar{X}_2$ from $\bar{X}_1$, but in the one-tailed test we *always* subtract in the direction of our prediction. Of course, if the difference turns out to be negative, this means that our results are opposite to what we predicted, and we can forget about calculating the *t* test entirely.

Let us examine some of these concepts through the use of an example. An educational psychologist is interested in the effects of knowledge of results in a classroom setting. He assigns 10 children at random to the knowledge-of-results (KR) group and 10 to the no-knowledge-of-results (NKR) group. In the KR group each child's arithmetic paper is scored and returned immediately after the daily test is completed, while in the NKR group children do not get their tests back until the next day. After a 2-week period, a unit exam is given over the same material. The errors for each student are shown in Table 10-4. Is there a significant difference in errors between the two groups?

The researcher will likely use a one-tailed test in this situation, since KR has been shown in previous research to aid the learning process. Certainly, we would not expect KR to retard learning! So, he will assume the usual null hypothesis, $\mu_{NKR} = \mu_{KR}$, and the alternate hypothesis will be $\mu_{NKR} > \mu_{KR}$ (i.e., the mean number of errors for the population receiving NKR will be greater than that for the population receiving KR).

The calculations for the one-tailed t test are shown in Table 10-4. The procedure is identical to that for the two-tailed tests of Tables 10-1 and 10-2. The only difference is that $\bar{X}_1$ must be subtracted from $\bar{X}_2$ in computing t, since that was the direction hypothesized by the researcher.

After t is calculated, we enter Table E with $df = 18$ and obtain the one-tailed values. The tabled value at the .05 level is 1.73, and our t of 1.77 is larger, so we conclude that there is a significant difference in the number of errors between the NKR and KR groups.

It should be noted that a one-tailed t has more *power* than a two-tailed t; that is, with the one-tailed t test, the null hypothesis is more likely to be rejected if it should be rejected. This is true, however, *only if the direction of the difference is predicted in advance of collecting the data.* If the researcher on knowledge of results originally wanted to see if there was *any* kind of difference but, after seeing the first three exam papers, proposed a directional hypothesis, this would be an unacceptable foundation for a one-tailed test. A two-tailed test should have been run under those conditions. It is probably safe to conclude that a two-tailed test should be run in most situations.

A t Test for Correlated Samples

The t test that was described in previous sections is intended for samples that are *independent* samples or *uncorrelated* samples. But there are times when we would like to see if there is a significant difference between the means of *correlated* samples, and this section

Table 10-4
Calculating the One-tailed t Test for Error Scores
as a Function of Knowledge of Results

KR Group	NKR Group
1	4
2	3
2	1
2	2
4	4
2	7
2	3
1	2
2	1
2	4

$$\Sigma X = 20 \qquad \Sigma X = 31$$
$$\Sigma X^2 = 46 \qquad \Sigma X^2 = 125$$
$$\overline{X}_1 = 2.0 \qquad \overline{X}_2 = 3.1$$

$$S_1 = \frac{1}{N}\sqrt{N\Sigma X^2 - (\Sigma X)^2} \qquad S_2 = \frac{1}{N}\sqrt{N\Sigma X^2 - (\Sigma X)^2}$$

$$= \frac{1}{10}\sqrt{10(46) - (20)^2} \qquad = \frac{1}{10}\sqrt{10(125) - (31)^2}$$

$$= \frac{\sqrt{60}}{10} = \frac{7.74}{10} \qquad = \frac{\sqrt{289}}{10} = \frac{17}{10}$$

$$S_1 = 0.77 \qquad S_2 = 1.7$$

$$s_{D\overline{X}} = \sqrt{\frac{N_1 S_1^{\,2} + N_2 S_2^{\,2}}{N_1 + N_2 - 2}\left(\frac{1}{N_1} + \frac{1}{N_2}\right)} = \sqrt{\frac{10(0.77)^2 + 10(1.7)^2}{10 + 10 - 2}\left(\frac{1}{10} + \frac{1}{10}\right)}$$

$$s_{D\overline{X}} = \sqrt{\frac{5.9 + 28.9}{18}(0.2)} = \sqrt{.3867} = 0.62$$

$$t = \frac{\overline{X}_2 - \overline{X}_1}{s_{D\overline{X}}} = \frac{3.1 - 2.0}{.62} = 1.77$$

$t_{05}, df = 18$, is 1.73
Significant, $p < .05$

describes a *t* test for either *matched samples* or *repeated measurements of the same subject.*

Matched Samples

We noted in the *t* test for *independent* samples that subjects were assigned at *random* to one of two groups or *random* samples were taken from two populations. With matched samples, we do not depend on random assignment to get our samples but construct them carefully to make sure they are equal on any variables that affect what we are measuring. We can do this by matched pairs, split litters, and co-twin controls.

Matched pairs. When matched pairs are used, they are usually matched on the basis of some variable that correlates highly with what we are measuring. For example, if we wanted to see if college freshmen that come from metropolitan high schools get better grades in college than those that come from rural schools, we would probably decide to use college entrance exam scores as the matching variable. For example, a person with a high entrance exam score from an urban school would be matched with a person with a high score from a rural school. In this manner, we would feel quite certain that both groups of matched pairs are equal in ability at the start and that any differences in future college grades would be due to the environmental setting from which they came.

Split litters. Many animal experiments involve this method, which resembles the matched-pair method above. One member of a litter of kittens, for example, may be placed in an experimental group and another of the same litter placed in the control group. This method would ensure that both groups are alike with respect to certain hereditary and prenatal factors that might influence the variable that we are measuring.

Co-twin controls. The purpose of the co-twin control is very similar to that of the split-litter technique, except that human identical twins are used. In many studies of maturation and development, one child is assigned to a control group and its twin to the experimental group. Any differences between the groups as a result of some experimental procedure would then be attributed to the independent variable, since both groups are similar in hereditary and maturational factors.

Repeated Measures of the Same Subject

One way to ensure that both groups are equal before some experimental procedure is attempted would be to have the same person serve in both groups. For example, if we were to investigate whether a person has greater hand steadiness with the preferred or the non-preferred hand, we could test each subject under both conditions—once with the preferred hand and once with the nonpreferred hand. At least we do not have to worry about both groups being equal at the start, since both "groups" consist of the same people!

Calculating a Correlated t Test: Direct Difference Method

Whether we use matched pairs or repeated measurements, we wind up with one measurement in each condition. This is *correlated* data, since if one member of a pair scores high in one condition the matched partner would have a tendency to score high in the other condition. Obviously, the same would hold true for repeated measures, where a person scoring high in one condition would tend to score high in the other condition.

There are a number of computational methods for calculating a correlated *t* test, but one of the simplest is called the *direct difference* method, and it is shown in Table 10-5. A matched-group design was used to investigate reaction time under two different conditions. One group of subjects (two-choice condition) pressed a switch with their thumb whenever a red light came on and pushed another switch with their little finger whenever a green light came on. The other group (three-choice condition) had a similar task, but they also pressed a third switch with their middle finger whenever an amber light came on. The 20 subjects were grouped into 10 pairs on the basis of a pretest in which they pressed a button in response to a tone. Their reaction times for the two-choice and three-choice conditions are shown in hundredths of seconds in Table 10-5.

Note that in the direct difference method, we are working only with the differences between the pairs of observations in the difference column (*D*). The formula for the mean of the differences would be

$$\bar{D} = \frac{\Sigma D}{N} \tag{10-5}$$

where ΣD is the sum of the differences (*D*) column,
N is the number of pairs.

In Table 10-5, the algebraic sum of the *D* column is 27, so the mean of the differences, $\bar{D}$, is 2.7. As you can see, this is the same as the difference between the means of the scores, 39.9 and 37.2.

You calculate the standard deviation of the differences in the usual way, by squaring each difference to obtain the *D²* column and

Table 10-5
Direct Difference Method for Correlated t Test

Sub- ject Pair	Two- Choice	Three- Choice	D	D^2
A	37	39	2	4
B	39	45	6	36
C	35	34	-1	1
D	41	43	2	4
E	32	37	5	25
F	35	38	3	9
G	36	35	-1	1
H	39	45	6	36
I	40	42	2	4
J	38	41	3	9
	372	399	27	129
	$\bar{X}_1 = 37.2$	$\bar{X}_2 = 39.9$	$\bar{D} = 2.7$	

Mean of the Differences:

$$\bar{D} = \frac{\Sigma D}{N} = \frac{27}{10} = 2.7$$

Standard Deviation of the Differences:

$$S_D = \sqrt{\frac{\Sigma D^2}{N} - \bar{D}^2} = \sqrt{\frac{129}{10} - (2.7)^2}$$

$$= \sqrt{12.9 - 7.29} = \sqrt{5.61}$$

$$S_D = 2.37$$

Standard Error of the Mean for the Differences:

$$s_{\bar{X}_D} = \frac{S_D}{\sqrt{N-1}} = \frac{2.37}{\sqrt{10-1}} = \frac{2.37}{3} = 0.79$$

Correlated t Test:

$$t = \frac{\bar{D}}{s_{\bar{X}_D}} = \frac{2.7}{0.79} = 3.42$$

t_{01}, $df = 9$, is 3.250
Significant, $p < .01$

substituting ΣD^2 into the slightly modified version of our ordinary standard deviation formula,[2]

$$S_D = \sqrt{\frac{\Sigma D^2}{N} - \overline{D}^2} \qquad (10\text{-}6)$$

where ΣD^2 is the sum of the D^2 column,
$\overline{D}$ is the mean of the differences,
N is the number of pairs.

The standard deviation of the differences, S_D, in Table 10-5 is 2.37.

We next calculate the standard error of the mean for the differences, $s_{\overline{x}_D}$, using formula 10-7.

$$s_{\overline{x}_D} = \frac{S_D}{\sqrt{N-1}} \qquad (10\text{-}7)$$

where S_D is the standard deviation of differences,
N is the number of pairs.

Note that this formula is similar to an earlier one, for the standard error of the mean, where a standard deviation is divided by $\sqrt{N-1}$. In Table 10-5, $s_{\overline{x}_D}$ is calculated to be 0.79.

Finally, we calculate the correlated t test by formula 10-8,

$$t = \frac{\overline{D}}{s_{\overline{x}_D}} \qquad (10\text{-}8)$$

where $\overline{D}$ is the mean of the differences,
$s_{\overline{x}_D}$ is the standard error of the mean of the differences.

For the data of Table 10-5, $t = 3.42$. For 9 degrees of freedom and a two-tailed test, a t of 3.250 is significant at the .01 level, and so we declare our t significant, $p < .01$.

Correlated vs. Uncorrelated t Tests

If instead of using the direct difference method on the data of Table 10-5 we had mistakenly used the t test for random samples, our t value would have been 1.79, which is not significant ($p > .05$), rather than 3.42, which is significant at the .01 level. The reason for the larger t when we are using the correlated t test is that the method has a built-in correction for the amount of correlation between the matching variable and the actual measures. If it turned out that the correlation between the two were actually 0, both the direct difference method and the t test for random samples would yield the same value of t.

The larger t with the correlated t test means that you are more likely to reject the null hypothesis and *less likely to make a Type II*

[2]The machine formula for S (formula 5-4) could be used as well, with similar modifications for ΣD and ΣD^2.

error. You are more likely to pick up a difference, if it exists, with a correlated *t* test.

Then why not use a correlated design with its matched pairs all the time? The answer to this question lies in the number of degrees of freedom for the two different approaches. As we saw earlier in the chapter, the degrees of freedom for a *t* test for random samples was $df = (N_1 - 1) + (N_2 - 1)$. Note that this is twice as many degrees of freedom as we have in the correlated *t* test, where $df = N - 1$ and *N* is the number of pairs. As a result, a somewhat higher *t* value is needed for significance at a given level with the correlated *t* test.

Consequently, there should be a substantial correlation between the variable that is used for matching the pairs (the independent variable) and the variable that is used for the measurements to be made (the dependent variable). For example, a researcher studying the reading comprehension of adults in the Midwest vs. adults in the deep South would not match pairs on the basis of height or weight, since there is no relationship between reading comprehension and these physical measures. As explained in the previous paragraph, using these as a matching variable would only reduce the number of degrees of freedom in the *t* test.

Significant Differences between Other Statistics

This entire chapter has been devoted to testing the significance of the difference between means. A similar approach is used in testing the significance of a difference between medians, proportions, standard deviations, and other statistics. For example, we might want to know if our local political candidate has any chance to win the election if a sample of voters shows that 48% will vote for her. Since she needs 50% of the vote to win, we ask if 48% is only sampling error (we hope!) or if it is the real population value and our candidate stands to be defeated. A test for the significance of a proportion would help us answer our question.

A number of these significance tests are beyond the intended scope of this introductory text, and you are referred to one of the more advanced texts listed in the References, Glass and Stanley (1970), for example.

Sample Problem #1

A social psychologist is investigating the development of "generosity" in preschool children and would like to see if girls are more generous than boys at age 4. Each child at a day care center is given 16 small pieces of candy and is asked to "put some in a sack for your very best friend." The numbers of candies set aside for "friends" by 12 girls and 10 boys are shown below. Calculate a *t* test for random samples to see if there is a significant sex difference in generosity.

Girls			Boys	
X	X²		X	X²
7	49		2	4
3	9		3	9
6	36		5	25
9	81		3	9
3	9		4	16
8	64		2	4
6	36		2	4
7	49		1	1
5	25		2	4
9	81		3	9
8	64		27	85
7	49			
78	552			

Means:

$$\overline{X}_1 = \frac{78}{12} = 6.5 \qquad\qquad \overline{X}_2 = \frac{27}{10} = 2.7$$

Standard Deviations:

$$S_1 = \frac{1}{N}\sqrt{N\Sigma X^2 - (\Sigma X)^2} \qquad S_2 = \frac{1}{N}\sqrt{N\Sigma X^2 - (\Sigma X)^2}$$

$$= \frac{1}{12}\sqrt{12(552) - (78)^2} \qquad = \frac{1}{10}\sqrt{10(85) - (27)^2}$$

$$= \frac{\sqrt{540}}{12} = \frac{23.24}{12} \qquad = \frac{\sqrt{121}}{10} = \frac{11}{10}$$

$$S_1 = 1.94 \qquad\qquad S_2 = 1.10$$

Standard Error of the Difference:

$$s_{D\overline{X}} = \sqrt{\frac{N_1 S_1^2 + N_2 S_2^2}{N_1 + N_2 - 2}\left(\frac{1}{N_1} + \frac{1}{N_2}\right)}$$

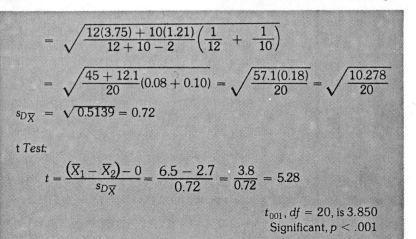

$$= \sqrt{\frac{12(3.75) + 10(1.21)}{12 + 10 - 2}\left(\frac{1}{12} + \frac{1}{10}\right)}$$

$$= \sqrt{\frac{45 + 12.1}{20}(0.08 + 0.10)} = \sqrt{\frac{57.1(0.18)}{20}} = \sqrt{\frac{10.278}{20}}$$

$$s_{D\overline{X}} = \sqrt{0.5139} = 0.72$$

t Test:

$$t = \frac{(\overline{X}_1 - \overline{X}_2) - 0}{s_{D\overline{X}}} = \frac{6.5 - 2.7}{0.72} = \frac{3.8}{0.72} = 5.28$$

t_{001}, $df = 20$, is 3.850
Significant, $p < .001$

Since our calculated t of 5.28 is greater than the value for the .001 level for 20 degrees of freedom in Table E, we would conclude that the girls set aside significantly more candies than the boys and that the difference in means was significant at the .001 level.

Sample Problem #2

Eight novice bowlers are dissatisfied with their present bowling averages and decide to take a lesson from a professional bowler. For a month after the lesson they calculate their bowling averages again and compare them with the averages before the lesson. Use a t test for correlated samples to see if there was a significant difference between the bowling averages before the lesson and after the lesson.

Bowler	Before	After	D	D²
A	144	151	7	49
B	126	120	−6	36
C	132	137	5	25
D	143	154	11	121
E	133	132	−1	1
F	128	131	3	9
G	152	149	−3	9
H	126	130	4	16
	1,084	1,104	20	266

$\overline{X}_1 = 135.5$ $\overline{X}_2 = 138$ $\overline{D} = 2.5$

Mean of the Differences:

$$\overline{D} = \frac{\Sigma D}{N} = \frac{20}{8} = 2.5$$

Standard Deviation of the Differences:

$$S_D = \sqrt{\frac{\Sigma D^2}{N} - \overline{D}^2} = \sqrt{\frac{266}{8} - (2.5)^2}$$

$$= \sqrt{33.25 - 6.25} = \sqrt{27}$$

$$S_D = 5.20$$

Standard Error of the Mean for the Differences:

$$s_{\overline{X}_D} = \frac{S_D}{\sqrt{N-1}} = \frac{5.20}{\sqrt{8-1}} = \frac{5.20}{2.65} = 1.96$$

Correlated t Test:

$$t = \frac{\overline{D}}{s_{\overline{X}_D}} = \frac{2.5}{1.96} = 1.28$$

t_{05}, $df = 7$, is 2.365
Not significant, $p > .05$

Since our calculated t of 1.28 is less than that required for significance at the .05 level for a two-tailed test, we conclude that there was no significant difference in the average bowling scores after the lesson.

Study Questions

1. What is a sampling distribution of differences between means? What is the standard deviation of this distribution called?
2. The null hypothesis states that $\mu_1 - \mu_2 = 0$. What does this mean? How is this statement related to the assumption that $\overline{D}_{\overline{X}} = 0$?
3. What is the region of rejection?
4. What do we mean when we say that a difference is not significant?
5. A difference between means is labeled "significant at the .01 level." What does this mean?
6. What is the difference between the t distribution and the normal curve?
7. A researcher has seven children in an experimental group and nine children in a control group. She obtains a t value of 2.56. Is

this significant at the .05 level? At the .01 level?

8. What are the assumptions for the t test?
9. What is a Type I error? A Type II error? Under what conditions would you prefer one to the other?
10. Why is the probability of making a Type I error the same as the significance level (α) chosen by the experimenter?
11. What is meant by the term *power* as applied to a statistical test? Why is power so important to the researcher?
12. What is the difference between a one-tailed test and a two-tailed test?

Exercises

1. A college dean wanted to know if married students participated in college activities as much as single students. From a random sample of each group she tallied the number of extracurricular activities participated in by each student for the previous year. On the basis of the following results, what would you conclude? (Use a two-tailed test.)

Married	Single
$N_1 = 10$	$N_2 = 17$
$\bar{X}_1 = 3.2$	$\bar{X}_2 = 5.4$
$S_1 = 2.4$	$S_2 = 3.6$

2. A wheat farmer wanted to see if there was any difference between using expensive certified seed and using his own wheat. He planted 5 fields with the certified seed and 6 fields with his own wheat. At harvest he determined the yield in bushels per acre for the 11 fields. Was there any difference between the certified seed and the farmer's own wheat? (Use a two-tailed test.)

Certified	Own
35	32
29	27
34	30
34	29
33	26
	30

3. An electronics firm wanted to market a micro-miniature recorder. The engineers devised two prototypes that were similar in cost. The products manager had to decide which one to produce and devised

an experiment to test the intelligibility of the recorded message. Twenty subjects were divided into two groups and each one heard a number of taped words played back on that recorder. The number of words correctly identified from the two instruments is given below. Was there a significant difference between the two recorders? (Use a two-tailed test.)

Model 1	Model 2
15	12
13	10
13	11
12	13
12	14
11	10
9	7
9	6
8	5
8	2

4. Fifteen experienced typists were tested for speed of typing on two brands of electric typewriters. Was there a significant difference in the average number of words per minute typed on the two machines? (Use a two-tailed test.)

Typist	Brand A	Brand B
A	89	86
B	88	84
C	87	86
D	85	86
E	84	82
F	83	82
G	83	83
H	83	81
I	83	82
J	82	82
K	81	81
L	81	78
M	80	80
N	78	80
O	78	77

5. A developmental psychologist was interested in the developmental lag of male infants. He investigated sex differences in the age at

which certain developmental skills began in infancy. A sample of 10 boys and 10 girls was assessed for the age (in weeks) when they could first sit alone. Use a one-tailed t test to see if there was a significant difference between boys and girls.

Girls	Boys
28	30
25	27
34	35
30	31
29	31
26	27
27	31
28	30
29	31
27	31

11 One-Way Analysis of Variance

The *t* tests described in the last chapter have one very serious limitation—they are restricted to tests of the significance of the difference between only *two* groups. Certainly, there are many times when we would like to see if there are significant differences among three, four, or even more groups. For example, we may want to investigate which of three teaching methods (lecture, discussion, or programmed textbook) is best for a first-year algebra class or which of four brands of pain killers works best for dental trauma. In these cases we cannot use the ordinary *t* test, because more than two groups are involved.

We *cannot* solve the problem by running a *t* test on two groups at a time. If we have three means, $\overline{X}_1$, $\overline{X}_2$, and $\overline{X}_3$, we cannot use the ordinary *t* test first on $\overline{X}_1$ and $\overline{X}_2$, then on $\overline{X}_1$ and $\overline{X}_3$, and finally on $\overline{X}_2$ and $\overline{X}_3$. The reason this is an invalid procedure is that the probabilities associated with obtaining various *t* values given in Table E are for pairs of means from *random* samples. If we have a number of pairs of means to be compared, we definitely are *not* choosing two of them at random for the *t* test since, if we have chosen to compare, say, $\overline{X}_1$ with $\overline{X}_2$ first, then our next two choices must necessarily be $\overline{X}_1$ with $\overline{X}_3$ and $\overline{X}_2$ with $\overline{X}_3$. Thus, the probability values given in Table E in Appendix 2 are not applicable.

It is for this reason that we now consider one of the most useful techniques in statistics — the analysis of variance (abbreviated AOV or ANOVA). This technique allows us to compare two or more means to see if there are significant differences between or among them. The analysis of variance is used in a wide variety of applications and in varying degrees of complexity by researchers in such diverse fields as psychology, agriculture, education, and industrial engineering. It is such an important part of the professional's repertoire that at least superficial acquaintance with ANOVA is essential for anyone in education and the behavioral sciences. Since there are entire textbooks and two-semester courses devoted to ANOVA, we will just barely scratch the surface in applying this statistical tool. But we will become acquainted with the introductory concepts and build a foundation for further course work. In this chapter we will consider the most elementary form of ANOVA — the *simple analysis of variance*, sometimes called the *one-way classification analysis of variance*.

The Concept of Variance Revisited

Before we jump into the topic, it might be a good idea to review briefly the concept of variance. We noted in Chapter 5 that the variance is a measure of variability based on the squared deviations from the mean. The numerator of the formula is the familiar Σx^2, which is called *the sum of squares*. You will recall from Chapter 5 that the sum of squares is the result of subtracting the mean from each score to obtain the deviation (x), squaring each deviation (x^2), and finally summing the squared deviations to obtain Σx^2. In the example of Table 11-1, $\Sigma x^2 = 118$.

The denominator of the variance formula, for the unbiased estimate, is the degrees of freedom, $N - 1$. As you can see from Table 11-1, the variance, s^2, is obtained by division of the sum of squares by the degrees of freedom, or $118/9 = 13.11$. This value is a measure of variability for these 10 scores, and s^2 would be smaller for a group of scores that deviated less from the mean and larger for a group that deviated more.

Note that the sum of squares, Σx^2, is not itself a measure of variability, since the size of Σx^2 depends not only on the extent of the devi-

Table 11-1
Calculating the Unbiased Estimate of the Population Variance

X	x	x^2
12	6	36
7	1	1
9	3	9
2	-4	16
10	4	16
7	1	1
1	-5	25
3	-3	9
4	-2	4
5	-1	1
60	0	$\Sigma x^2 = 118$

$\bar{X} = 6$

$$s^2 = \frac{\Sigma x^2}{N-1} = \frac{118}{9} = 13.11$$

ations from the mean but also on the size of the sample. Thus the necessity of dividing by the degrees of freedom to obtain a sort of average.

Sources of Variation

Let us use a hypothetical example to show graphically the basic structure of the one-way classification ANOVA. A researcher wants to know which of four methods of teaching introductory psychology produces the best results: (1) lecture, (2) films and videotapes, (3) discussion groups, or (4) self-study with a programmed text. A total of 200 college students is available for the research project, and 50 are assigned at random to each of the four groups. After the semester's course work is completed under each of the four different techniques, all students are given a final exam covering basic psychological principles.

To make our graphic analysis easier, let us assume that the 50 scores in each group are normally distributed and that there is no overlapping of any of the groups. This nonoverlapping, of course, would never happen in practice, but it is easier to see the *sources of variation* in this way.

Figure 11-1 shows the four frequency polygons for the final exam-

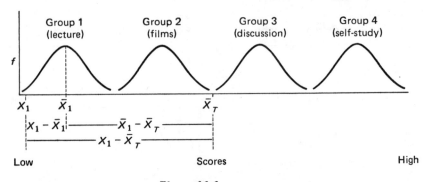

Figure 11-1
Within-groups variability and between-groups variability equals total variability.

ination scores. Note that the self-study group had the highest scores and the lecture group (this is a hypothetical example!) had the lowest exam scores. Also shown on the polygon is a score (X_1) made by a student in group 1, the mean of group 1 $(\overline{X}_1)$, and the mean of all 200 students, called the total mean $(\overline{X}_T)$. Examining Figure 11-1 carefully, we see that there are really three kinds of variability shown.

Total Variability

We can see that there is variability in the distribution of all 200 scores, which is exemplified by the deviation of a score in group 1 from the total mean, or $X_1 - \overline{X}_T$. This $X_1 - \overline{X}_T$ shown in Figure 11-1 would be the contribution to *total* variability of the single score X_1. There would, of course, be 199 others $(X_2 - \overline{X}_T, X_3 - \overline{X}_T,$ etc.), and each deviation of a score from the total mean contributes to the *total variability* in the combined distribution.

But note in Figure 11-1 that the deviation of a single score from the total mean, $X_1 - \overline{X}_T$, can be broken down into two separate components. The first component is the deviation of a given score from its group mean, $X_1 - \overline{X}_1$, and the second component is the deviation of the group mean from the total mean, $\overline{X}_1 - \overline{X}_T$. Note that these are additive, both graphically in Figure 11-1 and algebraically, since $(X_1 - \overline{X}_1) + (\overline{X}_1 - \overline{X}_T) = X_1 - \overline{X}_T$.

Variability within Groups

The deviation of a score from its group mean is part of the variability *within groups*, that is, the amount each score in any group deviates from its own mean. The deviation of $X_1 - \overline{X}_1$ in Figure 11-1 would be one part of the variability within group 1, and each of the other 49 scores would contribute its deviation to the variability within group 1. There would be a similar variability in the other three groups.

Variability between Groups

The deviation of a group mean from the total mean contributes to the *variability between groups*. Again looking at Figure 11-1, we see that the deviation of the mean of group 1 from the total mean, $\overline{X}_1 - \overline{X}_T$, is part of the variability between groups. Note that the term *between groups* is used despite the fact that the actual deviation is not between the individual means themselves but between the group mean and the total mean ($\overline{X}_1 - \overline{X}_T, \overline{X}_2 - \overline{X}_T$, etc.).

Significant Differences between Means

The aim of our analysis, of course, is to determine whether there are significant differences between the group means. We will do this

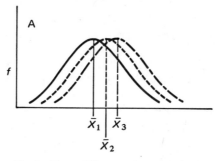

No significant differences between the means

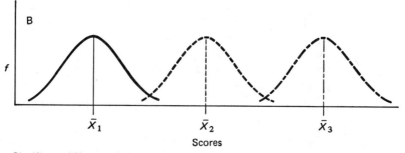

Significant differences between the means

Figure 11-2
Possible relationship between three group means for significant and nonsignificant differences.

eventually by comparing the variability between groups with the vari-ability within groups. We know that in any single distribution of scores there will be variability, so we will always expect to find *variability within groups*.

However, if there are no significant differences between the means of the groups, we expect that there will be very little variability between groups—only the small amount we expect to find by sampling error.

This point is illustrated in Figure 11-2 for three distributions. Note that in Figure 11-2A the three groups differ very little from each other and their means differ only slightly due to sampling error. There is still variability *within each group,* of course, but there is much less *variability between groups* than in Figure 11-2B, where the means of the groups differ markedly. Eventually we will be able to use the comparison of the *variability between groups* to the *variability within groups* to show whether there are significant differences between the means.

Calculating the Sums of Squares

Before we can calculate some variances to analyze, we need to develop formulas to calculate the sums of squares, which will be the numerators of the various variance formulas. Remembering that the *total variability* is composed of variability *within groups* and variability *between groups,* we can express this as we did before, in Figure 11-1, as

$$(X - \overline{X}_T) = (X - \overline{X}_1) + (\overline{X}_1 - \overline{X}_T)$$

As we noted before, this expresses the contribution to the total variability of *one* score in group 1, and the deviation of this score from the total mean is composed of the deviation of the score from its group mean plus the deviation of the group mean from the total mean.

However, the deviation from the mean must be squared before we can arrive at the sums of squares, so we must square both sides of the above expression to obtain

$$(X - \overline{X}_T)^2 = (X - \overline{X}_1)^2 + 2(X - \overline{X}_1)(\overline{X}_1 - \overline{X}_T) + (\overline{X}_1 - \overline{X}_T)^2$$

This represents the squared deviation of *one* score in group 1. We now have to sum for *all* of the scores in group 1. Summing both sides of the equation gives

$$\sum^{N_1} (X - \overline{X}_T)^2 = \sum^{N_1}(X - \overline{X}_1)^2 + 2(\overline{X}_1 - \overline{X}_T)\sum^{N_1}(X - \overline{X}_1) + N_1(\overline{X}_1 - \overline{X}_T)^2$$

Note that $\overset{N_1}{\Sigma}$ means that we are summing the various deviations for all the scores in group 1. Note also that in the second term on the right-hand side of the equation, both 2 and $(\overline{X}_1 - \overline{X}_T)$ are constants, so they appear in front of the summation sign, since the sum of a constant times a variable is equal to the constant times the sum of the variable. Note also that, in the third term on the right-hand side, we finish up with $N(\overline{X}_1 - \overline{X}_T)^2$, since the sum of a constant is equal to N times the constant.

Examining the second term again, we note that it contains $\overset{N_1}{\Sigma} (X - \overline{X}_1)$. This is nothing more than our old Σx, which we know is equal to 0 for a given group of scores. Thus, the entire second term drops out, and we are left with

$$\overset{N_1}{\Sigma} (X - \overline{X}_T)^2 = \overset{N_1}{\Sigma} (X - \overline{X}_1)^2 + N_1(\overline{X}_1 - \overline{X}_T)^2$$

In a verbal description of this formula, along with the graphical representation of Figure 11-1, we would say that the squared deviations of the scores in group 1 from the total mean are made up of the squared deviations of the scores from the mean of group 1 plus the size of group 1 times the squared deviation of the mean of group 1 from the total mean.

There remains one additional step. The formula given is for scores in one group only. We now need to sum over all the groups (k = number of groups), to obtain

$$
\begin{array}{ccc}
\textit{Total} & \textit{Within-Groups} & \textit{Between-Groups} \\
\textit{Sum of Squares} & \textit{Sum of Squares} & \textit{Sum of Squares}
\end{array}
$$

$$\overset{k}{\Sigma}\overset{N_G}{\Sigma}(X - \overline{X}_T)^2 = \overset{k}{\Sigma}\overset{N_G}{\Sigma}(X - \overline{X}_G)^2 + \overset{k}{\Sigma}N_G(\overline{X}_G - \overline{X}_T)^2 \quad \textbf{(11-1)}$$

Note that the subscript G refers to the number of the group. For example, N_3 refers to the number of scores in group 3, while $\overline{X}_2$ would be the mean of group 2.

The formula above is one of the most complex formulas we have encountered in this text, but it is probably one of the most important, so let us examine each component in detail. Remember that each is a sum of squares (abbreviated SS), that is, the sum of squared deviations from a mean (Σx^2).

Total Sum of Squares (SS_T)

$$SS_T = \overset{k}{\Sigma}\overset{N_G}{\Sigma} (X - \overline{X}_T)^2 \quad \textbf{(11-2)}$$

This term represents the squared deviations of *all* scores from the total mean. The expression $(X - \overline{X}_T)^2$ is the squared deviation of a score from the total mean. $\overset{N_G}{\Sigma}$ indicates that these squared deviations are to be summed for all the scores in each group. $\overset{k}{\Sigma}$ indicates that the sums of the squared deviations from each group are to be added together finally to give the total sum of the squared deviations.

Within-Groups Sum of Squares (SS$_{WG}$)

$$SS_{WG} = \overset{k}{\Sigma}\,\overset{N_G}{\Sigma}\,(X - \overline{X}_G)^2 \tag{11-3}$$

This term represents the squared deviations of scores from their respective group means. $(X - \overline{X}_G)^2$ is the squared deviation of a score from its group mean. $\overset{N_G}{\Sigma}$ indicates that the squared deviations are to be summed for each group, and $\overset{k}{\Sigma}$ indicates that the sums for each group are to be added together to give the within-groups sum of squares for all groups.

Between-Groups Sum of Squares (SS$_{BG}$)

$$SS_{BG} = \overset{k}{\Sigma}\,N_G(\overline{X}_G - \overline{X}_T)^2 \tag{11-4}$$

This term represents the squared deviation of each group mean from the total mean. $(\overline{X}_G - \overline{X}_T)^2$ indicates this squared deviation. N_G indicates that each squared deviation is to be multiplied by the size of its group (this is called "weighted by N"), and $\overset{k}{\Sigma}$ indicates that the sums for each group are to be added together to give the weighted squared deviations for all groups.

So we conclude that the sum of squares from the total mean is composed of the sum of squares within the groups plus the sum of squares between groups, or

$$SS_T = SS_{WG} + SS_{BG}$$

Let us see how the formulas that we have developed work in a hypothetical example. Table 11-2 shows three groups of scores and the calculation of SS_T, SS_{BG}, and SS_{WG}.

Note that the calculations in Table 11-2 are simply the arithmetic counterpart of the logic of ANOVA developed in the previous sections. The calculation of SS_T is the sum of the squared deviations of each score from the total mean of 5. The SS_{BG} value shows the deviation of

Table 11-2
Calculation of Sums of Squares: Deviation Formulas

I		II		III	
3		11		2	
1	$\bar{X}_1 = 2$	6	$\bar{X}_2 = 8$	6	$\bar{X}_3 = 4$
2		5		4	
6		10		12	
		32			

$$\bar{X}_T = \frac{\Sigma X_T}{N_T} = \frac{6 + 32 + 12}{10} = 5$$

$SS_T:$

$$\overset{k}{\underset{}{\Sigma}} \overset{N_G}{\underset{}{\Sigma}} (X - \bar{X}_T)^2 = (3-5)^2 + (1-5)^2 + (2-5)^2 = 29$$

$$(11-5)^2 + (6-5)^2 + (5-5)^2 + (10-5)^2 = 62$$

$$(2-5)^2 + (6-5)^2 + (4-5)^2 = 11$$

$$SS_T = 29 + 62 + 11 = 102$$

$SS_{BG}:$

$$\overset{k}{\underset{}{\Sigma}} N_G (\bar{X}_G - \bar{X}_T)^2 = N_1 (\bar{X}_1 - \bar{X}_T)^2 + N_2 (\bar{X}_2 - \bar{X}_T)^2 + N_3 (\bar{X}_3 - \bar{X}_T)^2$$

$$SS_{BG} = 27 + 36 + 3 = 66$$

$SS_{WG}:$

$$\overset{k}{\underset{}{\Sigma}} \overset{N_G}{\underset{}{\Sigma}} (X - \bar{X}_G)^2 = (3-2)^2 + (1-2)^2 + (2-2)^2 = 2$$

$$(11-8)^2 + (6-8)^2 + (5-8)^2 + (10-8)^2 = 26$$

$$(2-4)^2 + (6-4)^2 + (4-4)^2 = 8$$

$$SS_{WG} = 2 + 26 + 8 = 36$$

Summary:

$$SS_T = SS_{BG} + SS_{WG}$$

$$102 = 66 + 36$$

each group mean from the total mean, each deviation being squared and multiplied by its sample size N. And, finally, the SS_{WG} value shows that within each group the deviation of each score from its mean is squared and the squares are summed for the entire group and that these sums are themselves summed over all three groups. And, of course, the last statement in Table 11-2 shows that $SS_{BG} + SS_{WG} = SS_T$.

Calculating the Variances

The previous sections have dealt with the sums of squares, which we noted earlier are the numerators of the variances we wish to calculate. Before we can calculate these variances, we need to deal now with the denominators of the variances, or the *degrees of freedom*, in order to have a variance of the form $\Sigma x^2/(N - 1)$. Just as we found that the total sum of squares could be partitioned into a between-groups and a within-groups sum of squares, we now observe that the total degrees of freedom can be partitioned in the same way.

Total df. The degrees of freedom associated with the entire group of observations is equal to $N_T - 1$, where N_T is the total number of observations. The data of Table 11-2 consisted of 10 scores, so the total $df = 9$.

Between-groups df. The degrees of freedom associated with the between-groups component is equal to $k - 1$, where k is the number of groups. For the data of Table 11-2, the df for between groups would be 2.

Within-groups df. The degrees of freedom within *one* group would be one less than the N of that group. Combining them for all groups would give $(N_1 - 1) + (N_2 - 1) + (N_3 - 1)$ and so on for as many groups as required, which would equal $N_T - k$. For the example in Table 11-2, the within-groups $df = 10 - 3 = 7$.

Note that the degrees of freedom are additive in the same way that the sums of squares were; that is,

$$df_T = df_{BG} + df_{WG}$$
$$N_T - 1 = (k - 1) + (N_T - k)$$

For the data of Table 11-2, $2 + 7 = 9$.

The Mean Squares

We are now ready to calculate the variance estimates associated with the between-groups component and the within-groups component. These variance estimates are called *mean squares.* Mean squares are variance estimates, and they consist of a sum of squares divided by the appropriate degrees of freedom. Since we will eventually want to compare the variance estimate based on the between-groups component with the variance estimate based on the within-groups component, we will focus our attention on the mean square between groups, MS_{BG}, and the mean square within groups, MS_{WG}. The formulas for these variance estimates are:

$$MS_{BG} = \frac{SS_{BG}}{k-1} \tag{11-5}$$

$$MS_{WG} = \frac{SS_{WG}}{N_T - k} \tag{11-6}$$

For the data of Table 11-2, the mean squares would be

$$MS_{BG} = \frac{66}{3-1} = 33$$

$$MS_{WG} = \frac{36}{10-3} = 5.14$$

Variance Estimates and the Null Hypothesis

Now that we have spent considerable time and energy on the calculation of MS_{WG} and MS_{BG}, just what are they? What do they represent? Since they have a sum of squares in the numerator and a df term in the denominator, they certainly must be variance estimates of some sort.

MS_{WG} and MS_{BG} as Variance Estimates

We have already stated that the sums of squares within groups, SS_{WG}, was composed of squared deviations from the various group means. For a *single* group, then, SS_{WG_1} would be the sum of squared deviations from the mean of group 1. And if we calculated

$$MS_{WG_1} = \frac{SS_{WG_1}}{N_1 - 1}$$

we would have the mean square within group 1, *which is an unbiased estimate of the population variance from which group 1 came.* To refer back to Figure 11-1, the lecture group, group 1, is a random sample from a population of available college students, and MS_{WG_1} is an estimate of the variance of that population.

We could also calculate MS_{WG_2} by dividing SS_{WG_2} by $N_2 - 1$. This would be an unbiased estimate of the variance of the population from which group 2 came.

We could do this in a similar manner for MS_{WG_3} and MS_{WG_4} or for as many groups as we had. Each one is an unbiased estimate of the variance of the different populations from which the samples came. *However, under the null hypothesis, these various estimates are all estimating the same thing!* Since the null hypothesis states that $\mu_1 = \mu_2 = \mu_3 = \mu_4$, we assume that the populations from which the various samples have been drawn are identical and that MS_{WG_1}, MS_{WG_2}, MS_{WG_3}, and MS_{WG_4} are just estimates of the same population variance. Since we are rather knowledgeable on the topic of sampling by now, we know that a *mean* of these estimates would give us a very accurate overall estimate of the population variance, *if the null hypothesis is true*. So, if we take an average of MS_{WG_1}, MS_{WG_2}, and so on, we wind up with our familiar MS_{WG}, the average unbiased estimate of the variance of the population from which the samples came.

Let us get back to the mean square between groups, MS_{BG}. It can be shown that, if the null hypothesis is true ($\mu_1 = \mu_2 = \mu_3$, etc.), then MS_{BG} is *also an unbiased estimate of the variance of the population from which the samples came.* The mathematical proof for this statement is beyond the scope of this textbook, but we will accept it on faith.

The Ratio MS_{BG}/MS_{WG}

Since MS_{BG} and MS_{WG} are estimates of the same population variance, we would expect that if the null hypothesis is true the ratio MS_{BG}/MS_{WG} will be equal to 1.0. Of course, we do not expect it to be *exactly* 1.0, since we know that there will be some fluctuations due to sampling error.

However, if the ratio is quite a bit larger than 1.0, we reject the null hypothesis and conclude that there is a real difference between the means of the populations from which the samples were drawn ($\mu_1 \neq \mu_2 \neq \mu_3$, etc.). If the ratio is such that it would happen less than 5% or 1% or 0.1% of the time by sampling error alone, we conclude that there is a significant difference between the means. The statistical procedure for determining whether the ratio MS_{BG}/MS_{WG} is significant is called the F test.

The F Test

The F test (named after a British statistician, Sir Ronald Fisher) consists of examining the ratio of two variances to see if the departure from 1.0 is sufficiently large so it is not likely due to sampling error. The F test (or F ratio), as indicated above, is the ratio

$$F = \frac{MS_{BG}}{MS_{WG}} \tag{11-7}$$

But how large must F be before we reject the null hypothesis? We noted earlier with the t test that the value to be equaled or exceeded in Table E depended upon the degrees of freedom on which the t test had been computed. The F value to be equaled or exceeded depends upon the degrees of freedom also, but *both* the numerator and denominator of the F test determine the degrees of freedom. You will notice in Table F in Appendix 2 a list of various values of F that need to be equaled or exceeded for the given significance levels. As with the t distributions, these values are points that mark off the 5% and 1% points in the sampling distribution of F. These values are determined by the degrees of freedom associated with both the numerator and the denominator of the F ratio. For example, if you have 4 degrees of freedom in the numerator and 20 degrees of freedom in the denominator you would need an F value of at least 2.87 for the ratio to be significant at the .05 level and 4.43 for it to be significant at the .01 level. For the data shown in Table 11-2, the F value would be

$$F = \frac{MS_{BG}}{MS_{WG}} = \frac{33}{5.14} = 6.42$$

Remembering that the *df* for MS_{BG} was $k - 1 = 2$ and the *df* for MS_{WG} was $N_T - k = 7$, we would proceed to Table F and note that for 2 and 7 degrees of freedom F_{05} is 4.74 and F_{01} is 9.55. We would then conclude that $p < .05$ that our F of 6.42 happened by sampling error and would state that there is a significant difference between the means of the three groups.

Computational Formulas

The deviation formulas used in Table 11-2 demonstrate the logic of ANOVA very clearly, but they are rather cumbersome to work with. Subtracting a mean from each score and squaring the deviation is very time-consuming, and for this reason computational formulas have been developed. (You may remember we did the same thing for the standard deviation in Chapter 5.) These formulas for the sums of squares deal with the raw scores rather than the deviations. The *raw score* formula for the total sum of squares is as follows:

$$SS_T = \sum^{N_T} X^2 - N_T \overline{X}_T^2 \tag{11-8}$$

In this formula, $\overset{N_T}{\underset{}{\Sigma}} X^2$ indicates that *all* scores are squared and then summed, and $N_T \overline{X}_T^2$ indicates that the total mean is squared and multiplied by the total number of observations and this result is then subtracted from $\overset{N_T}{\underset{}{\Sigma}} X^2$.

$$SS_{BG} = N_1 \overline{X}_1^2 + N_2 \overline{X}_2^2 + N_3 \overline{X}_3^2 + \ldots - N_T \overline{X}_T^2 \qquad (11\text{-}9)$$

This formula for the between-groups sum of squares indicates that each group mean is squared and then multiplied by the size of that group and that these products are added together for as many groups as there are. The quantity $N_T \overline{X}_T^2$, which is the same value calculated previously in the formula for SS_T, is then subtracted.

$$SS_{WG} = \left(\overset{N_1}{\underset{}{\Sigma}} X^2 - N_1 \overline{X}_1^2 \right) + \left(\overset{N_2}{\underset{}{\Sigma}} X^2 - N_2 \overline{X}_2^2 \right)$$
$$+ \left(\overset{N_3}{\underset{}{\Sigma}} X^2 - N_3 \overline{X}_3^2 \right) + \ldots \qquad (11\text{-}10)$$

The formula for the within-groups sum of squares shows that the mean of group 1 is squared, multiplied by the size of group 1, and subtracted from the sum of the squared scores in group 1. This procedure is repeated for as many groups as there are, and the sums of squares for each group are then added together to yield SS_{WG}.

To illustrate the use of the computational formulas, let us consider

Table 11-3
Using the Computational Formulas for ANOVA

Squirrels		Cats		Guinea Pigs		Rats	
X	X²	X	X²	X	X²	X	X²
9	81	17	289	12	144	10	100
9	81	16	256	10	100	8	64
3	9	14	196	14	196	7	49
5	25	15	225	36	440	9	81
6	36	10	100			12	144
32	232	6	36			8	64
		78	1,102			54	502
$\overline{X}_1 = 6.4$		$\overline{X}_2 = 13$		$\overline{X}_3 = 12$		$\overline{X}_4 = 9$	

Table 11-3 (continued)

$$*\bar{X}_T = \frac{\Sigma X_T}{N_T} = \frac{32 + 78 + 36 + 54}{5 + 6 + 3 + 6} = \frac{200}{20} = 10.0$$

$$**\Sigma X^2 = 232 + 1{,}102 + 440 + 502 = 2{,}276$$

Sums of Squares:

$$SS_T = \overset{N_T}{\Sigma X^2} - N_T \bar{X}_T{}^2 = 2{,}276 - 20(10.0)^2$$

$$= 2{,}276 - 2{,}000$$

$$SS_T = 276$$

$$SS_{BG} = N_1 \bar{X}_1{}^2 + N_2 \bar{X}_2{}^2 + N_3 \bar{X}_3{}^2 + N_4 \bar{X}_4{}^2 - N_T \bar{X}_T{}^2$$

$$= 5(6.4)^2 + 6(13)^2 + 3(12)^2 + 6(9)^2 - 2{,}000$$

$$= 204.8 + 1{,}014 + 432 + 486 - 2{,}000$$

$$SS_{BG} = 136.8$$

$$***SS_{WG} = \left(\overset{N_1}{\Sigma X^2} - N_1 \bar{X}_1{}^2\right) + \left(\overset{N_2}{\Sigma X^2} - N_2 \bar{X}_2{}^2\right)$$

$$+ \left(\overset{N_3}{\Sigma X^2} - N_3 \bar{X}_3{}^2\right) + \left(\overset{N_4}{\Sigma X^2} - N_4 \bar{X}_4{}^2\right)$$

$$= (232 - 204.8) + (1{,}102 - 1{,}014) + (440 - 432) + (502 - 486)$$

$$= 27.2 + 88 + 8 + 16$$

$$SS_{WG} = 139.2$$

Check:

$$SS_{BG} + SS_{WG} = SS_T$$

$$136.8 + 139.2 = 276$$

Mean Squares and the F *Test:*

$$MS_{BG} = \frac{SS_{BG}}{k - 1} = \frac{136.8}{3} = 45.6$$

$$MS_{WG} = \frac{SS_{WG}}{N_T - k} = \frac{139.2}{16} = 8.7$$

$$F = \frac{MS_{BG}}{MS_{WG}} = \frac{45.6}{8.7} = 5.24$$

$$F_{05}, df = 3/16, \text{ is } 3.24$$

Significant, $p < .05$

the data of Table 11-3. An investigator was studying the learning abilities of four species of laboratory animals. She taught 5 squirrels, 6 cats, 3 guinea pigs, and 6 rats a simple maze response and kept track of the errors each animal made. Were there significant differences in the learning ability of these four species?

In applying the raw score formulas for the sums of squares, we should note the starred items in Table 11-3:

*Remember that you cannot simply take an average of the four means to obtain $\overline{X}_T$. You must divide the total ΣX by the total N.

**The total ΣX^2 is the sum of the individual ΣX^2 columns.

***Note that the quantities $N_1\overline{X}_1{}^2$, $N_2\overline{X}_2{}^2$, and so on, have already been calculated in the previous SS_{BG} formula. So, each component is simply the ΣX^2 of each group minus the $N\overline{X}^2$ for that group.

The main interest, of course, is in the F value, and we see that the calculated F is 5.24, which is greater than the tabled value at the 5% level for 3 and 16 degrees of freedom. We would conclude that there are significant differences between the means of the maze errors committed by the different laboratory animals.

The ANOVA Summary Table

In the professional literature, you will find that, when ANOVA is used for determining the significance of the differences among means, all the computational steps of Table 11-3 are not shown. Instead, a *summary table* is used which lists the *source of variance, degrees of freedom, sums of squares,* and *mean squares,* as well as the value of F. Such a summary table has been prepared for the data of Table 11-3 and is shown in Table 11-4. Note that this table contains all the necessary information for the reader of a book or a journal article, including a probability statement on the value of F.

Table 11-4
ANOVA Summary Table for Animal Learning Experiment

Source of Variance	df	SS	MS	F
Between groups	3	136.8	45.6	5.24
Within groups	16	139.2	8.7	
Total	19	276.0		

Significant, $p < .05$

Testing for Differences among Pairs of Means

After a significant F has been obtained, we are faced with the question of *which* differences between means are significant. If there are three means, $\bar{X}_1$, $\bar{X}_2$, and $\bar{X}_3$, it is possible that they are all significantly different from each other. On the other hand, maybe $\bar{X}_1$ and $\bar{X}_2$ are about the same, but $\bar{X}_3$ is significantly different from those two. With a little imagination, you can see how these comparisons could become complex with as many as five or six or even more groups to be compared.

Clearly, what is needed is a technique that will enable us to determine which differences between means are significant and which are not. A number of techniques have been developed, and you may run across a reference to Duncan's multiple-range test, the Newman-Keuls procedure, the Scheffé method, Tukey's procedure, and others. Each of these methods has been developed for a particular purpose, and your instructor may have a personal bias for or against a particular technique. We will confine our discussion to Tukey's procedure, at the same time remembering that your instructor or an advanced text might prefer another approach. The Tukey procedure may be used in all cases where a significant F was obtained in the ANOVA calculation. And even when F was not significant, the procedure may be used on those mean differences *predicted to be significant prior to collection of the data.*

The Tukey Method — Unequal N's

The statistic that will enable us to evaluate differences among pairs of means is called the *studentized range statistic*, q, whose general formula is

$$q = \frac{\bar{X}_L - \bar{X}_S}{\sqrt{\dfrac{MS_{WG}}{2}\left(\dfrac{1}{N_L} + \dfrac{1}{N_s}\right)}} \tag{11-11}$$

where $\bar{X}_L$ is the larger of the two means,
   $\bar{X}_S$ is the smaller of the two means,
   MS_{WG} is the mean square within groups from the ANOVA calculations,
   N_L is the size of the group with the larger mean,
   N_S is the size of the group with the smaller mean.

If q is large enough, we can reject the hypothesis that the difference between two means is due only to sampling erroi, and we pronounce the difference as significant. How large does q have to be?

Table M in Appendix 2 lists the values for the .05 and .01 significance levels (i.e., for α). If these tabled values are equaled or exceeded by our calculated q, they are significant at the stated level. Table M is entered by using (1) the appropriate value of k, the number of means in the ANOVA, and (2) the df for the MS_{WG}, the number of degrees of freedom in the calculation of MS_{WG}.

Let us use the animal learning data shown in Table 11-5 to help clarify the procedure. Note that each mean is paired with every other mean, and the calculated q is compared with the tabled values from Table M. Since we have four means and $df = 16$ for the MS_{WG}, we enter Table M to find that $q_{05} = 4.05$ and $q_{01} = 5.19$. In Table 11-5 we see that the mean error score for squirrels ($\bar{X} = 6.4$) is significantly less than the mean error score for cats ($\bar{X} = 13$), with a q value of 5.22, $p < .01$. However, we would have to conclude that the rest of the means are not significantly different, $p > .05$.

The Tukey Method – Equal N's

The procedure described above is greatly simplified if all the groups are of equal size. If $N_1 = N_2 = N_3$, and so on, then formula 11-11 reduces to

$$q = \frac{\bar{X}_L - \bar{X}_S}{\sqrt{\dfrac{MS_{WG}}{N_G}}} \tag{11-12}$$

where N_G is the size of any group and the rest of the terms are as described earlier. When the groups are of equal size, we begin the Tukey procedure by selecting the *largest* difference between means, applying formula 11-12, and evaluating our value of q in Table M. We then repeat the procedure with the next largest difference and continue until our q is no longer significant. Obviously, since the denominator remains the same, once we have a difference between means that is not large enough to yield a significant q, it is pointless to test smaller differences. This procedure is illustrated in the **Sample Problem** at the end of this chapter.[1]

It must be emphasized that the Tukey method is only one of many methods for making multiple comparisons, and your instructor may wish to pursue one or more of the other methods mentioned earlier. An excellent resource is a summary article by Hopkins and Anderson (1973).

---

[1]It is possible to find a significant F value in your ANOVA computation and not find any q values to be significant. Such an occurrence is quite rare, however.

Table 11-5
The Tukey Method for Animal Learning Data (Errors)

Squirrels	*Cats*	*Guinea Pigs*	*Rats*
$\overline{X}$ = 6.4	$\overline{X}$ = 13	$\overline{X}$ = 12	$\overline{X}$ = 9
N = 5	N = 6	N = 3	N = 6

$$MS_{WG} = 8.7$$

$$df = N_T - k = 16$$

Squirrels–Cats:

$$q = \frac{\overline{X}_L - \overline{X}_S}{\sqrt{\frac{MS_{WG}}{2}\left(\frac{1}{N_L}+\frac{1}{N_S}\right)}} = \frac{13 - 6.4}{\sqrt{\frac{8.7}{2}\left(\frac{1}{6}+\frac{1}{5}\right)}} = \frac{6.6}{\sqrt{4.35\ (.367)}}$$

$$= \frac{6.6}{\sqrt{1.596}} = \frac{6.6}{1.26} = 5.24 \qquad\qquad \text{Significant, } p < .01$$

Squirrels–Guinea Pigs:

$$q = \frac{12 - 6.4}{\sqrt{\frac{8.7}{2}\left(\frac{1}{3}+\frac{1}{5}\right)}} = \frac{5.6}{\sqrt{4.35\ (.533)}} = \frac{5.6}{\sqrt{2.319}} = \frac{5.6}{1.52} = 3.68$$

$$\text{Not significant, } p > .05$$

Squirrels–Rats:

$$q = \frac{9 - 6.4}{\sqrt{\frac{8.7}{2}\left(\frac{1}{6}+\frac{1}{5}\right)}} = \frac{2.6}{\sqrt{4.35\ (.367)}} = \frac{2.6}{\sqrt{1.596}} = \frac{2.6}{1.26} = 2.06$$

$$\text{Not significant, } p > .05$$

Cats–Guinea Pigs:

$$q = \frac{13 - 12}{\sqrt{\frac{8.7}{2}\left(\frac{1}{6}+\frac{1}{3}\right)}} = \frac{1}{\sqrt{4.35\ (.5)}} = \frac{1}{\sqrt{2.175}} = \frac{1}{1.47} = .68$$

$$\text{Not significant, } p > .05$$

Cats–Rats:

$$q = \frac{13 - 9}{\sqrt{\frac{8.7}{2}\left(\frac{1}{6}+\frac{1}{6}\right)}} = \frac{4}{\sqrt{4.35\ (.333)}} = \frac{4}{\sqrt{1.449}} = \frac{4}{1.20} = 3.33$$

$$\text{Not significant, } p > .05$$

Guinea Pigs–Rats:

$$q = \frac{12 - 9}{\sqrt{\frac{8.7}{2}\left(\frac{1}{3}+\frac{1}{6}\right)}} = \frac{3}{\sqrt{4.35\ (.5)}} = \frac{3}{\sqrt{2.175}} = \frac{3}{1.47} = 2.04$$

$$\text{Not significant, } p > .05$$

Assumptions for the Analysis of Variance

In order for the F test to be a valid procedure for determining the significance of the differences between means, the following assumptions or restrictions must be met. These assumptions are identical to those listed in Chapter 10 for the t test.

1. The scores must be interval or ratio in nature.
2. The scores must be measures on random samples from the respective populations.
3. The populations from which the samples were drawn must be normally distributed.
4. The populations from which the samples were drawn must have approximately the same variability (homogeneity of variance).

Concluding Remarks

This elementary introduction to the analysis of variance barely touches on the use of a highly popular and versatile statistical tool. Almost any professional journal in education or the behavioral sciences will contain one or more studies where ANOVA has been used for the data analysis. The reasons for its popularity have not been obvious in our examination of the single classification method, which may appear to be nothing more than an extension of the t test for more than two means. One of the unique features of the more complex ANOVA designs is its measurement of an *interaction* effect, the relationship that one variable has to another variable in producing a significant difference. This form of ANOVA will be treated in detail in the next chapter.

Sample Problem

An industrial psychologist was investigating three different training methods for speeding up assembly line production. Thirty workers were assigned at random to three groups, and each group was trained in a different method for completing the assemblies. Each worker's performance was then measured in number of units assembled per hour. These measurements are shown below for each of the three different methods. Was there a significant difference in the workers' performance in the three training methods? If so, which differences were significant?

Method A		Method B		Method C	
X	X^2	X	X^2	X	X^2
52	2,704	61	3,721	76	5,776
54	2,916	62	3,844	65	4,225
49	2,401	68	4,624	66	4,356
62	3,844	58	3,364	76	5,776
45	2,025	43	1,849	84	7,056
47	2,209	39	1,521	83	6,889
31	961	41	1,681	78	6,084
35	1,225	50	2,500	66	4,356
41	1,681	50	2,500	73	5,329
40	1,600	53	2,809	62	3,844
456	21,566	525	28,413	729	53,691

$$\bar{X}_1 = \frac{456}{10} = 45.6 \qquad \bar{X}_2 = \frac{525}{10} = 52.5 \qquad \bar{X}_3 = \frac{729}{10} = 72.9$$

$$\bar{X}_T = \frac{\Sigma X_T}{N_T} = \frac{456 + 525 + 729}{30} = \frac{1,710}{30} = 57.0$$

$$\overset{N_T}{\Sigma} X^2 = 21,566 + 28,413 + 53,691 = 103,670$$

Sums of Squares:

$$SS_T = \overset{N_T}{\Sigma} X^2 - N_T \bar{X}_T^2 = 103,670 - 30(57)^2$$
$$= 103,670 - 97,470$$
$$SS_T = 6,200$$

$$SS_{BG} = N_1 \bar{X}_1^2 + N_2 \bar{X}_2^2 + N_3 \bar{X}_3^2 - N_T \bar{X}_T^2$$
$$= 10(45.6)^2 + 10(52.5)^2 + 10(72.9)^2 - 97,470$$
$$= 20,793.6 + 27,562.5 + 53,144.1 - 97,470$$
$$SS_{BG} = 4,030.2$$

$$SS_{WG} = \left(\overset{N_1}{\Sigma} X^2 - N_1 \bar{X}_1^2 \right) + \left(\overset{N_2}{\Sigma} X^2 - N_2 \bar{X}_2^2 \right) + \left(\overset{N_3}{\Sigma} X^2 - N_3 \bar{X}_3^2 \right)$$
$$= (21,566 - 20,793.6) + (28,413 - 27,562.5)$$
$$+ (53,691 - 53,144.1)$$
$$= 772.4 + 850.5 + 546.9$$
$$SS_{WG} = 2,169.8$$

Check:

$$SS_{BG} + SS_{WG} = SS_T$$
$$4,030.2 + 2,169.8 = 6,200$$

Mean Squares and the F Test:

$$MS_{BG} = \frac{SS_{BG}}{k-1} = \frac{4{,}030.2}{2} = 2{,}015.1$$

$$MS_{WG} = \frac{SS_{WG}}{N_T - k} = \frac{2{,}169.8}{27} = 80.36$$

$$F = \frac{MS_{BG}}{MS_{WG}} = \frac{2{,}015.1}{80.36} = 25.08$$

Source of Variance	df	SS	MS	F
Between groups	2	4,030.2	2,015.1	25.08
Within groups	27	2,169.8	80.36	
Total	29	6,200.0		

$$F_{01}, df = 2/27, \text{ is } 5.49$$
$$\text{Significant}, p < .01$$

Since an F value of 25.08 would happen less than 1% of the time by sampling error, we conclude that there is a significant difference between the means of the three training groups.

Tukey's Procedure:

Method A	Method B	Method C
$\bar{X}_1 = 45.6$	$\bar{X}_2 = 52.5$	$\bar{X}_3 = 72.9$

$$MS_{WG} = 80.36; df = 27; k = 3$$

Methods A and C: $q = \dfrac{\bar{X}_L - \bar{X}_S}{\sqrt{\dfrac{MS_{WG}}{N}}} = \dfrac{72.9 - 45.6}{\sqrt{\dfrac{80.36}{10}}} = \dfrac{27.3}{\sqrt{8.036}}$

$$= \frac{27.3}{2.83} = 9.65 \qquad\qquad \text{Significant}, p < .01$$

Methods B and C: $q = \dfrac{72.9 - 52.5}{2.83} = \dfrac{20.4}{2.83} = 7.21$

$$\text{Significant}, p < .01$$

Methods A and B: $q = \dfrac{52.5 - 45.6}{2.83} = \dfrac{6.9}{2.83} = 2.44$

$$\text{Not significant}, p > .05$$

And we conclude that method C is superior to methods A and B, while there appears to be no significant difference between methods A and B. Note that we used formula 11-12 for Tukey's procedure, since there were an equal number of subjects in the three groups.

Study Questions

1. Why is the t test inappropriate for testing the significance of the difference between more than two means?
2. Define the term *sum of squares*. Is this a good measure of variability?
3. Define the term *variance*.
4. Describe in your own words what is meant by the expression $(X_1 - \bar{X}_1) + (\bar{X}_1 - \bar{X}_T) = (X_1 - \bar{X}_T)$.
5. Which type of variability (between groups or within groups) will always be present, even if there are no significant differences between the means? Why is this so?
6. What does MS_{WG} represent? MS_{BG}? Why should the ratio MS_{BG}/MS_{WG} equal 1.0 under the null hypothesis?
7. A researcher has seven subjects in group 1, five in group 2, and eight in group 3. How large must the F value be to be significant at the .05 level?
8. You are running an analysis of variance on data from four groups of subjects with seven subjects in each group. If you use Tukey's procedure to test for significant differences among the means, how large a q value will you need for significance at the .05 level?

Exercises

1. Use the deviation formulas (as in Table 11-2) to obtain SS_T, SS_{BG}, and SS_{WG} for the data below.

Group 1	Group 2	Group 3
6	7	11
3	9	11
8	7	9
2	8	6
1	9	8

2. Calculate MS_{BG}, MS_{WG}, and the F test for the data above. Is there a significant difference between the means?
3. Use the computational formulas for SS_T, SS_{BG}, and SS_{WG} on the data in exercise 1, and check your results against the deviation method.
4. In a study on warning signal systems in aircraft, an investigator compared three methods of alerting the operator to a potentially dangerous situation. In one method the pointer on a dial changed its position by 30°. In the second method a warning light changed

its color from red to green. In the third method the dial pointer changed position *and* the color of the illumination changed. Seven subjects served in each condition, and their reaction times were measured in hundredths of seconds. Was there a significant difference between the methods? If so, which differences between means were significant?

Pointer	Light	Light and Pointer
78	68	54
72	69	48
70	72	50
70	74	50
55	60	35
57	50	34
60	48	51

5. A social psychologist was interested in seeing if there were differences in tipping behavior in restaurants among cigarette smokers, pipe smokers, and nonsmokers. The value (in cents) of tips left by a sample from each category is shown below. Was there a significant difference? If so, which differences were significant?

Cigarette Smokers	Pipe Smokers	Non- smokers
75	50	85
65	55	75
65	50	80
80	60	65
85	45	70
85	45	75
80	30	60
70	35	90
75	40	60
60	40	95

12 Two-Way Analysis of Variance

The preceding chapter was devoted entirely to the *one-way* ANOVA. If, for example, we want to see which of three teaching methods (lecture, discussion, or programmed workbook) is best for teaching freshman English to college students, we can assign freshmen at random to one of three groups. Each group can then learn under its designated instructional method, and we can use final test scores as our criterion measure. We can diagram the results schematically as below, where the blanks are final exam scores, and $\bar{X}_1$, $\bar{X}_2$, and $\bar{X}_3$ are the group means for the three instructional methods.

Lecture	Discussion	Workbook
——	——	——
——	——	——
——	——	——
——	——	——
$\bar{X}_1 =$	$\bar{X}_2 =$	$\bar{X}_3 =$

The null hypothesis would state that $\mu_1 = \mu_2 = \mu_3$ and any difference between $\bar{X}_1$, $\bar{X}_2$, and $\bar{X}_3$ is due to sampling error. This design is called a one-way or single-classification ANOVA because only *one* variable (teaching method) is being tested. In this example, we are comparing three levels (lecture, discussion, and workbook) of a single variable. We might have 3 or 7 or 15 different levels, but we still are dealing with only one variable, that of teaching method.

However, we may sometimes want to investigate the effects of *two* variables simultaneously. We may wish to see if the teaching methods above have different effects with superior students than with average students. We could do such an analysis by conducting two separate experiments — one with superior students and one with average students. This, however, would be inefficient, since it would require twice as much effort as a single experiment. And, unfortunately, we would not be able to get a direct measure of the *interaction effect*: one teaching method might be better for superior students, while another method might work better for average students! In the material to follow we will develop a method for looking at the effects of two variables simultaneously, the two-way ANOVA.

Factorial Designs

The two-way ANOVA that we will be examining is called a factorial design, indicating that we are looking at the effects of two factors (variables) simultaneously. For example, let us suppose that we have 60 superior students (determined by their college entrance exam scores) and 60 average students, and we assign 20 of each at random to each of the three English teaching methods mentioned earlier. Since we have two ability levels (superior and average) and three teaching methods (lecture, discussion, and workbook), we have a 2×3 (say "two by three") factorial design. Factorial designs come in all shapes and sizes (3×7, 2×4, and so on), depending on how many levels we have for each of the two variables.

The 2×3 factorial design for the ability level and teaching method experiment is presented in Table 12-1. Each compartment is called a *cell* and will contain the final exam scores for the 20 students in that cell. For example, the upper left cell would have the final exam scores for the 20 superior students taught under the lecture method. After the data have been tabulated into rows and columns as in Table 12-1, a factorial design is always analyzed in terms of two components — main effects and interaction effects.

Table 12-1
An Illustration of a Two-Factor Experiment

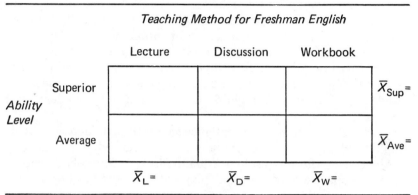

Teaching Method for Freshman English

	Lecture	Discussion	Workbook	
Superior				$\bar{X}_{Sup} =$
Average				$\bar{X}_{Ave} =$
	$\bar{X}_L =$	$\bar{X}_D =$	$\bar{X}_W =$	

Ability Level (labels to the left of the Superior/Average rows)

Main Effects

Obviously, we are interested in the effects of our variables or factors, and these are called *main* effects. In this example, we are looking at the possible effects of teaching method and ability level.

Let us first consider the variable of *ability level*, indicated by the row means. If we disregard which teaching method is used, we have a mean for 60 superior students ($\bar{X}_{Sup}$) and a mean for 60 average students ($\bar{X}_{Ave}$). Even if there were no *real* difference between the performance of superior and average students, we still would expect a slight difference in the sample means, $\bar{X}_{Sup}$ and $\bar{X}_{Ave}$, due to sampling error, so we will use the null hypothesis that these two sample means are random samples from populations with identical means. Later on, we will develop an F test to see if we can reject the null hypothesis that there is no difference in ability level (i.e., that there is a main effect of ability level).

Similarly, we now consider the variable of teaching method, indicated by the column means. We disregard the ability level of the students and note that we have three means — one for the 40 students in the lecture method ($\bar{X}_L$), one for the 40 in the discussion method ($\bar{X}_D$), and one for the 40 using the workbook ($\bar{X}_W$). Under the null hypothesis there is no real difference in the populations from which the sample means were drawn, and differences between $\bar{X}_L$, $\bar{X}_D$, and $\bar{X}_W$ are simply due to sampling error. Again, an F test is used to see if these differences are large enough to be significant, that is, if there is a main effect of teaching method.

Interaction Effects

An important purpose of the factorial design is to explore possible *interaction effects*. For example, variable A may have a different effect at one level of variable B than it does at another level of variable B. In the teaching method example, it might be that average students do better than superior students when using the programmed workbook (the superior students might find it boring and not do their best work) while superior students might do better than average students in the discussion group method.

This state of affairs is an interaction effect: one variable is behaving differently at one level of the other variable. When an interaction effect occurs, our interest in any main effects is diminished, since the effect of one main variable is dependent upon the level of the other main variable. In our example, if there were a significant interaction effect and someone asked, "Which teaching method is best for freshman English?" we would answer, "It depends on whether you are working with superior or average students." Conversely, if the question were which students do better in freshman English, we would have to say that it would depend on which teaching method is used.

Graphical Methods to Illustrate Interaction

A graph of the result of a factorial experiment is often helpful in understanding the concept of interaction. Let us first consider an experiment where there is no significant interaction effect.

An example of a nonsignificant interaction. A developmental psychologist is studying differences in reading ability between boys and girls and is also interested in whether these differences change with age. She administers a reading test to students in the fourth, fifth, and sixth grades. This is a 2×3 factorial design — two levels of sex (boys and girls) and three levels of grade placement (fourth, fifth, and sixth) — and the reading test scores are tabulated for each cell. The means for each cell, as well as row and column means, are shown in Table 12-2.

After completing our table of means, we construct a graph with the dependent variable (reading scores) on the y-axis and one of the main variables (let us use grade level) on the x-axis. The cell means are plotted for both boys and girls and the resultant graph is shown in Figure 12-1. Any main effects can easily be seen, so if sex differences are significant we conclude that girls had higher reading scores at all grade levels. Similarly, if there is a significant difference between grade levels, we conclude that reading scores are lowest at the fourth grade and highest at the sixth.

Table 12-2
Table of Means for Reading Scores of
Boys and Girls in Grades 4-6

		Girls	Boys	
			Sex	
Grade	4	$\bar{X} = 29$	$\bar{X} = 19$	$\bar{X}_{R_1} = 24$
	5	$\bar{X} = 40$	$\bar{X} = 30$	$\bar{X}_{R_2} = 35$
	6	$\bar{X} = 42$	$\bar{X} = 32$	$\bar{X}_{R_3} = 37$
		$\bar{X}_{C_1} = 37$	$\bar{X}_{C_2} = 27$	

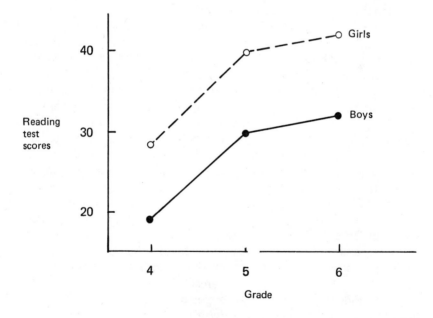

Figure 12-1
Reading test scores: an example of a
nonsignificant interaction.

However, our main interest in drawing the graph is to examine any possible interaction effect. We note that there is a separation between the curves for girls and boys, but the separation is the same at all three grades; that is, the curves are parallel. If the curves are parallel, *there is no interaction effect*, since the reading scores are not affected by the sex of the student more at one grade level than another. An examination of the table of means in Table 12-2 is also helpful. We note that the differences between the column means (girls and boys) is $37 - 27 = 10$ points, and this difference is the same at all grade levels. And this, by definition, means that there is no interaction effect.

An example of a significant interaction. An educational psychologist was investigating characteristics of creative children. One of her tests for creativity presented the subject with a number of small circles, and the subject was asked to draw as many things using these circles as possible. The psychologist wanted to know what effect there would be if the students were given examples to start them out. She then developed two sets of instructions for the creativity test — one in which the student was shown two examples of drawings from circles and one in which the student was shown no examples at all.

She also wanted to see what effect the two sets of instructions had on "creative" and "noncreative" children. She asked several elementary school teachers to identify which of their children were creative and which were not creative, based strictly on classroom observation.

This design is, of course, a 2×2 factorial design. One factor is *instructions* (the two levels are "examples" and "no examples") and the other is *type of student* (the two levels are "creative" and "noncreative"). The elementary school teachers identified 20 creative and 20 noncreative students. Ten of each were assigned at random to the group that was given examples, and ten of each were also assigned to the group that was not given examples. The creativity test was administered and scored for the number of objects drawn from the circles in 5 minutes. The mean number of objects drawn by each group is shown in Table 12-3 and Figure 12-2.

It is obvious from the column means of Table 12-3 that creative students produced more drawings ($\bar{X}_{C_1} = 9$) than noncreative students ($\bar{X}_{C_2} = 4$). But of greater interest is a possible interaction effect shown in Figure 12-2. When examples were used in the instructions, there was not much difference between creative and noncreative students (who had means of 7 and 5, respectively). However, when no examples were given, creative students produced more drawings, while noncreative students were much less productive (with means of 11 and 3, respectively).

Table 12-3
Number of Original Drawings by "Creative" and "Noncreative" Students with Different Instructional Sets

Type of Student

	Creative	Noncreative	
Examples	$\bar{X} = 7$	$\bar{X} = 5$	$\bar{X}_{R_1} = 6$
No examples	$\bar{X} = 11$	$\bar{X} = 3$	$\bar{X}_{R_2} = 7$
	$\bar{X}_{C_1} = 9$	$\bar{X}_{C_2} = 4$	

Instructions

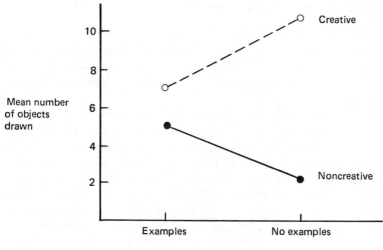

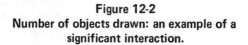

Figure 12-2
Number of objects drawn: an example of a significant interaction.

Here we have a clear interaction effect. The curves in Figure 12-2 are obviously not parallel. The instructions given had different effects, depending on the type of student. It is possible that the creative students were blocked or inhibited by the examples while the noncreative students were helped by the examples. However, when no examples were given, the noncreative students were definitely handicapped, while the creative students were free to use their inventive abilities to create new forms.

A Definition of Interaction

Interaction can be defined as a significant departure from a parallel relationship of two or more curves. Even if there is no real interaction between the two variables, we, of course, do not expect to get perfectly parallel curves. The cell means will fluctuate just by sampling error, causing some degree of divergence or convergence from a parallel relationship. However, at some point the deviation from parallelism may be so great that we reject the notion of no interaction and say that we have a significant interaction effect. The sections that follow describe the approach we will use to determine significance.

Calculating the Sums of Squares

As with the one-way ANOVA, we eventually need to calculate variance estimates of the form $\Sigma x^2 / (N - 1)$, so we need to find various values of Σx^2 or sums of squares. We will consider only the computational formulas in this chapter and not develop the deviation formulas as in the last chapter.

The formulas are easier to understand in terms of an example, so let us suppose that the topic of perceptual-motor skills with preferred or nonpreferred hand was investigated by an experimental psychologist. The motor skills performance was measured by pursuit rotor. The apparatus is something like a phonograph turntable that has a small disk about the size of a dime on it. The subject attempted to follow this disk with a stylus as it went around. An electronic timer kept track of the time that the stylus was in contact with the disk. This measurement, called "time on target," was recorded to the nearest second. The greater the time on target, the better the performance.

The experimenter was interested in seeing how performance was affected at different pursuit rotor speeds and chose 20, 40, and 60 revolutions per minute (RPM) as the three levels of task difficulty.

Table 12-4
Time on Target (Seconds) for Preferred or Nonpreferred Hand
at Three Pursuit Rotor Speeds

	Preferred Hand			Nonpreferred Hand		
	20	*40*	*60*	*20*	*40*	*60*
	8	9	6	5	1	2
	7	5	5	5	2	0
	8	7	4	7	4	1
	6	4	5	6	2	1
	6	5	5	7	6	1
ΣX:	35	30	25	30	15	5
ΣX^2:	249	196	127	184	61	7
$\overline{X}$:	7	6	5	6	3	1

$$\overline{X}_T = \frac{35 + 30 + 25 + 30 + 15 + 5}{30} = 4.67$$

$$\overset{N_T}{\Sigma} X^2 = 249 + 196 + 127 + 184 + 61 + 7 = 824$$

Since there were two levels of hand used (preferred vs. nonpreferred) and three levels of task difficulty (20, 40, and 60 RPM), this was a 2×3 factorial design.

Thirty subjects volunteered for the experiment and were assigned at random to *one* of the six combinations of pursuit rotor speed and hand used. Thus, there were five subjects in each combination. Each subject's time on target during a 20-second trial is shown in Table 12-4. As we have done so many times before, we calculate ΣX, ΣX^2, and $\overline{X}$ for each column. For the first step, we will be using the computational formulas for the one-way ANOVA from the last chapter, so we also need the total mean ($\overline{X}_T$) and the sum of all the squared scores ($\overset{N_T}{\Sigma} X^2$).

To begin our two-way ANOVA, we first calculate SS_T, SS_{BG}, and SS_{WG} as we did in the last chapter.

$$SS_T = \sum^{N_T} X^2 - N_T\bar{X}_T{}^2 = 824 - (30)(4.67)^2$$

$$= 824 - 654.27 = 169.73$$

$$SS_{BG} = N_1\bar{X}_1{}^2 + N_2\bar{X}_2{}^2 + \ldots + N_6\bar{X}_6{}^2 - N_T\bar{X}_T{}^2$$

$$= 5(7)^2 + 5(6)^2 + 5(5)^2 + 5(6)^2 + 5(3)^2 + 5(1)^2 - 654.27$$

$$= 780 - 654.27 = 125.73$$

$$SS_{WG} = SS_T - SS_{BG} = 169.73 - 125.73 = 44.0$$

Note that we calculated SS_{WG} by simply subtracting SS_{BG} from SS_T. We could, of course, have calculated SS_{WG} directly using formula 11-10.

Now that we have our sums of squares separated into the familiar SS_{BG} and SS_{WG}, we need to consider their meaning in a two-way ANOVA. As in the one-way ANOVA, SS_{WG} will be used to calculate a variance estimate, an estimate of the variance of the population from which the samples came. We will have more to say about this estimate later. And what about SS_{BG}? In the one-way ANOVA of the last chapter, SS_{BG} was used to calculate a variance estimate which, under the null hypothesis, was estimating the same variance as that based on SS_{WG}.

But, in the two-way ANOVA, SS_{BG} reflects *both* the effects of the row variable (speed) and the column variable (hand used), *as well as* the interaction effect, if any. This is easiest to understand if we present the results of Table 12-4 in the form of a table of means. This 2×3 table in Table 12-5 shows 5 subjects in each of the 6 combinations of hand used and pursuit rotor speed. Each of the 6 cells shows the N of 5 in the corner and the mean time on target for the 5 subjects. Note also the row and column means, which indicate performance by a particular row or column. For example, $\bar{X}_{R_2} = 4.5$ is the mean time on target for the 10 subjects at 40 RPM, while $\bar{X}_{C_1} = 6.0$ is the mean for the 15 subjects using preferred hands.

We are now ready to begin calculating the sums of squares which will be used directly in our two-way ANOVA. The formula for the sum of squares for the row variable, SS_R, is

$$SS_R = N_{R_1}\bar{X}_{R_1}{}^2 + N_{R_2}\bar{X}_{R_2}{}^2 + N_{R_3}\bar{X}_{R_3}{}^2 - N_T\bar{X}_T{}^2 \qquad \textbf{(12-1)}$$

Plugging in the values from Table 12-5, we get

$$SS_R = 10(6.5)^2 + 10(4.5)^2 + 10(3.0)^2 - 30(4.67)^2$$

Table 12-5
**Mean Time on Target as a Function of Hand Used
and Pursuit Rotor Speed**

Hand

		Preferred		Nonpreferred		

	Preferred	Nonpreferred	
20	$\bar{X} = 7$ 5	$\bar{X} = 6$ 5	$\bar{X}_{R_1} = 6.5$
40	$\bar{X} = 6$ 5	$\bar{X} = 3$ 5	$\bar{X}_{R_2} = 4.5$
60	$\bar{X} = 5$ 5	$\bar{X} = 1$ 5	$\bar{X}_{R_3} = 3.0$

Speed (revolutions per minute)

$\bar{X}_{C_1} = 6.0$ $\bar{X}_{C_2} = 3.33$ $\bar{X}_T = 4.67$

$$= 422.5 + 202.5 + 90 - 654.27$$
$$= 60.73$$

The formula for the sum of squares for the column variable, SS_C, is

$$SS_C = N_{C_1}\bar{X}_{C_1}{}^2 + N_{C_2}\bar{X}_{C_2}{}^2 - N_T\bar{X}_T{}^2 \tag{12-2}$$

Plugging in the values from Table 12-5, we get

$$SS_C = 15(6.0)^2 + 15(3.33)^2 - 30(4.67)^2$$
$$= 540 + 166.33 - 654.27$$
$$= 52.06$$

The formula for the sum of squares for interaction, $SS_{R \times C}$ (say "rows by columns"), is

$$SS_{R \times C} = SS_{BG} - SS_R - SS_C \tag{12-3}$$

Plugging in the values already obtained, we get

$$SS_{R \times C} = 125.73 - 60.73 - 52.06$$
$$= 12.94$$

Calculating the Variances

The previous section dealt with the calculation of the sums of squares, which are the numerators of the variances we wish to calculate. We noted in the last chapter that variances are sums of squares divided by their respective degrees of freedom (df). We are now interested in the total df ($N_T - 1$) and also in the df associated with the two main variables (rows and columns) and the interaction between the two (rows by columns).

The df for the row variable is one less than the number of rows, or $r - 1$.

$$df_R = r - 1 \tag{12-4}$$

In the example, the row variable is pursuit rotor speed at three levels (20, 40, and 60 RPM), so the df for speed is

$$df_R = 3 - 1 = 2$$

The df for the column variable is one less than the number of columns, or $c - 1$.

$$df_C = c - 1 \tag{12-5}$$

In the example, the column variable is the hand used with two levels (preferred or nonpreferred), so the df for hand used is

$$df_C = 2 - 1 = 1$$

The df for the interaction of the row variable and column variable is one less than the number of levels of the row variable multiplied by one less than the number of levels of the column variable, or $(r - 1)(c - 1)$. The formula for the df for interaction is

$$df_{R \times C} = (r - 1)(c - 1) \tag{12-6}$$

In the example there are three speeds and two hands, so

$$df_{R \times C} = (3 - 1)(2 - 1) = 2$$

In the last chapter the formula for the within-groups df was given as $N_T - k$, where k was the number of groups. We use the same approach in the two-way ANOVA except that the number of groups is now the number of cells. Since we have r rows and c columns, the number of groups would be $r \times c$, or rc. Thus, the within-groups df would be $N_T - rc$.

$$df_{WG} = N_T - rc \tag{12-7}$$

In the example there were 30 subjects divided among three rows and two columns so the within-groups df is

$$df_{WG} = 30 - (3)(2) = 24$$

We again expect that the addition of the various degrees of freedom should equal the total df, $N_T - 1$. Using the symbolic notation of the previous paragraphs, we would have $df_T = df_R + df_C + df_{R \times C} + df_{WG}$. Gathering the numbers we just calculated for the pursuit rotor experiment, we have $2 + 1 + 2 + 24 = 29$, which is the same as $N_T - 1 = 30 - 1 = 29$.

The Mean Squares

We can now calculate the variance estimates, or mean squares, by dividing each sum of squares by its appropriate df. We will have four mean squares in a two-way ANOVA, one each for rows, columns, rows by columns, and within groups. The formulas are:

$$MS_R = \frac{SS_R}{r - 1} \tag{12-8}$$

$$MS_C = \frac{SS_C}{c - 1} \tag{12-9}$$

$$MS_{R \times C} = \frac{SS_{R \times C}}{(r - 1)(c - 1)} \tag{12-10}$$

$$MS_{WG} = \frac{SS_{WG}}{N_T - rc} \tag{12-11}$$

From the pursuit rotor data, we would calculate the following mean squares.

$$MS_R = \frac{60.73}{2} = 30.365$$

$$MS_C = \frac{52.06}{1} = 52.06$$

$$MS_{R \times C} = \frac{12.94}{(2)(1)} = 6.47$$

$$MS_{WG} = \frac{44}{30 - (3)(2)} = 1.83$$

The Meaning of the Variance Estimates

As in the last chapter, we stop momentarily after calculating the mean squares in order to reflect on their meaning. They obviously are variance estimates of some sort, since they have a sum of squares in the numerator and degrees of freedom in the denominator. But just what are they estimating?

MS_{WG}. In the one-way ANOVA of the last chapter, MS_{WG} was a combined estimate of the variance of the populations from which each sample came. Under the null hypothesis, the population means are identical so MS_{WG_1}, MS_{WG_2}, and so on were estimates of the same population variance, and MS_{WG} was the average of these individual estimates from each group. However, in a two-way ANOVA each cell corresponds to a single "group," and we again could consider MS_{WG} for cell 1, MS_{WG} for cell 2, and so on as individual estimates of the same population variance. Thus, MS_{WG} in a two-way ANOVA is a combined estimate of the variance of the population from which each sample came.

MS_R. The variance estimate based on the row means is *also* an estimate of the population variance, *if the null hypothesis is true*. In other words, if $\mu_{R_1} = \mu_{R_2} = \mu_{R_3}$, and so on, the variance estimate (MS_R) derived from the sample row means ($\bar{X}_{R_1}$, $\bar{X}_{R_2}$, etc.) is estimating the same population variance as MS_{WG}. We expect, of course, that the sample row means will vary just by sampling error and MS_R will reflect this sampling variation among $\bar{X}_{R_1}$, $\bar{X}_{R_2}$, and so on. However, if the row variable is exerting a significant effect, the row means will vary more than what would be expected by chance, and MS_R will be larger than the variance estimate, MS_{WG}. With the pursuit rotor data of Table 12-5, we are saying under the null hypothesis that the sample row means of 6.5, 4.5, and 3.0 seconds on target for the various pursuit rotor speeds are different simply because of chance variation.

MS_C. Using the same logic we applied to MS_R, we note that under the null hypothesis, MS_C is also an estimate of the population variance calculated from the column means. If $\mu_{C_1} = \mu_{C_2} = \mu_{C_3}$, and so on, we expect that the column means ($\bar{X}_{C_1}$, $\bar{X}_{C_2}$, etc.) will vary only by sampling error, and the variance estimate, MS_C, will be an estimate of the same population variance as MS_{WG}. However, if the column variable is exerting a significant effect, the column means will vary more than what would be expected by chance, and MS_C will be larger than the variance estimate, MS_{WG}. In the example, we are saying under the null hypothesis that the sample column means of 6.0 and 3.33 for the preferred and nonpreferred hands are different only because of chance variation.

$MS_{R \times C}$. Before investigating what the remaining variance estimate, $MS_{R \times C}$, is estimating, let us review the concept of interaction. In Table 12-2 we saw that there was no interaction effect of reading test scores of boys and girls in fourth, fifth, and sixth grades. We stressed that the graph in Figure 12-1 showed *parallel* lines, indicating that the difference between boys and girls was consistent at the three grade levels. Note that, when there is no interaction, we can predict the value of the cell means from the column and row means alone. For example, the girls' mean and boys' mean are 37 and 27, respectively. The total mean would be 32, and these two column means are 5 points on each side of the total mean. Now, looking at the row mean of 24 for fourth-graders, we note that if there is no interaction present at this level the cell means for fourth-grade girls and fourth-grade boys should be 5 points on each side of the row mean for fourth-graders. This would yield means of 29 and 19, respectively, and is exactly what is shown in the fourth-grade cells of Table 12-2. The same calculations could be done, of course, to obtain the means in the remaining cells. In general, we note that for any table of results we have now established what the cell means should be when there is no interaction present. We need only remember that the sample cell means could be expected to deviate from these expected values because of sampling error. $MS_{R \times C}$ is a variance estimate based on the deviations from these expected values, and under the null hypothesis (no significant interaction) $MS_{R \times C}$ is also an estimate of the variance of the population from which the samples came. And using our usual logic, if the deviations from these expected values are significant (i.e., if the interaction is exerting a significant effect), we note that $MS_{R \times C}$ will be larger than it would if the deviation of the cell means about their expected values were due to chance variation. As a result, the variance estimate of $MS_{R \times C}$ will be larger than the estimate given by MS_{WG}. In the pursuit rotor example of Table 12-5, we are saying under the null hypothesis that the sample cell means of 7, 6, 6, 5, 3, and 1 are deviating from their expected values by an amount due only to chance variation.

The F Tests

Finally, we are ready to attempt what we set out to do at the beginning of this chapter, to see if one or both of the variables or their interaction in a two-factor experiment has had a significant effect. As with the one-way ANOVA, we will set up a ratio of two variance estimates and see if the resulting F value is significant. Note that the denominator in each case is MS_{WG}, the estimate of the population variance that is *not* affected by the action of the row variable or column variable or by their interaction. The numerator in each case will be a mean square of the row variable or column variable or their interaction. As we noted in the preceding section, these variance estimates are also estimates of the population variance if the null hypothesis is true. However, if the variable is exerting a significant effect, the respective variance estimate will be larger than the estimate given by MS_{WG}, and the F value will be significantly greater than 1. The formula for the row effect is

$$F_R = \frac{MS_R}{MS_{WG}} \tag{12-12}$$

The formula for the column effect is

$$F_C = \frac{MS_C}{MS_{WG}} \tag{12-13}$$

The formula for the interaction effect is

$$F_{R \times C} = \frac{MS_{R \times C}}{MS_{WG}} \tag{12-14}$$

And the calculations for the pursuit rotor data are, for the row effect:

$$F_R = \frac{30.365}{1.83} = 16.59$$

for the column effect:

$$F_C = \frac{52.06}{1.83} = 28.45$$

and for the interaction effect:

$$F_{R \times C} = \frac{6.47}{1.83} = 3.54$$

We now summarize the results of all our computational efforts in the typical ANOVA summary table shown in Table 12-6.

Each F value is evaluated by entering Table F in Appendix 2 with the df associated with the numerator and the df associated with the denominator. For example, the main effect of speed is tested by the F ratio of MS_R/MS_{WG}, with 2 and 24 df, respectively. In Table F we note that for 2 and 24 df, our F needs to exceed 3.40 at the 5% level and 5.61 at the 1% level. Since our calculated value of 16.59 exceeds 5.61, we conclude that our F is significant beyond the .01 level. We evaluate the other F values and note their probability levels as shown in Table 12-6.

We are now ready to analyze the results of the pursuit rotor experiment. Our first task is to graph the means shown earlier in Table 12-5, and this graph is shown in Figure 12-3. We see from the ANOVA

Table 12-6
ANOVA Summary Table for Pursuit Rotor Data

Source of Variance	df	SS	MS	F
Speed (R)	2	60.73	30.36	16.59*
Hand (C)	1	52.06	52.06	28.45*
Speed by hand (R x C)	2	12.94	6.47	3.54**
Within groups	24	44.00	1.83	
Totals	29	169.73		

* Significant, $p < .01$ ** Significant, $p < .05$

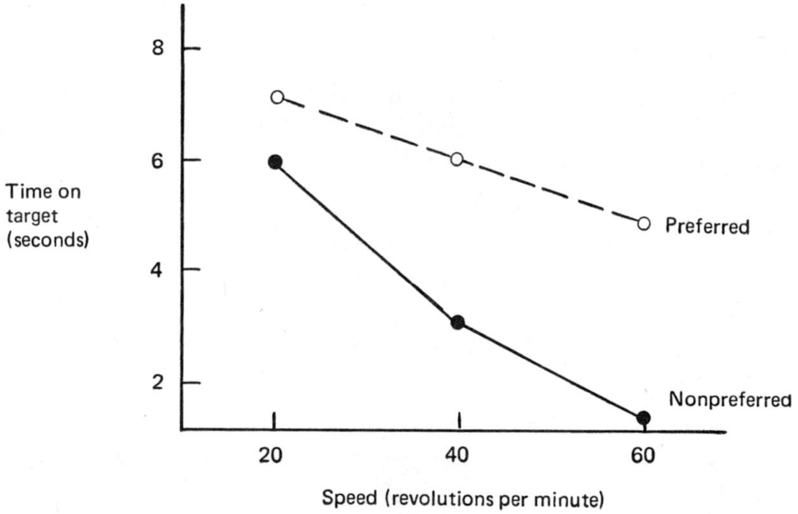

Figure 12-3
Time on target as a function of hand used
at three pursuit rotor speeds

summary table that the main effect of pursuit rotor speed is significant, and a glance at Figure 12-3 shows that performance with both pre-ferred and nonpreferred hands decreased as the speed increased from 20 to 60 RPM. The summary table also shows a significant effect of handedness, and the separation of the curves shows better performance for subjects using their preferred hand than subjects using their nonpreferred hand.

And, finally, the interaction effect is significant ($p < .05$), which is shown on the graph by the curves diverging as pursuit rotor speed increases. The interaction simply says that at the 20 RPM speed there was not much difference in the performance between preferred and nonpreferred hands. However, as the speed increased, performance of the nonpreferred hand deteriorated more rapidly than performance with the preferred hand. As we noted earlier, a significant interaction effect always modifies our interpretation of the main effects. For example, in response to the question "Does an increase in pursuit rotor speed interfere with performance?" we would answer that the amount of interference depends on whether one is using the preferred or nonpreferred hand.

Assumptions for the Two-Way ANOVA

The assumptions for the two-way ANOVA are identical to those for the one-way ANOVA described in the last chapter, except that we are now talking about cells rather than groups.

1. Data must be in interval or ratio form.
2. Subjects must be assigned at random to cells.
3. The populations from which the samples are drawn must be normal.
4. The populations from which the samples are drawn must have equal variances.

In addition to the familiar assumptions listed, the ANOVA procedure described in this chapter assumes *an equal number of observations per cell*. In our pursuit rotor experiment shown in Table 12-5, there were 5 subjects in each of the 6 cells for a total of 30. It is essential for this ANOVA procedure that there be an equal number of subjects in each cell. There are methods for handling ANOVA with unequal numbers in the cells, but the procedures are beyond the scope of this text. If you are interested, consult an advanced statistics text (e.g., Glass and Stanley, 1970) for details of the method used.

Multiple Comparisons

After a significant F has been obtained with either of the two variables or with their interaction, a logical step is to investigate which differences between means are significant. Referring to the ANOVA summary table of our pursuit rotor results in Table 12-6, we note that there is a significant main effect of hand used. Looking at Table 12-5 and Figure 12-3, we note that the preferred hand was compared with the nonpreferred hand at three different speeds and that the difference between preferred and nonpreferred hand increases as pursuit rotor speed increases. But are the differences at all three speeds significant? There is not much of a difference at 20 RPM, and this difference might not be significant, while the differences at 40 and 60 RPM may indeed be significant. To test for significant differences among these and other pairs of differences, a test for *multiple comparisons* is needed. As was pointed out in the last chapter, tests developed by Scheffé, Duncan, and others can be used, and the article by Hopkins and Anderson (1973) will provide you with the necessary information about these.

Concluding Remarks

In two rather concentrated chapters we have covered only a small fraction of the possible ANOVA designs. Our interest in an introductory level statistics text is to become familiar with some of the basic concepts underlying this powerful statistical technique. Should you take another statistics course, you will undoubtedly spend much of the time on a variety of ANOVA designs, some of which are mentioned in **Note 12-1.** When you see how ANOVA can be used to analyze complex relationships among variables, it is easy to understand its wide popularity among researchers.

Note 12-1
Split-Plot Designs?

A casual glance at journal articles, books, and other publications in education and the behavioral sciences shows a wide variety of applications of the analysis of variance — and it is easy to develop the misconception that the analysis of variance is the unique province of these fields. However, much of the theory and application of ANOVA grew out of agricultural and biological research. R. A. Fisher (the *F* test bears his initial) and his associates at the Rothamsted Experiment Station, in England, were initially responsible for developing much of the experimental design and analysis used in assessing the effects of soil conditions, types of fertilizer, time of planting, amount of moisture, and a host of other conditions related to agricultural productivity.

Randomized blocks, split-plots, factorial design, and other such exotic terms were the result of early agricultural and biological research. Gradually, Fisher's applications and ideas were adopted and expanded by researchers in other fields, and present-day research efforts are greatly simplified by the early work of Fisher and the work of subsequent theorists.

Sample Problem

A researcher is interested in characteristics of obesity and is studying the amount of effort expended by obese subjects and normal-weight subjects to obtain food. A subject enters the laboratory and is told to fill out an attitude questionnaire. At the table where the subject sits is a bowl of peanuts. For half the subjects the bowl contains shelled peanuts, and for the other half the peanuts are in the shells. The experimenter chooses 20 obese and 20 normal-weight subjects from a pool of volunteers and records the number of peanuts each subject eats while filling out the questionnaire. This is a 2×2 factorial design (obese and normal subjects with shelled and unshelled peanuts), with 10 subjects of each weight assigned at random to the shelled or unshelled condition. The results are shown below.

	Obese		*Normal*	
	Shelled	*Unshelled*	*Shelled*	*Unshelled*
	16	4	10	7
	17	2	5	9
	12	2	9	6
	14	0	10	4
	13	1	9	3
	10	3	7	8
	9	2	6	7
	17	1	8	10
	16	1	5	4
	16	4	11	2
ΣX:	140	20	80	60
ΣX^2:	2,036	56	682	424
$\bar{X}$:	14	2	8	6

$$\bar{X}_T = \frac{140 + 20 + 80 + 60}{40} = 7.5$$

$$\sum^{N_T} X^2 = 2,036 + 56 + 682 + 424 = 3,198$$

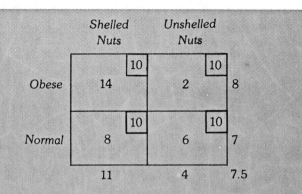

Sums of Squares:

$$SS_T = \overset{N_T}{\Sigma} X^2 - N_T \bar{X}_T^2 = 3{,}198 - 40(7.5)^2 = 3{,}198 - 2{,}250 = 948$$

$$SS_{BG} = N_1\bar{X}_1^2 = N_2\bar{X}_2^2 + N_3\bar{X}_3^2 + N_4\bar{X}_4^2 - N_T\bar{X}_T^2$$

$$= 10(14)^2 + 10(2)^2 + 10(8)^2 + 10(6)^2 - 40(7.5)^2$$

$$= 3{,}000 - 2{,}250 = 750$$

$$SS_{WG} = SS_T - SS_{BG} = 948 - 750 = 198$$

$$SS_R = N_{R_1}\bar{X}_{R_1}^2 + N_{R_2}\bar{X}_{R_2}^2 - N_T\bar{X}_T^2 = 20(8)^2 + 20(7)^2 - 40(7.5)^2 = 10$$

$$SS_C = N_{C_1}\bar{X}_{C_1}^2 + N_{C_2}\bar{X}_{C_2}^2 - N_T\bar{X}_T^2 = 20(11)^2 + 20(4)^2 - 40(7.5)^2 = 490$$

$$SS_{R \times C} = SS_{BG} - SS_R - SS_C = 750 - 10 - 490 = 250$$

Mean Squares and F Tests:

$$MS_R = \frac{SS_R}{r-1} = \frac{10}{1} = 10$$

$$MS_C = \frac{SS_C}{c-1} = \frac{490}{1} = 490$$

$$MS_{R \times C} = \frac{SS_{R \times C}}{(r-1)(c-1)} = \frac{250}{1} = 250$$

$$MS_{WG} = \frac{SS_{WG}}{N_T - rc} = \frac{198}{40-4} = 5.5$$

$$F_R = \frac{MS_R}{MS_{WG}} = \frac{10}{5.5} = 1.82$$

$$F_C = \frac{MS_C}{MS_{WG}} = \frac{490}{5.5} = 89.10$$

$$F_{R \times C} = \frac{MS_{R \times C}}{MS_{WG}} = \frac{250}{5.5} = 45.45$$

ANOVA Summary Table

Sources of Variance	df	SS	MS	F
Weight (R)	1	10	10	1.82*
Nut type (C)	1	490	490	89.10**
Weight by nut type (R × C)	1	250	250	45.45**
Within groups	24	198	5.5	

*Not significant
**Significant, $p < .01$

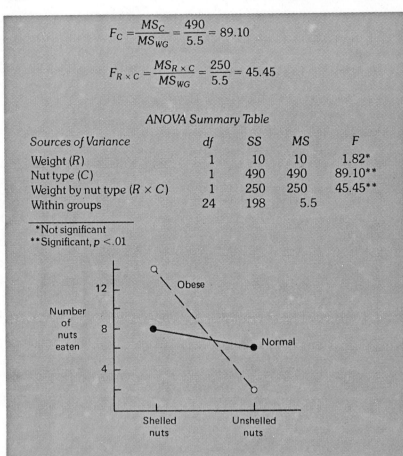

We see in the ANOVA summary table a significant F for nut type and note from the graph and the table of means that more shelled peanuts were eaten than unshelled peanuts. However, this is of minor importance because our main interest is in the interaction effect indicated by a significant F for weight by nut type. As you can see from the graph, when the peanuts were shelled the obese subjects ate more than the normal-weight subjects (means of 14 and 8, respectively). However, when the peanuts were not shelled the normal-weight subjects ate more than the obese subjects (means of 6 and 2, respectively).

Study Questions

1. How does the two-way ANOVA differ from the one-way ANOVA?
2. What are main effects? Interaction effects?

3. What does the phrase "2 × 4 factorial design" mean?
4. Describe the construction of a graph in a two-way ANOVA. How would that graph demonstrate that there was no interaction effect? That there was an interaction effect?
5. How would the relative sizes of MS_R and MS_{WG} indicate whether there was a significant row effect? How about MS_C and MS_{WG}?
6. "If there is a significant interaction the variance estimate of $MS_{R \times C}$ will be larger than the estimate given by MS_{WG}." What does this statement mean?

Exercises

1. A researcher in social psychology studied sex differences in an individual's personal space. A male or female confederate stood in a large room while male or female subjects were asked to approach the person and start a conversation. The researcher (by means of a hidden optical system) measured the distance in inches between the subject and the stationary person to see how close together they were when conversation initiated. Twenty male and 20 female college students were assigned at random to one of four groups — male approaching male, male approaching female, female approaching male, and female approaching female. The distances between the approaching subjects and the stationary person are shown below in inches. What did the experiment show regarding the sex of the approaching person and the sex of the stationary person? Complete a two-way ANOVA, including a table of means and a graph.

Approaching Male		Approaching Female	
Stationary Male	Stationary Female	Stationary Male	Stationary Female
11	16	15	13
14	11	16	11
11	13	14	14
15	12	15	13
16	14	17	14
14	14	15	13
14	15	13	12
13	14	16	14
14	15	15	11
14	14	14	13

2. An experimental psychologist is studying the effects of stress on visual perception. In one experiment 80 decibels of white noise was used as the stressor while subjects proofread a prose passage projected on a screen. The projected image was sharp for some subjects and was slightly blurred for other subjects. Ten subjects were assigned to each of four combinations of stress and image quality — clear image with no stress, blurred image with no stress, clear image with stress, and blurred image with stress. The number of errors made in proofreading a 100-word paragraph by each subject is shown below. What effects of stress and image quality were demonstrated in this experiment? Run a two-way ANOVA, and show a table of means and a graph.

	No Stress			Stress	
	Clear	*Blurred*		*Clear*	*Blurred*
	3	7		5	11
	6	8		7	11
	3	5		4	9
	4	8		7	12
	5	4		8	8
	5	7		4	7
	1	9		8	12
	3	3		3	8
	7	5		7	11
	3	4		5	9

13 Some Nonparametric Statistical Tests

The t test and the F test, described in the two previous chapters, are called *parametric* tests; that is, they assume certain conditions about the *parameters* of the populations from which the samples are drawn. We have spent considerable time discussing these conditions, noting, for example, that the populations must be normal and must have equal variances. These conditions are not ordinarily tested themselves but are assumed to hold, and the meaningfulness that we attach to a particular value of t or F depends on whether these assumptions are valid. In addition, we have also emphasized that the data must be at least interval in nature before the operations necessary to calculate means and standard deviations can be performed and a t or F value obtained.

But what is the researcher to do when he or she knows that a set of data cannot meet these requirements? Even if assured that the normality and homogeneity of variance assumptions are valid, the researcher may frankly admit that the data in question are only nominal or, at best, ordinal in nature. Some measurement purists will go so far as to say that the *majority* of data in education and the behavioral sciences does not reach the precision of an interval scale. We may be able to tell that individual A has more of something than individual B, but we are not sure just *how much* more of it individual A has! Data such as this would be ordinal in nature.

For these reasons, a number of *nonparametric* statistical methods have been developed that allow us to run significance tests on data that do not meet the assumptions of the parametric tests. There is a wide variety of nonparametric tests, but we will be able to include only a small sample of them—just enough to demonstrate their ease of computation and wide applicability. We will consider the appropriate techniques for two general classes of data—independent samples and correlated samples.

Nonparametric Tests Using Independent Samples

The nonparametric tests to be treated in this section require *independent* samples. This simply means that the placement of subjects in one category does not affect the occurrence of subjects in another category. If John Doe turns up in one category or if he is assigned at random to a particular group, the selection has no bearing on any other category. In short, our observation of John Doe is independent of any other observation.

The Chi Square: One-Way Classification

Suppose that we flip a coin 20 times and record the frequency of occurrence of heads and tails. We know from the laws of probability that we should expect 10 heads and 10 tails. We also know that because of sampling error, we could easily come up with 9 heads and 11 tails or 12 heads and 8 tails. As we asked ourselves in **Note 7-1,** at what point do we say that an observed deviation from a 50-50 split is *not* sampling error but is due to some other factor, such as a biased coin? At what point do we say that there is a *significant* deviation between the theoretical 50-50 split and our observed frequency distribution?

A technique that can be used to determine whether there is a significant difference between some *theoretical* or *expected* frequencies and the corresponding *observed* frequencies in two or more categories is the *chi square test* (chi is denoted by the Greek letter χ). The formula for the calculation of chi square is

$$\chi^2 = \sum \frac{(O - E)^2}{E} \qquad \text{(13-1)}$$

where O is the observed frequency in a given category,
  E is the expected frequency in a given category.

Let us suppose our coin-flipping experiment yielded 12 heads and 8 tails. We would enter our expected frequencies (10-10) and our observed frequencies in a table resembling Table 13-1.

The calculation of χ^2 in a one-way classification is very straightforward. The expected frequency in a category (e.g., "heads") is subtracted from the observed frequency, the difference is squared, and the square is divided by its expected frequency. This is repeated for the remaining categories, and, as the formula for χ^2 indicates, these results are summed for all the categories.

The chi square distribution. How does a calculated χ^2 of 0.8 tell us if our observed results of 12 heads and 8 tails represent a significant deviation from an expected 10-10 split? To answer this question, we again resort to the concept of a sampling distribution.

In the same way that we had a sampling distribution of t or F, we are now concerned with the sampling distribution of chi square. The shape of the chi square sampling distribution depends upon the number of degrees of freedom, and the distribution for $df = 6$ shown in Figure 13-1 illustrates this. As with other sampling distributions, we can mark off the different values that would be equaled or exceeded by sampling error a given percentage of the time. Note in Figure 13-1 that for 6 degrees of freedom χ^2 values of 12.59 or greater happen less than 5% of the time by chance, so we conclude that a χ^2 of 12.59 or greater is significant at the .05 level.

Since the shape of the sampling distribution depends on the number of degrees of freedom, the χ^2 value to be equaled or exceeded a given percentage of the time also depends on the degrees of freedom. Table G in Appendix 2 shows these values for the usual .05, .01, and .001 significance levels. For example, for 1 degree of freedom, we see that our calculated χ^2 must equal or exceed 3.84 to be significant at the .05 level.

Table 13-1
Calculating a χ^2: One-Way Classification

	Observed	Expected	(O – E)	(O – E)²		(O – E)²/E
Heads	12	10	2	4		0.4
Tails	8	10	-2	4		0.4
	20	20			χ^2 =	0.8

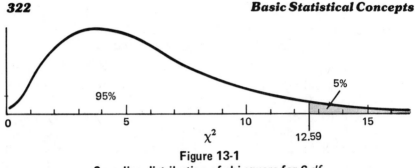

Figure 13-1
Sampling distribution of chi square for 6 *df*.

The degrees of freedom for a one-way classification x^2 is $r - 1$, *where r is the number of categories.* Since the one-way classification x^2 is often presented in the tabular form of Table 13-1, r can be thought of as the number of rows. In the coin-flipping experiment of Table 13-1, there are two categories ($r = 2$), so there would obviously be 1 degree of freedom. From Table G we see that a x^2 of 3.84 or greater is needed for x^2 to be significant at the .05 level, so we conclude that our x^2 of 0.8 in the coin-flipping experiment could have happened by sampling error and that the deviations between the observed frequencies and expected frequencies are not significant.

Let us consider another example that involves more than just two categories. A psychology instructor makes out his final grades for 200 students in an introductory psychology class. He is curious to see if his grade distribution resembles the "normal curve" and notes from the college catalog that in a normal distribution of grades 45% of them would be C's, 24% of them would be B's and 24% D's, and 3.5% of them would be A's and 3.5% F's. Table 13-2 shows the chi square table with the instructor's observed grade distribution and the distribu-tion of letter grades that could be expected according to the normal curve model. Note that the professor obtained the expected distribution by multiplying the class size of 200 by the percentage for that letter grade (e.g., 3.5% × 200 = 7 A's).

Note in the data of Table 13-2 that there are 4 degrees of freedom, since $df = r - 1$, where r is the number of categories. From Table G we see that for $df = 4$, a chi square value of 13.28 is needed for x^2 to be significant at the .01 level, so we conclude that our x^2 of 18.02 is significant.

When a significant x^2 occurs, we know that the deviation between the observed frequencies and the expected frequencies is larger than what we expect by chance. But in a chi square table involving a number of categories, such as Table 13-2, we would expect that the frequencies

Table 13-2
Using χ^2 to Check "Normality" of a Grade Distribution

Grades	Observed	Expected	(O - E)	(O - E)²	(O - E)²/E
A (3.5%)	15	7	8	64	64/7 = 9.14
B (24%)	53	48	5	25	25/48 = 0.52
C (45%)	87	90	-3	9	9/90 = 0.10
D (24%)	33	48	-15	225	225/48 = 4.69
F (3.5%)	12	7	5	25	25/7 = 3.57
	200	200			χ^2 = 18.02

$\chi^2_{.01}$, *df* = 4, is 13.28
Significant, *p* < .01

in some categories might deviate more from what is expected by chance than others. In looking at the grade distribution data of Table 13-2, we note that the A, D, and F categories each contribute substantially to the χ^2 value (9.14, 4.69, and 3.57), while the B and C categories contribute very little. The reason can be seen in an inspection of the data: there were many more A's given than what would be expected by chance (15 observed vs. 7 expected), there were fewer D's (33 observed vs. 48 expected), and there were more F's (12 observed vs. 7 expected).

Effect of sample size on one-way classification χ^2. We must make certain in our calculation of χ^2 that when *df* = 1 (as in the coin-flipping data, where there are only two categories) the *expected frequencies are at least 5*. If values of *E* are less than 5, the χ^2 value is invalid.

When *df* > 1 (i.e., when you have more than two categories), the χ^2 technique should not be used when more than 20% of the expected frequencies are less than 5 or when any *single* expected frequency is less than 1. This problem can sometimes be eliminated by *combination* of adjacent categories. For example, if in the grade distribution data of Table 13-2 there had been only 100 students, there would have been two expected frequencies of less than 5 (3.5 in both the A and F categories). But the data could be combined into three categories instead of five (A with B, C, and D with F) and the problem of expected frequencies would be eliminated. There are a number of other restrictions governing the use of chi square, and we will consider these at length after the next section.

The Chi Square: Two-Way Classification

The two-way chi square is a convenient technique for determining the *significance of the difference* between the frequencies of occurrence in two or more categories with two or more groups. For example, we may ask if there is any difference in the number of freshmen, sophomores, juniors, or seniors as to their preference for spectator sports (football, basketball, or baseball). This is called a two-way classification, since we would need two bits of information from the students in our sample—their class and their sports preference.

Another use for a two-way classification chi square would be to see if there are sex differences for some variable. For example, Table 13-3 shows the educational level of 180 faculty members at a midwestern liberal arts college. The two elements of this two-way classification are, of course, sex and highest degree earned. This type of a two-way table is called a *contingency table,* and each entry is called a *cell.*

Determining the expected frequencies. In the one-way classification, the expected frequencies are determined by some *a priori* hypothesis—a 50-50 split in coin flipping or a normal distribution of grades. However, in the two-way classification, the expected values

Table 13-3
Sex Differences in Educational Level of Faculty Members

		Highest Earned Degree			
		Bachelor's	Master's	Doctorate	Totals
Sex	Men	5 (11)	68 (75)	61 (48)	134
	Women	10 (4)	33 (26)	3 (16)	46
	Totals	15	101	64	N = 180

O	E	(O - E)	(O - E)²	(O - E)²/E
5	11	- 6	36	36/11 = 3.27
10	4	6	36	36/4 = 9.00
68	75	- 7	49	49/75 = 0.65
33	26	7	49	49/26 = 1.88
61	48	13	169	169/48 = 3.52
3	16	-13	169	169/16 = 10.56

$$\chi^2 = 28.88$$

$\chi^2_{.001}$, $df = 2$, is 13.82
Significant, $p < .001$

(sometimes called *independence values*) are calculated from the marginal totals of the contingency table. For example, the total number of faculty holding only a bachelor's degree is 15. Since there is a total of 180 faculty members, we know that 15/180 or 8% of the total group, both men and women, have only a bachelor's degree. Now, if the null hypothesis were true (i.e., if there were no difference in the frequency of men and women holding only a bachelor's degree), we would expect 8% of the men and 8% of the women to have only a bachelor's degree. Since there are 134 men, we simply multiply 8% by 134 to obtain 11. Thus, if there were no sex differences, we would expect 11 men to have only a bachelor's degree. Similarly, 8% times 46 yields an expected value of 4. We expect 4 women to have only a bachelor's degree. These values are entered in parentheses for each cell of the contingency table.

A quick and handy way of calculating each of the expected values is to multiply the column total by the row total for each cell and divide by the total N. The expected values for each cell in Table 13-3 would be:

$(15 \times 134)/180 = 11$ $(101 \times 134)/180 = 75$ $(64 \times 134)/180 = 48$
$(15 \times 46)/180 = 4$ $(101 \times 46)/180 = 26$ $(64 \times 46)/180 = 16$

After the expected values for each cell have been calculated, the same computational procedures for χ^2 are used as in the one-way classification. The differences between the observed and expected frequencies are found, the differences are squared, the squared difference is divided by its expected value, and the results of all the cells are summed. Notice that the *expected* values in each column or row add up to the same column or row total as the *observed* frequencies. This is an essential requirement for chi square, as we shall see in a later section.

Determining the degrees of freedom. It was easy to see that the *df* for the one-way classification was $r - 1$, because in order for the category frequencies to add up to the total number of cases all the frequencies could vary but one. For example, in the grade distribution data of Table 13-2, there were five categories, and $5 - 1 = 4$ degrees of freedom. That is, four of the category frequencies could take any value, while the fifth, in order for the total to be 200, would be dependent on the first four.

A similar technique is used in the two-way classification, but the number of degrees of freedom depends on both the number of rows *and* the number of columns. For the two-way classification chi square, $df = (r - 1)(c - 1)$, where *r* is the number of rows and *c* is the number of columns. For the example in Table 13-3, $df = (2 - 1)(3 - 1) = 2$. In other words, only two cell frequencies are free to vary; after two are given, the remaining frequencies are fixed so that the row and column totals will be correct. You may already have discovered this in examining the calculation of the expected values in Table 13-3. You would only have to calculate the expected values for Men-Bachelor's and Men-Master's, and the rest of the expected values could be obtained by subtraction. While this is a tempting and arithmetically sound shortcut, it might be a good idea to actually calculate several other expected values, in the event that you made a computational error on the first two!

What does a significant χ^2 mean? In Table G we find that with $df = 2$ a chi square of 13.82 is needed for the difference to be significant at the .001 level. Since chi squares of 13.82 or larger happen by chance less than 0.1% of the time, we conclude that our χ^2 of 28.88 is significant beyond the .001 level. Given the data in a contingency table, such as the sex and educational level tabulation of Table 13-3, what does a significant chi square mean? Besides indicating a significant deviation between observed and expected cell frequencies, it means that we can treat a significant χ^2 as either a *significant difference* between levels of one of the variables or as a *significant relationship* between the two variables.

In Table 13-3, our significant χ^2 tells us that there is a significant difference between men and women faculty members in their highest earned degrees. By inspecting the differences between observed and expected cell frequencies, we can see that the greatest contribution to the total χ^2 value comes from the fact that there are more women who have only a bachelor's degree than the number that would be expected by chance (10 vs. 4) and far fewer women who have a doctorate than the number that would be expected by chance (3 vs. 16). These two cells alone contribute 19.56 (9.00 and 10.56) to the total χ^2 of 28.88.

Another way of describing our significant χ^2 would be to say that there is a significant relationship between the sex of a faculty member and the highest earned degree. An inspection of the contingency table shows that the relationship is due to the fact that more women than expected by chance have only a bachelor's degree, while more men and fewer women than expected by chance have a doctorate.

Although both of the above explanations are used, the *significant difference* approach is the more common.

The 2×2 contingency table. When there are two levels of both variables in the two-way classification, the computational effort of calculating the χ^2 value is greatly reduced. The data are tabulated in a 2×2 (say "two by two") contingency table with the cell frequencies labeled *A* through *D*, along with the marginal totals and total *N*, as shown:

A	B	$A+B$
C	D	$C+D$

$A+C \qquad B+D \qquad\qquad N$

The computational formula is:

$$\chi^2 = \frac{N\left(|AD-BC|-\frac{N}{2}\right)^2}{(A+B)(C+D)(A+C)(B+D)} \qquad (13\text{-}2)$$

where the letters A through D refer to the cell frequencies,

N is the total number of observations,

$(A+B)$ and $(C+D)$ are row totals,

$(A+C)$ and $(B+D)$ are column totals.

Note that the quantity $N/2$ is to be subtracted from the *absolute value* of $AD - BC$. The degrees of freedom for the χ^2 calculated from this formula is always 1, since in a 2×2 table the quantity $(r-1)$ $(c-1)$ is, of course, 1.

As an illustration of the 2×2 contingency table let us consider a college campus survey which dealt with, among many other topics, the student's place of residence. A random sample of 350 students was asked whether they lived on campus or off campus, and the results are tabulated in Table 13-4. Was there a significant difference in the place of residence of men and women?

The χ^2 of 8.54 is significant at the .01 level, so we conclude that there is a significant difference in the place of residence for men and women students. By inspecting the contingency table we see that proportionately more women live on campus and more men live off campus.

This computational formula for the 2×2 table eliminates the separate steps involved in calculating the expected values and performing the arithmetic operations for each step. However, the numbers do get unwieldy at times, and a calculator is almost a necessity.

Assumptions necessary for chi square. Even though a nonparametric statistic does not require assumptions regarding the population, there still are some restrictions regarding its use. Assumptions necessary for use of the chi square technique are:

1. *The data must be in frequency form.* The entries in the cells indicate *how many* are in a given category and involve only a counting procedure. This is, basically, a technique for nominal data.

Table 13-4
College Residence of Men and Women Students

Place of Residence

		On Campus	Off Campus	
Sex	Men	104 (A)	52 (B)	156 (A + B)
	Women	157 (C)	37 (D)	194 (C + D)
		261 (A + C)	89 (B + D)	350 (N)

$$\chi^2 = \frac{N\left(|AD - BC| - \dfrac{N}{2}\right)^2}{(A+B)(C+D)(A+C)(B+D)} = \frac{350\left(|104\,(37) - 52\,(157)| - \dfrac{350}{2}\right)^2}{(156)(194)(261)(89)}$$

$$= \frac{350\,(4{,}316 - 175)^2}{703{,}002{,}456} = \frac{6{,}001{,}758{,}350}{703{,}002{,}456} = 8.54$$

$\chi^2_{.01}$, $df = 1$, is 6.64
Significant, $p < .01$

2. *The individual observations must be independent of each other.* This means, for example, that you cannot "inflate" χ^2 by asking each of 10 people to guess the suit of a playing card on four successive draws and then claim that you have an N of 40. Since a given person is making four guesses, we could expect that guesses on one occasion might be influenced by the guesses on previous occasions. Clearly, the four observations would be related and not independent of each other.

3. *Sample size must be adequate.* We have already noted that there were restrictions on the size of sample for the one-way classification χ^2. For the two-way classification we need to remember that:

   a. In a 2×2 table, chi square should not be used if N is less than 20. (See Siegel [1956] for alternate methods.)

   b. In a larger table, no cell should have an expected value of less than 1, and no more than 20% of the cells can have expected values of less than 5. For example, the data of Table 13-3 has one cell with an expected value of only 4. However, there are six cells, and, since only one is short, $1/6 = 16.7\%$, or less than 20%, as required.

There is not complete agreement among statisticians on this

requirement, and your instructor may have a different view than that presented here. A correction is sometimes applied to the basic chi square formula, called a "correction for continuity," and your instructor or advanced text may develop this concept further. The computational formula for the 2×2 contingency table presented earlier has the correction for continuity built in. Statisticians generally agree that a correction for continuity is always necessary in a 2×2 table.

4. *Distribution basis must be decided on before the data are collected.* In the grade distribution of Table 13-2, our psychology instructor was testing the deviation of his final grade distribution from a normal distribution. You can see that it would be inappropriate for him to "eyeball" his data and choose some kind of a distribution (i.e., rectangular, bimodal, or skewed) to compare with his distribution. Obviously, he could come up with a distribution that would yield nonsignificant or significant results to please his fancy. There must be a logical basis for his choosing the categories before he collects his data.

5. *The sum of the observed frequencies must equal the sum of the expected frequencies.* In order for the chi square formula to "work," the sums of the observed and expected frequencies have to be equal. Tables 13-1, 13-2, and 13-3 all show the expected and observed sums to be the same. Suppose we rolled a die 60 times and observed the frequency with which a "2" appeared. We could *not* use chi square to see whether there is a significant difference between the 14, for example, observed "2's" and the 10 expected by chance, because 14 and 10 are not the same. What is missing, of course, are the "non-2's." We can indeed run a chi square if we have 14 observed "2's" and 46 "non-2's," with expected values of 10 and 50, respectively, since now the sum of the observed frequencies is equal to the sum of the expected frequencies.

The Median Test

We can use this handy nonparametric test with two independent groups to see if they differ with respect to a combined median. The null hypothesis would state that both groups are samples from populations with the same median. The scores (which must be ordinal or above) for both groups are used to calculate a combined median, and then the numbers of scores above and below the group median are tabulated. If there is no difference between the two groups, we would expect that about half of the scores in each group would be above this median and half below. On the other hand, if a majority of one group scores above the combined median while a majority of the other group scores below, we would have reason to believe that the two groups are different with respect to what is being measured. The following example should help clarify these preliminary statements.

A child psychologist was studying frustration in children and noticed that the maturity of a child's play activities decreased when the child was frustrated. She had a group of 30 nursery school children and divided them into two groups of 15 each. One group ate their noon lunch at the usual time (the satiated group), and the other group did not eat until mid-afternoon (the hungry group). Starting at 2:00 P.M. four nursery school teachers rated each child on "maturity of play activity" on a scale of 1 (very immature play) to 20 (extremely mature play). The scores are listed in the two columns at the top of Table 13-5. The psychologist hypothesized that the maturity scores would be higher for the satiated group than for the hungry group.

The first step in the median test is to calculate the median of *both groups combined*. The median for the group of 30 scores is 9.5. The next step in the median test is to tabulate the number from each group scoring above and below this combined median to see if there is a significant deviation from the 50-50 split that we would expect just by chance.

The numbers of each group scoring above or below the median are entered in a 2×2 contingency table, as shown in Table 13-5, and the computational formula for a 2×2 chi square is used as before. The calculated $\chi^2 = 0.53$ is not large enough for the difference to be significant at the .05 level, so we would conclude that the distribution of frequencies in the contingency table could have happened by chance. In terms of the experiment, not enough hungry children scored below the combined median and not enough satiated children scored above the combined median for us to attribute the difference to something other than chance.

The median test is easy to use, and you can modify it slightly to avoid troublesome complications. For example, if a number of scores are equal to the median, you can simply eliminate them from the analysis. This, of course, reduces the number of scores, which may not be desirable. If too many scores are at the median, you can avoid that problem by using the labels "number above the median" and "number *not* above the median" instead of the usual "above" and "below" dichotomy.

Since the 2×2 contingency table for chi square is used in the

Table 13-5
Median Test on the Maturity of Play Activity

Hungry Group	Satiated Group
14	15
13	14
12	14
11	13
11	12
10	12
9	11
9	11
8	10
8	9
7	9
7	7
6	4
5	3
4	3

Combined $Med = 9.5$

	Hungry	Satiated	
Number above the median	A 6	B 9	15 $(A + B)$
Number below the median	C 9	D 6	15 $(C + D)$
	15 $(A + C)$	15 $(B + D)$	30 (N)

$$\chi^2 = \frac{N\left(|AD - BC| - \frac{N}{2}\right)^2}{(A + B)(C + D)(A + C)(B + D)} = \frac{30\left(|36 - 81| - \frac{30}{2}\right)^2}{(15)(15)(15)(15)}$$

$$= \frac{30(30)^2}{50,625} = \frac{27,000}{50,625} = 0.53$$

$\chi^2_{.05}, df = 1$, is 3.84
Not significant, $p > .05$

median test, the same restrictions apply to the median test as affected the 2×2 chi square. That is, the median test cannot be used when N is less than 20.

The Mann-Whitney U Test

The Mann-Whitney test is a very powerful nonparametric technique for determining whether two independent samples have been drawn from the same population. The measurements in both groups must be at least of an ordinal nature. The logic of the method is simple enough: if you have two populations from which you are drawing your two samples, the null hypothesis would state that both populations have the same distribution. That is, if you selected a score from one population, the probability that it would be larger than a score from another population would be $p = .50$. However, if we found that more scores from one population were larger than scores from the other population than would be expected by chance, we would reject the null hypothesis. We would conclude that there was a significant difference between the two populations.

Table 13-6
Mann-Whitney U Test on Government Efficiency Data

Community A	Community B
8	10
11	13
6	16
9	12
	18
$N_1 = 4$	$N_2 = 5$

6	8	9	10	11	12	13	16	18
A	A	A	B	A	B	B	B	B

A precedes B nineteen times, $U' = 19$

B precedes A once, $U = 1$

$p = .016 \times 2 = .032$
Significant

Small samples. To see how the method works with small samples, let us consider the data of Table 13-6. An interviewer at a state political rally asked four people from community A and five people from community B to rate the efficiency of their local government on a scale from 1 (very inefficient) to 20 (extremely efficient). Was there a significant difference in the ratings of the two local governments?

The Mann-Whitney test requires only three bits of information:

1. $N_1 =$ sample size of smaller group,
2. $N_2 =$ sample size of larger group,
3. $U =$ number of times a score in the larger group precedes a score in the smaller group when both groups are ranked together.

As shown in Table 13-6, we take the scores from the columns and rank them from smallest to largest, keeping their identities (A or B) intact. We then simply count the number of times that B (the largest group) precedes A. The only B preceding an A is the B of 10, which precedes an A of 11. Since this is the only B in front of an A, our $U = 1$.

We can check the accuracy of our counting by tabulating *the number of times A precedes B.* We see that the first B (10) is preceded by three A's, the second B (12) by four A's, and the remaining B's each by four A's. The total would be $3 + 4 + 4 + 4 + 4 = 19$, and this statistic is denoted U'. This can be a check on the accuracy of our tabulation of U, since there is a relationship between U and U', in that

$$U = N_1N_2 - U'$$

For the data of Table 13-6,

$$U = (4)(5) - 19$$
$$U = 1$$

It must be remembered that U is *always* smaller than U'. In fact, if we tabulate both, we can tell which value is U because it is the smaller of the two.

Once we have tabulated U, we again resort to a sampling distribution, and the probabilities or critical values are shown in Tables H and I in Appendix 2. Table H is to be used when neither N_1 nor N_2 is larger than 8, and Table I can be used when N_2 (the size of the larger group) is between 9 and 20.

Since the data of Table 13-6 has a small sample size, with $N_2 = 5$, we will use Table H to determine whether our $U = 1$ is statistically significant. The first page of Table H shows a table of $N_2 = 5$, and we go down the left-hand column to a U of 1. With $N_1 = 4$, the probability associated with values this small is $p = .016$. However, the probabilities given in Table H are for a *one-tailed test*. This means that whenever a two-tailed test is used, *these probabilities must be doubled*. Since we did not predict in advance which community would be rated more efficient, we have to make a two-tailed test, and the probability of obtaining a U as small as 1 in a two-tailed test is $.016 \times 2 = .032$. Since this probability is less than the usual .05, we conclude that there is a significant difference between the ratings of the two communities.

Using Table I with larger samples. When N_2 (the larger of the two samples) is between 9 and 20, we cannot use Table H to determine the exact probability of obtaining a value as small as U. With these larger samples, one of the tables from Table I must be used which shows the value of U needed for the difference to be significant at the .001, .01, .025, and .05 levels for a one-tailed test and the .002, .02, .05, and .10 levels for a two-tailed test.

As an example let us consider the data of Table 13-7, where a sample of 7 women drivers and 10 men drivers were assigned safe driving scores based on a complex formula involving accident rate and miles traveled. A higher score indicates a poorer driver. Was there a significant difference between the driving scores of men and women?

Since U is the number of times scores from the larger sample precede scores from the smaller sample, we tabulate the number of times a woman's score (W) is preceded by a man's score (M). We see in Table 13-7 that the women's scores of 22, 27, 32, and 37 are each preceded by one man's score, a woman's score of 52 is preceded by two men's scores, and a woman's score of 67 is preceded by three men's scores. This gives a total of $U = 1 + 1 + 1 + 1 + 2 + 3 = 9$.

As a check on our calculations we tabulate U' and find that a man's score of 17 is preceded by one woman's score, a man's score of 42 is preceded by five women's scores, a man's score of 62 is preceded by six women's scores, and the remaining seven men's scores are each preceded by seven women's scores. This would give a total of $U' = 1 + 5 + 6 + 7 + 7 + 7 + 7 + 7 + 7 + 7 = 61$. Applying the check for accuracy:

$$U = N_1N_2 - U'$$
$$U = (7)(10) - 61$$
$$U = 9$$

Keeping in mind that we are running a two-tailed test, we now consult Table I and find the value of U for $N_2 = 10$ and $N_1 = 7$ in the four tables. We note that our value of $U = 9$ is between the tabled U of 5 in the .002 table and the U of 11 in the .02 table. Since our value of 9 is less than the tabled value of 11 in the .02 table, we say that our

Table 13-7
Mann-Whitney *U* Test on Safe Driving Scores

Women	*Men*
37	17
52	72
67	62
27	75
32	69
22	85
13	42
	77
	71
	81
$N_1 = 7$	$N_2 = 10$

13	17	22	27	32	37	42	52	62	67	69	71	72	75	77	81	85
W	M	W	W	W	W	M	W	M	W	M	M	M	M	M	M	M

$$U = 1 + 1 + 1 + 1 \quad + \quad 2 \quad + \quad 3 = 9$$

Significant, $p < .02$ (two-tailed test)

U is significant between the .02 and the .002 levels. (Note that with the Mann-Whitney test the smaller the value of *U* the greater the level of significance.) In terms of the experimental data, we conclude that the women's safe driving scores are significantly lower (indicating better drivers) than the men's scores.

The Mann-Whitney test can also be used for samples larger than 20, but space does not permit inclusion of the procedure in this introductory text. Other sources (e.g., Siegel, 1956) can provide you with this technique, as well as alternate ways of computing *U* and *U'* without going through the laborious (especially if *N* is large) counting procedure. It should be mentioned again that the Mann-Whitney test is one of the most powerful nonparametric tests, and it is strongly recommended when the assumptions cannot be met for the parametric *t* test.

The Kruskal-Wallis One-Way Analysis of Variance

The last nonparametric technique for independent samples to be discussed in this chapter is one that is markedly different from the procedures described earlier. Like the parametric analysis of variance, the Kruskal-Wallis test can be used *for more than just two samples*. This test assumes that the data are at least ordinal in nature so they can be converted to ranks.

The procedure requires converting the scores of the individual groups to one *overall* set of ranks. The data of Table 13-8 show the scores for four separate groups ($k = 4$), and their ranks in a single over-all series. The smallest score is given a rank of 1, the next smallest a rank of 2, and so on. In Table 13-8, the freshman score of 2 has a rank of 1 and the senior score of 21 has a rank of 28. As with the Spearman method of correlation, from Chapter 8, scores that are tied are given the average ranking. For example, there are two scores of 3, which would be tied for second and third rank, so both scores of 3 are given a rank of 2.5, and the next score is given a rank of 4. Similarly, there are three scores of 8, tied for ranks of 11, 12, and 13, so each score of 8 has a rank of 12, and the next score is given a rank of 14.

The null hypothesis for the Kruskal-Wallis test should be obvious now that we have converted all the scores to ranks. If there were no differences between the groups, the sums of the ranks for each group would be about the same. That is, if only sampling error were respon-sible for differences in *scores* among the groups, the *sums of the ranks* for each group would only differ because of sampling error—and we would conclude that the samples had been drawn from the *same* popu-lation. On the other hand, if the sums of the ranks for each group differ from each other by more than we would expect by sampling error, we would conclude that these groups were samples from *different* popula-tions, and we would have demonstrated that there is a significant dif-ference between the populations.

The statistic to be evaluated in the Kruskal-Wallis test is H, and it is given by

$$H = \frac{12}{N(N+1)} \sum \frac{R_G{}^2}{N_G} - 3(N+1) \qquad \textbf{(13-3)}$$

where N is the total number of scores,

$R_G{}^2$ is the squared sum of the ranks in a group,

N_G is the number of scores in a group.

While the formula for H looks somewhat imposing, it requires only that after ranking the scores in the manner described above we

1. Add the ranks for group 1 to obtain R_1.
2. Square this sum of ranks to obtain $R_1{}^2$.
3. Divide $R_1{}^2$ by N_1, the number of scores in group 1.

Table 13-8
Kruskal-Wallis Test on Personal Concerns Inventory

Freshman		Sophomore		Junior		Senior	
Score	*Rank*	*Score*	*Rank*	*Score*	*Rank*	*Score*	*Rank*
7	9.5	9	14	17	23	21	28
6	7.5	7	9.5	12	18.5	20	27
8	12	6	7.5	19	25.5	18	24
12	18.5	11	17	10	15.5	19	25.5
5	5.5	10	15.5	8	12	16	22
3	2.5	5	5.5	14	20	15	21
8	12	3	2.5				
2	1						
4	4						
$R_1 = 72.5$		$R_2 = 71.5$		$R_3 = 114.5$		$R_4 = 147.5$	
$N_1 = 9$		$N_2 = 7$		$N_3 = 6$		$N_4 = 6$	

$$H = \frac{12}{N(N+1)} \sum \frac{R_G{}^2}{N_G} - 3(N+1)$$

$$= \frac{12}{28(28+1)} \left[\frac{(72.5)^2}{9} + \frac{(71.5)^2}{7} + \frac{(114.5)^2}{6} + \frac{(147.5)^2}{6} \right] - 3(28+1)$$

$$= \frac{12}{812} (584.03 + 730.32 + 2{,}185.04 + 3{,}626.04) - 87$$

$$= 0.0148 (7{,}125.43) - 87$$

$$H = 105.46 - 87 = 18.46$$

$\chi^2_{.001}$, $df = 3$, is 16.27
Significant, $p < .001$

4. Since the above steps give us R^2/N for the first group only, we repeat these steps for all k groups ($k =$ number of groups).
5. We sum the individual R^2/N for all groups, multiply by $12/N(N+1)$, and subtract the quantity $3(N+1)$.
6. If there are at least five cases in every group, the resultant statistic, H, is distributed as chi square with $df = k - 1$. H is also distributed as chi square if $k = 3$ and there are *more* than five cases in every group. For times when $k = 3$ and there are five cases or fewer in any group, Siegel (1956) has a special table, since the chi square distribution cannot be used.

Table 13-8 shows the results of a "Personal Concerns" question-naire given to a sample of 28 college students. A personnel dean had predicted earlier that as the students got nearer to receiving their col-lege degrees, they would check more and more items on the question-naire that dealt with vocational and marital decisions. The sample con-sisted of 9 freshmen, 7 sophomores, 6 juniors, and 6 seniors. Was there a significant difference between the groups on the number of items checked relating to future decisions?

Since the value of H is greater than the tabled chi square value for $df = 3$ of 16.27, we conclude that our samples are from different pop-ulations, with $p < .001$ that such a result would happen by sampling error alone. In terms of the data, the seniors seem to have checked a significantly greater number of items relating to future vocational and marriage plans than have the freshmen and sophomores.

The problem of tied ranks. When the number of tied ranks be-comes quite large, the value of H calculated by the formula is some-what smaller than it should be. Siegel (1956) presents a correction for tied ranks which we will not consider here, since H is not seriously affected unless the tied ranks are unusually severe. In the data of Table 13-8, for example, 14 of the 28 scores are tied, and the corrected H is 18.52 instead of the 18.46 calculated in Table 13-8. Obviously, this did not affect our decision to reject the null hypothesis and conclude that the differences were significant. The Kruskal-Wallis test is a "conserva-tive" test with respect to tied scores; that is, when the correction is made, it tends to make the test even more powerful in its rejection of a false null hypothesis.

In conclusion, we must note that the Kruskal-Wallis test is a rea-sonable alternative to the one-way analysis of variance when we can-not meet the assumptions of the parametric F test.[1]

Nonparametric Tests Using Related Samples

The nonparametric tests in this section are alike in that they all require *correlated data.* As you may remember from Chapter 10, we noted that one type of t test (the direct difference method) used cor-related samples. We further noted that correlated data could involve matched samples (split litters, co-twin controls, or matched pairs) or repeated measurements of the same subjects. The nonparametric tests to be described in the following pages are designed for use with such correlated data.

[1]As with the parametric F test, there is also a procedure following a Kruskal-Wallis test to see which groups are significantly different. The technique is beyond the scope of this introductory text but is described in a text by Daniel (1978).

The McNemar Test of Changes

The McNemar test uses the chi square distribution in situations where we have nominal data from related samples. It is particularly useful in applications where we have groups of subjects tabulated *before* and *after* some specific experimental treatment. For example, let us suppose that a municipal park board is proposing a bond issue to finance a new swimming pool. A survey of 25 voters (shown in the *Before* column of Table 13-9) indicates that only 8 out of the 25 would vote for the bond issue. An advertising campaign is planned and the brochures and other material are shown to these 25 voters. Now, a total of 16 out of the 25 indicate they will vote for the bond issue. Is this a significant change in the direction of voters passing the bond issue? The null hypothesis would state that of those who change their attitude, about half should change from For to Against while the other half should change from Against to For.

You can use the McNemar test on this data by first tabulating the voters' preferences before the advertising campaign is begun. As mentioned earlier, these responses are in the *Before* column. Voters' responses are again tabulated after the campaign, in the *After* column.

You then set up a 2 × 2 contingency table by counting the number of voters who remained the same (6 were for the bond issue both before and after, 7 were against both before and after). Note that these frequencies appear in cells B and C respectively. In cells A and D are the voters who changed their minds after the advertising campaign. Two voters changed from For to Against (cell A) and 10 changed from Against to For (cell D).

Since we are interested in the *changes*, we concentrate on cells A and D. The formula for the McNemar test is:

$$\chi^2 = \frac{(|A - D| - 1)^2}{A + D} \qquad (13\text{-}4)$$

Note that 1 is subtracted from the absolute value of $A - D$ before the numerator is squared.

We see that our calculated $\chi^2 = 4.08$ is significant at the .05 level since it exceeds the tabled value for $df = 1$ of 3.84, so we know that there were a significant number of changes in one direction. In terms of the experimental data, we would conclude that a significant number of voters changed from Against to For after the advertising campaign.

There is one caution in the use of the McNemar test: we must avoid using the technique if the *expected* frequency in cells A or D is less than 5. Fortunately, we can calculate the expected frequency very

Table 13-9
McNemar Test of Changes Applied to Voting Preferences
before and after an Advertising Campaign

Voter	Before	After	Voter	Before	After
A	For	For	N	Against	Against
B	Against	For	O	For	For
C	Against	Against	P	Against	For
D	Against	Against	Q	Against	For
E	For	Against	R	Against	For
F	Against	For	S	Against	Against
G	Against	For	T	For	For
H	Against	Against	U	For	For
I	For	For	V	Against	For
J	Against	Against	W	Against	For
K	For	For	X	Against	Against
L	Against	For	Y	For	Against
M	Against	For			

After

		Against	For	
Before	For	A: 2	B: 6	8
	Against	C: 7	D: 10	17
		9	16	

$$\chi^2 = \frac{(|A - D| - 1)^2}{A + D} = \frac{(|2 - 10| - 1)^2}{2 + 10}$$

$$= \frac{(7)^2}{12} = \frac{49}{12} = 4.08$$

$\chi^2_{.05}$, $df = 1$, is 3.84
Significant, $p < .05$

simply by $\frac{1}{2}(A + D)$. In Table 13-9 we see that $\frac{1}{2}(A + D) = \frac{1}{2}(2 + 10)$ = 6, so we can legitimately use the McNemar test on this data.

The Sign Test

A very convenient test using matched pairs or repeated measurements is the sign test (so called because plus and minus signs are used to indicate changes). Each pair of measures is considered separately, and, if the second score is *greater* than the first, a minus sign is entered in the *Sign* column. If the second score is *smaller* than the first, a plus sign is entered. And, if both observations are the same, a 0 is entered. Since we must be able to tell which of the two scores is greater in a given pair, data must be at least ordinal. A typical sign test is shown in Table 13-10.

It should be obvious from Table 13-10 that the null hypothesis would state that half the signs would be positive and half would be negative. In other words, if there are no significant differences between the pairs of measurements, about half of the changes should occur in a positive direction and half should be in a negative direction.

The example in Table 13-10 shows the results of a study involving the amount of negative, self-deprecating statements made by clients in a psychotherapeutic setting. Tape recordings of the first therapy session for 14 clients were studied, and the number of negative statements

Table 13-10
Sign Test on Number of Negative Statements Made during Therapy

Client	First Session	Eighth Session	Sign
A	35	23	+
B	17	17	0
C	14	6	+
D	18	12	+
E	14	10	+
F	36	26	+
G	27	24	+
H	10	14	−
I	16	20	−
J	15	2	+
K	36	13	+
L	25	18	+
M	10	17	−
N	16	14	+

$$N = 13$$
$$x = 3$$

Significant, $p = .046$

made during therapy were tabulated. Eight sessions later a similar tabulation was made. Was there a significant reduction in the number of negative statements made?

The sign test makes use of two bits of information:

1. N is the number of changes. If there are any pairs that show a 0, they are subtracted from the total number of pairs. In the data of Table 13-10, there is one pair with a 0, so $N = 14 - 1 = 13$.
2. x is the frequency of occurrence of the sign that appears the least. There are 10 plus signs and 3 minus signs, so $x = 3$.

When N and x have been determined, we need to consult Table J in Appendix 2 to determine the probability of obtaining an x as small as our obtained value. Table J can be used for N values as large as 25. With $N = 13$ and $x = 3$, we see that the one-tailed probability of obtaining an x as small as 3 is .046. Since .046 is less than the conventional .05, we state that $p < .05$, and we conclude that there was a significant reduction in the number of negative statements made by clients in the therapy sessions.

We must remember that Table J shows *one-tailed* probabilities, meaning that the researcher is specifying in advance of collecting the data that the change will be in a specific direction. If the researcher is not specifying the direction of the difference, a two-tailed probability is needed, and the values in Table J must be *doubled*. Our researcher in the therapy survey *was* predicting a reduction in the number of negative statements, so she used the one-tailed probabilities in Table J.

The Wilcoxon Matched-Pairs Signed-Ranks Test

The sign test discussed in the previous section requires that we merely be able to tell whether one of a pair of scores is greater or less than the other. There may be times when our measuring scale is such that the difference between the two itself can be measured. For example, if pair A has a small difference between the two scores and pair B has a large difference, we would certainly attach more meaning to the larger difference. The sign test, of course, is not sensitive to the magnitude of the differences but only to the *direction* of the differences (plus or minus).

The Wilcoxon test uses the size of each difference. It requires that we determine the size of each difference, rank each difference without regard to its algebraic sign (smallest difference gets a rank of one), and then give each rank the sign of the original difference. Thus, if a rank is associated with a positive difference, it is given a plus sign. If the rank is associated with a negative difference, it is given a minus sign.

If the null hypothesis were true and the differences between paired values were due to sampling error, we would expect about as many small positive differences as small negative differences and about as many large positive differences as large negative differences. We would also expect the sum of the positive ranks to be about the same as the sum of the negative ranks. However, if we found one of these sums to be much smaller than the other, we would suspect that there was a significant difference between the two sets of scores.

Before we examine an example using the Wilcoxon test, we have to agree on how to handle the equivalent pairs and the tied values. If both scores in a single pair are the same, their difference is 0, and such pairs are eliminated from the data analysis, just as with the sign test. That is, N = the number of pairs minus the number of pairs whose difference is 0. In Table 13-11, pairs K and O were eliminated because both differences were 0, so $N = 20 - 2 = 18$.

To handle ties when we are ranking the individual differences, we again use the technique we used in the Spearman rank-difference method of correlation and in the Kruskal-Wallis test: each tied difference is given the average rank. For example, in Table 13-11, differences of 6 and -6 are tied for fourth and fifth ranks, so each is given a rank of 4.5, and the next score is given a rank of 6. (Remember that in the Wilcoxon test the differences are ranked without regard to sign.)

The data in Table 13-11 show the results of the project of an educational psychologist who was studying the effect that knowledge of results has on the learning process. Forty high school sophomores were used to form 20 pairs that were matched for sex, grade-point average, and manual dexterity. All students were tested on a tracking device, called a pursuit rotor, that tested motor coordination skills. Each member of the experimental group heard a click and saw an indicator light flash every time he or she made an error, while members of the control group had no extra information when they strayed off-target. Was there a significant difference between the number of errors made by the students who had immediate knowledge of results (experimental group) and the number made by those who did not receive additional knowledge of results (control group)?

The paired scores are first listed in columns, as shown in Table 13-11. The differences (D) are then found, the second score being subtracted from the first score in each pair, and the difference, with its algebraic sign, is placed in the D column. These differences are now ranked, *without regard to sign,* and each rank is placed in the appropriate column. As mentioned earlier, zero differences are eliminated from the analysis, and tied differences are given the average of the ranks for which they are tied.

Table 13-11
The Wilcoxon Test on Knowledge-of-Results Data

Pair	Control Group	Experimental Group	D	Rank of D	Rank with Less Frequent Sign
A	80	45	35	17	
B	24	62	-38	18	18
C	40	45	- 5	2.5	2.5
D	46	30	16	9	
E	85	56	29	13	
F	52	31	21	11	
G	55	35	20	10	
H	29	36	- 7	6	6
I	77	46	31	14	
J	59	49	10	7	
K	26	26	0	—	
L	46	35	11	8	
M	57	51	6	4.5	
N	46	52	- 6	4.5	4.5
O	69	69	0	—	
P	88	56	32	15	
Q	49	44	5	2.5	
R	49	25	24	12	
S	93	60	33	16	
T	35	39	- 4	1	1

$$T = 32.0$$

$$N = 18$$

$$T = 32$$

Significant, $p < .01$

After the ranking is completed, we look at the D column again and note the differences that have the less frequent sign. In Table 13-11, these are the differences with the minus sign, *and the ranks corresponding to these differences* are then placed in the last column on the right. There are only five minus differences in the D column; their ranks are 18, 2.5, 6, 4.5, and 1, and the total of these ranks with the less frequent sign is 32.0. The total of this column is T, the statistic to be evaluated in the Wilcoxon test.

Table K in Appendix 2 contains the critical values of T necessary for significance at the customary significance levels for values of N up to 25. Since our researcher specified in advance that the knowledge-of-results group would have fewer errors, we use the values for the one-tailed test. We see that for $N = 18$, a T of 33 is significant at the .01 level. Since values smaller than the tabled values of T have a smaller probability of occurrence, our T of 32 is significant beyond the .01 level, and $p < .01$.

We noted earlier that the Wilcoxon test is preferred to the sign test when the magnitude of the differences between paired scores can be measured. If we were to apply the sign test to the data of Table 13-11, with $N = 18$ and $x = 5$, we would see from Table J that the one-tailed probability is .048. This is considerably larger than the probability reported by the Wilcoxon test in Table 13-11, reflecting the fact that the Wilcoxon test is a more powerful test when the magnitude as well as the direction of the differences can be measured.

The Friedman Two-Way Analysis of Variance by Ranks

The Friedman test is a useful nonparametric test when we have *more* than two related samples. If our data is at least ordinal in nature, we can use the Friedman test to test the null hypothesis that our samples have been drawn from the same population. Although this procedure can be used for matched samples, it probably has its greatest application in situations where repeated measurements have been made on the same individual.

The rationale for the analysis is reasonably straightforward. If a table is constructed with the usual columns and rows, the rows correspond to individuals, and the columns are the experimental conditions. In the Friedman test, N is the number of rows, and k is the number of columns. The scores in the different conditions for each individual are entered in the appropriate columns in the row for that individual. Another table is now constructed which shows these scores converted to ranks, and the scores for *each* individual are ranked from 1 to k, where k is the number of conditions. That is, the ranks in each row should go from 1 to k. For example, in Table 13-12, student A has scores of 82, 57, 67, and 60 on four tests ($k = 4$), and these are ranked as 4, 1, 3, and 2 in the table of ranks. Similar rankings have been done for the other nine students.

Under the null hypothesis, the sums of the ranks should be about the same for each column. That is, if there are no differences in the experimental conditions, the ranks should be distributed evenly over the k conditions. However, if one of the conditions, let us say, has consistently lower scores, there will obviously be more ranks of 1 in the column corresponding to that condition, resulting in a smaller sum of the ranks for that column.

Let us consider an example to clarify some of these points. A freshman advisor at a small liberal arts college was curious about the special academic abilities of students who had decided to major in psychology. He wanted to know if beginning freshmen who chose psychology as a major had strong abilities in some special area such as mathematics or the natural sciences. To help answer this question he chose 10 freshman psychology majors and examined their college entrance examination scores. This particular exam yielded a student's percentile rank in the areas of English, mathematics, social science, and natural science. The data for the 10 students are shown in Table 13-12. The first part of the table shows the percentile ranks in each of the four ability areas, and the second part of the table shows the four percentiles ranked for each student. Note that the null hypothesis would state that if there are no differences between the four ability areas the ranks will be distributed in such a way that the sums of the columns are about the same.

The ranks are assigned for each student's scores, with the smallest score being given a rank of 1. If there are tied scores, the familiar procedure of averaging the tied ranks is used. The ranks in the first column are then summed, yielding R_1. The sums are also calculated for the remaining columns. These values of R, along with N (the number of

Table 13-12
The Friedman Analysis of Variance on
Special Abilities of Psychology Majors

College Entrance Exam Percentile Ranks

Student	English	Mathematics	Social Science	Natural Science
A	82	57	67	60
B	61	95	79	92
C	88	82	99	70
D	86	98	77	97
E	77	89	72	97
F	99	85	95	98
G	77	46	95	87
H	61	71	79	56
I	10	30	28	19
J	61	34	54	57

Table 13-12 (continued)

		Ranks		
Student	E	M	SS	NS
A	4	1	3	2
B	1	4	2	3
C	3	2	4	1
D	2	4	1	3
E	2	3	1	4
F	4	1	2	3
G	2	1	4	3
H	2	3	4	1
I	1	4	3	2
J	4	1	2	3
	$R_1 = 25$	$R_2 = 24$	$R_3 = 26$	$R_4 = 25$

$$\chi_r^2 = \frac{12}{Nk(k+1)} \Sigma (R_G)^2 - 3N(k+1)$$

$$= \frac{12}{10(4)(4+1)} \left[(25)^2 + (24)^2 + (26)^2 + (25)^2 \right] - 3(10)(4+1)$$

$$= \frac{12}{200} (625 + 576 + 676 + 625) - 150$$

$$= 0.06 (2,502) - 150$$

$$\chi_r^2 = 0.12$$

$\chi_{.05}^2$, $df = 3$, is 7.82
Not significant, $p > .05$

rows) and k (the number of columns) are then substituted into Friedman's formula:

$$\chi_r^2 = \frac{12}{Nk(k+1)} \Sigma (R_G)^2 - 3N(k+1) \qquad (13\text{-}5)$$

Note that the sum of ranks for each column is squared, these squares are added, this sum is multiplied by $12/Nk(k+1)$, and, finally, the quantity $3N(k+1)$ is subtracted from the above.

The resulting statistic is χ_r^2 (read "chi square for ranks"), and it is distributed approximately as chi square with $k-1$ degrees of freedom.

From Table G we see that, for $df = 3$, a chi square of 7.82 is needed for the difference to be significant at the .05 level. Our $\chi_r^2 = 0.12$ does not come close to being significant, so we must accept the null hypothesis that there are no differences between the conditions. This does not surprise us, since a glance at the first part of Table 13-12 shows that the ranks for the ability levels are spread out among the 10 students and that there are an approximately equal number of ranks of 1, 2, 3, and 4 in all four conditions. So, we conclude that, at least for this group of students, no ability area seemed to rank consistently high or low among those students choosing a psychology major.

It turns out that the statistic χ_r^2 is distributed as chi square with $df = k - 1$ only if the number of columns or the number of rows is not too small. Siegel (1956) states that if k is 3 and N is less than 10, or if k is 4 and N is less than 5, you cannot use the usual chi square table to determine significance levels. For these smaller samples, a special table of critical values of χ_r^2 is available (Siegel, 1956).

Note 13-1

Nonparametric Statistical Tests and How They Grew

Compared to the parametric techniques, which evolved early in this century, nonparametric statistical methods have been developed in recent years. Frank Wilcoxon (1892-1965), an industrial chemist, proposed the test bearing his name in 1945, which helped to stimulate a variety of researchers in the development of other nonparametric methods. These methods found extensive use in education and the behavioral sciences, because much of the data of rating scales, surveys, and other scaling techniques yielded data which was on an ordinal scale and did not meet the assumptions of the usual parametric tests. This interest in small-group interactions and measurements of attributes was a primary factor in the immediate popularity of the techniques.

Concluding Remarks

At the beginning of the chapter we noted that the nonparametric tests were necessary for situations in which (1) the parametric assumptions regarding normality and homogeneity of variance of populations could not be met or (2) data were from a nominal or ordinal scale. We have seen in this chapter a wide variety of statistical tests that are appropriate for just these situations. A convenient way to remember the various nonparametric tests is to study them in tabular form according to the level of measurement (nominal or ordinal) and type of situation (independent samples or related samples). Table 13-13 summarizes these characteristics in a convenient form.

The main weakness of nonparametric tests is that they are less powerful than parametric tests; that is, they are less likely to reject the null hypothesis when it is false. We must remember that when the assumptions of parametric tests can be met, parametric tests should definitely be used, because they are the most powerful tests available. However, if these assumptions cannot be met, we simply do not have any choice in the matter. We are left with nonparametric tests alone, and we must do the best we can.

But this is a rather negative approach, and it has led to the feeling that nonparametric tests are not quite legitimate and should be avoided whenever possible. This feeling is entirely unwarranted, because nonparametric tests can be just as powerful as parametric tests if *the size of the samples* is increased. A researcher who had planned initially on using 40 subjects in her project might increase her sample size to 50 if she knew that her data could not meet the assumptions of a parametric test. The precise increases in sample size needed to achieve similar power in nonparametrics are discussed by Siegel (1956).

In some of the tests described in this chapter, there have been restrictions placed on the size of samples that could be used. In an introductory text it is just impossible to list all the alternative ways of handling very small samples or samples with an N of more than 25. The texts by Daniel (1978) and Siegel (1956) are excellent resources for these special situations, and the researcher can find in them answers to just about any question on statistical analysis by nonparametric procedures.

Table 13-13
Level of Measurement and Application for
Selected Nonparametric Tests

	Independent Samples	*Related Samples*
Nominal	Chi square	McNemar test of changes
Ordinal	Median test	Sign test
	Mann-Whitney U test	Wilcoxon matched-pairs test
	Kruskal-Wallis ANOVA	Friedman ANOVA

Sample Problem

In a test of a new drug intended to increase the attention span of hyper-
active children, a neurologist asked the mothers of 16 children to observe their child's TV viewing for a period of 1 week prior to the onset
of medication. After each child had been on medication for 10 days,
the mother was again asked to monitor the child's TV viewing for 1
week and to indicate to the neurologist whether she felt that the
child's attention span was shorter than, the same as, or longer than
when the child received no medication. Which of the nonparametric
tests should be used to analyze the data?

Since each child was "measured" twice we have *related* samples, and the designation of "Greater" or "Lesser" attention span
indicates that we have ordinal data. Referring to Table 13-13, we see
that we can consider the sign test, the Wilcoxon test, or the Friedman
ANOVA. Since we have only two conditions (before medication and
after medication), we can eliminate the Friedman test, which is for
more than two conditions. And we can eliminate the Wilcoxon test
because we do not know *how much* of a difference a judgment of
"Greater" indicates. This leaves the sign test, and we next set up a
table similar to Table 13-10. However, we do not need to have the
Before and *After* columns, since we already have the information
regarding the change implicit in the statements "Greater," "Same,"
or "Lesser."

Child	Attention Span after Medication	Sign
A	Greater	−
B	Same	0
C	Greater	−
D	Greater	−
E	Lesser	+
F	Same	0
G	Same	0
H	Greater	−
I	Lesser	+
J	Greater	−
K	Same	0
L	Greater	−
M	Same	0
N	Greater	−
O	Greater	−
P	Greater	−

$$N = 11$$
$$x = 2$$

Significant, $p = .033$

We note that the attention span of 5 of the 16 children was judged "Same," so the N for the sign test is 11. Only two of the children (E and I) had a shorter attention span than before medication, so $x = 2$.

From Table J we see that $p = .033$ (one-tailed probability) for an N of 11 and $x = 2$. Since the neurologist was predicting that attention span would be *increased* by the medication, a one-tailed test is called for, and the results are significant, since $p < .05$.

Study Questions

1. What is the difference between parametric and nonparametric statistics?

2. What are the two main categories for nonparametric tests?

3. How are the expected frequencies determined in a one-way chi square? In a two-way chi square?

4. How does sample size affect the use of one-way chi-square?

5. How are the degrees of freedom determined for a one-way chi square? For a two-way chi square?

6. What are the assumptions for the chi square?

7. Explain the relationship of the null hypothesis to the median test.

8. How is the method of the Mann-Whitney U test related to the null hypothesis?

9. In the Kruskall-Wallis test, observations in each category are given an overall rank. Why should the rank sums of each category be the same under the null hypothesis?

10. How do related samples differ from independent samples?

11. Under the null hypothesis what can you say regarding the changes in the McNemar test of changes?

12. In what ways are the sign test and the Wilcoxon test alike? How are they different?

13. How is the method of the Friedman test related to the null hypothesis?

14. What is the main weakness of the nonparametric tests? How might this be overcome?

Exercises

1. In a survey of special education facilities in a midwestern school district, there were 80 students identified as learning disabled — 62 boys and 18 girls. Use the chi square to test the null hypothesis that there should be an equal number of each sex.

2. A mathematics professor wanted to see if there was any difference in the final grades obtained by students who did the majority of the assigned problems and those who rarely handed in the problems. She tabulated the final grades from her grade book and then counted those who had handed in at least 75% of the assigned problems and those who had handed in less than 25% of the problems. Was there a significant difference between these two groups of students on their final grades?

Final Grade

		A or B	D or F
Problems	Under 25%	8	22
	Over 75%	28	12

3. A sample of 100 college graduates, 100 individuals with some college training, and 100 individuals with no training beyond high school were asked about the frequency with which they read the editorial page of the local newspaper. The tabulations are shown below. Was there a significant difference in the habits of individuals at various educational levels?

Response

		"Rarely, if ever"	"About half the time"	"Just about always"
Educa-tional Level	College grad	5	30	65
	Some college	25	60	15
	High school grad	50	40	10

4. A college football coach was interested in the relative abilities of recruits from small high schools and large high schools. He first ranked his 52 players on general ability and then examined the college records to find out the size of each player's high school graduating class. All schools with a graduating class of 200 or larger were designated as large schools. The coach then determined whether each player was in the top 50% or bottom 50% in ability and tabulated each according to the size of the graduating class. Was there a significant difference in ability between players from large schools and players from small schools?

	Small School	Large School
Above median ability	12	14
Below median ability	17	9

5. Five children from families where each is an only child and four children with at least one brother or sister were rated for "maturity of verbal expression." Each child was given a rating from 1 (few verbalizations) to 20 (many verbalizations) during a 30-minute evaluation period. The results are shown below. Use the Mann-Whitney U test to determine if there were significantly more verbal expressions by only children.

Only Children	Other Children
11	8
15	10
12	7
17	5
9	

6. Studies on creativity have shown that children taught by a teacher who encourages divergent thinking (arriving at multiple solutions for a problem instead of a single correct answer) are more likely to display creative behavior. One investigator, in trying to locate such teachers for participation in a research project, noted that some elementary schools seemed to encourage the teaching of divergent thinking more than others. The researcher chose eight teachers at random from each of three schools and assessed each teacher's classroom behavior on the amount of divergent problem-solving behavior displayed (on a scale from 1 to 50). Use the Kruskal-Wallis procedure to see if there was a significant difference between the schools on this variable.

School A	*School B*	*School C*
41	48	30
43	46	49
30	43	30
32	40	25
45	47	31
28	45	29
42	40	27
25	35	34

7. Seventy households were asked their preferences for one of two popular brands of laundry detergent. The manufacturer of Brand A then conducted an intensive advertising campaign. The 70 nouseholds were again asked their preferences. Was there a significant change in their preferences after the advertising campaign?

		After	
		Brand A	Brand B
Before	Brand B	38	10
	Brand A	10	12

8 The director of campus police at a university noted that the majority of parking tickets seemed to be issued to a small minority of students. He selected 15 from this group and gave them a lecture on the philosophy of parking regulations. He then compared the number of parking tickets each had received 2 months prior to the lecture with the number of tickets issued for the 2-month period after the lecture. Use the sign test to see if there was a significant reduction in the amount of tickets issued during the second 2-month period.

Student	*Before*	*After*	*Student*	*Before*	*After*
A	5	4	I	4	4
B	3	3	J	3	4
C	4	5	K	2	6
D	2	2	L	5	4
E	8	2	M	3	2
F	7	6	N	2	3
G	4	0	O	4	3
H	6	5			

9. An investigator was studying problem-solving ability under quiet surroundings and under noisy surroundings. Twelve subjects were tested under both conditions, with the scores below. Use the Wilcoxon method to determine if there was a significant difference in performance under the two conditions.

Subject	Quiet	Noisy	Subject	Quiet	Noisy
A	37	32	G	39	33
B	38	38	H	30	30
C	34	35	I	32	31
D	34	33	J	45	40
E	36	34	K	29	27
F	40	42	L	37	34

10. A supermarket promotion for different brands of yogurt invited customers to sample three brands and rank them according to taste. Twelve customers yielded the data shown below. Use the Friedman analysis of variance to determine if there was a significant difference in the ranks given the three brands.

Customer	Brand A	Brand B	Brand C
1	2	3	1
2	3	2	1
3	2	1	3
4	1	3	.2
5	2	3	1
6	1	3	2
7	3	2	1
8	1	3	2
9	3	1	2
10	3	2	1
11	1	2	3
12	3	2	1

14 Statistical Methods in Test Construction

The inclusion of the following material in this introductory text in statistics is somewhat arbitrary—and also a little strange, since it is the only chapter devoted entirely to an *application* of statistical methods to a content field. But, since we are bombarded with tests almost from birth to death, any self-respecting student of education and the behavioral sciences should be acquainted with some of the statistical concepts that are important in test construction.

The application of statistics to testing is a broad subject, its topics ranging from construction of an individual test item all the way to mathematical theory about the accuracy of a test score. We can by no means cover all the statistical applications in a single chapter, or in a single volume for that matter. If you are interested in the subject, a textbook on tests and measurements (e.g., Anastasi, 1976) or a statistical treatment on the order of Guilford and Fruchter (1978) may be helpful. Moreover, these may be able to point out additional sources for more specialized topics.

Our main interest in this chapter will be to examine two character-istics of a measuring instrument and to see how a statistical approach can be used to assess these characteristics. Specifically, we are inter-ested in the *reliability* and the *validity* of a test.

Reliability

One important characteristic of any measuring device, be it a bathroom scale or a reading readiness test, is its *reliability*. That is, we expect the measurements yielded by any instrument to be *consistent* or *repeatable*. If Johnny's weight as taken at 1-hour intervals on the same scale were 75, 98, and 36 pounds, or his I.Q. scores as measured at 1-month intervals by the same test were 126, 180, and 92, we would seriously doubt the reliability of the bathroom scale and the particular I.Q. test. We expect a reliable instrument to give us consistent results. We do not, of course, expect to get *identical* results each time we mea-sure some human characteristic more than once, because most instru-ments are not perfectly reliable, but we do expect a certain degree of "sameness" in our measurements.

It does not take a great deal of imagination to see that the meth-ods of correlation discussed in Chapter 8 could be used to determine the reliability of a test. If we gave the same test twice to the same group of students, we would expect a high positive correlation if the test were reliable. If the measurements were consistent, those pupils who scored high on one administration of the test would tend to score high on the second administration, and those making low scores the first time should also score low the second time. The coefficient of correlation, the Pearson r, for example, would be a direct indicator of the amount of reliability. If r were high, it would indicate a great degree of consistency between the two administrations of the test. If some students who scored high on the first testing scored low on the second, the value of r would be lower, indicating a lower degree of reliability.

However, determining the reliability of a test is not quite as simple as it may first appear, and a number of special methods have been de-veloped. We will consider three general methods often used by test writers and publishers to determine the reliability of their tests—the test-retest, the parallel forms, and the internal consistency methods.

Test-Retest Method

The simplest and most straightforward method for determining reliability would be to give the test twice to the same group of individ-uals. We could then use the Pearson r to determine the correlation between the two administrations of the test. As we noted earlier, the coefficient of correlation yielded by this method would indicate the amount of relationship. If *r* were high, the measurements would be consistent and the test would be considered reliable.

Despite its simplicity, there are a number of problems involved in the test-retest method. If the test is repeated within a short time interval, many individuals might be able to recall answers that they had given previously and could spend more time on the more difficult material. Not all individuals would do this, of course, so this would increase some scores and not others and would lower the coefficient of correlation. The type of test would determine the amount of transfer from one test administration to the next.

On the other hand, if the time interval between the initial administration of the test and its repetition is too long, growth and maturity (especially if the examinees are children) would affect performance on the second administration. Certain experiences by different individuals during this interval might influence their performance also—again tending to lower the correlation coefficient.

Because of the difficulty in controlling these conditions, the test-retest method is not often used. It is always included in a discussion of reliability, however, since it *defines* the term. Theoretically, a reliable test should always give consistent results from one administration to the next.

Parallel Forms Method

One obvious way to avoid the practice effect of the test-retest method for short time intervals would be to use another form of the same test. This parallel forms method (also called alternate forms or comparable forms) means that a test author would have to write twice as many items as would be needed for just a single test and two separate tests, for example, Form A and Form B, would be constructed. Both forms of the test would then be given to a sample of individuals. A time interval of 5 days to 2 weeks might separate the two administrations, but there should be very little practice effect since the two forms contain completely different items. The reliability of the test is given by the Pearson *r* calculated between the two sets of test scores.

When accurate parallel forms have been constructed (such as Form L and Form M of one of the earlier editions of the Stanford-Binet I.Q. test), they have provided a very useful research tool and a defensible definition of reliability. Nevertheless, it is imperative to keep in mind that the use of parallel forms does not really eliminate the problem of growth or maturity over longer time intervals that we encountered in the test-retest method. As individuals change, so do their responses to an identical item or to a completely different item that is testing the same content. What the use of parallel forms does do is eliminate the *need* for long time intervals between two administrations of a test.

The greatest drawback to the parallel forms method lies in the sheer amount of labor required for an author to construct the parallel form. Writing good items for one test is a difficult task (as you may have learned in a tests-and-measurements course), and writing twice as many is a real problem. There may be a number of occasions when we would like to determine the reliability of a test we have constructed for classroom purposes but when the extra time and effort involved would prevent us from using the parallel forms approach.

Internal Consistency Methods

The two methods described above are similar in that they both involve *two* administrations — either of the same test or of parallel forms. However, methods involving *internal consistency* are based on a *single* administration of the test. For example, in the *split-half method*, the test is divided into two parts (such as two subsections, with random assignment of items into the two parts), and a correlation coefficient is calculated between the two portions of the test. Obviously, this correlation coefficient has a different interpretation from the coefficient for the test-retest and parallel forms methods: it describes *internal consistency*.

One commonly used technique for obtaining split halves in order to determine internal consistency is the *odd-even method*. With this method, each individual has two scores — a score on the odd-numbered items in a test and a score on the even-numbered items. It is necessary to go through the answer sheet for each individual and tabulate the number of items correct on the odd items and the number correct on the even items. The scores are then placed in the familiar X and Y columns of the Pearson correlation method, as shown in Table 14-1. For example, suppose that we gave a 30-item multiple choice test to 10 students. (The examples in this chapter will, by necessity, involve small samples. Much larger numbers of examinees are used in actual situations.) Student A received a score of 22 on the test, so we go through the answer sheet and find that he got 12 of the odd-numbered items correct and 10 of the even-numbered items correct. These scores, and the odd and even scores for the remaining students, are shown in Table 14-1.

Table 14-1
Calculating a Reliability Coefficient by the Odd-Even Method

Student	X (Odd)	Y (Even)	X^2	Y^2	XY
A	12	10	144	100	120
B	10	8	100	64	80
C	9	11	81	121	99
D	14	11	196	121	154
E	13	10	169	100	130
F	8	8	64	64	64
G	12	11	144	121	132
H	11	10	121	100	110
I	11	11	121	121	121
J	10	10	100	100	100
	110	100	1,240	1,012	1,110

Correlation Coefficient:

$$r_{oe} = \frac{N\Sigma XY - \Sigma X\Sigma Y}{\sqrt{N\Sigma X^2 - (\Sigma X)^2}\sqrt{N\Sigma Y^2 - (\Sigma Y)^2}}$$

$$= \frac{10(1,110) - (110)(100)}{\sqrt{10(1,240) - (110)^2}\sqrt{10(1,012) - (100)^2}}$$

$$r_{oe} = \frac{100}{189.65} = .53$$

Spearman-Brown:

$$r_{tt} = \frac{2r_{oe}}{1 + r_{oe}} = \frac{2(.53)}{1 + .53} = \frac{1.06}{1.53} = .69$$

As you see from Table 14-1, the computational steps are identical to those for the correlation coefficients that you calculated in Chapter 8. However, $r_{oe} = .53$ is *not* the reliability coefficient but only the correlation between the two halves of the test. It has been demonstrated that reliability is directly related to the *length* of the test, and we have, in effect, cut our test in half by separating odd and even items.

Our r_{oe} of .53 is artificially low as an estimate of the reliability of the original test.

For this reason it is necessary to correct for the effective length of the test by using the Spearman-Brown formula:

$$r_{tt} = \frac{2r_{oe}}{1 + r_{oe}} \qquad\qquad (14\text{-}1)$$

where r_{tt} is the reliability coefficient of the entire test,

r_{oe} is the coefficient of correlation between the two halves.

Using this formula with the data of Table 14-1, we see that the reliability of the entire test, r_{tt}, is .69, quite low as reliability coefficients go We will have occasion later in this chapter to discuss the relative sizes of reliability coefficients.

But what is the rationale for the odd-even method of determining reliability? The test-retest and parallel forms methods were straightforward: if the test were reliable, an individual would make comparable scores relative to the rest of the group on both administrations. Is there similar reasoning behind the odd-even method (and other internal consistency methods)? When we separate an individual's total score into odd and even correct, we expect to see similar results on the odd and even items (if odd and even items are of similar difficulty) relative to the rest of the group. If this is the case, the test is reliable; that is, its measurements are consistent. If the individual does not do equally well on the odd and even halves, the test is not measuring consistently and, therefore, is not reliable. However, this "split-half" method for determining reliability is not measuring the same concept as the test-retest and parallel forms methods. It measures internal consistency and not consistency from administration to administration.

The split-half method should not be used on what are termed "speed tests." Theoretically, most tests are timed tests, in that a student does not have an infinite amount of time to complete them. But a speed test, strictly speaking, is one where every examinee would get *all* the items correct if enough time were allowed. Obviously, this would lead to problems with internal consistency, since every examinee would have the same score (i.e., 100% correct) on each half.

Comparing the Three Methods

The test-retest, parallel forms, and internal consistency methods for estimating the reliability of a test will result in different estimates for the same test. This does not surprise us, since we know that there are specific characteristics that are unique to each method. For example, we have already noted that the test-retest method can be affected by practice and lengthy time intervals, the parallel forms method is sensitive to lengthy time intervals, and internal consistency methods are different from stability (test-retest) or equivalency (parallel forms) methods. In fact, split-half reliability coefficients tend to be higher than those obtained by either of the other two methods. For these reasons, it is important that the type of method used be cited in test manuals and journal articles, so the reader can interpret the results correctly.

Since all the methods have their shortcomings, is there any one method that is preferred? The answer to this question lies in the purpose of the investigator. Since the test-retest approach has limited use because of the practice effect, we are often left with a choice between parallel forms or internal consistency methods. If the investigator is involved in test theory—for example, development of alternative methods for estimating reliability, or effect of test length or item difficulty on reliability—he or she will probably choose one of the internal consistency methods. On the other hand, the *test user* (clinical psychologist, educational consultant) might be more interested in a parallel forms approach, since he or she may be running *before* and *after* studies where the same test is given a second time but in a different form.

We are likely to see both methods cited frequently in the literature; however, the fact that internal consistency tests are well suited for computer analysis makes them very desirable. There are many different methods for analyzing internal consistency, and our odd-even illustration is just one of these methods. There are several methods employing *item statistics*, which do not require that the test be split into separate halves. Some of these methods require information on how each student did on every test item, but this approach generally requires electronic scoring by a computer. We must note again, however, that internal consistency methods are generally not for use with speed tests. You will find additional information on these methods in most tests-and-measurements texts, and the statistics text by Guilford and Fruchter (1978) is an excellent source.

One last word about reliability: it is not something "possessed" by a test, like an answer sheet or a title or a scoring key. There is nothing about the test itself that has the quality "reliability," because reliability is partly a function of *how* a test is used and on *whom* it is used. We would be more accurate in our discussion if we talked about a test yielding "reliable results" or said, "The scores on such and such a test were reliable." Technically, we can talk of a "reliable test" only when we specify the conditions under which it was administered and the sample to whom it was given.

Standard Error of Measurement

Correlation coefficients and their interpretation may be difficult to apply in specific settings, especially for the person who has relatively little training in statistics. An alternative approach to using the reliability coefficient, r_{tt}, as an index of accuracy is the *standard error of measurement*. It is unaffected by certain characteristics of the data used to calculate r_{tt}, and it makes a certain amount of intuitive sense. It is used, basically, to set up a confidence interval which allows us to interpret a single individual's score with a certain degree of precision.

Suppose, for example, that a student scores 79 on an examination. How much confidence do we have in this score? How much confidence do we have that our test is measuring accurately and that 79 is the individual's *true* score? (By a *true score*, we mean one in whose determination there are no errors of measurement present.) We assume that, if we could somehow measure this student over and over again, the mean of the student's scores would be the *true* score. The standard deviation of the distribution of scores would be called the *standard error of measurement*.

It is impractical to administer a test enough times to find a mean of the distribution to identify the student's true score. It is also unnecessary, for we can *estimate* the standard deviation of this distribution of repeated measurements and use a confidence interval approach to make a probability statement about the individual's true score. This estimate is the standard error of measurement, and it is given by

$$S_{EM} = S_T\sqrt{1 - r_{tt}} \qquad (14\text{-}2)$$

where S_T is the standard deviation of the original test scores,

  r_{tt} is the reliability coefficient of the test.

For example, suppose that, in the situation above, the standard deviation of the test scores was 6.45 and the reliability coefficient of the test was .87. The standard error of measurement would then be

$$
\begin{aligned}
S_{EM} &= S_T\sqrt{1 - r_{tt}} \\
&= 6.45\sqrt{1 - .87} \\
&= 6.45\sqrt{.13} \\
&= 6.45(.36) \\
S_{EM} &= 2.33
\end{aligned}
$$

We can now use S_{EM} just like any other standard error to determine a 95% confidence interval in which we expect the true mean (the individual's true score) to fall. That is, we could mark off $X \pm 1.96 S_{EM}$

or $X \pm 2.58S_{EM}$, and these intervals would give probabilities of .95 and .99 that the individual's true score is in the interval. However, it has been conventional in test theory to mark off $1S_{EM}$ above and below the individual's observed score to obtain $X \pm S_{EM}$. This, of course, gives the 68% confidence interval. For the situation above, with the individual's score of 79 and $S_{EM} = 2.33$, the confidence interval would be

$$X \pm S_{EM} = 79 \pm 2.33$$
$$= 76.67 \text{ to } 81.33$$

We interpret this by saying that we are 68% certain that the true score is in the interval 76.67 to 81.33 or that the chances are 2 out of 3 that the true score is in that interval. Table 14-2 shows the standard error of measurement based on the data of Table 14-1. As an example, student H had a total score of 21 (11 on the odd items and 10 on the even items). What does the standard error of measurement tell us about the accuracy of this score?

Note in Table 14-2 that, before we can calculate S_{EM}, we have to determine S_T, the standard deviation of the original test scores. (The subscript, T, denotes the original test scores, so S_T is the standard deviation of the test scores, *not* of the odd or even scores.) We first calculate ΣX_T, the sum of the test scores, by simply adding ΣX and ΣY, where X and Y denote the odd and even data from Table 14-1. We then determine ΣX_T^2, the sum of the squared test scores, by finding $\Sigma X^2 + 2\Sigma XY + \Sigma Y^2$, where X and Y again refer to the odd and even values in Table 14-1. We then use the machine formula to obtain $S_T = 2.49$. The remaining steps to determine S_{EM} and the confidence interval are shown in Table 14-2.

We would conclude that the chances are 2 out of 3 that the student's true score lies between 19.61 and 22.39. We have done what we set out to do: even though we cannot know what the true score may be for any examinee, we can state the probability that the true score is included in a certain interval.

The confidence interval for the true score has been used by some test publishers in constructing norms, and we noted in Chapter 4 that the use of percentile bands aided us in interpreting an individual's score. For example, we noted that a test score of 157 on the Cooperative English Test had a percentile band of from 29 to 52. This means that we are 68% certain that the individual's true score would lie in such a way that from 29% to 52% of the norm distribution was below the true score.

It should be obvious that errors of measurement are related to the size of the reliability coefficient. The greater the value of r_{tt}, the smaller

Table 14-2

Calculation of the True Score Interval for Student H

Test Data:

$$\Sigma X_T = \Sigma X + \Sigma Y = 110 + 100 = 210$$

$$\Sigma X_T^2 = \Sigma X^2 + 2\Sigma XY + \Sigma Y^2 = 1{,}240 + 2(1{,}110) + 1{,}012 = 4{,}472$$

$$S_T = \frac{1}{N}\sqrt{N\Sigma X_T^2 - (\Sigma X_T)^2} = \frac{1}{10}\sqrt{10(4{,}472) - (210)^2}$$

$$= \frac{\sqrt{620}}{10} = 2.49$$

$$r_{tt} = .69 \quad \text{(calculated previously)}$$

Standard Error of Measurement:

$$S_{EM} = S_T\sqrt{1 - r_{tt}} = 2.49\sqrt{1 - .69} = 2.49\,(0.56) = 1.39$$

Confidence Interval for Student H:

$$X \pm S_{EM} = 21 \pm 1.39 = 19.61 \text{ to } 22.39$$

the standard error of measurement and the greater the accuracy of the score. This is illustrated quite simply by the formula for S_{EM}. The size of the confidence interval indicates the amount of error, which is directly dependent upon $S_T\sqrt{1 - r_{tt}}$. If there is perfect reliability, $r_{tt} = 1.0$, S_{EM} is 0, and there is no error at all. And, if $r_{tt} = 0$, S_{EM} becomes the same as the standard deviation of the test. We can see that the higher the reliability of the test, the smaller the standard error of measurement.

Validity

When we ask the question "Are these test results consistent and repeatable?" we are talking about reliability. But when we ask, "Is this test testing what it is supposed to test?" we are concerned with *validity*, or the purpose of the test. Various tests may yield valid measures of intelligence, manual dexterity, vocational interest, and a host of other traits that are amenable to measurement. Basically, we say that a test is valid if it measures what it purports to measure.

A test can be highly reliable without being valid. With a primitive I.Q. test which consisted of measuring the circumference of the head with a tape measure, we might get very *reliable* (i.e., consistent) measurements. However, such measurements would not be *valid* for esti-mating intelligence.

Test theorists have identified three basic types of validity—content validity, construct validity, and criterion-related validity. These terms all represent different ways of determining whether a test is "testing what it is supposed to test." Since the purpose of this chapter is to illustrate some of the statistical methods in test construction, we will confine our discussion to the third type, the *criterion-related* validity, because statistical analysis is a major factor in this method.

In order to determine whether a test is testing what it is supposed to test, we need to have some other measurement that is totally independent with which to compare our test. This independent "other measurement" is called the *criterion,* and the proper selection of a criterion is a vital part of criterion-related validity. The criterion must be a valid and reliable measure of what we are interested in measuring with our own test. For example, if we are constructing a new intelligence test, we would probably choose a test like the Stanford-Binet or one of the Wechsler tests as our criterion. These tests have been shown previously to be valid and reliable measures of intellectual ability. If our new test compares favorably with the criterion, we can say that our test is also a valid measure of intelligence.

But a criterion need not necessarily be another test. If our task was to construct a test that would predict success in soldering electronic parts in an assembly line procedure, we would need some independent measure of job success as a criterion. Since job "success" is quite often defined in terms of production, we could use the number of parts produced by a worker per hour or per day as the criterion.

The criterion may take many forms in validity studies. For a college entrance examination the criterion might be GPA at the end of the freshman year, for a personality inventory the criterion might be a clinical evaluation by a psychiatrist or clinical psychologist, and for a mechanical aptitude test the criterion might be supervisor ratings of a group of diesel mechanics. Many tests have been validated against multiple criteria, and one aptitude test was validated against such diverse criteria as typing speed of women bank clerks, ground-school grades of naval aviation cadets, and posting machine speed for experienced bookkeepers!

The precise *amount* of validity shown by a test in a given situation is the *statistical correlation* between the test and its criterion. If the co-efficient is positive and relatively high, we would conclude that both the test and the criterion are yielding similar results, so *both must be measuring the same traits.* In other words, a test is valid in a given situation to the extent that it is yielding the same results as the criterion. The logical tool for measuring how pairs of scores are related is the Pearson r, and we call the result a validity coefficient.

There are two ways of looking at criterion-related validity: we can speak of *predictive validity* or *concurrent validity*. These two methods are distinguished by the difference in the amount of time elapsing between the test administration and the measurement of the criterion.

Predictive Validity

Establishment of the *predictive* validity for a test in a given situation means that there will be a significant period of time between the test administration and the criterion measurement. This time interval must be of sufficient length that progress in the trait that is being predicted can be evaluated. Suppose, for example, that a college entrance exam is to be validated. Most exams are given to high school seniors during the fall of their senior year, so if the criterion were college GPA at the end of the freshman year there would be a time interval of at least a year and a half between the test administration and the correlation of the test scores with GPA.

We have already discussed an example of predictive validity back in Chapter 9, again using college entrance exams and GPA. The data is reproduced in Figure 14-1, and the validity coefficient is $r = .53$. By inspecting the scattergram, we see that, *in general,* those with higher entrance scores tended to make higher grades and those with the lower entrance scores tended to make lower grades.

Time intervals in predictive validity studies can be quite lengthy. It is not unusual to see validity coefficients reported on performance tests of intelligence given to 4-year-olds with the criterion of high school or college grades. Of course, any longitudinal study of this sort has problems—not the least of which is the dropout rate of the examinees, whose families may move away before the study is completed.

Concurrent Validity

There are times when the investigator does not have the luxury of months or years elapsing between the administration of the test and the measurement of criterion performance. It might be too expensive to gather data and then wait until the examinee reaches the criterion, or maybe the results are needed immediately and a lengthy time interval is just not a possibility.

In such cases, *concurrent* validity is the alternate procedure; it involves administering the test and measuring the criterion within a very short time interval. For example, a personnel director of a business

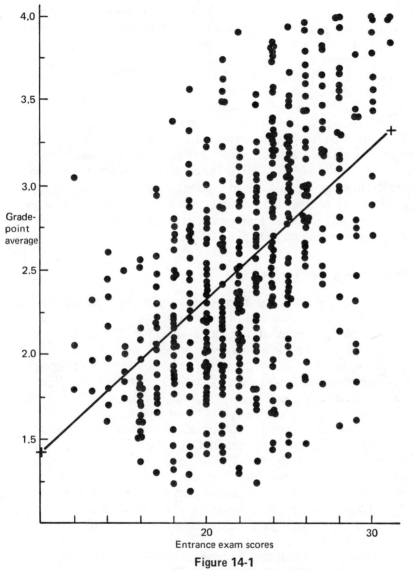

Figure 14-1
Scattergram for examining the validity of a college entrance exam.

firm may want to develop a clerical aptitude test that will predict how well an applicant will do as a clerk-typist in the office. If she were using a predictive validity approach, she would administer the test to applicants for typing jobs and then wait months (or even longer, if other specialized skills are involved) before measuring their criterion performance, such as on-the-job ratings by a supervisor. However, using a concurrent validity approach, she administers the test to typists *already* employed by the company and has a supervisor rate the typists on their job performance. The Pearson method of correlation then yields a validity coefficient for the test.

Concluding the topic of validity, we should note that it is somewhat misleading to say that "such and such a test is valid." A test is not valid in itself but is valid *for* a particular purpose. A given set of items may be *invalid* for most purposes but could be valid *for* assessing clerical skills, English vocabulary, or knowledge of internal combustion engines. In summary, we would say that validity is a *specific* characteristic of a test rather than a general one. For a good discussion of validity, as well as other topics in tests and measurements, see the excellent paperback by Tyler and Walsh (1979).

Concluding Remarks

We noted in an earlier section that a test could be reliable (i.e., consistent in its measurement of some attribute) but still not be a valid instrument for testing what it is supposed to test. But what about the reverse? Can a test be valid in a given situation without being reliable? The answer is no, of course, since an unreliable test is not giving you very much information about what it is supposed to be testing. If an unreliable I.Q. test tells you that your I.Q. is 127 or 83 or 159 in three testings, you certainly would have doubts about what it is really measuring.

This last point can be demonstrated mathematically, and test theorists have shown that the size of the validity coefficient depends on the reliability of *both* the test *and* the criterion. This is an important point to remember, since many test constructors take great pains to devise a reliable test but then choose a criterion with questionable reliability. To obtain maximum predictive efficiency with a validity coefficient, you must have high reliability in both your test and the criterion.

Nothing has been said so far about the relative sizes of reliability and validity coefficients, and a complete discussion of this topic more properly belongs in a textbook on tests and measurements. However, you probably can get an idea of relative sizes by referring to the data of some representative tests shown in Table 14-3.

Reliability coefficients are usually higher than validity coefficients, and it is not unusual to find split-half coefficients in the .90 to .95 range. And we noted earlier that these internal consistency coefficients are generally higher than those found by either the parallel forms or test-

Table 14-3
Some Reliability and Validity Coefficients for Selected Tests

Test	Reliability	Validity
Differential Aptitude Test, Form L, Verbal Reasoning	Split-half $r = .92$	With high school English grades $r = .63$
Minnesota Paper Form Board	Parallel forms $r = .78$	With freshman mechanical drawing grades $r = .49$
Peabody Picture Vocabulary Test, Age Level 18	Parallel forms $r = .84$	With Stanford-Binet $r = .71$
Purdue Pegboard	Test-retest $r = .84$	With radio tube assemblers $r = .64$
Stanford-Binet I.Q., Form L-M	Test-retest (Age 3 and 1 year later) $r = .83$	Subtest with full test I.Q. $r = .61$

retest methods. Not all reliability coefficients are as high as those shown in Table 14-3, however, and the reliability of such measures as supervisor or interview ratings are much lower.

Validity coefficients may range anywhere from .20 and up, with the .60 to .70 range considered quite high. Since the validity coefficient is an index of how well the test predicts future performance, we are naturally interested in having r as large as possible. We must remember, though, that *any* significant validity coefficient indicates that the test is better than nothing. If a manual dexterity test correlates only .35 with some industrial job, it is still better to use the test as a means of screening new workers than just to give the job to any warm body that happens to wander in. If the turnover rate for a particular job was 19% before the test was used for screening and drops to 17% after the test is adopted, the difference of 2% may save the company thousands of dollars in supervisor time, reduce the waste of materials, and increase production during training.

We should also call attention to the fact that in many statistical studies of reliability and validity, relatively large numbers of examinees are used. The illustrative examples and problems in this chapter have used a very small N to prevent us from getting bogged down in computational procedures, but real-life situations demand as large a sample as possible to reduce measurement error. Most popular standardized tests have been evaluated on the basis of thousands of examinees.

We started this chapter with the reservation that we would be discussing only a small sample of statistical applications in test construction. If these selected topics have aroused your curiosity about the test construction field, you are referred to traditional texts on tests and measurements or educational statistics (e.g., Guilford and Fruchter, 1978) for a more thorough treatment of these and related topics.

Sample Problem #1

A graduate class in educational testing constructed a short test that was designed to measure arithmetic skills. The test was given to 21 eighth-graders, and their scores on odd and even items are shown below. Calculate r_{tt}, S_{EM}, and the confidence interval for student L.

Student	X(Odd)	Y(Even)	X^2	Y^2	XY
A	15	14	225	196	210
B	15	16	225	256	240
C	16	16	256	256	256
D	17	18	289	324	306
E	13	12	169	144	156
F	15	16	225	256	240
G	16	16	256	256	256
H	16	15	256	225	240
I	16	18	256	324	288
J	19	18	361	324	342
K	16	11	256	121	176
L	13	13	169	169	169
M	15	15	225	225	225
N	12	11	144	121	132
O	17	15	289	225	255
P	14	12	196	144	168
Q	12	11	144	121	132
R	15	14	225	196	210
S	11	7	121	49	77
T	12	12	144	144	144
U	9	5	81	25	45
$N = 21$	304	285	4,512	4,101	4,267

Correlation Coefficient:

$$r_{oe} = \frac{N\Sigma XY - \Sigma X\Sigma Y}{\sqrt{N\Sigma X^2 - (\Sigma X)^2}\ \sqrt{N\Sigma Y^2 - (\Sigma Y)^2}}$$

$$= \frac{21(4,267) - (304)(285)}{\sqrt{21(4,512) - (304)^2}\ \sqrt{21(4,101) - (285)^2}}$$

$$= \frac{2,967}{3,381.65} = .88$$

Spearman-Brown:

$$r_{tt} = \frac{2r_{oe}}{1 + r_{oe}} = \frac{2(.88)}{1 + .88} = \frac{1.76}{1.88} = .94$$

Whole Test Data:

$$\Sigma X_T = \Sigma X + \Sigma Y = 304 + 285 = 589$$

$$\Sigma X_T{}^2 = \Sigma X^2 + 2\Sigma XY + \Sigma Y^2 = 4,512 + 2(4,267) + 4,101 = 17,147$$

$$S_T = \frac{1}{N}\sqrt{N\Sigma X_T{}^2 - (\Sigma X_T)^2} = \frac{1}{21}\sqrt{21(17,147) = (589)^2}$$

$$= \frac{\sqrt{13,166}}{21} = 5.46$$

Standard Error of Measurement:

$$S_{EM} = S_T\sqrt{1 - r_{tt}} = 5.46\sqrt{1 - .94} = 5.46(.24) = 1.31$$

Confidence Interval for Student L:

$$X \pm S_{EM} = 26 \pm 1.31 = 24.69 \text{ to } 27.31$$

We conclude that the chances are 2 out of 3 that L's true score is included in the interval 24.69 to 27.31.

Sample Problem #2

The arithmetic skills test described above was found to be highly reliable, with $r_{tt} = .94$. The class then proceeded to determine the validity of this test by comparing it with a nationally standardized arithmetic achievement test. Both tests were administered to another group of 20 eighth-graders. Use the Pearson method of correlation to determine the validity of the class-made test.

Student	Class Test X	National Y	X^2	Y^2	XY
A	31	24	961	576	744
B	32	18	1,024	324	576
C	33	29	1,089	841	957
D	34	23	1,156	529	782
E	36	26	1,296	676	936
F	35	32	1,225	1,024	1,120
G	34	23	1,156	529	782
H	34	30	1,156	900	1,020
I	34	26	1,156	676	884
J	37	27	1,369	729	999
K	35	37	1,225	1,369	1,295
L	36	34	1,296	1,156	1,224
M	34	31	1,156	961	1,054
N	37	32	1,369	1,024	1,184
O	37	31	1,369	961	1,147
P	37	25	1,369	625	925
Q	37	35	1,369	1,225	1,295
R	37	32	1,369	1,024	1,184
S	38	31	1,444	961	1,178
T	38	29	1,444	841	1,102
N = 20	706	575	24,998	16,951	20,388

Validity Coefficient:

$$r = \frac{N\Sigma XY - \Sigma X \Sigma Y}{\sqrt{N\Sigma X^2 - (\Sigma X)^2} \ \sqrt{N\Sigma Y^2 - (\Sigma Y)^2}}$$

$$= \frac{20(20,388) - (706)(575)}{\sqrt{20(24,998) - (706)^2} \ \sqrt{20(16,951) - (575)^2}}$$

$$= \frac{1,810}{(39.04)(91.62)} = .51$$

With a validity coefficient of .51, we would conclude that the class-constructed test is measuring to a moderate extent what the national test is measuring.

Study Questions

1. What is meant by the *reliability* of a test?

2. Describe the three methods for determining the reliability of a test.

3. In what major way are the internal consistency methods for determining reliability different from the other two?

4. Why is the Spearman-Brown formula necessary when the split-half method is used?

5. What does the interval $X \pm S_{EM}$ represent?

6. What is meant by the *validity* of a test?

7. What is the difference between predictive validity and concurrent validity?

8. How can a test be reliable without being valid?

Exercises

1. A communications instructor wanted to determine the reliability of her final examination. She broke down each student's score into odd-numbered answers (X) and even-numbered answers (Y) correct. The results for her 60 students are shown below. Determine r_{tt} for her exam.

$$\Sigma X = 1,161 \qquad \Sigma Y = 1,290$$
$$\Sigma X^2 = 23,499 \qquad \Sigma Y^2 = 28,860$$
$$\Sigma XY = 25,778$$
$$N = 60$$

2. One of the students scored 41 on the communications exam described in exercise 1. Determine the 68% confidence interval for her score.

3. A mathematics achievement test is given to 15 eighth-graders, and their scores are broken down into odd (X) and even (Y) answers correct. Calculate r_{tt} for this test.

Student	X (Odd)	Y (Even)	Student	X (Odd)	Y (Even)
A	12	13	I	9	10
B	15	14	J	8	9
C	13	14	K	4	4
D	11	12	L	7	8
E	11	11	M	10	11
F	9	8	N	4	7
G	8	8	O	6	12
H	8	9			

4. One eighth-grader scored 29 on the mathematics test in exercise 3. Calculate the 68% confidence interval for his score.

5. A high school guidance counselor is dissatisfied with present college entrance exams and decides to construct his own. He administers his own exam (X) to 15 college-bound high school seniors and, one year later, tabulates their college GPA's (Y). Calculate the Pearson r to determine the validity of his exam.

Student	X	Y	Student	X	Y
A	22	2.8	I	16	2.8
B	21	2.6	J	15	2.8
C	20	3.2	K	14	2.7
D	18	3.2	L	14	2.4
E	17	3.2	M	13	2.6
F	16	2.8	N	11	3.0
G	16	2.3	O	11	2.9
H	16	2.7			

6. The personnel manager of a large insurance company is developing a new clerical aptitude test and wants to validate the test against the well-known Minnesota Clerical Aptitude Test. He administers both tests to a group of 20 clerical employees, and the scores (number of errors) on both tests are shown below. Use the Pearson r to determine the validity of this new test.

Employee	Local Test	Minnesota Clerical	Employee	Local Test	Minnesota Clerical
A	14	9	K	14	8
B	14	9	L	12	7

C	13	9	M	12	7
D	14	8	N	11	8
E	14	8	O	13	7
F	13	9	P	13	8
G	13	9	Q	12	7
H	12	7	R	13	5
I	14	7	S	10	7
J	13	7	T	10	6

Appendix 1: Formulas

Name	Formula	First appears on page:
Arithmetic mean (3-1)	$\overline{X} = \dfrac{\Sigma X}{N}$	47
Combined mean (3-2)	$\overline{X} = \dfrac{N_1\overline{X}_1 + N_2\overline{X}_2 + N_3\overline{X}_3 + \ldots}{N_1 + N_2 + N_3 + \ldots}$	56
Arithmetic mean— grouped data (3-3)	$\overline{X} = MP + i\left(\dfrac{\Sigma fd}{N}\right)$	59
Median— grouped data (3-4)	$Med = L + i\left(\dfrac{0.5N - \mathrm{cum}f}{f_{50}}\right)$	62
Percentiles (4-1)	$P_p = L + i\left(\dfrac{pN - \mathrm{cum}f}{f_p}\right)$	81
Percentile rank (4-2)	$PR = \dfrac{\left(\mathrm{cum}\,f\,\mathrm{to}\,L + \dfrac{(X-L)}{i}f\right)}{N} \times 100$	84

Name	Formula	First appears on page:
Average deviation (5-1)	$AD = \dfrac{\Sigma |x|}{N}$	100
Standard deviation— deviation formula (5-2)	$S = \sqrt{\dfrac{\Sigma x^2}{N}}$	101
Standard deviation— mean formula (5-3)	$S = \sqrt{\dfrac{\Sigma X^2}{N} - \bar{X}^2}$	103
Standard deviation— machine formula (5-4)	$S = \dfrac{1}{N}\sqrt{N\Sigma X^2 - (\Sigma X)^2}$	104
z score (5-5)	$z = \dfrac{X - \bar{X}}{S}$	110
Semi-interquartile range (5-6)	$Q = \dfrac{P_{75} - P_{25}}{2}$	116
Standard deviation— grouped data (5-7)	$S = i\sqrt{\dfrac{N\Sigma fd^2 - (\Sigma fd)^2}{N^2}}$	117
Standard error of the mean—with population standard deviation (7-1)	$\sigma_X = \dfrac{\sigma}{\sqrt{N}}$	157
Standard error of the mean—with sample standard deviation (7-2)	$s_{\bar{X}} = \dfrac{S}{\sqrt{N-1}}$	158
z score—sampling distribution of means (7-3)	$z = \dfrac{\bar{X} - \bar{X}_{\bar{X}}}{s_{\bar{X}}}$	160

Name	Formula	*First appears on page:*
95% confidence interval for population mean (7-4)	$\bar{X} \pm 1.96\, s_{\bar{x}}$	166
99% confidence interval for population mean (7-5)	$\bar{X} \pm 2.58\, s_{\bar{x}}$	166
Biased estimate of population variance (7-6)	$S^2 = \dfrac{\Sigma x^2}{N}$	175
Unbiased estimate of population variance (7-7)	$s^2 = \dfrac{\Sigma x^2}{N-1}$	175
Pearson r—z score method (8-1)	$r = \dfrac{\Sigma z_X z_Y}{N}$	188
Pearson r—mean and S formula (8-2)	$r = \dfrac{\dfrac{\Sigma XY}{N} - \bar{X}\bar{Y}}{S_X S_Y}$	189
Pearson r—machine formula (8-3)	$r = \dfrac{N\Sigma XY - \Sigma X \Sigma Y}{\sqrt{N\Sigma X^2 - (\Sigma X)^2}\sqrt{N\Sigma Y^2 - (\Sigma Y)^2}}$	191
Standard error of Pearson r (8-4)	$s_r = \dfrac{1}{\sqrt{N-1}}$	194
Spearman rank-difference correlation coefficient (8-5)	$r_s = 1 - \dfrac{6\Sigma D^2}{N(N^2-1)}$	197
Regression equation (9-1)	$Y' = \left(\dfrac{rS_Y}{S_X}\right)X - \left(\dfrac{rS_Y}{S_X}\right)\bar{X} + \bar{Y}$	214
Standard error of estimate (9-2)	$s_E = S_Y\sqrt{1-r^2}$	220

Name	*Formula*	*First appears on page:*
68% confidence interval for Y' (9-3)	$Y' \pm 1s_E$	220
z score—sampling distribution of differences (10-1)	$z = \dfrac{(\bar{X}_1 - \bar{X}_2) - 0}{\sigma_{D\bar{X}}}$	239
Standard error of the difference between means—population standard deviation (10-2)	$\sigma_{D\bar{X}} = \sqrt{\sigma_{\bar{X}_1}{}^2 + \sigma_{\bar{X}_2}{}^2}$	242
Standard error of the difference between means—sample standard deviation (10-3)	$s_{D\bar{X}} = \sqrt{\dfrac{N_1 S_1{}^2 + N_2 S_2{}^2}{N_1 + N_2 - 2}\left(\dfrac{1}{N_1} + \dfrac{1}{N_2}\right)}$	242
t test—independent samples (10-4)	$t = \dfrac{(\bar{X}_1 - \bar{X}_2) - 0}{s_{D\bar{X}}}$	243
Mean of the differences—direct difference method for correlated t test (10-5)	$\bar{D} = \dfrac{\Sigma D}{N}$	261
Standard deviation—direct difference method for correlated t test (10-6)	$S_D = \sqrt{\dfrac{\Sigma D^2}{N} - \bar{D}^2}$	263
Standard error—direct difference method for correlated t test (10-7)	$s_{\bar{X}_D} = \dfrac{S_D}{\sqrt{N - 1}}$	263

Name	Formula	*First appears on page:*
t test—correlated samples (10-8)	$$t = \frac{\overline{D}}{s_{\overline{X}_D}}$$	263
Total sum of squares—deviation formula (11-2)	$$SS_T = \sum^{k} \sum^{N_G} (X - \overline{X}_T)^2$$	277
Within-groups sum of squares—deviation formula (11-3)	$$SS_{WG} = \sum^{k} \sum^{N_G} (X - \overline{X}_G)^2$$	278
Between-groups sum of squares—deviation formula (11-4)	$$SS_{BG} = \sum^{k} N_G(\overline{X}_G - \overline{X}_T)^2$$	278
Mean square between groups (11-5)	$$MS_{BG} = \frac{SS_{BG}}{k - 1}$$	281
Mean square within groups (11-6)	$$MS_{WG} = \frac{SS_{WG}}{N_T - k}$$	281
F test (11-7)	$$F = \frac{MS_{BG}}{MS_{WG}}$$	283
Total sum of squares—computational formula (11-8)	$$SS_T = \sum^{N_T} X^2 - N_T \overline{X}_T^2$$	283
Between-groups sum of squares—computational formula (11-9)	$$SS_{BG} = N_1\overline{X}_1^2 + N_2\overline{X}_2^2 + N_3\overline{X}_3^2 + \ldots - N_T\overline{X}_T^2$$	284
Within-groups sum of squares—computational formula (11-10)	$$SS_{WG} = \left(\sum^{N_1} X^2 - N_1\overline{X}_1^2 \right) + \left(\sum^{N_2} X^2 - N_2\overline{X}_2^2 \right) + \left(\sum^{N_3} X^2 - N_3\overline{X}_3^2 \right) + \ldots$$	284

Name	Formula	First appears on page:
Tukey's method— unequal N's (11-11)	$q = \dfrac{\bar{X}_{L\cdot\cdot} - \bar{X}_S}{\sqrt{\dfrac{MS_{WG}}{2}\left(\dfrac{1}{N_L} + \dfrac{1}{N_S}\right)}}$	287
Tukey's method— equal N's (11-12)	$q = \dfrac{\bar{X}_L - \bar{X}_S}{\sqrt{\dfrac{MS_{WG}}{N_G}}}$	288
Sum of squares for row variable (12-1)	$SS_R = N_{R_1}\bar{X}_{R_1}{}^2 + N_{R_2}\bar{X}_{R_2}{}^2 + \ldots - N_T\bar{X}_T{}^2$	304
Sum of squares for column variable (12-2)	$SS_C = N_{C_1}\bar{X}_{C_1}{}^2 + N_{C_2}\bar{X}_{C_2}{}^2 + \ldots - N_T\bar{X}_T{}^2$	305
Sum of squares for interaction (12-3)	$SS_{R \times C} = SS_{BG} - SS_R - SS_C$	305
df for rows (12-4)	$df_R = r - 1$	306
df for columns (12-5)	$df_C = c - 1$	306
df for interaction (12-6)	$df_{R \times C} = (r - 1)(c - 1)$	306
Within-groups df (12-7)	$df_{WG} = N_T - rc$	306
Mean square for rows (12-8)	$MS_R = \dfrac{SS_R}{r - 1}$	307
Mean square for columns (12-9)	$MS_C = \dfrac{SS_C}{c - 1}$	307
Mean square for interaction (12-10)	$MS_{R \times C} = \dfrac{SS_{R \times C}}{(r - 1)(c - 1)}$	307

Name	Formula	First appears on page:
Within-groups mean square (12-11)	$MS_{WG} = \dfrac{SS_{WG}}{N_T - rc}$	307
F for row effect (12-12)	$F_R = \dfrac{MS_R}{MS_{WG}}$	310
F for column effect (12-13)	$F_C = \dfrac{MS_C}{MS_{WG}}$	310
F for interaction effect (12-14)	$F_{R \times C} = \dfrac{MS_{R \times C}}{MS_{WG}}$	310
Chi square (13-1)	$\chi^2 = \sum \dfrac{(O - E)^2}{E}$	320
Chi square—2 × 2 table (13-2)	$\chi^2 = \dfrac{N\left(\lvert AD - BC \rvert - \dfrac{N}{2}\right)^2}{(A + B)(C + D)(A + C)(B + D)}$	327
Kruskal-Wallis test (13-3)	$H = \dfrac{12}{N(N + 1)}\sum \dfrac{R_G^2}{N_G} - 3(N + 1)$	336
McNemar test of changes (13-4)	$\chi^2 = \dfrac{(\lvert A - D \rvert - 1)^2}{A + D}$	339
Friedman analysis of variance (13-5)	$\chi_r^2 = \dfrac{12}{Nk(k + 1)}\sum (R_G)^2 - 3N(k + 1)$	347
Spearman-Brown formula (14-1)	$r_{tt} = \dfrac{2r_{oe}}{1 + r_{oe}}$	362
Standard error of measurement (14-2)	$S_{EM} = S_T\sqrt{1 - r_{tt}}$	364

Appendix 2: Tables

Table A
Squares and Square Roots of Numbers from 1 to 1,000

N	N^2	$\sqrt{N}$	$\sqrt{10N}$	N	N^2	$\sqrt{N}$	$\sqrt{10N}$
1	1.	1.000	3.162	45	2025.	6.708	21.213
2	4.	1.414	4.472	46	2116.	6.782	21.448
3	9.	1.732	5.477	47	2209.	6.856	21.679
4	16.	2.000	6.325	48	2304.	6.928	21.909
5	25.	2.236	7.071	49	2401.	7.000	22.136
6	36.	2.449	7.746	50	2500.	7.071	22.361
7	49.	2.646	8.367	51	2601.	7.141	22.583
8	64.	2.828	8.944	52	2704.	7.211	22.804
9	81.	3.000	9.487	53	2809.	7.280	23.022
10	100.	3.162	10.000	54	2916.	7.348	23.238
11	121.	3.317	10.488	55	3025.	7.416	23.452
12	144.	3.464	10.954	56	3136.	7.483	23.664
13	169.	3.606	11.402	57	3249.	7.550	23.875
14	196.	3.742	11.832	58	3364.	7.616	24.083
15	225.	3.873	12.247	59	3481.	7.681	24.290
16	256.	4.000	12.649	60	3600.	7.746	24.495
17	289.	4.123	13.038	61	3721.	7.810	24.698
18	324.	4.243	13.416	62	3844.	7.874	24.900
19	361.	4.359	13.784	63	3969.	7.937	25.100
20	400.	4.472	14.142	64	4096.	8.000	25.298
21	441.	4.583	14.491	65	4225.	8.062	25.495
22	484.	4.690	14.832	66	4356.	8.124	25.690
23	529.	4.796	15.166	67	4489.	8.185	25.884
24	576.	4.899	15.492	68	4624.	8.246	26.077
25	625.	5.000	15.811	69	4761.	8.307	26.268
26	676·	5.099	16.125	70	4900.	8.367	26.458
27	729.	5.196	16.432	71	5041.	8.426	26.646
28	784.	5.292	16.733	72	5184.	8.485	26.833
29	841.	5.385	17.029	73	5329.	8.544	27.019
30	900.	5.477	17.321	74	5476.	8.602	27.203
31	961.	5.568	17.607	75	5625.	8.660	27.386
32	1024.	5.657	17.889	76	5776.	8.718	27.568
33	1089.	5.745	18.166	77	5929.	8.775	27.749
34	1156.	5.831	18.439	78	6084.	8.832	27.928
35	1225.	5.916	18.708	79	6241.	8.888	28.107
36	1296.	6.000	18.974	80	6400.	8.944	28.284
37	1369.	6.083	19.235	81	6561.	9.000	28.460
38	1444.	6.164	19.494	82	6724.	9.055	28.636
39	1521.	6.245	19.748	83	6889.	9.110	28.810
40	1600.	6.325	20.000	84	7056.	9.165	28.983
41	1681.	6.403	20.248	85	7225.	9.220	29.155
42	1764.	6.481	20.494	86	7396.	9.274	29.326
43	1849.	6.557	20.736	87	7569.	9.327	29.496
44	1936.	6.633	20.976	88	7744.	9.381	29.665

Table A (continued)

N	N²	√N	√10N	N	N²	√N	√10N
89	7921.	9.434	29.833	134	17956.	11.576	36.606
90	8100.	9.487	30.000	135	18225.	11.619	36.742
91	8281.	9.539	30.166	136	18496.	11.662	36.878
92	8464.	9.592	30.332	137	18769.	11.705	37.014
93	8649.	9.644	30.496	138	19044.	11.747	37.148
94	8836.	9.695	30.659	139	19321.	11.790	37.283
95	9025.	9.747	30.822	140	19600.	11.832	37.417
96	9216.	9.798	30.984	141	19881.	11.874	37.550
97	9409.	9.849	31.145	142	20164.	11.916	37.683
98	9604.	9.899	31.305	143	20449.	11.958	37.815
99	9801.	9.950	31.464	144	20736.	12.000	37.947
100	10000.	10.000	31.623	145	21025.	12.042	38.079
101	10201.	10.050	31.780	146	21316.	12.083	38.210
102	10404.	10.100	31.937	147	21609.	12.124	38.341
103	10609.	10.149	32.094	148	21904.	12.166	38.471
104	10816.	10.198	32.249	149	22201.	12.207	38.601
105	11025.	10.247	32.404	150	22500.	12.247	38.730
106	11236.	10.296	32.558	151	22801.	12.288	38.859
107	11449.	10.344	32.711	152	23104.	12.329	38.987
108	11664.	10.392	32.863	153	23409.	12.369	39.115
109	11881.	10.440	33.015	154	23716.	12.410	39.243
110	12100.	10.488	33.166	155	24025.	12.450	39.370
111	12321.	10.536	33.317	156	24336.	12.490	39.497
112	12544.	10.583	33.466	157	24649.	12.530	39.623
113	12769.	10.630	33.615	158	24964.	12.570	39.749
114	12996.	10.677	33.764	159	25281.	12.610	39.875
115	13225.	10.724	33.912	160	25600.	12.649	40.000
116	13456.	10.770	34.059	161	25921.	12.689	40.125
117	13689.	10.817	34.205	162	26244.	12.728	40.249
118	13924.	10.863	34.351	163	26569.	12.767	40.373
119	14161.	10.909	34.496	164	26896.	12.806	40.497
120	14400.	10.954	34.641	165	27225.	12.845	40.620
121	14641.	11.000	34.785	166	27556.	12.884	40.743
122	14884.	11.045	34.928	167	27889.	12.923	40.866
123	15129.	11.091	35.071	168	28224.	12.961	40.988
124	15376.	11.136	35.214	169	28561.	13.000	41.110
125	15625.	11.180	35.355	170	28900.	13.038	41.231
126	15876.	11.225	35.496	171	29241.	13.077	41.352
127	16129.	11.269	35.637	172	29584.	13.115	41.473
128	16384.	11.314	35.777	173	29929.	13.153	41.593
129	16641.	11.358	35.917	174	30276.	13.191	41.713
130	16900.	11.402	36.056	175	30625.	13.229	41.833
131	17161.	11.446	36.194	176	30976.	13.266	41.952
132	17424.	11.489	36.332	177	31329.	13.304	42.071
133	17689.	11.533	36.469	178	31684.	13.342	42.190

Table A (continued)

N	N²	√N	√10N	N	N²	√N	√10N
179	32041.	13.379	42.308	224	50176.	14.967	47.329
180	32400.	13.416	42.426	225	50625.	15.000	47.434
181	32761.	13.454	42.544	226	51076.	15.033	47.539
182	33124.	13.491	42.661	227	51529.	15.067	47.645
183	33489.	13.528	42.778	228	51984.	15.100	47.749
184	33856.	13.565	42.895	229	52441.	15.133	47.854
185	34225.	13.601	43.012	230	52900.	15.166	47.958
186	34596.	13.638	43.128	231	53361.	15.199	48.062
187	34969.	13.675	43.243	232	53824.	15.232	48.166
188	35344.	13.711	43.359	233	54289.	15.264	48.270
189	35721.	13.748	43.474	234	54756.	15.297	48.374
190	36100.	13.784	43.589	235	55225.	15.330	48.477
191	36481.	13.820	43.704	236	55696.	15.362	48.580
192	36864.	13.856	43.818	237	56169.	15.395	48.683
193	37249.	13.892	43.932	238	56644.	15.427	48.785
194	37636.	13.928	44.045	239	57121.	15.460	48.888
195	38025.	13.964	44.159	240	57600.	15.492	48.990
196	38416.	14.000	44.272	241	58081.	15.524	49.092
197	38809.	14.036	44.385	242	58564.	15.556	49.193
198	39204.	14.071	44.497	243	59049.	15.588	49.295
199	39601.	14.107	44.609	244	59536.	15.620	49.396
200	40000.	14.142	44.721	245	60025.	15.652	49.497
201	40401	14.177	44.833	246	60516.	15.684	49.598
202	40804.	14.213	44.944	247	61009.	15.716	49.699
203	41209.	14.248	45.056	248	61504.	15.748	49.800
204	41616	14.283	45.166	249	62001.	15.780	49.900
205	42025.	14.318	45.277	250	62500.	15.811	50.000
206	42436.	14.353	45.387	251	63001.	15.843	50.100
207	42849.	14.387	45.497	252	63504.	15.875	50.200
208	43264.	14.422	45.607	253	64009.	15.906	50.299
209	43681.	14.457	45.717	254	64516.	15.937	50.398
210	44100.	14.491	45.826	255	65025.	15.969	50.498
211	44521.	14.526	45.935	256	65536.	16.000	50.596
212	44944.	14.560	46.043	257	66049.	16.031	50.695
213	45369.	14.595	46.152	258	66564.	16.062	50.794
214	45796.	14.629	46.260	259	67081.	16.093	50.892
215	46225.	14.663	46.368	260	67600.	16.125	50.990
216	46656.	14.697	46.476	261	68121.	16.155	51.088
217	47089.	14.731	46.583	262	68644.	16.186	51.186
218	47524.	14.765	46.690	263	69169.	16.217	51.284
219	47961.	14.799	46.797	264	69696.	16.248	51.381
220	48400.	14.832	46.904	265	70225.	16.279	51.478
221	48841.	14.866	47.011	266	70756.	16.310	51.575
222	49284.	14.900	47.117	267	71289.	16.340	51.672
223	49729.	14.933	47.223	268	71824.	16.371	51.769

Table A (continued)

N	N²	√N	√10N		N	N²	√N	√10N
269	72361.	16.401	51.865		314	98596.	17.720	56.036
270	72900.	16.432	51.962		315	99225.	17.748	56.125
271	73441.	16.462	52.058		316	99856.	17.776	56.214
272	73984.	16.492	52.154		317	100489.	17.804	56.303
273	74529.	16.523	52.249		318	101124.	17.833	56.391
274	75076.	16.553	52.345		319	101761.	17.861	56.480
275	75625.	16.583	52.440		320	102400.	17.889	56.569
276	76176.	16.613	52.536		321	103041.	17.916	56.657
277	76729.	16.643	52.631		322	103684.	17.944	56.745
278	77284.	16.673	52.726		323	104329.	17.972	56.833
279	77841.	16.703	52.820		324	104976.	18.000	56.921
280	78400.	16.733	52.915		325	105625.	18.028	57.009
281	78961.	16.763	53.009		326	106276.	18.055	57.096
282	79524.	16.793	53.104		327	106929.	18.083	57.184
283	80089.	16.823	53.198		328	107584.	18.111	57.271
284	80656.	16.852	53.292		329	108241.	18.138	57.359
285	81225.	16.882	53.385		330	108900.	18.166	57.446
286	81796.	16.912	53.479		331	109561.	18.193	57.533
287	82369.	16.941	53.572		332	110224.	18.221	57.619
288	82944.	16.971	53.666		333	110889.	18.248	57.706
289	83521.	17.000	53.759		334	111556.	18.276	57.793
290	84100.	17.029	53.852		335	112225.	18.303	57.879
291	84681.	17.059	53.944		336	112896.	18.330	57.966
292	85264.	17.088	54.037		337	113569.	18.358	58.052
293	85849.	17.117	54.129		338	114244.	18.385	58.138
294	86436.	17.146	54.222		339	114921.	18.412	58.224
295	87025.	17.176	54.314		340	115600.	18.439	58.310
296	87616.	17.205	54.406		341	116281.	18.466	58.395
297	88209.	17.234	54.498		342	116964.	18.493	58.481
298	88804.	17.263	54.589		343	117649.	18.520	58.566
299	89401.	17.292	54.681		344	118336.	18.547	58.652
300	90000.	17.321	54.772		345	119025.	18.574	58.737
301	90601.	17.349	54.863		346	119716.	18.601	58.822
302	91204.	17.378	54.955		347	120409.	18.628	58.907
303	91809.	17.407	55.045		348	121104.	18.655	58.992
304	92416.	17.436	55.136		349	121801.	18.682	59.076
305	93025.	17.464	55.227		350	122500.	18.708	59.161
306	93636.	17.493	55.317		351	123201.	18.735	59.245
307	94249.	17.521	55.408		352	123904.	18.762	59.330
308	94864.	17.550	55.498		353	124609.	18.788	59.414
309	95481.	17.578	55.588		354	125316.	18.815	59.498
310	96100.	17.607	55.678		355	126025.	18.841	59.582
311	96721.	17.635	55.767		356	126736.	18.868	59.666
312	97344.	17.664	55.857		357	127449.	18.894	59.749
313	97969.	17.692	55.946		358	128164.	18.921	59.833

Table A (continued)

N	N²	√N	√10N	N	N²	√N	√10N
359	128881.	18.947	59.917	404	163216.	20.100	63.561
360	129600.	18.974	60.000	405	164025.	20.125	63.640
361	130321.	19.000	60.083	406	164836.	20.149	63.718
362	131044.	19.026	60.166	407	165649.	20.174	63.797
363	131769.	19.053	60.249	408	166464.	20.199	63.875
364	132496.	19.079	60.332	409	167281.	20.224	63.953
365	133225.	19.105	60.415	410	168100.	20.248	64.031
366	133956.	19.131	60.498	411	168921.	20.273	64.109
367	134689.	19.157	60.581	412	169744.	20.298	64.187
368	135424.	19.183	60.663	413	170569.	20.322	64.265
369	136161.	19.209	60.745	414	171396.	20.347	64.343
370	136900.	19.235	60.828	415	172225.	20.372	64.420
371	137641.	19.261	60.910	416	173056.	20.396	64.498
372	138384.	19.287	60.992	417	173889.	20.421	64.576
373	139129.	19.313	61.074	418	174724.	20.445	64.653
374	139876.	19.339	61.156	419	175561.	20.469	64.730
375	140625.	19.365	61.237	420	176400.	20.494	64.807
376	141376.	19.391	61.319	421	177241.	20.518	64.885
377	142129.	19.416	61.400	422	178084.	20.543	64.962
378	142884.	19.442	61.482	423	178929.	20.567	65.038
379	143641.	19.468	61.563	424	179776.	20.591	65.115
380	144400.	19.494	61.644	425	180625.	20.616	65.192
381	145161.	19.519	61.725	426	181476.	20.640	65.269
382	145924.	19.545	61.806	427	182329.	20.664	65.345
383	146689.	19.570	61.887	428	183184.	20.688	65.422
384	147456.	19.596	61.968	429	184041.	20.712	65.498
385	148225.	19.621	62.048	430	184900.	20.736	65.574
386	148996.	19.647	62.129	431	185761.	20.761	65.651
387	149769.	19.672	62.209	432	186624.	20.785	65.727
388	150544.	19.698	62.290	433	187489.	20.809	65.803
389	151321.	19.723	62.370	434	188356.	20.833	65.879
390	152100.	19.748	62.450	435	189225.	20.857	65.955
391	152881.	19.774	62.530	436	190096.	20.881	66.030
392	153664.	19.799	62.610	437	190969.	20.905	66.106
393	154449.	19.824	62.690	438	191844.	20.928	66.182
394	155236.	19.849	62.769	439	192721.	20.952	66.257
395	156025.	19.875	62.849	440	193600.	20.976	66.332
396	156816.	19.900	62.929	441	194481.	21.000	66.408
397	157609.	19.925	63.008	442	195364.	21.024	66.483
398	158404.	19.950	63.087	443	196249.	21.048	66.558
399	159201.	19.975	63.166	444	197136.	21.071	66.633
400	160000.	20.000	63.246	445	198025.	21.095	66.708
401	160801.	20.025	63.325	446	198916.	21.119	66.783
402	161604.	20.050	63.403	447	199809.	21.142	66.858
403	162409.	20.075	63.482	448	200704.	21.166	66.933

Table A (continued)

N	N²	√N	√10N	N	N²	√N	√10N
449	201601.	21.190	67.007	494	244036.	22.226	70.285
450	202500.	21.213	67.082	495	245025.	22.249	70.356
451	203401.	21.237	67.157	496	246016.	22.271	70.427
452	204304.	21.260	67.231	497	247009.	22.293	70.498
453	205209.	21.284	67.305	498	248004.	22.316	70.569
454	206116.	21.307	67.380	499	249001.	22.338	70.640
455	207025.	21.331	67.454	500	250000.	22.361	70.711
456	207936.	21.354	67.528	501	251001.	22.383	70.781
457	208849.	21.378	67.602	502	252004.	22.405	70.852
458	209764.	21.401	67.676	503	253009.	22.428	70.922
459	210681.	21.424	67.750	504	254016.	22.450	70.993
460	211600.	21.448	67.823	505	255025.	22.472	71.063
461	212521.	21.471	67.897	506	256036.	22.494	71.134
462	213444.	21.494	67.971	507	257049.	22.517	71.204
463	214369.	21.517	68.044	508	258064.	22.539	71.274
464	215296.	21.541	68.118	509	259081.	22.561	71.344
465	216225.	21.564	68.191	510	260100.	22.583	71.414
466	217156.	21.587	68.264	511	261121.	22.605	71.484
467	218089.	21.610	68.337	512	262144.	22.627	71.554
468	219024.	21.633	68.411	513	263169.	22.650	71.624
469	219961.	21.656	68.484	514	264196.	22.672	71.694
470	220900.	21.679	68.557	515	265225.	22.694	71.764
471	221841.	21.703	68.629	516	266256.	22.716	71.833
472	222784.	21.726	68.702	517	267289.	22.738	71.903
473	223729.	21.749	68.775	518	268324.	22.760	71.972
474	224676.	21.772	68.848	519	269361.	22.782	72.042
475	225625.	21.794	68.920	520	270400.	22.804	72.111
476	226576.	21.817	68.993	521	271441.	22.825	72.180
477	227529.	21.840	69.065	522	272484.	22.847	72.250
478	228484.	21.863	69.138	523	273529.	22.869	72.319
479	229441.	21.886	69.210	524	274576.	22.891	72.388
480	230400.	21.909	69.282	525	275625.	22.913	72.457
481	231361.	21.932	69.354	526	276676.	22.935	72.526
482	232324.	21.954	69.426	527	277729.	22.956	72.595
483	233289.	21.977	69.498	528	278784.	22.978	72.664
484	234256.	22.000	69.570	529	279841.	23.000	72.732
485	235225.	22.023	69.642	530	280900.	23.022	72.801
486	236196.	22.045	69.714	531	281961.	23.043	72.870
487	237169.	22.068	69.785	532	283024.	23.065	72.938
488	238144.	22.091	69.857	533	284089.	23.087	73.007
489	239121.	22.113	69.929	534	285156.	23.108	73.075
490	240100.	22.136	70.000	535	286225.	23.130	73.144
491	241081.	22.159	70.071	536	287296.	23.152	73.212
492	242064.	22.181	70.143	537	288369.	23.173	73.280
493	243049.	22.204	70.214	538	289444.	23.195	73.348

Table A (continued)

N	N²	√N	√10N	N	N²	√N	√10N
539	290521.	23.216	73.417	584	341056.	24.166	76.420
540	291600.	23.238	73.485	585	342225.	24.187	76.485
541	292681.	23.259	73.553	586	343396.	24.207	76.551
542	293764.	23.281	73.621	587	344569.	24.228	76.616
543	294849.	23.302	73.689	588	345744.	24.249	76.681
544	295936.	23.324	73.756	589	346921.	24.269	76.746
545	297025.	23.345	73.824	590	348100.	24.290	76.811
546	298116.	23.367	73.892	591	349281.	24.310	76.877
547	299209.	23.388	73.959	592	350464.	24.331	76.942
548	300304.	23.409	74.027	593	351649.	24.352	77.006
549	301401.	23.431	74.095	594	352836.	24.372	77.071
550	302500.	23.452	74.162	595	354025.	24.393	77.136
551	303601.	23.473	74.229	596	355216.	24.413	77.201
552	304704.	23.495	74.297	597	356409.	24.434	77.266
553	305809.	23.516	74.364	598	357604.	24.454	77.330
554	306916.	23.537	74.431	599	358801.	24.474	77.395
555	308025.	23.558	74.498	600	360000.	24.495	77.460
556	309136.	23.580	74.565	601	361201.	24.515	77.524
557	310249.	23.601	74.632	602	362404.	24.536	77.589
558	311364.	23.622	74.699	603	363609.	24.556	77.653
559	312481.	23.643	74.766	604	364816.	24.576	77.717
560	313600.	23.664	74.833	605	366025.	24.597	77.782
561	314721.	23.685	74.900	606	367236.	24.617	77.846
562	315844.	23.707	74.967	607	368449.	24.637	77.910
563	316969.	23.728	75.033	608	369664.	24.658	77.974
564	318096.	23.749	75.100	609	370881.	24.678	78.038
565	319225.	23.770	75.166	610	372100.	24.698	78.102
566	320356.	23.791	75.233	611	373321.	24.718	78.166
567	321489.	23.812	75.299	612	374544.	24.739	78.230
568	322624.	23.833	75.366	613	375769.	24.759	78.294
569	323761.	23.854	75.432	614	376996.	24.779	78.358
570	324900.	23.875	75.498	615	378225.	24.799	78.422
571	326041.	23.896	75.565	616	379456.	24.819	78.486
572	327184.	23.917	75.631	617	380689.	24.839	78.549
573	328329.	23.937	75.697	618	381924.	24.860	78.613
574	329476.	23.958	75.763	619	383161.	24.880	78.677
575	330625.	23.979	75.829	620	384400.	24.900	78.740
576	331776.	24.000	75.895	621	385641.	24.920	78.804
577	332929.	24.021	75.961	622	386884.	24.940	78.867
578	334084.	24.042	76.026	623	388129.	24.960	78.930
579	335241.	24.062	76.092	624	389376.	24.980	78.994
580	336400.	24.083	76.158	625	390625.	25.000	79.057
581	337561.	24.104	76.223	626	391876.	25.020	79.120
582	338724.	24.125	76.289	627	393129.	25.040	79.183
583	339889.	24.145	76.354	628	394384.	25.060	79.246

Table A (continued)

N	N²	√N	√10N	N	N²	√N	√10N
629	395641.	25.080	79.310	674	454276.	25.962	82.098
630	396900.	25.100	79.373	675	455625.	25.981	82.158
631	398161.	25.120	79.436	676	456976.	26.000	82.219
632	399424.	25.140	79.498	677	458329.	26.019	82.280
633	400689.	25.159	79.561	678	459684.	26.038	82.341
634	401956.	25.179	79.624	679	461041.	26.058	82.401
635	403225.	25.199	79.687	680	462400.	26.077	82.462
636	404496.	25.219	79.750	681	463761.	26.096	82.523
637	405769.	25.239	79.812	682	465124.	26.115	82.583
638	407044.	25.259	79.875	683	466489.	26.134	82.644
639	408321.	25.278	79.937	684	467856.	26.153	82.704
640	409600.	25.298	80.000	685	469225.	26.173	82.765
641	410881.	25.318	80.062	686	470596.	26.192	82.825
642	412164.	25.338	80.125	687	471969.	26.211	82.885
643	413449.	25.357	80.187	688	473344.	26.230	82.946
644	414736.	25.377	80.250	689	474721.	26.249	83.006
645	416025.	25.397	80.312	690	476100.	26.268	83.066
646	417316.	25.417	80.374	691	477481.	26.287	83.126
647	418609.	25.436	80.436	692	478864.	26.306	83.187
648	419904.	25.456	80.498	693	480249.	26.325	83.247
649	421201.	25.475	80.561	694	481636.	26.344	83.307
650	422500.	25.495	80.623	695	483025.	26.363	83.367
651	423801.	25.515	80.685	696	484416.	26.382	83.427
652	425104.	25.534	80.747	697	485809.	26.401	83.487
653	426409.	25.554	80.808	698	487204.	26.420	83.546
654	427716.	25.573	80.870	699	488601.	26.439	83.606
655	429025.	25.593	80.932	700	490000.	26.458	83.666
656	430336.	25.612	80.994	701	491401.	26.476	83.726
657	431649.	25.632	81.056	702	492804.	26.495	83.785
658	432964.	25.652	81.117	703	494209.	26.514	83.845
659	434281.	25.671	81.179	704	495616.	26.533	83.905
660	435600.	25.690	81.240	705	497025.	26.552	83.964
661	436921.	25.710	81.302	706	498436.	26.571	84.024
662	438244.	25.729	81.363	707	499849.	26.589	84.083
663	439569.	25.749	81.425	708	501264.	26.608	84.143
664	440896.	25.768	81.486	709	502681.	26.627	84.202
665	442225.	25.788	81.548	710	504100.	26.646	84.261
666	443556.	25.807	81.609	711	505521.	26.665	84.321
667	444889.	25.826	81.670	712	506944.	26.683	84.380
668	446224.	25.846	81.731	713	508369.	26.702	84.439
669	447561.	25.865	81.792	714	509796.	26.721	84.499
670	448900.	25.884	81.854	715	511225.	26.739	84.558
671	450241.	25.904	81.915	716	512656.	26.758	84.617
672	451584.	25.923	81.976	717	514089.	26.777	84.676
673	452929.	25.942	82.037	718	515524.	26.796	84.735

Table A (continued)

N	N^2	$\sqrt{N}$	$\sqrt{10N}$	N	N^2	$\sqrt{N}$	$\sqrt{10N}$
719	516961.	26.814	84.794	764	583696.	27.641	87.407
720	518400.	26.833	84.853	765	585225.	27.659	87.464
721	519841.	26.851	84.912	766	586756.	27.677	87.521
722	521284.	26.870	84.971	767	588289.	27.695	87.579
723	522729.	26.889	85.029	768	589824.	27.713	87.636
724	524176.	26.907	85.088	769	591361.	27.731	87.693
725	525625.	26.926	85.147	770	592900.	27.749	87.750
726	527076.	26.944	85.206	771	594441.	27.767	87.807
727	528529.	26.963	85.264	772	595984.	27.785	87.864
728	529984.	26.981	85.323	773	597529.	27.803	87.920
729	531441.	27.000	85.381	774	599076.	27.821	87.977
730	532900.	27.019	85.440	775	600625.	27.839	88.034
731	534361.	27.037	85.499	776	602176.	27.857	88.091
732	535824.	27.055	85.557	777	603729.	27.875	88.148
733	537289.	27.074	85.615	778	605284.	27.893	88.204
734	538756.	27.092	85.674	779	606841.	27.911	88.261
735	540225.	27.111	85.732	780	608400.	27.928	88.318
736	541696.	27.129	85.790	781	609961.	27.946	88.374
737	543169.	27.148	85.849	782	611524.	27.964	88.431
738	544644.	27.166	85.907	783	613089.	27.982	88.487
739	546121.	27.185	85.965	784	614656.	28.000	88.544
740	547600.	27.203	86.023	785	616225.	28.018	88.600
741	549081.	27.221	86.081	786	617796.	28.036	88.657
742	550564.	27.240	86.139	787	619369.	28.054	88.713
743	552049.	27.258	86.197	788	620944.	28.071	88.769
744	553536.	27.276	86.255	789	622521.	28.089	88.826
745	555025.	27.295	86.313	790	624100.	28.107	88.882
746	556516.	27.313	86.371	791	625681.	28.125	88.938
747	558009.	27.331	86.429	792	627264.	28.142	88.994
748	559504.	27.350	86.487	793	628849.	28.160	89.051
749	561001.	27.368	86.545	794	630436.	28.178	89.107
750	562500.	27.386	86.603	795	632025.	28.196	89.163
751	564001.	27.404	86.660	796	633616.	28.213	89.219
752	565504.	27.423	86.718	797	635209.	28.231	89.275
753	567009.	27.441	86.776	798	636804.	28.249	89.331
754	568516.	27.459	86.833	799	638401.	28.267	89.387
755	570025.	27.477	86.891	800	640000.	28.284	89.443
756	571536.	27.495	86.948	801	641601.	28.302	89.499
757	573049.	27.514	87.006	802	643204.	28.320	89.554
758	574564.	27.532	87.063	803	644809.	28.337	89.610
759	576081.	27.550	87.121	804	646416.	28.355	89.666
760	577600.	27.568	87.178	805	648025.	28.373	89.722
761	579121.	27.586	87.235	806	649636.	28.390	89.778
762	580644.	27.604	87.293	807	651249.	28.408	89.833
763	582169.	27.622	87.350	808	652864.	28.425	89.889

Table A (continued)

N	N²	√N	√10N	N	N²	√N	√10N
809	654481.	28.443	89.944	854	729316.	29.223	92.412
810	656100.	28.460	90.000	855	731025.	29.240	92.466
811	657721.	28.478	90.056	856	732736.	29.257	92.520
812	659344.	28.496	90.111	857	734449.	29.275	92.574
813	660969.	28.513	90.167	858	736164.	29.292	92.628
814	662596.	28.531	90.222	859	737881.	29.309	92.682
815	664225.	28.548	90.277	860	739600.	29.326	92.736
816	665856.	28.566	90.333	861	741321.	29.343	92.790
817	667489.	28.583	90.388	862	743044.	29.360	92.844
818	669124.	28.601.	90.443	863	744769.	29.377	92.898
819	670761.	28.618	90.499	864	746496.	29.394	92.952
820	672400.	28.636	90.554	865	748225.	29.411	93.005
821	674041.	28.653	90.609	866	749956.	29.428	93.059
822	675684.	28.671	90.664	867	751689.	29.445	93.113
823	677329.	28.688	90.719	868	753424.	29.462	93.167
824	678976.	28.705	90.774	869	755161.	29.479	93.220
825	680625.	28.723	90.830	870	756900.	29.496	93.274
826	682276.	28.740	90.885	871	758641.	29.513	93.327
827	683929.	28.758	90.940	872	760384.	29.530	93.381
828	685584.	28.775	90.995	873	762129.	29.547	93.434
829	687241.	28.792	91.049	874	763876.	29.563	93.488
830	688900.	28.810	91.104	875	765625.	29.580	93.541
831	690561.	28.827	91.159	876	767376.	29.597	93.595
832	692224.	28.844	91.214	877	769129.	29.614	93.648
833	693889.	28.862	91.269	878	770884.	29.631	93.702
834	695556.	28.879	91.324	879	772641.	29.648	93.755
835	697225.	28.896	91.378	880	774400.	29.665	93.808
836	698896.	28.914	91.433	881	776161.	29.682	93.862
837	700569.	28.931	91.488	882	777924.	29.698	93.915
838	702244.	28.948	91.542	883	779689.	29.715	93.968
839	703921.	28.965	91.597	884	781456.	29.732	94.021
840	705600.	28.983	91.652	885	783225.	29.749	94.074
841	707281.	29.000	91.706	886	784996.	29.766	94.128
842	708964.	29.017	91.761	887	786769.	29.783	94.181
843	710649.	29.034	91.815	888	788544.	29.799	94.234
844	712336.	29.052	91.869	889	790321.	29.816	94.287
845	714025.	29.069	91.924	890	792100.	29.833	94.340
846	715716.	29.086	91.978	891	793881.	29.850	94.393
847	717409.	29.103	92.033	892	795664.	29.866	94.446
848	719104.	29.120	92.087	893	797449.	29.883	94.499
849	720801.	29.138	92.141	894	799236.	29.900	94.552
850	722500.	29.155	92.195	895	801025.	29.917	94.604
851	724201.	29.172	92.250	896	802816.	29.933	94.657
852	725904.	29.189	92.304	897	804609.	29.950	94.710
853	727609.	29.206	92.358	898	806404.	29.967	94.763

Table A (continued)

N	N^2	$\sqrt{N}$	$\sqrt{10N}$	N	N^2	$\sqrt{N}$	$\sqrt{10N}$
899	808201.	29.983	94.816	944	891136.	30.725	97.160
900	810000.	30.000	94.868	945	893025.	30.741	97.211
901	811801.	30.017	94.921	946	894916.	30.757	97.263
902	813604.	30.033	94.974	947	896809.	30.773	97.314
903	815409.	30.050	95.026	948	898704.	30.790	97.365
904	817216.	30.067	95.079	949	900601.	30.806	97.417
905	819025.	30.083	95.131	950	902500.	30.822	97.468
906	820836.	30.100	95.184	951	904401.	30.838	97.519
907	822649.	30.116	95.237	952	906304.	30.854	97.570
908	824464.	30.133	95.289	953	908209.	30.871	97.622
909	826281.	30.150	95.341	954	910116.	30.887	97.673
910	828100.	30.166	95.394	955	912025.	30.903	97.724
911	829921.	30.183	95.446	956	913936.	30.919	97.775
912	831744.	30.199	95.499	957	915849.	30.935	97.826
913	833569.	30.216	95.551	958	917764.	30.952	97.877
914	835396.	30.232	95.603	959	919681	30.968	97.929
915	837225.	30.249	95.656	960	921600.	30.984	97.980
916	839056.	30.265	95.708	961	923521.	31.000	98.031
917	840889.	30.282	95.760	962	925444.	31.016	98.082
918	842724.	30.299	95.812	963	927369.	31.032	98.133
919	844561.	30.315	95.864	964	929296.	31.048	98.184
920	846400.	30.332	95.917	965	931225.	31.064	98.234
921	848241.	30.348	95.969	966	933156.	31.081	98.285
922	850084.	30.364	96.021	967	935089.	31.097	98.336
923	851929.	30.381	96.073	968	937024.	31.113	98.387
924	853776.	30.397	96.125	969	938961.	31.129	98.438
925	855625.	30.414	96.177	970	940900.	31.145	98.489
926	857476.	30.430	96.229	971	942841.	31.161	98.539
927	859329.	30.447	96.281	972	944784.	31.177	98.590
928	861184.	30.463	96.333	973	946729.	31.193	98.641
929	863041.	30.480	96.385	974	948676.	31.209	98.691
930	864900.	30.496	96.437	975	950625.	31.225	98.742
931	866761.	30.512	96.488	976	952576.	31.241	98.793
932	868624.	30.529	96.540	977	954529.	31.257	98.843
933	870489.	30.545	96.592	978	956484.	31.273	98.894
934	872356.	30.561	96.644	979	958441.	31.289	98.944
935	874225.	30.578	96.695	980	960400.	31.305	98.995
936	876096.	30.594	96.747	981	962361.	31.321	99.045
937	877969.	30.610	96.799	982	964324.	31.337	99.096
938	879844.	30.627	96.850	983	966289.	31.353	99.146
939	881721.	30.643	96.902	984	968256.	31.369	99.197
940	883600.	30.659	96.954	985	970225.	31.385	99.247
941	885481.	30.676	97.005	986	972196.	31.401	99.298
942	887364.	30.692	97.057	987	974169.	31.417	99.348
943	889249.	30.708	97.108	988	976144.	31.432	99.398

Table A (continued)

N	N²	√N	√10N		N	N²	√N	√10N
989	978121.	31.448	99.448		995	990025.	31.544	99.750
990	980100.	31.464	99.499		996	992016.	31.559	99.800
991	982081.	31.480	99.549		997	994009.	31.575	99.850
992	984064.	31.496	99.599		998	996004.	31.591	99.900
993	986049.	31.512	99.649		999	998001.	31.607	99.950
994	988036.	31.528	99.700		1000	1000000.	31.623	100.000

Table B
Areas under the Normal Curve between the Mean and z

z	Area from Mean to z	z	Area from Mean to z	z	Area from Mean to z
0.00	.0000	0.35	.1368	0.70	.2580
0.01	.0040	0.36	.1406	0.71	.2611
0.02	.0080	0.37	.1443	0.72	.2642
0.03	.0120	0.38	.1480	0.73	.2673
0.04	.0160	0.39	.1517	0.74	.2704
0.05	.0199	0.40	.1554	0.75	.2734
0.06	.0239	0.41	.1591	0.76	.2764
0.07	.0279	0.42	.1628	0.77	.2794
0.08	.0319	0.43	.1664	0.78	.2823
0.09	.0359	0.44	.1700	0.79	.2852
0.10	.0398	0.45	.1736	0.80	.2881
0.11	.0438	0.46	.1772	0.81	.2910
0.12	.0478	0.47	.1808	0.82	.2939
0.13	.0517	0.48	.1844	0.83	.2967
0.14	.0557	0.49	.1879	0.84	.2995
0.15	.0596	0.50	.1915	0.85	.3023
0.16	.0636	0.51	.1950	0.86	.3051
0.17	.0675	0.52	.1985	0.87	.3078
0.18	.0714	0.53	.2019	0.88	.3106
0.19	.0753	0.54	.2054	0.89	.3133
0.20	.0793	0.55	.2088	0.90	.3159
0.21	.0832	0.56	.2123	0.91	.3186
0.22	.0871	0.57	.2157	0.92	.3212
0.23	.0910	0.58	.2190	0.93	.3238
0.24	.0948	0.59	.2224	0.94	.3264
0.25	.0987	0.60	.2257	0.95	.3289
0.26	.1026	0.61	.2291	0.96	.3315
0.27	.1064	0.62	.2324	0.97	.3340
0.28	.1103	0.63	.2357	0.98	.3365
0.29	.1141	0.64	.2389	0.99	.3389
0.30	.1179	0.65	.2422	1.00	.3413
0.31	.1217	0.66	.2454	1.01	.3438
0.32	.1255	0.67	.2486	1.02	.3461
0.33	.1293	0.68	.2517	1.03	.3485
0.34	.1331	0.69	.2549	1.04	.3508

Table B (continued)

z	Area from Mean to z	z	Area from Mean to z	z	Area from Mean to z
1.05	.3531	1.40	.4192	1.75	.4599
1.06	.3554	1.41	.4207	1.76	.4608
1.07	.3577	1.42	.4222	1.77	.4616
1.08	.3599	1.43	.4236	1.78	4625
1.09	.3621	1.44	.4251	1.79	4633
1.10	.3643	1.45	.4265	1.80	4641
1.11	.3665	1.46	.4279	1.81	.4649
1.12	.3686	1.47	.4292	1.82	.4656
1.13	.3708	1.48	.4306	1.83	.4664
1.14	.3729	1.49	.4319	1.84	.4671
1.15	.3749	1.50	.4332	1.85	.4678
1.16	.3770	1.51	.4345	1.86	.4686
1.17	.3790	1.52	.4357	1.87	.4693
1.18	.3810	1.53	.4370	1.88	.4699
1.19	.3830	1.54	.4382	1.89	.4706
1.20	.3849	1.55	.4394	1.90	.4713
1.21	.3869	1.56	.4406	1.91	.4719
1.22	3888	1.57	.4418	1.92	.4726
1.23	.3907	1.58	.4429	1.93	.4732
1.24	3925	1.59	.4441	1.94	.4738
1.25	.3944	1.60	.4452	1.95	.4744
1.26	.3962	1.61	.4463	1.96	.4750
1.27	.3980	1.62	.4474	1.97	.4756
1.28	.3997	1.63	.4484	1.98	.4761
1.29	.4015	1.64	.4495	1.99	.4767
1.30	.4032	1.65	.4505	2.00	.4772
1.31	.4049	1.66	.4515	2.01	.4778
1.32	.4066	1.67	.4525	2.02	.4783
1.33	.4082	1.68	.4535	2.03	.4788
1.34	.4099	1.69	.4545	2.04	.4793
1.35	.4115	1.70	.4554	2.05	.4798
1.36	.4131	1.71	.4564	2.06	.4803
1.37	.4147	1.72	.4573	2.07	.4808
1.38	.4162	1.73	.4582	2.08	.4812
1.39	.4177	1.74	.4591	2.09	.4817

Table B (continued)

z	Area from Mean to z	z	Area from Mean to z	z	Area from Mean to z
2.10	.4821	2.45	.4929	2.80	.4974
2.11	.4826	2.46	.4931	2.81	.4975
2.12	.4830	2.47	.4932	2.82	.4976
2.13	.4834	2.48	.4934	2.83	.4977
2.14	.4838	2.49	.4936	2.84	.4977
2.15	.4842	2.50	.4938	2.85	.4978
2.16	.4846	2.51	.4940	2.86	.4979
2.1	.4850	2.52	.4941	2.87	.4979
2.18	.4854	2.53	.4943	2.88	.4980
2.19	.4857	2.54	.4945	2.89	.4981
2.20	.4861	2.55	.4946	2.90	.4981
2.21	.4864	2.56	.4948	2.91	.4982
2.22	.4868	2.57	.4949	2.92	.4982
2.23	.4871	2.58	.4951	2.93	.4983
2.24	.4875	2.59	.4952	2.94	.4984
2.25	.4878	2.60	.4953	2.95	.4984
2.26	.4881	2.61	.4955	2.96	.4985
2.27	.4884	2.62	.4956	2.97	.4985
2.28	.4887	2.63	.4957	2.98	.4986
2.29	.4890	2.64	.4959	2.99	.4986
2.30	.4893	2.65	.4960	3.00	.4987
2.31	.4896	2.66	.4961	3.01	.4987
2.32	.4898	2.67	.4962	3.02	.4987
2.33	.4901	2.68	.4963	3.03	.4988
2.34	.4904	2.69	.4964	3.04	.4988
2.35	.4906	2.70	.4965	3.05	.4989
2.36	.4909	2.71	.4966	3.06	.4989
2.37	.4911	2.72	.4967	3.07	.4989
2.38	.4913	2.73	.4968	3.08	.4990
2.39	.4916	2.74	.4969	3.09	.4990
2.40	.4918	2.75	.4970	3.10	.4990
2.41	.4920	2.76	.4971	3.11	.4991
2.42	.4922	2.77	.4972	3.12	.4991
2.43	.4925	2.78	.4973	3.13	.4991
2.44	.4927	2.79	.4974	3.14	.4992

Table B (continued)

z	Area from Mean to z	z	Area from Mean to z
3.15	.4992	3.25	.4994
3.16	.4992	3.26	.4994
3.17	.4992	3.27	.4995
3.18	.4993	3.28	.4995
3.19	.4993	3.29	.4995
3.20	.4993	3.30	.4995
3.21	.4993	3.40	.4997
3.22	.4994	3.50	.4998
3.23	.4994	3.60	.4998
3.24	.4994	3.70	.4999

Table C
Values of *r* for the .05 and .01 Levels of Significance

df (N - 2)	.05	.01	df (N - 2)	.05	.01
1	.997	1.000	31	.344	.442
2	.950	.990	32	.339	.436
3	.878	.959	33	.334	.430
4	.812	.917	34	.329	.424
5	.755	.875	35	.325	.418
6	.707	.834	36	.320	.413
7	.666	.798	37	.316	.408
8	.632	.765	38	.312	.403
9	.602	.735	39	.308	.398
10	.576	.708	40	.304	.393
11	.553	.684	41	.301	.389
12	.533	.661	42	.297	.384
13	.514	.641	43	.294	.380
14	.497	.623	44	.291	.376
15	.482	.606	45	.288	.372
16	.468	.590	46	.285	.368
17	.456	.575	47	.282	.365
18	.444	.562	48	.279	.361
19	.433	.549	49	.276	.358
20	.423	.537	50	.273	.354
21	.413	.526	60	.250	.325
22	.404	.515	70	.232	.302
23	.396	.505	80	.217	.283
24	.388	.496	90	.205	.267
25	.381	.487	100	.195	.254
26	.374	.479	200	.138	.181
27	.367	.471	300	.113	.148
28	.361	.463	400	.098	.128
29	.355	.456	500	.088	.115
30	.349	.449	1000	.062	.081

Adapted from A. L. Sockloff and J. N. Edney, Some extension of Student's *t* and Pearson's *r* central distributions, Technical Report (May, 1972), Measurement and Research Center, Temple University, Philadelphia.

Table D
Values of Spearman r_s for the .05 and .01 Levels of Significance

N	.05	.01	N	.05	.01·
6	.886	—	19	.462	.608
7	.786	—	20	.450	.591
8	.738	.881	21	.438	.576
9	.683	.833	22	.428	.562
10	.648	.818	23	.418	.549
11	.623	.794	24	.409	.537
12	.591	.780	25	.400	.526
13	.566	.745	26	.392	.515
14	.545	.716	27	.385	.505
15	.525	.689	28	.377	.496
16	.507	.666	29	.370	.487
17	.490	.645	30	.364	.478
18	.476	.625			

From E. G. Olds, Distribution of sums of squares of rank differences for small numbers of individuals, *Annals of Mathematical Statistics 9:* 133-48 (1938), and E. G. Olds, The 5% significance levels for sums of squares of rank differences and a correction, *Annals of Mathematical Statistics 20:* 117-18 (1949). Copyright 1938 and Copyright 1949 by the Institute of Mathematical Statistics, San Francisco, Calif. Reprinted by permission of the publisher.

Table E
Values of t at the .05, .01, and .001 Levels of Significance

	Two-tailed				One-tailed		
df	.05	.01	.001	df	.05	.01	.001
1	12.706	63.657	636.619	1	6.314	31.821	318.309
2	4.303	9.925	31.599	2	2.920	6.965	22.327
3	3.183	5.841	12.924	3	2.353	4.541	10.215
4	2.777	4.604	8.610	4	2.132	3.747	7.173
5	2.571	4.032	6.869	5	2.015	3.365	5.893
6	2.447	3.707	5.959	6	1.943	3.143	5.208
7	2.365	3.500	5.408	7	1.895	2.998	4.785
8	2.306	3.355	5.041	8	1.860	2.897	4.501
9	2.262	3.250	4.781	9	1.833	2.821	4.297
10	2.228	3.169	4.587	10	1.813	2.764	4.144

Table E (continued)

	Two-tailed				One-tailed		
df	.05	.01	.001	df	.05	.01	.001
11	2.201	3.106	4.437	11	1.796	2.718	4.025
12	2.179	3.055	4.318	12	1.782	2.681	3.930
13	2.160	3.012	4.221	13	1.771	2.650	3.852
14	2.145	2.977	4.141	14	1.761	2.625	3.787
15	2.132	2.947	4.073	15	1.753	2.603	3.733
16	2.120	2.921	4.015	16	1.746	2.584	3.686
17	2.110	2.898	3.965	17	1.740	2.567	3.646
18	2.101	2.879	3.922	18	1.734	2.552	3.611
19	2.093	2.861	3.883	19	1.729	2.540	3.579
20	2.086	2.845	3.850	20	1.725	2.528	3.552
21	2.080	2.831	3.819	21	1.721	2.518	3.527
22	2.074	2.819	3.792	22	1.717	2.508	3.505
23	2.069	2.807	3.768	23	1.714	2.500	3.485
24	2.064	2.797	3.745	24	1.711	2.492	3.467
25	2.060	2.787	3.725	25	1.708	2.485	3.450
26	2.056	2.779	3.707	26	1.706	2.479	3.435
27	2.052	2.771	3.690	27	1.703	2.473	3.421
28	2.048	2.763	3.674	28	1.701	2.467	3.408
29	2.045	2.756	3.659	29	1.699	2.462	3.396
30	2.042	2.750	3.646	30	1.697	2.457	3.385
40	2.021	2.705	3.551	40	1.684	2.423	3.307
50	2.009	2.678	3.496	50	1.676	2.403	3.261
60	2.000	2.660	3.460	60	1.671	2.390	3.232
70	1.994	2.648	3.435	70	1.667	2.381	3.211
80	1.990	2.639	3.416	80	1.664	2.374	3.195
90	1.987	2.632	3.402	90	1.662	2.369	3.183
100	1.984	2.626	3.391	100	1.660	2.364	3.174
∞	1.960	2.576	3.292	∞	1.645	2.327	3.091

Adapted from A. L. Sockloff and J. N. Edney, Some extension of Student's *t* and Pearson's *r* central distributions, Technical Report (May, 1972), Measurement and Research Center, Temple University, Philadelphia.

Table F
Values of *F* at the 5% and 1% Levels of Significance

df Associated with the Denominator		df Associated with the Numerator								
		1	2	3	4	5	6	7	8	9
1	5%	161	200	216	225	230	234	237	239	241
	1%	4052	5000	5403	5625	5764	5859	5928	5982	6022
2	5%	18.5	19.0	19.2	19.2	19.3	19.3	19.4	19.4	19.4
	1%	98.5	99.0	99.2	99.2	99.3	99.3	99.4	99.4	99.4
3	5%	10.1	9.55	9.28	9.12	9.01	8.94	8.89	8.85	8.81
	1%	34.1	30.8	29.5	28.7	28.2	27.9	27.7	27.5	27.3
4	5%	7.71	6.94	6.59	6.39	6.26	6.16	6.09	6.04	6.00
	1%	21.2	18.0	16.7	16.0	15.5	15.2	15.0	14.8	14.7
5	5%	6.61	5.79	5.41	5.19	5.05	4.95	4.88	4.82	4.77
	1%	16.3	13.3	12.1	11.4	11.0	10.7	10.5	10.3	10.2
6	5%	5.99	5.14	4.76	4.53	4.39	4.28	4.21	4.15	4.10
	1%	13.7	10.9	9.78	9.15	8.75	8.47	8.26	8.10	7 98
7	5%	5.59	4.74	4.35	4.12	3.97	3.87	3.79	3.73	3.68
	1%	12.2	9.55	8.45	7.85	7.46	7.19	6.99	6.84	6.72
8	5%	5.32	4.46	4.07	3.84	3.69	3.58	3.50	3.44	3.39
	1%	11.3	8.65	7.59	7.01	6.63	6.37	6.18	6.03	5.91
9	5%	5.12	4.26	3.86	3.63	3.48	3.37	3.29	3.23	3.18
	1%	10.6	8.02	6.99	6.42	6.06	5.80	5.61	5.47	5.35
10	5%	4.96	4.10	3.71	3.48	3.33	3.22	3.14	3.07	3.02
	1%	10.0	7.56	6.55	5.99	5.64	5.39	5.20	5.06	4.94
11	5%	4.84	3.98	3.59	3.36	3.20	3.09	3.01	2.95	2.90
	1%	9.65	7.21	6.22	5.67	5.32	5.07	4.89	4.74	4.63
12	5%	4.75	3.89	3.49	3.26	3.11	3.00	2.91	2.85	2.80
	1%	9.33	6.93	5.95	5.41	5.06	4.82	4.64	4.50	4.39
13	5%	4.67	3.81	3.41	3.18	3.03	2.92	2.83	2.77	2.71
	1%	9.07	6.70	5.74	5.21	4.86	4.62	4.44	4.30	4.19
14	5%	4.60	3.74	3.34	3.11	2.96	2.85	2.76	2.70	2.65
	1%	8.86	6.51	5.56	5.04	4.70	4.46	4.28	4.14	4.03

From M. Merrington and C. M. Thompson, Tables of percentage points of the inverted beta (F) distribution, *Biometrika* 33: 73-88 (1943). Copyright 1943 by the Biometrika Trust, London. Reprinted by permission of the publisher.

Table F (continued)

df Associated with the Denominator		df Associated with the Numerator								
		1	2	3	4	5	6	7	8	9
15	5%	4.54	3.68	3.29	3.06	2.90	2.79	2.71	2.64	2.59
	1%	8.68	6.36	5.42	4.89	4.56	4.32	4.14	4.00	3.89
16	5%	4.49	3.63	3.24	3.01	2.85	2.74	2.66	2.59	2.54
	1%	8.53	6.23	5.29	4.77	4.44	4.20	4.03	3.89	3.78
17	5%	4.45	3.59	3.20	2.96	2.81	2.70	2.61	2.55	2.49
	1%	8.40	6.11	5.18	4.67	4.34	4.10	3.93	3.79	3.68
18	5%	4.41	3.55	3.16	2.93	2.77	2.66	2.58	2.51	2.46
	1%	8.29	6.01	5.09	4.58	4.25	4.01	3.84	3.71	3.60
19	5%	4.38	3.52	3.13	2.90	2.74	2.63	2.54	2.48	2.42
	1%	8.18	5.93	5.01	4.50	4.17	3.94	3.77	3.63	3.52
20	5%	4.35	3.49	3.10	2.87	2.71	2.60	2.51	2.45	2.39
	1%	8.10	5.85	4.94	4.43	4.10	3.87	3.70	3.56	3.46
21	5%	4.32	3.47	3.07	2.84	2.68	2.57	2.49	2.42	2.37
	1%	8.02	5.78	4.87	4.37	4.04	3.81	3.64	3.51	3.40
22	5%	4.30	3.44	3.05	2.82	2.66	2.55	2.46	2.40	2.34
	1%	7.95	5.72	4.82	4.31	3.99	3.76	3.59	3.45	3.35
23	5%	4.28	3.42	3.03	2.80	2.64	2.53	2.44	2.37	2.32
	1%	7.88	5.66	4.76	4.26	3.94	3.71	3.54	3.41	3.30
24	5%	4.26	3.40	3.01	2.78	2.62	2.51	2.42	2.36	2.30
	1%	7.82	5.61	4.72	4.22	3.90	3.67	3.50	3.36	3.26
25	5%	4.24	3.39	2.99	2.76	2.60	2.49	2.40	2.34	2.28
	1%	7.77	5.57	4.68	4.18	3.86	3.63	3.46	3.32	3.22
26	5%	4.23	3.37	2.98	2.74	2.59	2.47	2.39	2.32	2.27
	1%	7.72	5.53	4.64	4.14	3.82	3.59	3.42	3.29	3.18
27	5%	4.21	3.35	2.96	2.73	2.57	2.46	2.37	2.31	2.25
	1%	7.68	5.49	4.60	4.11	3.78	3.56	3.39	3.26	3.15
28	5%	4.20	3.34	2.95	2.71	2.56	2.45	2.36	2.29	2.24
	1%	7.64	5.45	4.57	4.07	3.75	3.53	3.36	3.23	3.12
29	5%	4.18	3.33	2.93	2.70	2.55	2.43	2.35	2.28	2.22
	1%	7.60	5.42	4.54	4.04	3.73	3.50	3.33	3.20	3.09
30	5%	4.17	3.32	2.92	2.69	2.53	2.42	2.33	2.27	2.21
	1%	7.56	5.39	4.51	4.02	3.70	3.47	3.30	3.17	3.07

Table F (continued)

df Associated with the Denominator		df Associated with the Numerator								
		1	2	3	4	5	6	7	8	9
40	5%	4.08	3.23	2.84	2.61	2.45	2.34	2.25	2.18	2.12
	1%	7.31	5.18	4.31	3.83	3.51	3.29	3.12	2.99	2.89
60	5%	4.00	3.15	2.76	2.53	2.37	2.25	2.17	2.10	2.04
	1%	7.08	4.98	4.13	3.65	3.34	3.12	2.95	2.82	2.72
120	5%	3.92	3.07	2.68	2.45	2.29	2.18	2.09	2.02	1.96
	1%	6.85	4.79	3.95	3.48	3.17	2.96	2.79	2.66	2.56

Table G

Values of Chi Square at the .05, .01, and .001 Levels of Significance

df	.05	.01	.001	df	.05	.01	.001
1	3.84	6.64	10.83	16	26.30	32.00	39.29
2	5.99	9.21	13.82	17	27.59	33.41	40.75
3	7.82	11.34	16.27	18	28.87	34.80	42.31
4	9.49	13.28	18.46	19	30.14	36.19	43.82
5	11.07	15.09	20.52	20	31.41	37.57	45.32
6	12.59	16.81	22.46	21	32.67	38.93	46.80
7	14.07	18.48	24.32	22	33.92	40.29	48.27
8	15.51	20.09	26.12	23	35.17	41.64	49.73
9	16.92	21.67	27.88	24	36.42	42.98	51.18
10	18.31	23.21	29.59	25	37.65	44.31	52.62
11	19.68	24.72	31.26	26	38.88	45.64	54.05
12	21.03	26.22	32.91	27	40.11	46.96	55.48
13	22.36	27.69	34.53	28	41.34	48.28	56.89
14	23.68	29.14	36.12	29	42.56	49.59	58.30
15	25.00	30.58	37.70	30	43.77	50.89	59.70

From R. A Fisher, *Statistical methods for research workers*, 14th ed. (New York, 1970, [1st ed., Edinburgh: Oliver and Boyd, 1932]), pp. 112-13. Copyright 1970 by Hafner Press. Reprinted by permission of the publisher.

Table H
Probabilities Associated with Values as Small as Observed Values of U in the Mann-Whitney U Test

$N_2 = 3$

U \ N_1	1	2	3
0	.250	.100	.050
1	.500	.200	.100
2	.750	.400	.200
3		.600	.350
4			.500
5			.650

$N_2 = 4$

U \ N_1	1	2	3	4
0	.200	.067	.028	.014
1	.400	.133	.057	.029
2	.600	.267	.114	.057
3		.400	.200	.100
4		.600	.314	.171
5			.429	.243
6			.571	.343
7				.443
8				.557

$N_2 = 5$

U \ N_1	1	2	3	4	5
0	.167	.047	.018	.008	.004
1	.333	.095	.036	.016	.008
2	.500	.190	.071	.032	.016
3	.667	.286	.125	.056	.028
4		.429	.196	.095	.048
5		.571	.286	.143	.075
6			.393	.206	.111
7			.500	.278	.155
8			.607	.365	.210
9				.452	.274
10				.548	.345
11					.421
12					.500
13					.579

$N_2 = 6$

U \ N_1	1	2	3	4	5	6
0	.143	.036	.012	.005	.002	.001
1	.286	.071	.024	.010	.004	.002
2	.428	.143	.048	.019	.009	.004
3	.571	.214	.083	.033	.015	.008
4		.321	.131	.057	.026	.013
5		.429	.190	.086	.041	.021
6		.571	.274	.129	.063	.032
7			.357	.176	.089	.047
8			.452	.238	.123	.066
9			.548	.305	.165	.090
10				.381	.214	.120
11				.457	.268	.155
12				.545	.331	.197
13					.396	.242
14					.465	.294
15					.535	.350
16						.409
17						.469
18						.531

Table H (continued)

$$N_2 = 7$$

U \ N₁	1	2	3	4	5	6	7
0	.125	.028	.008	.003	.001	.001	.000
1	.250	.056	.017	.006	.003	.001	.001
2	.375	.111	.033	.012	.005	.002	.001
3	.500	.167	.058	.021	.009	.004	.002
4	.625	.250	.092	.036	.015	.007	.003
5		.333	.133	.055	.024	.011	.006
6		.444	.192	.082	.037	.017	.009
7		.556	.258	.115	053	.026	.013
8			.333	.158	074	.037	.019
9			.417	.206	.101	.051	.027
10			.500	.264	.134	.069	.036
11			.583	.324	.172	.090	.049
12				.394	.216	.117	.064
13				.464	.265	.147	.082
14				.538	.319	.183	.104
15					.378	.223	.130
16					.438	.267	.159
17					.500	.314	.191
18					.562	.365	.228
19						.418	.267
20						.473	.310
21						.527	.355
22							.402
23							.451
24							.500
25							.549

Table H (continued)

$$N_2 = 8$$

U \ N_1	1	2	3	4	5	6	7	8	t	Normal
0	.111	.022	.006	.002	.001	.000	.000	.000	3.308	.001
1	.222	.044	.012	.004	.002	.001	.000	.000	3.203	.001
2	.333	.089	.024	.008	.003	.001	.001	.000	3.098	.001
3	.444	.133	.042	.014	.005	.002	.001	.001	2.993	.001
4	.556	.200	.067	.024	.009	.004	.002	.001	2.888	.002
5		.267	.097	.036	.015	.006	.003	.001	2.783	.003
6		.356	.139	.055	.023	.010	.005	.002	2.678	.004
7		.444	.188	.077	.033	.015	.007	.003	2.573	.005
8		.556	.248	.107	.047	.021	.010	.005	2.468	.007
9			.315	.141	.064	.030	.014	.007	2.363	.009
10			.387	.184	.085	.041	.020	.010	2.258	.012
11			.461	.230	.111	.054	.027	.014	2.153	.016
12			.539	.285	.142	.071	.036	.019	2.048	.020
13				.341	.177	.091	.047	.025	1.943	.026
14				.404	.217	.114	.060	.032	1.838	.033
15				.467	.262	.141	.076	.041	1.733	.041
16				.533	.311	.172	.095	.052	1.628	.052
17					.362	.207	.116	.065	1.523	.064
18					.416	.245	.140	.080	1.418	.078
19					.472	.286	.168	.097	1.313	.094
20					.528	.331	.198	.117	1.208	.113
21						.377	.232	.139	1.102	.135
22						.426	.268	.164	.998	.159
23						.475	.306	.191	.893	.185
24						.525	.347	.221	.788	.215
25							.389	.253	.683	.247
26							.433	.287	.578	.282
27							.478	.323	.473	.318
28							.522	.360	.368	.356
29								.399	.263	.396
30								.439	.158	.437
31								.480	.052	.481
32								.520		

Table I
Critical Values of *U* in the Mann-Whitney *U* Test

*Critical Values of U for a One-tailed Test at α = .001 or
for a Two-tailed Test at α = .002*

N_1 \ N_2	9	10	11	12	13	14	15	16	17	18	19	20
1												
2												
3									0	0	0	0
4		0	0	0	1	1	1	2	2	3	3	3
5	1	1	2	2	3	3	4	5	5	6	7	7
6	2	3	4	4	5	6	7	8	9	10	11	12
7	3	5	6	7	8	9	10	11	13	14	15	16
8	5	6	8	9	11	12	14	15	17	18	20	21
9	7	8	10	12	14	15	17	19	21	23	25	26
10	8	10	12	14	17	19	21	23	25	27	29	32
11	10	12	15	17	20	22	24	27	29	32	34	37
12	12	14	17	20	23	25	28	31	34	37	40	42
13	14	17	20	23	26	29	32	35	38	42	45	48
14	15	19	22	25	29	32	36	39	43	46	50	54
15	17	21	24	28	32	36	40	43	47	51	55	59
16	19	23	27	31	35	39	43	48	52	56	60	65
17	21	25	29	34	38	43	47	52	57	61	66	70
18	23	27	32	37	42	46	51	56	61	66	71	76
19	25	29	34	40	45	50	55	60	66	71	77	82
20	26	32	37	42	48	54	59	65	70	76	82	88

Table I (continued)

Critical Values of U for a One-tailed Test at α = .01 or
for a Two-tailed Test at α = .02

N_1 \ N_2	9	10	11	12	13	14	15	16	17	18	19	20
1												
2					0	0	0	0	0	0	1	1
3	1	1	1	2	2	2	3	3	4	4	4	5
4	3	3	4	5	5	6	7	7	8	9	9	10
5	5	6	7	8	9	10	11	12	13	14	15	16
6	7	8	9	11	12	13	15	16	18	19	20	22
7	9	11	12	14	16	17	19	21	23	24	26	28
8	11	13	15	17	20	22	24	26	28	30	32	34
9	14	16	18	21	23	26	28	31	33	36	38	40
10	16	19	22	24	27	30	33	36	38	41	44	47
11	18	22	25	28	31	34	37	41	44	47	50	53
12	21	24	28	31	35	38	42	46	49	53	56	60
13	23	27	31	35	39	43	47	51	55	59	63	67
14	26	30	34	38	43	47	51	56	60	65	69	73
15	28	33	37	42	47	51	56	61	66	70	75	80
16	31	36	41	46	51	56	61	66	71	76	82	87
17	33	38	44	49	55	60	66	71	77	82	88	93
18	36	41	47	53	59	65	70	76	82	88	94	100
19	38	44	50	56	63	69	75	82	88	94	101	107
20	40	47	53	60	67	73	80	87	93	100	107	114

Table I (continued)

*Critical Values of U for a One-tailed Test at α = .025 or
for a Two-tailed Test at α = .05*

N_1 \ N_2	9	10	11	12	13	14	15	16	17	18	19	20
1												
2	0	0	0	1	1	1	1	1	2	2	2	2
3	2	3	3	4	4	5	5	6	6	7	7	8
4	4	5	6	7	8	9	10	11	11	12	13	13
5	7	8	9	11	12	13	14	15	17	18	19	20
6	10	11	13	14	16	17	19	21	22	24	25	27
7	12	14	16	18	20	22	24	26	28	30	32	34
8	15	17	19	22	24	26	29	31	34	36	38	41
9	17	20	23	26	28	31	34	37	39	42	45	48
10	20	23	26	29	33	36	39	42	45	48	52	55
11	23	26	30	33	37	40	44	47	51	55	58	62
12	26	29	33	37	41	45	49	53	57	61	65	69
13	28	33	37	41	45	50	54	59	63	67	72	76
14	31	36	40	45	50	55	59	64	67	74	78	83
15	34	39	44	49	54	59	64	70	75	80	85	90
16	37	42	47	53	59	64	70	75	81	86	92	98
17	39	45	51	57	63	67	75	81	87	93	99	105
18	42	48	55	61	67	74	80	86	93	99	106	112
19	45	52	58	65	72	78	85	92	99	106	113	119
20	48	55	62	69	76	83	90	98	105	112	119	127

Table I (continued)

*Critical Values of U for a One-tailed Test at α = .05 or
for a Two-tailed Test at α = .10*

N_1 \ N_2	9	10	11	12	13	14	15	16	17	18	19	20
1											0	0
2	1	1	1	2	2	2	3	3	3	4	4	4
3	3	4	5	5	6	7	7	8	9	9	10	11
4	6	7	8	9	10	11	12	14	15	16	17	18
5	9	11	12	13	15	16	18	19	20	22	23	25
6	12	14	16	17	19	21	23	25	26	28	30	32
7	15	17	19	21	24	26	28	30	33	35	37	39
8	18	20	23	26	28	31	33	36	39	41	44	47
9	21	24	27	30	33	36	39	42	45	48	51	54
10	24	27	31	34	37	41	44	48	51	55	58	62
11	27	31	34	38	42	46	50	54	57	61	65	69
12	30	34	38	42	47	51	55	60	64	68	72	77
13	33	37	42	47	51	56	61	65	70	75	80	84
14	36	41	46	51	56	61	66	71	77	82	87	92
15	39	44	50	55	61	66	72	77	83	88	94	100
16	42	48	54	60	65	71	77	83	89	95	101	107
17	45	51	57	64	70	77	83	89	96	102	109	115
18	48	55	61	68	75	82	88	95	102	109	116	123
19	51	58	65	72	80	87	94	101	109	116	123	130
20	54	62	69	77	84	92	100	107	115	123	130	138

Table J
Probabilities Associated with Values as Small as Observed Values
of x in the Binomial Test

N \\ x	0	1	2	3	4	5	6	7	8	9	10	11	12	13	14	15
5	031	188	500	812	969	†										
6	016	109	344	656	891	984	†									
7	008	062	227	500	773	938	992	†								
8	004	035	145	363	637	855	965	996	†							
9	002	020	090	254	500	746	910	980	998	†						
10	001	011	055	172	377	623	828	945	989	999	†					
11		006	033	113	274	500	726	887	967	994	†	†				
12		003	019	073	194	387	613	806	927	981	997	†	r			
13		002	011	046	133	291	500	709	867	954	989	998	ı	†		
14		001	006	029	090	212	395	605	788	910	971	994	999	†	†	
15			004	018	059	151	304	500	696	849	941	982	996	†	†	†
16			002	011	038	105	227	402	598	773	895	962	989	998	†	†
17			001	006	025	072	166	315	500	685	834	928	975	994	999	†
18			001	004	015	048	119	240	407	593	760	881	952	985	996	999
19				002	010	032	084	180	324	500	676	820	916	968	990	998
20				001	006	021	058	132	252	412	588	748	868	942	979	994
21				001	004	013	039	095	192	332	500	668	808	905	961	987
22					002	008	026	067	143	262	416	584	738	857	933	974
23					001	005	017	047	105	202	339	500	661	798	895	953
24					001	003	011	032	076	154	271	419	581	729	846	924
25						002	007	022	054	115	212	345	500	655	788	885

†p = 1.0 or approximately 1.0.

From *Statistical inference* by Helen M. Walker and Joseph Lev. Copyright 1953 by Holt, Rinehart and Winston, Inc. Reprinted by permission of Holt, Rinehart and Winston, Inc.

Table K
Critical Values of T in the Wilcoxon
Matched-Pairs Signed-Ranks Test

N	Level of significance for one-tailed test		
	.025	*.01*	*.005*
	Level of significance for two-tailed test		
	.05	*.02*	*.01*
6	1	—	—
7	2	0	—
8	4	2	0
9	6	3	2
10	8	5	3
11	11	7	5
12	14	10	7
13	17	13	10
14	21	16	13
15	25	20	16
16	30	24	19
17	35	28	23
18	40	33	28
19	46	38	32
20	52	43	37
21	59	49	43
22	66	56	49
23	73	62	55
24	81	69	61
25	90	77	68

From F. Wilcoxon and R. Wilcox, *Some rapid approximate statistical procedures* (New York, 1964), p. 28. Copyright 1964 by the American Cyanamid Co. Reprinted by permission of the publisher.

Table L
Random Numbers

Col. 1	Col. 2	Col. 3	Col. 4	Col. 5	Col. 6	Col. 7	Col. 8
3831	7167	1540	1532	6617	1845	3162	0210
6019	4242	1818	4978	8200	7326	5442	7766
6653	7210	0718	2183	0737	4603	2094	1964
8861	5020	6590	5990	3425	9208	5973	9614
9221	6305	6091	8875	6693	8017	8953	5477
2809	9700	8832	0248	3593	4686	9645	3899
1207	0100	3553	8260	7332	7402	9152	5419
6012	3752	2074	7321	5964	7095	2855	6123
0300	0773	5128	0694	3572	5517	3689	7220
1382	2179	5685	9705	9919	1739	0356	7173
0678	7668	4425	6205	4158	6769	7253	8106
8966	0561	9341	8986	8866	2168	7951	9721
6293	3420	9752	9956	7191	1127	7783	2596
9097	7558	1814	0782	0310	7310	5951	8147
3362	3045	6361	4024	1875	4124	7396	3985
5594	1248	2685	1039	0129	5047	6267	0440
6495	8204	9251	1947	9485	3027	9946	7792
9378	0804	7233	2355	1278	8667	5810	8869
2932	4490	0680	8024	4378	9543	4594	8392
2868	7746	1213	0396	9902	4953	2261	8117
3047	6737	5434	9719	8026	9283	6952	1883
3673	2265	5271	4542	2646	1744	2684	4956
0731	8278	9597	0745	9682	8007	7836	2771
2666	3174	0706	6224	4595	2273	0802	9402
5879	3349	9239	2808	8626	8569	6660	9683
7228	8029	3633	6194	9030	1279	2611	3805
4367	2881	3996	8336	7933	6385	5902	1664
1014	9964	1346	4850	1524	1919	7355	4737
6316	4356	7927	6709	1375	0375	8855	3632
2302	6392	5023	8515	1197	9182	4952	1897
7439	5567	1156	9241	0438	0607	1962	0717
1930	7128	6098	6033	5132	5350	1216	0518
4598	6415	1523	4012	8179	9934	8863	8375
2835	5888	8616	7542	5875	2859	6805	4079
4377	5153	9930	0902	8208	6501	9593	1397
3725	7202	6551	7458	4740	8234	4914	0878

Table L (continued)

Col. 1	Col. 2	Col. 3	Col. 4	Col. 5	Col. 6	Col. 7	Col. 8
7868	7546	5714	9450	6603	3709	7328	2835
2168	2879	8000	8755	5496	3532	5173	4289
1366	5878	6631	3799	2607	0769	8119	7064
7840	6116	6088	5362	7583	6246	9297	9178
1208	7567	2984	1555	5633	2676	8668	9281
5492	1044	2380	1283	4244	2667	5864	5325
1049	9457	3807	8877	6857	6915	6852	2399
7834	8324	6028	6356	2771	1686	1840	3035
5907	6128	9673	4251	0986	3668	1215	2385
3405	6830	2171	9447	4347	6948	2083	0697
1785	4670	1154	2567	8965	3903	4669	4275
6180	3600	8393	5019	1457	2970	9582	1658
4614	8527	8738	5658	4017	0815	0851	7215
6465	6832	7586	3595	9421	9498	8576	4256
0573	7976	3362	1807	2929	0540	8721	3133
7672	3912	8047	0966	6692	4444	7690	8525
9182	1221	2215	0590	4784	5374	7429	5422
2118	5264	7144	8413	4137	6178	8670	4120
0478	5077	0991	3657	9242	5710	2758	0574
3386	1570	5143	4332	2599	4330	4999	8978
2053	4196	1585	4340	1955	6312	7903	8253
0483	3044	4609	4046	4614	4566	7906	0892
3825	9228	2706	8574	0959	6456	7232	5838
3426	9307	7283	9370	5441	9659	6478	1734
8365	9252	5198	2453	7514	5498	7105	0549
7915	3351	8381	2137	9695	0358	5163	1556
7521	7744	2379	2325	3585	9370	4879	6545
1262	0960	5816	3485	8498	5860	5188	3178
9110	8181	0097	3823	6955	1123	6794	5076
9979	5039	0025	8060	2668	0157	5578	0243
2312	2169	5977	8067	2782	7690	4146	6110
3960	1408	3399	4940	3088	7546	1170	6054
5227	6451	4868	0977	5735	0359	7805	8250
2599	3800	9245	6545	6181	7300	2348	4378
9583	3746	4175	0143	3279	0809	7367	2923
8740	4326	1105	0498	3910	2074	3623	9890
6541	2753	2423	4282	2195	1471	0852	6604
1237	2419	4572	3829	1274	9378	2393	4028
7397	4135	8132	3143	3638	0515	1133	9975

Table L (continued)

Col. 1	Col. 2	Col. 3	Col. 4	Col. 5	Col. 6	Col. 7	Col. 8
9105	3396	9469	0966	6128	3808	7073	7779
3348	5436	1171	5853	2392	7643	2011	0538
7792	4714	5799	1211	0409	5036	7879	6173
7523	0348	5237	2533	0635	2382	5092	3497
2674	2435	5979	7697	3260	2939	2511	7318
6825	3660	2688	9560	1329	4268	2532	5024
0639	6884	8337	5308	2054	3454	8745	1877
2467	2505	4916	1683	0034	7758	4458	9918
9513	2949	9337	7234	8458	3329	9691	4278
9116	6846	0205	1158	6112	9916	0723	3769
4012	3863	4817	6294	7865	1672	0137	6557
7698	0651	9756	1816	1154	6708	2522	8296
7158	8463	6406	0779	1185	7660	3065	8941
8412	5905	5612	7028	2545	2392	8434	1551
3134	3962	3147	9631	2881	3091	4678	4465
5840	1940	0754	0457	9533	0108	4523	8441
3237	4236	5504	3282	2838	5002	6614	2463
1990	9392	4943	9505	4925	8313	3108	7681
6724	8147	1557	1342	3352	4421	3707	2445
6521	8766	0654	2300	1696	0145	3257	3496
1888	6629	5385	8725	7185	6826	2279	5200
5567	1138	7139	8157	4906	2872	8842	0890
4511	3021	7370	0264	2690	6187	9110	0941
2188	3642	8905	8172	3930	0152	6931	4340
4086	8745	0988	4815	6192	9608	8686	7459
6817	9456	9157	3036	4769	9362	0074	0837
2914	8776	4833	3214	7643	4345	3304	6137
9122	4766	1599	5271	2257	8502	9560	2833
3558	1472	7664	7256	7181	0088	2257	2503
1928	8097	3520	2187	5124	7295	2525	1891
8032	1390	6606	7195	2724	7239	3888	5582
1846	9648	8699	9716	7752	9886	6299	9129
8691	5849	1005	6629	1632	1463	9288	8600
1884	3228	6397	1733	9543	9868	3611	4828
8211	8273	3941	1484	2627	8257	8493	6354
4070	3899	3121	6736	0668	0782	1398	7729
4463	5758	3905	1545	4699	4338	1235	9547
9961	4716	1687	2448	0815	3022	1220	4055
0420	8921	1593	4599	3401	7209	7877	6001

Table L (continued)

Col. 1	Col. 2	Col. 3	Col. 4	Col. 5	Col. 6	Col. 7	Col. 8
7927	6608	5190	9268	8431	0324	6619	6159
4007	1367	5975	8972	6629	1259	7204	6556
9515	5611	3025	2016	9209	0290	6236	7360
6670	0458	2062	7235	6818	7619	8698	0110
7485	8847	7234	9278	9453	4900	9119	9216
9177	4212	3238	2358	1109	9441	7591	3901

Table M
Critical Values of the Studentized Range Statistic, q

df for denominator	a	k (Number of Means)								
		2	3	4	5	6	7	8	9	10
1	.05	18.0	27.0	32.8	37.1	40.4	43.1	45.4	47.4	49.1
	.01	90.0	13.5	164	186	202	216	227	237	246
2	.05	6.09	8.3	9.8	10.9	11.7	12.4	13.0	13.5	14.0
	.01	14.0	19.0	22.3	24.7	26.6	28.2	29.5	30.7	31.7
3	.05	4.50	5.91	6.82	7.50	8.04	8.48	8.85	9.18	9.46
	.01	8.26	10.6	12.2	13.3	14.2	15.0	15.6	16.2	16.7
4	.05	3.93	5.04	5.76	6.29	6.71	7.05	7.35	7.60	7.83
	.01	6.51	8.12	9.17	9.96	10.6	11.1	11.5	11.9	12.3
5	.05	3.64	4.60	5.22	5.67	6.03	6.33	6.58	6.80	6.99
	.01	5.70	6.97	7.80	8.42	8.91	9.32	9.67	9.97	10.2
6	.05	3.46	4.34	4.90	5.31	5.63	5.89	6.12	6.32	6.49
	.01	5.24	6.33	7.03	7.56	7.97	8.32	8.61	8.87	9.10
7	.05	3.34	4.16	4.69	5.06	5.36	5.61	5.82	6.00	6.16
	.01	4.95	5.92	6.54	7.01	7.37	7.68	7.94	8.17	8.37
8	.05	3.26	4.04	4.53	4.89	5.17	5.40	5.60	5.77	5.92
	.01	4.74	5.63	6.20	6.63	6.96	7.24	7.47	7.68	7.78
9	.05	3.20	3.95	4.42	4.76	5.02	5.24	5.43	5.60	5.74
	.01	4.60	5.43	5.96	6.35	6.66	6.91	7.13	7.32	7.49
10	.05	3.15	3.88	4.33	4.65	4.91	5.12	5.30	5.46	5.60
	.01	4.48	5.27	5.77	6.14	6.43	6.67	6.87	7.05	7.21

Table M (continued)

df for denominator	*a*	*k (Number of Means)*								
		2	3	4	5	6	7	8	9	10
11	.05	3.11	3.82	4.26	4.57	4.82	5.03	5.20	5.35	5.49
	.01	4.39	5.14	5.62	5.97	6.25	6.48	6.67	6.84	6.99
12	.05	3.08	3.77	4.20	4.51	4.75	4.95	5.12	5.27	5.40
	.01	4.32	5.04	5.50	5.84	6.10	6.32	6.51	6.67	6.81
13	.05	3.06	3.73	4.15	4.45	4.69	4.88	5.05	5.19	5.32
	.01	4.26	4.96	5.40	5.73	5.98	6.19	6.37	6.53	6.67
14	.05	3.03	3.70	4.11	4.41	4.64	4.83	4.99	5.13	5.25
	.01	4.21	4.89	5.32	5.63	5.88	6.08	6.26	6.41	6.54
16	.05	3.00	3.65	4.05	4.33	4.56	4.74	4.90	5.03	5.15
	.01	4.13	4.78	5.19	5.49	5.72	5.92	6.08	6.22	6.35
18	.05	2.97	3.61	4.00	4.28	4.49	4.67	4.82	4.96	5.07
	.01	4.07	4.70	5.09	5.38	5.60	5.79	5.94	6.08	6.20
20	.05	2.95	3.58	3.96	4.23	4.45	4.62	4.77	4.90	5.01
	.01	4.02	4.64	5.02	5.29	5.51	5.69	5.84	5.97	6.09
24	.05	2.92	3.53	3.90	4.17	4.37	4.54	4.68	4.81	4.92
	.01	3.96	4.54	4.91	5.17	5.37	5.54	5.69	5.81	5.92
30	.05	2.89	3.49	3.84	4.10	4.30	4.46	4.60	4.72	4.83
	.01	3.89	4.45	4.80	5.05	5.24	5.40	5.54	5.56	5.76
40	.05	2.86	3.44	3.79	4.04	4.23	4.39	4.52	4.63	4.74
	.01	3.82	4.37	4.70	4.93	5.11	5.27	5.39	5.50	5.60
60	.05	2.83	3.40	3.74	3.98	4.16	4.31	4.44	4.55	4.65
	.01	3.76	4.28	4.60	4.82	4.99	5.13	5.25	5.36	5.45
120	.05	2.80	3.36	3.69	3.92	4.10	4.24	4.36	4.48	4.56
	.01	3.70	4.20	4.50	4.71	4.87	5.01	5.12	5.21	5.30
∞	.05	2.77	3.31	3.63	3.86	4.03	4.17	4.29	4.39	4.47
	.01	3.64	4.12	4.40	4.60	4.76	4.88	4.99	5.08	5.16

Adapted from H Leon Harter, Tables of range and studentized range, *Annals of Mathematical Statistics 31:* 1,122-47 (1960). Copyright 1960 by the Institute of Mathematical Statistics, San Francisco, Calif. Reprinted by permission of the publisher.

Appendix 3: Answers to Selected Exercises

Chapter 1

1. a. R; b. I; c. O; d. R; e. O or I; f. N; g. I; h. N

2. a. $\displaystyle\sum_{i=5}^{21} X_i;$ b. $\displaystyle\sum_{i=1}^{N} X_i^2$ or $\sum X^2;$ c. $\displaystyle\sum_{i=1}^{6} X_i$

3. a. Add scores from the third through the eighth
   b. Add all squared Y scores
   c. Add all values of X

Chapter 2

3. a. 109.5-119.5, 114.5, 10
   b. 45.5-48.5, 47, 3
   c. 1.45-1.95, 1.7, 0.5
   d. 49.5-74.5, 62, 25
   e. 0.015-0.045, 0.03, 0.03
   f. 99.5-149.5, 124.5, 50
   g. 69.5-74.5, 72, 5
   h. 19.5-49.5, 34.5, 30
   i. 18.95-19.45, 19.2, 0.5
   j. 85.5-87.5, 86.5, 2

4. a. D; b. C; c. C or D; d. D; e. D; f. C; g. D; h. C   D·   D
7. a. +; b. −; c. +; d. N; e. −; f. N

Chapter 3

1. $\bar{X} = 74.5$
2. $\bar{X} = \$25,335$
3. A = 2.5, B = 1.83, X = 1.75, X is preferred
4. $\bar{X} = 11.4; Med = 10$; Mode = 8; positive skewness
5. $\bar{X} = 55.4; Med = 54.95$ or 55.0; Mode = 57
6. $\bar{X} = 33.65$ or $33.7; Med = 32.87$ or 32.9; Mode = 32
7. a. +; b. N; c. −; d. +; e. N

Chapter 4

1. a. Girls: $PR_{26} = 3.6, PR_{51} = 91.2$; boys. $PR_{26} = 17, PR_{51} = 95.5$
   b. Girls: $P_{20} = 35.3, P_{62} = 43.1$; boys: $P_{20} = 26.8, P_{62} = 35.0$

Chapter 5

1. $S = 4.25$ for all three methods
2. $\bar{X} = 12.27$ or $12.3, S = 1.40$
3. $\bar{X} = 14.65$ or $14.7, S = 2.66$
4. a. 1.25; b. −.75; c. 128; d. 76; e. 84 to 116; f. 68 to 132
5. GATB = .75; CEEB = 1.27; $T = 1.10$; CEEB is best
6. $\bar{X} = 26; S = 10.01$

Chapter 6

1. a. 34.13; b. 47.5; c. 88; d. 6.56; e. 0.49; f. 94.84; g. 87.49
2. a. 6.68; b. 97.72; c. 62.8; d. 44.8; e. 30.4 to 69.6; f. 60.4;
   g. .0446; h. 4 to 96
3. 8/52 or .15
4. a. .22; b. .36; c. 18 to 32 and 32 to 18
5. a. .1587; b. .95; c. .0049; d. .99; e. .025

Chapter 7

1. .05
2. 4.56

3. 2.82 to 3.02
4. No, since 75 is outside 67.08 to 74.92
5. 69.96 to 70.04
6. 2.68 vs. 2.41

Chapter 8

1. a. +; b. −; c. +; d. +; e. −; f. 0; g. −
2. .08
3. .32
4. .62; .63
5. No
6. $N = 102$
7. −.96, significantly different from 0 at .01 level

Chapter 9

1. $Y' = .2X - 2.1$
2. 11.5
3. $s_E = 1.7$; 9.8 to 13.2
4. b. $Y' = .44X + 4.07$; c. 5.83; d. $s_E = 1.37$, 4.46 to 7.20
5. a. .78; c. Significantly different from 0 at .01 level; d. $Y' = .42X + 4.73$; e. 10.61; f. $s_E = 1.35$, 9.26 to 11.96

Chapter 10

1. $t = -1.65, p > .05$
2. $t = 2.92, p < .05$
3. $t = 1.39, p > .05$
4. $t = -2.44, p < .05$
5. $t = 1.96$, one-tailed, $p < .05$

Chapter 11

1. $SS_T = 126; SS_{WG} = 56; SS_{BG} = 70$
2. $MS_{BG} = 35; MS_{WG} = 4.67; F = 7.49, p < .01$
4. $F = 9.78, p < .01; \bar{X}_1$ and $\bar{X}_3$: $q = 5.78, p < .01; \bar{X}_2$ and $\bar{X}_3$: $q = 4.91, p < .01; \bar{X}_1$ and $\bar{X}_2$: $q = .87, p > .05$
5. $F = 28.95, p < .01; \bar{X}_2$ and $\bar{X}_3$: $q = 9.53, p < .01; \bar{X}_1$ and $\bar{X}_2$: $q = 9.06, p < .01; \bar{X}_1$ and $\bar{X}_3$: $q = .47, p > .05$

Chapter 12

1.

Source	df	SS	MS	F
Sex of stationary person	1	10	10	$5.49, p < .05$
Sex of approaching person	1	0.4	0.4	$< 1, p > .05$
Interaction	1	14.4	14.4	$7.93, p < .01$
Within groups	36	65.6	1.82	

2.

Source	df	SS	MS	F
Image quality	1	90	90	$25.86, p < .01$
Stress	1	78.4	78.4	$22.53, p < .01$
Interaction	1	10	10	$2.87, p > .05$
Within groups	36	125.2	3.48	

Chapter 13

1. $\chi^2 = 24.2, p < .001$
2. $\chi^2 = 11.21, p < .001$
3. $\chi^2 = 110.52, p < .001$
4. $\chi^2 = 1.25, p > .05$
5. $U = 1, p = .016$
6. $H = 7.27, p < .05$
7. $\chi^2 = 12.5, p < .001$
8. $x = 4, p = .194$
9. $T = 7$, two-tailed, $p < .05$
10. $\chi_r^2 = 2.11, p > .05$

Chapter 14

1. $r_{oe} = .76; r_{tt} = .86$
2. $S_{EM} = 2.94; 38.06$ to 43.94
3. $r_{oe} = .84; r_{tt} = .91$
4. $S_{EM} = 1.65; 27.35$ to 30.65
5. $r = .15$
6. $r = .44$

References

Anastasi, A. *Psychological testing.* New York: Macmillan, 1976.

Bobko, P., Sapinkoff, R., and Anderson, N. A lack of confidence about formulae for regression confidence intervals. *Teaching of Psychology* 5: 102–3 (1978).

Daniel, W. W. *Applied nonparametric statistics.* Boston: Houghton Mifflin, 1978.

Glass, G. V., and Stanley, J. C. *Statistical methods in education and psychology.* Englewood Cliffs, N.J.: Prentice-Hall, 1970.

Guilford, J. P., and Fruchter, B. *Fundamental statistics in psychology and education.* New York: McGraw-Hill, 1978.

Hopkins, K. D., and Anderson, B. L. Multiple comparisons guide. *Journal of Special Education* 7: 319–28 (1973).

Siegel, S. *Nonparametric statistics for the behavioral sciences.* New York: McGraw-Hill, 1956.

Tyler, L. E., and Walsh, W. B. *Tests and measurements.* Englewood Cliffs, N.J.: Prentice-Hall, 1979.

Index